LOGICAL STUDIES

BY THE LATE

HAROLD H. JOACHIM

Formerly Wykeham Professor of Logic
in the University of Oxford

OXFORD
AT THE CLARENDON PRESS
1948

Oxford University Press, Amen House, London E.C. 4

EDINBURGH GLASGOW NEW YORK TORONTO MELBOURNE
WELLINGTON BOMBAY CALCUTTA MADRAS CAPE TOWN

Geoffrey Cumberlege, Publisher to the University

PRINTED IN GREAT BRITAIN

PREFACE

'LOGICAL STUDIES' was the title given to a set of lectures, usually spread over two Terms, which the Wykeham Professor of Logic, the late H. H. Joachim, delivered yearly during the period 1927–35. As is evident from the manuscript, these lectures were revised before each series and whole sections were recast and rewritten, and it would seem that, even after his retirement, Professor Joachim had read over the text and made alterations and notes for a future rewriting. At the time of his death he was working on his commentary on Spinoza's *Tractatus de Intellectus Emendatione* (published posthumously in 1940 at the Clarendon Press). His colleagues and friends asked him at this period if he had considered preparing 'Logical Studies' for publication when the work on Spinoza was completed. The answer was usually non-committal and this was perhaps not unexpected, since the work on Spinoza was itself a strain on a failing eyesight. Nevertheless, when pressed by those who knew how much thought and care had already gone into the drafting of the lectures, Joachim would generally agree that, provided his health permitted, he would be able to revise and prepare 'Logical Studies' for publication without completely rewriting the whole text. He would also agree, with his characteristic modesty and directness, that these 'Studies' contained in fact the fullest written expression of his own philosophical position and that he saw nothing which would have materially altered this expression when he came to revise his manuscript. But it was clear to all those who knew Joachim's high standards that the revision of 'Logical Studies' would have led in practice to a complete rewriting of the major portion of the lectures and, as in the case of his commentary on Spinoza's *Tractatus*, he would probably have radically altered the whole work or at least a major portion of it. He would never have agreed to publish these 'Studies' as they now appear.

On the other hand, there are many who, having either listened to or read these lectures, have expressed their firm opinion that it would be a disservice to both teachers and students of philosophy not to allow both present and future generations of philosophers to read these lectures, even though they have not the final polish of their author's critical and searching revision. Moreover, it can be fairly stated that, however complete the rewriting might have been, the alterations introduced would not have affected the fundamental principles of the doctrine upheld and defended in the lectures. A comparison of the various versions of the text, altered from year to year, shows that Joachim's main theses were themselves unaltered and that the changes were merely in the detail of emphasis and expression. If I may express a personal opinion, I believe that Joachim would have written of 'Logical Studies', as he did when asked to revise *The Nature of Truth* (Preface to the Second Edition: unfinished):

'Accordingly I set to work to re-read the book: and the result, though not decisive, was to myself surprising. If I may speak frankly, and without fear of vanity or conceit, I can only say that the book is still not only alive, but kicking. The criticism, for example, of the metaphysics behind the theory of truth as a quality of independent entities is still unanswered; and until it is answered the whole recent development of logic—what is known as logical analysis and logical positivism —is, so far as I can see, worthless, however ingenious, and rooted in sheer confusion.'

In a similar contention lies the actuality of 'Logical Studies'.

My aim, in preparing the manuscript for publication, has been first and foremost to interfere as little as possible with Joachim's text. Where there was more than one version of the same passage the general principle adopted has been to choose the latest version of the text or portion of the text. This task has been, on the whole, comparatively easy, since the writer usually dated the different versions, when he had not already crossed out the older text. The only alterations made have been the omission of certain paragraphs obviously designed to link one lecture to a previous lecture, and a few parenthetical notes of an historical nature, inserted for the benefit of a student audience. A number of underlinings, inverted commas, and other marks of emphasis, meant entirely to help the lecturer himself, have also been omitted. There has only been some doubt in deciding on certain paragraphs, or series of paragraphs, which Joachim had bracketed, and, as is clear from pencil notes in the margin, sometimes left out in a given set of lectures. On the whole, I have followed the cuts suggested in this manner but I have not considered all such bracketings as indicative of a fixed determination on the part of the writer to be rid of the marked paragraphs. In many cases the cuts seem to have been imposed by the necessity of adapting the lectures to a given number of hours and not because the passages in question were considered superfluous or verbose. There are, in the text as printed, a number of words or phrases within brackets which may perhaps give the reader the impression that his continuous perusal of the argument is being interrupted and broken, unnecessarily, by synonymous words or phrases. It will be found, I think, that this is not so and that the brackets do contain words which modify, develop, or at least clarify the preceding word or words. Had Professor Joachim rewritten 'Logical Studies', I have no doubt that he would have recast the sentences in such a way as often to employ a single expression where he has now been forced, in his zeal for precision, to use several. It should be added that another set of lectures in manuscript, 'Universal and Individual', and a paper, 'What is a Category?', have been given to the Bradley Library at Merton College, Oxford, by Mrs. Joachim. They form a further development of the doctrine contained in these 'Logical Studies'.

I wish to thank Mr. W. H. Walsh, Fellow of Merton College, who has kindly helped in the revision of the proofs.

L. J. BECK

MERTON COLLEGE,
 OXFORD

CONTENTS

In it we have found a *datum*—viz. that immediate yet necessary nexus between self-consciousness and existence which Descartes discovered and formulated in the principle '*cogito, dubito, ergo sum*'.

But an examination of Descartes's exposition in the Second Meditation shows that the *datum*—the incontestable fact which affirms and guarantees itself as truth—is not the existence of a mind, or self, or self-conscious subject of experiences: but only the existence while it is thinking of an *x* which thinks (i.e. is conscious that it is experiencing). The *x*, which thus incontestably exists, is exhausted, both in its character and in the duration of its existence, in the single flash of self-conscious experience, of which it is postulated as the subject or originating power.

And even this meagre *datum*, which we have found, is found by an act of thought essentially discursive or inferential as well as immediate 134

In the former description the moment of return was confused with the (total) activity of the mind (*Note* on Descartes's and Spinoza's conceptions of the *Actus Reflexus*).

But, even when this confusion has been corrected, the description must be radically altered to meet two difficulties. It must be made clear (i) that there is a level or power of reflection, but no special reflective act and no special set of reflective experiences; (ii) that the objects of reflective study are not actual and individual as constituent events of the historical process, but as universal (intelligible) species and individual types of knowledge-or-truth.

Even then there remains an insuperable difficulty. For it is self-contradictory to ask—and that in effect is what we have been doing—whether the mind can reflectively study the subjective moment of knowledge *qua* subjective

3. Modern logical analysis, it may be suggested, distinguishes, amongst the structural elements and contents of any body of knowledge, three kinds of *cognita* which have a prima facie claim to be regarded as intelligible *data*; viz. (*a*) Fundamental principles, or formulations of the basal character of all-being and all-knowing—i.e. of the mere form of a structure or system in general; (*b*) Axioms, or formulations of the fundamental concepts of a particular science

I

THE SUBJECT-MATTER AND METHOD OF LOGIC

§ 1

1. IN the first of these Logical Studies I shall try to sketch the subject-matter and method of logic. The result will bring us into conflict with a number of generally accepted divisions—supposedly fundamental antitheses. And in the remaining two Logical Studies I shall start from the chief of these generally accepted divisions, and the theories based upon them; develop and examine them in detail; and try to show that, and precisely why, it is not possible to acquiesce in them, and that in the end they lead us back to, and so confirm, the view of logic sketched in the Introductory Study.

We are to begin, then, with a descriptive sketch, a provisional outline, of the subject-matter and method of logic. And such a sketch must not be confused with a definition. It anticipates the reasoned and systematic account which the definition would have to conclude and summarize. It professes to mark out roughly an area of inquiry: not to be the adequate delimitation of a science.

2. A project of this kind is exposed to attack from two opposite quarters: (a) Why not start—some critics will say—with the definition of logic: with the summary statement of the truth: with that adequate conception of the science which it is presumably hoped to reach in the end, and which the author at all events must possess already if his sketch is to have any value?

The only adequate answer to the question what is logic would be the science itself *in propria persona*. The definition with which, according to this criticism, we ought to start, presupposes, and is the concentrated expression of, the systematic reasoned exposition which is the actual science of logic. The critic, in short, is making what is literally a preposterous demand: for he wants to begin with that which, in the nature of the case, can come only at the end.

There is no need to labour the point. In principle, the matter was settled once for all by Aristotle in his account of the adequate or scientific definition of an attribute and its relation to demonstration.[1] And the position I am affirming against the critic is common to all respectable writers on logic and other philosophical subjects.

[1] *Post. Anal. B* 8–10.

B

Thus—I quote from Prof. Reyburn's *Introduction to Psychology*,[1] where this familiar position is simply expressed: 'No science can define its subject-matter adequately at the beginning. The subject-matter of any science is best defined as the object possessing the characteristics which the science itself discloses; and obviously the definition should come at the end of the study.' If the critic persists—but the author presumably has come to the end and possesses an adequate conception of the science. He ought therefore to begin by enunciating his results in the form of a definition, which his readers can take as authoritative and final—the *real* answer is that the critic in arguing thus shows fundamental misunderstanding of the nature of a philosophical discipline, as will become clear in the sequel. For the moment, it is enough to point out that the definition would be unintelligible to the readers. They, at all events, have not come to the end. The concentrated expression of the sum and substance of the science could, at this stage, mean little or nothing to them.

(*b*) From the opposite quarter it may be objected that it is unnecessary to offer any description at all. It would be enough to rely upon a general familiarity with the field of logical inquiry; to give a reference, perhaps, to some recognized text-book or to quote some standard definition of the subject; and then to plunge straight into the discussion of this or that particular logical problem.

Let us develop this criticism. A writer on subjects belonging to the domain of one of the natural sciences can count upon a general familiarity with the field of his science. Even the mathematician has the same advantage, so far at any rate as he is dealing with problems of arithmetic and Euclidean geometry. He can safely take his domain for granted, assume a general agreement as to its central character and outlines, and 'put' his audience 'wise' in a couple of sentences. Everybody knows—more or less—what these sciences are about, what the field of study in each of them is. We all know, for example, what the heavenly bodies are, what plants and animals (living things) are; and we have long ago familiarized ourselves with the numbers of the multiplication table, and with the lines, plane figures, and solids of Euclidean geometry—difficult though it may have been for the general public to conceive these *abstracta* precisely, when Pythagoras and the early Pythagoreans first discovered them and thus inaugurated the sciences of arith-

[1] p. 7.

metic and geometry. If university lectures were announced under the title of, for example, 'Geometrical', 'Astronomical', 'Biological' Studies, nothing would be needed by way of preliminary description. It would be quite enough to open with the bare statement that we are to study 'problems connected with the properties and relations of lines, plane figures, and solids', or 'with the nature, movements, and history of the heavenly bodies', or 'with the evolution, structural forms, and functions of living things'.[1] 'Each science knows in a vague way what it wants to deal with, and plunges straight into its task. All that is needed or possible at the beginning is to erect a finger-post pointing out the proper direction.'[2]

In much the same way—so in effect a critic might argue—the lecturer on a philosophical subject can reckon upon a general familiarity with the facts that fall within his domain, and upon a general agreement as to its main character and outlines. The facts, indeed, that constitute the domain of philosophy, or of any of the philosophical disciplines—such facts, for example, as judgement, inference, knowledge, truth; or again, moral behaviour, rights and duties, responsibility, virtue and vice, &c.—are not perceptible like the heavenly bodies and their movements; or the plants and animals, their structure and reactions. Nor are they, like the numbers and figures, objects of thought so abstract and simple, so easy to formulate and define, that we may almost be said to see them with the mind's eye, to recognize them infallibly the moment we reflect upon our perceptual experience. The facts which the philosopher studies are amongst the most concrete of realities. They are spiritual facts—embodiments-of-mind, manifestations-to-mind; below or above the division (between perceiving, thinking, willing, &c., and their objects) which the mathematical and natural sciences presuppose—which they unconsciously assume, and within which they work.[3] Our familiarity with these spiritual facts, with these non-perceptible yet concrete realities, is of an intimate but elusive kind. Still, it may be said, they pervade and dominate all human experience; they are matters of universal concern and absorbing interest. Everybody knows, in a vague and general sense, what they are. And a vague knowledge of this kind is enough for the start. It is a mistake to suppose that the lecturer

---

[1] Cf. H. W. B. Joseph, *Introduction to Logic*, p. 1, from whom I have borrowed some phrases in the preceding sentence.

[2] Cf. Reyburn, *Introduction to Psychology*, p. 7.

[3] Cf. below, pp. 6 ff., 52 ff.

on, for example, metaphysics, logic, or moral philosophy is entangled *ab initio* in a difficulty of orientation from which the man
of science or the mathematician is free. We are all familiar, at any
rate, with certain fundamental antitheses: with the distinctions
indicated by 'real and apparent', 'true and false', 'right and wrong'
(or 'good and bad'). And we should all agree that each of these
antitheses outlines the field of a philosophical discipline. The
philosopher can use them to erect his finger-post, to convey in a
sentence, which everybody would understand, the general character of the domain he is to explore. The logician, for example, he
would say, is concerned with knowledge and error, with thought,
with judgement and inference, or whatever it may be which can
and must be true or false.

Now in this criticism there is much plausibility and some truth.
We may admit that everybody knows what, for example, arithmetic and geometry and the natural sciences are about ; and that
this general familiarity enables the lecturer to erect his finger-post
in the shape of a conventional formula of orientation, and then to
plunge headlong into this or that special problem. We may admit
so much for the sake of argument—for there is a good deal to be
said on the other side. But in the philosophical disciplines the
situation is very different. In logic at all events, to speak only of
that for the sake of brevity, a conventional formula of orientation
would resemble a finger-post at cross-roads, from which the inscrip-
tion had become obliterated. It would show the traveller the
parting of the ways; not which road he has to take.

For the student of logic is faced at the outset with different and
irreconcilable views of the subject-matter. There are, or seem to
be, many bodies of theory, separate from one another, each
claiming to be the science of logic. Formal logic, for example ;
deductive logic; inductive logic; symbolic logic; philosophical
logic[1]—each of these, perhaps, knows in a vague way what it wants
to deal with. But do they all want to deal with the same subject or
even with parts of the same ? Are they the complementary, though
different, parts of a single science, the chapters of a single book ; or
are they all, or some of them, false claimants and usurpers, not
logic itself nor proper parts of logic ?

The criticism, in short, does not hold against my project, for
a very simple reason. There is no recognized text-book of logic,
no standard definition, no conventional formula of orientation ; or

---

[1] For the title, cf. Bosanquet, *Logic*², e.g. ii. 270.

rather, and this is equally fatal to the critic's advice, there are many authoritative text-books, and many accepted formulae of orientation. But the many text-books embody rival, and often incompatible, conceptions of the science; while the formulae of orientation point the student in different, and sometimes contrary, directions.

§ 2. *Logic is neither art nor science, but philosophy*

1. Logic is a theoretical study; a speculative investigation, i.e. one that is freely and systematically pursued for the sake of understanding its subject-matter. It may be called a science in order both (*a*) to distinguish it from those intelligent activities which are directed to doing or making or altering (it is ἐπιστήμη θεωρητική, not πρακτική or ποιητική, not τέχνη), and also (*b*) to emphasize its systematic character (it is ἐπιστήμη, not ἐμπειρία ἄλογος, or τριβή). But it is not a science in the technical sense in which the term is often used. It is not a positive or a special science comparable, for example, with the mathematical or the natural sciences. It is essentially distinguished from these, and is philosophy, in virtue of the concreteness of its subject-matter and the consequent critical and reflective nature of its method, characteristics which will be explained later.

2. The statement that logic is philosophy sounds trivial. Yet to take it seriously and insist upon it is to break with an old tradition. According to an old tradition logic is not a theoretical study. Its object is practical, disciplinary or educational, not disinterested investigation for the sake of understanding. It is the art of thinking or a compendium of the rules for sound reasoning: a general or propaedeutic art, an instrumental discipline indispensable for the acquisition of every special art and every science or branch of philosophy.

Some such view of logic, for example, seems to have been taken by Aristotle himself.[1] It was the view, at any rate, which emerged triumphant from the ancient controversy as to whether logic is a science or an art,[2] and is expressed in the orthodox definition of logic in the old text-books. Logic, i.e. formal or scholastic logic, the stereotyped system of doctrines into which the contents of Aristotle's *Organon* had been perverted, is 'Ars instrumentalis

---

[1] Cf. W. D. Ross, *Aristotle*, p. 20.

[2] Those who are interested in the ancient controversy, which is still of importance for the history of philosophy, and in particular for the study of Aristotle, will find it well and thoroughly set out in Zabarella's *De natura logicae*, Book I.

dirigens mentem nostram in cognitionem omnium intelligibilium.'[1]
And the same view, the same insistence upon the instrumental and
disciplinary character of logic reappears in the work of Descartes
and the Port-Royal logicians. Not only the title, but the whole
treatment of the *Regulae ad directionem ingenii*, make this abundantly clear in regard to Descartes; while the opening sentence of
La Logique ou l'art de penser (the Port-Royal logic) declares that
'Logic is the art of guiding one's reason aright in the knowledge
of things, so that one may best be able both to acquire such
knowledge for oneself and to impart it to others'.[2]

In maintaining that logic is philosophy we are breaking with an
old tradition. For logic, according to the orthodox view, is not
primarily a theoretical or speculative study. It is, on the contrary,
practical, instrumental, disciplinary. It is not a science, but an art.
The logician's object is to train the mind for, and guide it in, its
speculative activities; not simply to elucidate a determinate subject-
matter, but to strengthen and develop our power of elucidating
whatever we may otherwise wish to study or understand.

On the whole this is the view of logic taken by Aristotle,
Descartes, the Port-Royal logicians, and the best of the recognized
text-books (e.g. Sanderson's) on Aristotelian or Formal Logic.
Without arguing at length against this traditional view, since a
long discussion of it would at this stage be unprofitable, I will try
in what follows to define the point at issue more clearly.

(i) It must be remembered that no such distinction as that
between theory and practice, science and art, &c., is absolute.
Every speculative investigation necessarily contributes to make
and alter something in the student himself and in the world he
studies—and so far necessarily is also educational, disciplinary,
practical. Indeed, since it is, on one side of itself, an activity of
the student he must be held to be, even in his speculative activities,
a moral agent, morally responsible for the part he plays, e.g. for
the energy or slackness, thoroughness or slovenliness, of his 'pure'
thinking. And, conversely, there is no art, however widely we
interpret the term, which does not inevitably depend upon,
embody, and contribute to the enrichment of 'pure theory', i.e. the
disinterested study of things in order simply to understand them.

All this is, or ought to be, common ground. But, on and within

---

[1] Bishop Sanderson's *Logicae Artis Compendium* (1672), p. 1.
[2] 'La logique est l'art de bien conduire sa raison dans la connaissance des choses,
tant pour s'instruire soi-même que pour en instruire les autres.

this common ground, the traditional view of logic is sharply opposed to the view we are to maintain.

According to the traditional view, logic is essentially and in principle practical. It is the art of thinking, or of learning to think and reason. And unless a man develops and increases his power of reasoning by the study, he is no logician and what he has studied is not logic. We, on the other hand, in these studies, are to maintain that essentially and in principle logic is theoretical, a philosophical or speculative investigation. And as students of logic, we have nothing whatever to do with any practical or educational consequences of our study.

(ii) The term 'science', I suggested,[1] is applicable to logic in a general sense, viz. to mark both the theoretical and the systematic character of the logician's activity. But 'systematic' is a dangerous epithet. It may suggest that logic is, what Kant believed the formal logic of tradition to be, a completed aggregate of final doctrines concerning a certain subject-matter; i.e. an exhaustive collection of dogmatic items, each an absolute truth, true *per se*, self-contained, rigid, and unalterable.[2]

Now no science, not even the mathematical or the natural sciences, least of all the critical or philosophical sciences, is, or aims at being, a system in that dead and mechanical sense. Logic is systematic speculation, and therefore the very antithesis of a set of final doctrines. A system is in no way analogous to an exhaustive collection, a sum-total, of unit truths. Speculation is systematic, in proportion as it takes nothing for granted or on faith, neglects nothing relevant and is continuous and coherent. If we speak of logic as a science or system of knowledge, we must not think of it as a completed tale of finally established doctrines, as

---

[1] Cf. p. 5.

[2] On Kant's faith in the finality of formal logic, his view of it as a science which Aristotle 'created complete and entire at a stroke'—cf. e.g. *Kritik der reinen Vernunft*, preface, 2nd edit., p. viii, and N. K. Smith's *Commentary on Kant's Critique*, pp. 21, 184-5. Smith rightly draws attention to the strangely perverse situation to which Kant is led. 'In the very act of revolutionising the traditional logic' (Smith, l.c., p. 184), 'Kant relies upon its prestige, and upon the assumed finality of its results, to make good the shortcomings of the [transcendental] logic which is to displace it.' . . . 'Since formal logic is a completed and perfectly *a priori* science, which has stood the test of 2,000 years, and remains practically unchanged to the present day', therefore (so Kant appears to have argued) 'its results can be accepted as final, and can be employed without question in all further inquiries.' Accordingly, as is well known, Kant used the traditional classification of the forms of judgement to guarantee the exhaustiveness of his table of the categories, with disastrous results.

an aggregation of bits of knowledge. We must think of it rather as a single truth gradually emerging and expanding, as a development, or growth, which in all its stages is self-adjusting, self-correcting, and self-fulfilling, but never self-fulfilled, i.e. frozen into the rigidity of a creed. Or we may think of it perhaps, though the analogy is very far from satisfactory, as an integral whole or unity, which nevertheless is such that it must show itself in our experience as an uncompleted and incompletable sequence of parts or components.[1]

Suppose, for example—for the sake of argument, since the view I am going to suppose is far from adequate[2]—suppose the subject-matter of logic is thought, and that thought is a function or activity of the mind in its endeavour after knowledge or truth. Suppose that the logician systematically investigates the nature and conditions of this function, the variety of the forms it assumes in exercise, their application and the conditions determining their truth or falsity or their comparative truth and falsity. No doubt he will be able, when his study has reached a certain stage, to arrest the movement of his speculative investigation, to crystallize it and to concentrate its 'results' in the shape of conclusions, positive theories, or summary doctrines. Such and such, he will be able to say, are the principles of sound thinking; the *conditiones sine quibus non* of a healthy exercise of the function of thought; rules which must be observed if we are to think truly, or at least if we are not to think falsely. And such and such are, in rough outline, at all events, the chief varieties of its forms; their structural affinities and divergencies; and their comparative merits and demerits when measured by the natural end or aim of thought, viz. the attainment and embodiment of truth, that being the standard by reference to which thought is a function, or functional activity, of the mind. But logic itself, the science which, as we are

---

[1] The view of a science as an aggregate of truths against which I have been protesting, seems to be the generally accepted and orthodox doctrine. It underlies a passage in the *Theaetetus* which is worth recalling because the absurdity of the view in principle leaps to the eye owing to the extreme simplicity and baldness of the formulation Plato there gives to it. In a context avowedly pictorial (mythical), and speaking no doubt more than half in jest, Plato there describes arithmetic (ἀριθμητικὴ τέχνη) as 'the hunt after the knowledge of every even and every odd' (198a), and lays it down that the perfect arithmetician 'knows all numbers, for knowledge of all numbers is in his soul' (198b). He has caught and keeps them all in his memory, in the aviary in his soul, and thus possesses that aggregate of knowledge which is arithmetic. (Cf. also below, Study II, pp. 167-8.)

[2] Cf. below, pp. 16-21.

for the moment supposing, is the systematic study of thought, is more and other than any set or collection of such summary doctrines. The principles of thought, the rules of sound thinking, are at most crystallized deposits of that speculative activity, that reasoned and reasoning account, which *is* the science; crystals which, to continue the metaphor, continue to grow, and may even change their forms, as the activity proceeds.[1]

(iii) If thus it is a mistake to identify a science with a sum-total of doctrines, the traditional view involves a still further confusion. For, having identified logic with a sum-total of conclusions, fixed and cut off from the speculative movement which alone gives to them whatever validity and value they possess; having reduced the science of logic to a compendious summary of doctrines professing to set forth the principles or rules and typical forms of thought; it proceeds to identify logic, so understood, with the art of thinking. But the art of thinking, if it exists, is no more to be identified with a set of rules than any other art—than, for example, the art of building, or of printing, or of playing the violin. If there is an art of thinking, we must look to the great thinkers, the masters of science and philosophy, as its chief possessors, its most conspicuous exponents, and obviously it is childish to suggest that a Newton or a Darwin, an Aristotle or a Kant, thought by rule, guided themselves in their speculative adventures and discoveries by the application of any rules of reasoning—by, for example, the rules of the syllogism, or the canons of induction, or the Cartesian rules of method. One might as well suggest that, for example, Shakespeare or Beethoven or Paganini guided themselves in writing, in composing, and in playing by a knowledge and application of the rules of grammar, or of harmony (or of 'the principles of literary and musical composition'), or of the precepts embodied in a manual for students of the violin.

The statement that logic is philosophy is not convertible *simpliciter*, and thus raises the very difficult problem to which I referred,[2] the problem of the articulation of philosophy.

Logic may be philosophy; but it certainly is not all the philosophy there is, not the whole of philosophy. For philosophy, it seems obvious, is in some sense a whole, articulated into a plurality

---

[1] This statement, I am aware, and especially the last clause of it, requires qualification and defence. The path to which it commits me runs beside a precipice; but I cannot at present spend time in fencing it. See below in Study III.

[2] Cf. p. 5.

of philosophical sciences or disciplines. But in what sense is it a whole? What is the principle of its articulation? What is the number, what the nature and mutual relations, of its parts or articulated members?

The problem, so stated, is more than very difficult. For us, at any rate, its solution is impossible. We are devoid of the very rudiments of the necessary equipment for discussing the articulation of philosophy; we have made no attempt to explain wherein philosophy consists, what constitutes a philosophical science. We have nothing to go upon at present but conventional titles and loose popular phraseology. There is demanded, for an adequate discussion and solution of the problem, nothing less than a reasoned outline of what Hegel has called 'the encyclopaedia of the philosophical sciences'. And for us, in our present ignorance, such an undertaking would be madness. We might as well try to reach the attic from the basement at a jump, forgetting or despising the stairs.[1]

Fortunately there is no need, in a preliminary description of logic, to discuss the problem in full. What is required is difficult enough, but not beyond all possibility of attainment. The meaning of the terms 'philosophy' and 'philosophical' must be further explained; and we must try to show the nature of the limitation which makes it impossible to convert *simpliciter* the statement that 'logic is philosophy'. In other words, some discussion is inevitable of the sense in which philosophy is a whole, of the principle of its articulation, and of the relation (so to call it) of logic to 'the whole'. But we need not attempt to determine the number, nature, and mutual relations of the philosophical sciences.

§ 3. *The subject-matter of logic is knowledge-or-truth*

1. Logic[2] is distinguished from the special sciences, and is philosophy, in virtue of the concreteness of its subject-matter and the consequent reflective and critical nature of its method.

I will try to elucidate this statement, beginning with the subject-matter of logic. And in doing so, I shall disregard an objection which will probably be made. The subject-matter and method in philosophy, it may be said, are so intimately connected, that it is wrong to attempt to treat them separately at all. For indeed each in a sense essentially determines the other. The subject-matter, on

---

[1] Cf. Descartes, *Reg. V. Exp.*, ed. Adam and Tannery, vol. x, p. 380.
[2] See above, p. 5.

the one hand, dictates the method; because it is neither simple (one, without variety) nor composite (one, by the colligation of a variety of constituents) but concrete, it can only be understood if studied in a certain way. Nothing but reflective and critical analysis can unlock the secrets of its being, can reveal it as it really is. On the other hand, the method contributes to make the subject-matter what it really is; because the speculative investigation is reflective and critical, its subject-matter is concrete. For, in philosophy at all events, the subject-matter can only mean that which emerges, and constitutes itself, in the speculative movement; its real being is self-revealing, its *esse* is *intelligi*.

In this objection there is, as I hope to show later, a substantial element of truth.[1] Nevertheless I propose to disregard it, and to discuss the subject-matter of logic first and then its method; remembering only that my account of the former will have to be supplemented and perhaps corrected by my account of the latter.

2. In calling the subject-matter of logic concrete, I am contrasting the kind of facts with which all philosophical and therefore all logical speculation is concerned, and the kind of facts that are studied in the special sciences. The facts which constitute the subject-matter of any special science presuppose a division between object and subject of experience. They are abstracted objects of cognizance, objects cut off from the knowing or other experiencing of them. But the facts which constitute the subject-matter of logic (or, for that matter, of any philosophical study) are neither abstracted objects of experience nor abstracted subjects (subjective states, processes, or activities). They are concrete or spiritual facts, totalities, so to say, or unities, underlying and overriding the division between, for example, what is known and the knowing of it; what is willed and the willing of it; or generally what is object of experience and the experiencing of it.

In view of the common use of the antithetical terms 'abstract' and 'concrete', it may seem at best a mere paradox to speak of the concreteness of the subject-matter of logic. And, apart from this question of terminology, these totalities, with which logic is supposed to be concerned, these spiritual facts which underlie and override the facts of the special sciences, require further explanation.

(*a*) On the terminological question not much need be said. According to the commonest use of the antithesis, thought or theory, all speculative thinking and knowing, scientific and philosophical alike, is always abstract and occupied with abstractions. Only that is concrete which is part and parcel of the present experience of some sentient being, that which is present in sense or feeling, my experiences, as I live them, this or that 'Erlebnis' in its unique actuality in the temporal flow. This is the contrast which is obviously assumed in a famous passage of Bradley's.[1] The whole point of that passionate protest lies in the assumption that thought or theory dissects and mutilates the 'concrete facts of life' and substitutes for their full-blooded reality a dreary tissue of abstractions.

'. . . the sensuous curtain is a deception and a cheat, if it hides some colourless movement of atoms, some spectral woof of impalpable abstractions, or unearthly ballet of bloodless categories. . . . Our principles may be true, but they are not reality. They no more *make* that Whole which commands our devotion, than some shredded dissection of human tatters *is* that warm and breathing beauty of flesh which our hearts found delightful.'

Now of course I am not suggesting that the subject-matter of logic, or the facts with which the logician is concerned, are concrete in this sense—leaves, so to say, of 'the golden tree of life', or sections and constituents of 'the moving show'. The common use of the antithesis to which I have been referring rests upon certain views of thought and of reality—antediluvian views which nobody has done more to discredit than Bradley himself. It would not be very difficult to show—using for the purpose Bradley's own criticisms—that concreteness, in this common usage, is a misnomer for confused togetherness; and that the so-called abstractness of thought or theory is in fact its determinateness or precision.[2] But no amount of philosophical criticism will remove, from everyday language and literature, so deeply ingrained a use (or misuse) of the terms. And our best course is simply to note it, and to admit that the subject-matter of logic is not concrete, nor yet, properly speaking, abstract, when the antithesis is thus applied.

The first is in principle concrete and the second in principle 'abstract'; because, whereas the first is relatively complete and self-subsistent, the second depends, for the being it is supposed to have, upon a condition it is taken to exclude. That condition,

---

[1] *The Principles of Logic*, 2nd edit., vol. ii, p. 591.
[2] Cf., e.g., Nettleship, *Philosophical Remains*, vol. i, pp. 114–15, on the sense in which all clear thinking is abstract.

ignored or suppressed, but essentially implied in the subject-matter of a science, is explicitly recognized as contributing to constitute the subject-matter of a philosophical study.

The facts of number and figure, and the facts of nature (the mathematical and physical facts, let us call them for short) are assumed by the sciences which study them to be what they are in independence of any experiencing (perception or thought) of them, and to involve no thought, no spiritual activity of any kind, in their constitution. As subjects of mathematical and physical study, they are taken to be cut off from all activities of mind. They are taken by the men of science to form self-contained systems or domains, which thought may be said to posit or to recognize, but only to posit or recognize as closed to, as excluding and excluded by, thought itself. In a word, they have their being and reality, their existence or subsistence and their nature or character, in themselves. Thought plays no part whatever in their constitution, neither the thought which posits and studies them, nor thought in any sense or of any kind. They stand there, so to speak, fixed and self-established, confronting the man of science. It is irrelevant to their being, that its independence has been posited by thought; a mere accident to it that, as the science progresses, it gets more fully known.

Now facts thus posited are, in truth, abstractions. And, in contrast to them, the facts which form the subject-matter of any philosophical study (including logic) are in principle concrete, the full or complete totalities, from which the former have been split off.

For thought is not only included within the entirety of things: not only something that occurs here and there, in patches (so to say) within the universe: not only the occasional activity of this or that thinker—the exercise of a function peculiar to certain individuals specially endowed or 'qualified' (as Alexander would say), the members of a privileged group of beings within the whole. So much, of course, even the special sciences and even a materialist or a realist philosophy would readily admit. But thought—to put it roughly and, for the present, dogmatically—is a power of the universe, a power rooted in the very nature of things; a spiritual force or energy which pervades, penetrates, and at least contributes to constitute the universe itself, both as a whole and in its detail. Nothing, I am suggesting, therefore, can be what the facts of the mathematical and physical sciences are posited as being. So to posit them—to take them as though they were in no sense related to, or constituted by, thought—is to omit a relevant and essential condition of their being. They are, i.e. as they are posited, in some degree unreal—in some degree shorn of their full being, mutilated results of inadequate conception, abstractions.

On the other hand, the philosopher (or the logician) expressly recognizes, and includes, in the conception of his subject-matter, its relation to thought, and the part thought plays in its constitution. And, in virtue precisely of that recognition, the facts he 'takes' to study (philosophical or logical facts, I will call them in future for short) may be said to be concrete in contrast to the mathematical and physical facts—to be (relatively and by contrast to the latter) complete and self-subsistent.

There is a passage in T. H. Green's posthumous lectures on logic[1] which expresses this contrast very simply and clearly.

'All thought', he says, 'must be conscious . . . but need not imply reflection on itself as thought. In ordinary knowledge there is no such reflection. Hence ordinary men are quite unaware of any activity of thought having contributed to constitute the things of which they have experience. When it comes to scientific inquiry they know they are thinking, but, from the preconceived idea that thought has contributed nothing to the constitution of the things thought about, they give a wrong account to themselves of what their scientific thought consists in, and regard it as mere methodic reception (suppose that the mind in scientific thought, as in ordinary experience, is merely receptive, but more methodically receptive).'

But, though the subject-matter of logic and all logical facts are in this sense concrete in principle, and the physical and mathematical facts, in principle, abstractions from them, logic, in yet another application of the antithesis, is the most abstract of philosophical studies and its subject-matter the barest skeleton of that Whole which (in Bradley's phrase) 'commands [the philosopher's] devotion', i.e. that concrete (or spiritual) reality with which philosophy is concerned. As contrasted with those concrete spiritual facts—those manifestations to, and embodiments of, mind—which form the subject-matters of (let us say) the philosophy of art, of conduct, of religion, the subject-matter of logic is 'a woof of impalpable abstractions', and 'logical' facts constitute 'a system of bloodless categories'.

'Impalpable' and 'bloodless', it is true, are misleading epithets.

[1] *Works*, vol. ii, p. 194.

For no philosophical fact is palpable if we are to press the literal (the sensuous) meaning of the term; and the categories, which are the facts of logic, convey (if we are to use these physiological metaphors) the life-blood of the Whole. Nevertheless, it is the business and the privilege of the logician to search out the universal conditions without which nothing can be or be known at all; to trace the bare and abstract structure, the structural principles or forms, of intelligibility and intelligence in one. His work is thus to explore the basal conditions of *all* being and knowing; not to study the rich and varied architecture of the Whole in any of its more *special* developments.

(*b*) What, then, are these spiritual (but abstract) facts, with which the logician is concerned? These categories, which are the structural principles of intelligibility and intelligence in one, these fundamental and indispensable conditions of all being and knowing?

At this point, the objection which was brushed aside[1] threatens to return upon us with its full force. If every philosophical subject-matter is concrete in the sense explained, then (it will be objected) clearly nothing short of the speculative movement, which is the science of logic itself, can be an adequate answer to the question 'What are the facts with which the logician is concerned?' For, whatever may be the case in science, in logic at any rate (since logic is philosophy) there are no fixed and self-established facts. Logical facts must clearly be inseparable from the logical speculation in which they are discovered or emerge—or rather which discovers them by constituting and establishing them. For a logical fact is not an object detached from the thought which posits and which studies it. It is not, as the physical and mathematical facts are or are taken to be, an independent entity (or thing-in-itself) confronting a merely receptive observer or student. On the contrary, the objector will say, a 'logical fact', it seems, *is* a spiritual (an intellectual) activity become self-explicit, manifest to, and conscious of, itself. For, according to the preceding account, the real being of every philosophical fact is a self-revealing: its *esse* is *intelligi*. And it seems clear that the *esse* of a logical fact is *fieri*; its being is an emerging; it *is*, in so far as it constitutes, or establishes, itself in a speculative movement. In its case, therefore, *intelligi* can only mean *explicari* or *explicitum fieri*; becoming known, becoming understood, in that the spiritual activity which

[1] Cf. above, p. 10.

constitutes the fact is in some sense one with the thought which studies it: in some sense is, or becomes, manifest to, and conscious of, itself in the medium and at the level of the explicit reflective thinking of the logician. Now, even if we accept the objection as it stands, even if we concede the full force of all the objector claims: there follows no more than what we knew already. Certainly, it is impossible, in a preliminary description like the present, to give an adequate account of the subject-matter of logic, to explain adequately what are the logical facts. For precisely the giving such an account constitutes the logician's end and aim, and is the whole of his work.

But, all this being admitted, something can still be done in preparation for an adequate account of that kind. For there are certain popular conceptions of the subject-matter of logic; and there is a general consensus that certain topics fall somewhere within it. (*a*) Logic, for example, it would commonly be said, is the science of thought, of the forms and principles of thought, of right thinking or of knowledge; and (*b*) the logician is concerned *inter alia* with the Laws of Identity, Contradiction, and Excluded Middle; with the proposition or judgement; with proof, reasoning, or inference. Now, it should be possible (*a*) to start with one or other of these popular conceptions, to show in what respects it needs correction or supplementation, and thus to determine the region within which the adequate account will have to move, the point at which it will start, and the lines along which it will proceed. And it should be possible (*b*) also to bring out more definitely the character of a logical fact, by considering one or more of these generally accepted topics and showing in what sense, for example, the 'law of contradiction' or the so-called laws of thought do indeed belong to the subject-matter of the science, are indeed 'logical facts'.

3. The most generally accepted description of logic[1] as the science of thought, 'of the forms and laws of right thinking', is apt to be misleading. For it at once suggests that logic is concerned with thought, but not with things; with a subjective faculty of thinking and its exercise, in contrast to the objective realities, the things and events of the real world, about which we think. And it suggests further that logic is concerned with thought, but not with sense or feeling; with one faculty of cognizance to the exclusion of another or others. Now a thought which is opposed to things, a

[1] Cf. above, pp. 8–9.

subjective faculty which is contrasted with the objects about which it is exercised, cannot possibly be the subject-matter of logic, if logic is a philosophical investigation in the sense explained. It cannot even be the subject-matter of a special science. For the subject-matter of a special science is the abstracted object of cognizance, but what is here in question is the abstracted subject (subjective faculty) of cognizance; and an entity of that kind (it must be insisted, whatever we may be told in text-books of psychology) is not a possible object of study in any sense or at all.

This criticism of the popular description of logic—though I believe it to be sound—will hardly carry conviction in the form in which I have stated it. Let me try therefore to amplify and confirm it. In saying that the popular description suggests an opposition between a subjective faculty and the real things about which it is exercised, and along with that a further opposition between thought and sense, I am referring to the conventional meaning which its terms have come to bear. For the terms 'thought' and 'thinking' have acquired, in ordinary usage, a fairly definite and restricted meaning, presupposing a certain philosophical position. That position is pre-Kantian, or even pre-Platonic. And it is rather difficult therefore to state it sympathetically and plausibly, though everybody (even Kant and Plato) lapses into it at times, and most of us acquiesce in it more or less unconsciously, assume it by implication, throughout our lives. Broadly, however, it may be sketched as follows:

There is the independent system of reality, the universe of self-existent reals; and, amongst these self-existent reals, are living and self-conscious organisms, specially privileged members of the system, equipped with the faculty of thinking about it and its constituents, including themselves. Coming thus, as it were, upon a ready-made world, upon a universe of things complete in their independent being, and indifferent to any intellectual activities which may be exercised about them, thought is of necessity both subjective and formal. It is subjective; i.e. an activity springing from and expressing a function of the finite subjects, the individual self-conscious organisms which are the only thinking things. Obviously, and on any view, there can be no thought without a thinker; but on this view the thinkers, the individual finite subjects, are the originative sources (the ἀρχαί) of thought. They are, so to say, the sufficient causes (not merely a *conditio sine qua non*) of thought; it is their special function and prerogative, their

C

spontaneous act. And it is formal; i.e. an activity of arranging (distinguishing, connecting) a material which it requires but cannot originate, a material which it must find presented or given to it. It is, in short, a function of the thinker which presupposes for its exercise another faculty in him, a faculty of receiving *data* (feelings, impressions, sensations) to be arranged (distinguished, connected).[1]

Now, if the preceding account of logic as a philosophical investigation is sound, it cannot be right to identify its subject-matter with thought so understood. The study of a faculty of thought, an intellect, thus subjective and formal, could not possibly enable the logician 'to trace the structural principles of intelligibility and intelligence in one', to exhibit those 'categorical forms' which are 'the fundamental conditions of all being and knowing'.[2]

The common description of logic as the science of thought is unsatisfactory. Thought, thinking, &c., have acquired a restricted meaning in current usage; and the description therefore tends to commit us to two assumptions. We tend to assume (1) that thought is subjective, i.e. a faculty of the finite self-conscious subject or subjects contrasted with the things and events of the real world, the objects or objective realities about which the subject thinks; and (2) that thought is formal, i.e. a faculty by which the thinker forms certain materials, or arranges certain *data*, which are presented to him, and received by his sense or feeling, i.e. by a second faculty independent of, and contrasted with, thought.

In regard to the first of these assumptions, it is of course true that those who describe logic as the science of the principles and forms of thought do not as a rule suppose that thought is the uniquely singular (the private and peculiar) power of this or that individual thinker: or at all events they do not mean that the logician is to study it in its uniquely singular character, as the function of this and no other subject. On the contrary, it is supposed that the intellect, or the faculty of thought, has the same nature (a common or universal nature) in all thinkers; and that it is with this common nature that the logician is concerned. He

---

[1] This is the view which, for example, Kant habitually takes for granted and starts from, e.g. *Kritik der reinen Vernunft*[2], p. 74 (Berlin ed., vol. iii, p. 74). 'Our knowledge originates from two basal sources in the Mind. The first of these is the faculty of receiving presentations (Receptivity of Impressions); the second is the faculty of knowing [recognizing] an object through these presentations (Spontaneity of Conceptions).'

[2] Cf. above, p. 15.

studies thought, a faculty subjective in the sense that it inheres in the individual subjects; and studies it in so far as it functions (or can, and ought to, function) uniformly, viz. in accordance with certain laws, the laws of thought. To think, in what for the logician is the proper or normal sense, is to arrange *data* in forms, and on principles, dictated by the very nature of the intellect—to realize or exercise the faculty of thought as such, not as mine-not-yours or as mine-not-his.

But the supposed common or universal faculty of thought is still subjective and formal: and it clearly will not do to describe logic as the science of thought, if, as I have been urging hitherto, the business of the logician is 'to trace the structural principles of intelligibility and intelligence in one'. For while, perhaps, it is necessary that the natural functioning of this common or universal faculty of thought, its exercise in conformity to its own laws, the laws of thought, should be valid, there is no necessity that it should be true. Its exercise is not necessarily knowledge, does not necessarily achieve or embody truth. If in the exercise of it, if by thinking, anything becomes intelligible, is known, made evident as truth, this is due in part to the character of the *data* (or materials) on which it is exercised, which it forms or arranges. And *ex hypothesi* the *data* or materials are presented to the thinker by another faculty, a faculty contrasted with thought, and therefore assumed on this view to be excluded from the subject-matter of logic.

There is a more fundamental objection to this description of logic. For what right have we to assume that thought is subjective and formal—that thought so conceived exists, or is a possible subject of study at all?

Nothing less, it seems to me, could justify these assumptions, or, as is more likely, could refute them, than a critical analysis of cognizant experience *as a whole*, of knowledge. And by knowledge or cognizant experience *as a whole*, I mean the concrete total fact of which the experiencing and what is experienced, or the knowing and the known, are not constituents, but inseparable (though distinguishable) 'sides' or 'moments'.

Nothing less than philosophical reflection upon the whole situation—upon, for example, the concrete fact which would be called this perception of fact or the demonstration of truth—(*a*) on the one hand could determine the character of what is perceived or demonstrated of the facts or truths which are commonly called the objects perceived or 'the realities known'; or (b) on the other hand could determine (if anything could determine) the character of the knowing subject, the character of the faculties or powers by which (as is commonly said) he perceives or reasons.

Such an analysis, I venture to think, is essentially logical, i.e. the work of the logician as such and of nobody else. And it is an analysis not of thought alone in contrast to sense, not of thought as a formal faculty, nor of thought apart from the reality which thought (whether alone, or with the co-operation of sense) endeavours to know, i.e. not of thought as a subjective faculty. Except through, and on the ground of, such an analysis, we have no right to take for granted either (i) that what is perceived, or otherwise known, is resoluble into a matter or a form, into elements and relations, or into *data* and modes of their arrangement; or (ii) that the part played by the knowing subject is, by the spontaneous activity of his thinking, to arrange a material he passively receives by sense or feeling.

To avoid committing ourselves at the start to these ungrounded and at least doubtful assumptions, it would be better therefore to describe logic as the science not of thought but of knowledge. For (a) knowledge does not (like thought) carry with it, in ordinary usage, any contrast with sense, or suggest the exclusion of any form or part of cognizant experience (of, for example, sensation or perception) from the purview of the logician; and (b) it may, not unnaturally, be used to cover the concrete whole, the 'total fact' (the total cognizant situation), within which the opposition between subject and object arises and exists.[1]

It is better then to describe logic as the science of the laws and forms, not of thought, but of knowledge; and best of all, I have now to add (in order to rule out *ab initio* a not improbable misunderstanding), to couple knowledge and truth together, and to speak of logic as the science of knowledge-or-truth. For truth is reality disclosed or evidencing itself to mind (i.e. to mind as such— to my, your, his, or any mind), and thus designates the same concrete or spiritual fact as knowledge, in the sense in which I propose to use the latter term; designates it, however, so as to

---

[1] Cf. R. L. Nettleship, *Philosophical Lectures and Remains*, vol. i, p. 125: 'To study the theory of knowledge should mean, accordingly, to realize gradually what the fact called knowledge means. The use of language; discovery, observation, experimentation; reasoning, judging, proof; force, space, time; causation, subject, object—these are all facts, parts (to speak roughly) of the great fact called knowledge.'

emphasize the objective side of the concrete fact, which in our common use of 'knowledge' tends to be ignored or merely implied. If we speak of truth, we think primarily of the evident or manifest to sense and reason, of the intuitable and intelligible. When, on the other hand, we speak of knowledge, we think primarily of the functions or acts of mind involved in the evidence or manifestation, of insight, intuition, intellection, demonstration. Hence, by coupling truth with knowledge, and describing the subject-matter of logic as the fundamental and indispensable conditions of knowledge-or-truth, we can safeguard ourselves against the misleading suggestions of either term when used alone.[1]

4. It will help to elucidate and confirm this description if I apply it to determine the sense in which certain familiar topics belong to the subject-matter of logic, are logical facts. Amongst these topics which, by general consensus, fall somewhere within the subject-matter of logic are the so-called 'Laws of Thought' (the Principles, for example, of Identity, Contradiction, and Excluded Middle).[2] In what sense are these logical facts? How are they to be conceived so as to fit within the subject-matter of logic, so as to belong unambiguously to knowledge-or-truth? In what sense are they proper parts or factors constituting that concrete reality, that total fact, with which the logician is concerned?

The Laws of Thought. Aristotle[3] enumerates certain problems which, as he thinks, should form the first subjects of discussion in metaphysics, that is, in the speculative study of 'Being as such and its essential attributes' (or of 'the first causes and principles of Being or Reality as a whole') to which he gives the names of 'First Philosophy' or 'Wisdom' or (in two passages only) 'Theology'.[4] The second of these problems[5] concerns the 'first principles' or 'axioms' of demonstration—the ἀποδεικτικαὶ ἀρχαί (or, in 1005ᵇ 7, συλλογιστικαὶ ἀρχαί), the ἀξιώματα or κοιναὶ δόξαι ἐξ ὧν ἅπαντες δεικνύουσιν ('the axioms or "common notions" which all men presuppose as the basis of their demonstrations'). Do these axioms, these principles, in accordance with which every inference must be drawn, and whose truth is the ultimate warrant of every sound

---

[1] The serious difficulties in this description—e.g. the inclusion under 'knowledge-or-truth' of 'error-or-falsity'—must be left at present without discussion. I shall attempt to deal with the chief of them in Studies II and III.

[2] Cf. above, p. 16.   [3] *Metaph. B.*

[4] πρώτη φιλοσοφία: σοφία: or (1026ᵃ 19, 1064ᵇ 3) θεολογική.

[5] Cf. 995ᵇ 6–10 and 996ᵇ 26–997ᵃ 15.

illation—the Principles, for example, of Excluded Middle and of Contradiction and any others there may be of the same basal character—do they fall within the domain of 'First Philosophy'?

Aristotle discusses this problem in *Metaphysics Γ*, and answers it in the affirmative. The Principles of Contradiction and Excluded Middle, the principles that 'the same thing cannot both be and not-be in the same respect' and that 'every predicate must be either affirmed or denied of any given subject'[1]—are basal principles of demonstration *because* they are basal ontological laws. They are the most assured and stable laws of that fact, that reality, which 'First Philosophy' has to study.[2] The Principle of Contradiction is the most assured and stable law of all, since it formulates a condition which must be satisfied if anything is to be in any sense and at all, and it must be known (or must in some way be possessed by the mind) if one is to know anything.[3] And the Principle of Excluded Middle follows at once from the definitions of 'the true' and 'the false'—i.e. from the fundamental condition under which alone what *is* (and what therefore is determined by the Principle of Contradiction) can be adequately expressed in judgement. If anything is in any sense and at all, it must be itself (Principle of Identity) and not itself and also other than itself (Principle of Contradiction); and if anything which is, is to be adequately expressed in judgement, so that there is to be a true assertion, and a truth asserted, it must be either *this* or *not this*, unambiguously possess or not-possess whatever may be offered as its character (proposed as a predicate of it in a judgement).[4]

The axioms of demonstration, then (the so-called 'Laws of Thought'), are, in Aristotle's view, basal ontological laws—definitions of 'what is' in respect to the primary or *minimum* conditions of its 'being'; and therefore also basal principles controlling all judgement and demonstration, conditions under which alone these can yield knowledge or be true.

On this interpretation of the so-called 'Laws of Thought', are they logical facts, do they belong to the subject-matter of logic as I have described it? The answer to such a question is neither

---

[1] ἀδύνατον ἅμα εἶναι καὶ μὴ εἶναι (996[b] 30) = τὸ αὐτὸ ἅμα ὑπάρχειν τε καὶ μὴ ὑπάρχειν ἀδύνατον τῷ αὐτῷ καὶ κατὰ τὸ αὐτὸ κτλ. (1005[b] 19). πᾶν ἀναγκαῖον ἢ φάναι ἢ ἀποφάναι (996[b] 29) = ἀνάγκη ἢ φάναι ἢ ἀποφάναι ἐν καθ' ἑνὸς ὁτιοῦν (1011[a] 24) = οὐδὲ μεταξὺ ἀντιφάσεως ἐνδέχεται εἶναι οὐθέν (1011[a] 23).

[2] Γ 1005[b] 8–11 (τὰς βεβαιοτάτας ἀρχὰς τοῦ πράγματος).

[3] Γ 1005[b] 11–17 (βεβαιοτάτη ἀρχὴ πασῶν . . . ἣν . . . ἀναγκαῖον ἔχειν τὸν ὁτιοῦν ξυνιέντα τῶν ὄντων κτλ.).   [4] Cf. *Metaph. Γ* 1011[b] 23–9.

simply 'Yes', nor simply 'No'. 'Yes,' we might say, 'subject to a reservation.' But this reservation cuts so deep that, strictly considered, the answer must be 'No'. For Aristotle's conception of these axioms of demonstration presupposes precisely that division which the logician must not make or accept. It pre-supposes a realm of Being-as-such, and (supervening upon it in its finished completeness) our intellectual powers of judgement and inference. The latter, no doubt, if they are to yield knowledge or attain truth, must operate in conformity to principles which formulate the barest, and most general, structural conditions of the former. The laws which control our thought in its pursuit of knowledge are dictated to it by the formal structural character of the independent reals it seeks to know. But still there is, and remains, a fundamental division; and the dependence is one-sided. There is a realm of independent entities determined by ontological laws, a reality which thought in no way conditions or helps to constitute; and there is a power of thought, rooted in, and exer-cised by, some amongst these entities, viz. the finite individual minds, and dependent in some (not in all) of its operations upon the ontological laws.

The *status* (so to call it) of these laws, or, rather, of the 'knowledge' or 'truth' which thought aims at achieving and cannot achieve unless *at least* it obeys them, is, throughout Aristotle's philosophy, ambiguous. There are passages which seem to say unequivocally that true judgement and the demonstrations in, and through, which alone we know are mental activities and products, realizations of psychical powers, of functions, aptitudes, and habits of mind; that truth and knowledge are representations, reproductions in the medium of thought, of a world of facts (τὰ πράγματα) complete without them. Truth and knowledge (the judgements and demon-strations of science) are conceived as 'replicas' or analogues of the real substances with their real qualities and relations. The analogues are conditioned, no doubt, by the originals to which they correspond, and adjusted to them; but they do not in any sense or degree contribute to constitute the latter. The analogues are mental—i.e. constructed by the mind and existing in the mind, made by thought and consisting of thoughts.[1]

On the other hand, some of Aristotle's statements seem to imply

---

[1] Cf. Aristotle's theory of the λόγος ἀποφαντικός (below, Study III, § 13. 2) and one side at any rate of his account of demonstrative knowledge in *Post. Anal.* Also his treatment (in *N. E.* vi and elsewhere) of ἐπιστήμη as a ἕξις, &c.

a very different conception of the status of truth and knowledge. To be completely real (he seems to assume with Plato)[1] is to be completely known; or at least the reality of anything is its definable being, its form (εἶδος) is its essential nature (its τὸ τί ἦν εἶναι). If one pressed to the full the implications (a) of Aristotle's treatment of definition in *Post. Anal. B* and in *Metaph. Z* and *H*); (b) of his occasional statements concerning the eternal and necessary cohesions and severances between things (essential natures) and their *Propria*;[2] and (c) of his conception of the oneness of thought and its object in the most perfect form and degree of knowledge (in νόησις or θεωρητικὴ ἐπιστήμη[3])—one would reach a conception of knowledge-or-truth akin to that which I have been trying to suggest. The fact itself (τὸ πρᾶγμα) would be completely itself, would be genuinely fact, only in that expression (in that unfolding and re-integration) which is accomplished in the definitions, the commensurate judgements, and the demonstrations of science. Truth (ἡ ἀλήθεια, τὸ ἀληθές, τὸ ὡς ἀληθὲς ὄν) would be neither a state (or an activity) of our intelligence; nor a structure made by thought, and out of thoughts, to correspond to the real relations of certain extra-mental substances and qualities—it would be the facts disclosing themselves to mind, and being facts (having their reality as facts) only in the disclosure. And the so-called 'Laws of Thought' would be, not principles dictated to our subjective faculty of thinking by the basal conditions of a self-existent world (by 'ontological' laws), but genuine laws of knowledge in the total or concrete sense. They would formulate the barest and most indispensable characters of *reality in the form of truth*. I do not suggest that Aristotle himself explicitly, still less consistently, maintains a view of this kind. He comes nearest to it, perhaps, in his doctrine of the infallible νόησις τῶν ἀσυνθέτων, the intellectual intuition of the simple or incomposite reals which, if (or when) it occurs, is *eo ipso* true or truth. I am reluctant to enter into any exposition of this doctrine at present, since it will be necessary to examine the conceptions of an immediate intellectual apprehension and of a truth which excludes the possibility of error, in some detail later.[4] But a brief digression on Aristotle's account of τὸ ὡς ἀληθὲς ὄν and τὸ μὴ ὂν ὡς ψεῦδος in *Metaph. E* 4 and *Θ* 10 is forced upon me, because the view I am taking of it disagrees with the interpretation

---

[1] τὸ παντελῶς ὂν παντελῶς γνωστόν. *Rep.* 477ᴀ.
[2] Cf., e.g., *Metaph. Θ* 1051ᵇ 9–17.   [3] Cf., e.g., *De anima* 430ᵃ 3–5.
[4] Cf. below, Study II, § 11 (pp. 152 ff.); and Study III, § 15.

of one of the best living exponents of Aristotle. Sir David Ross—
in his edition of the *Metaphysics*—treats the doctrines of a 'truth',
of which the opposite is not error but sheer nescience, as 'absurd'—
and denies that Aristotle can have meant to advocate it.[1]

In *E* 4 Aristotle says: 'The false and the true are not determined
by (do not depend upon) the facts—it is not the case, for example,
that "the good" is *eo ipso* true and "the bad" *eo ipso* false—but
by (upon) thought. And with regard to the simple reals—i.e. the
essential natures—truth does not depend upon, is not determined
by, thought either.'[2] In the first part of this passage, Aristotle
denies that things, apart from all relation to thought, are as such
(in themselves) true or false. And, consistently with this denial,
he goes on[3] to dismiss from metaphysics (i.e. from the study of τὸ
ὂν ᾗ ὄν) the consideration of τὸ ὡς ἀληθὲς ὄν. Reality in the form
of truth, that which *is* in the sense of *is true*, is no part of the metaphysician's subject-matter, because its cause is διανοίας τι πάθος.

But what are we to make of the reservation with regard to
τὰ ἁπλᾶ καὶ τὰ τί ἐστιν? 'Truth in regard to them', Aristotle says,
'is not determined by *thought* either (οὐδ' ἐν διανοίᾳ).' According to
Ross, this cryptic statement is equivalent to a denial that, in regard
to these simple reals, there can be truth at all.

'That which could not possibly be false', Ross says,[4] 'cannot without
tautology, and therefore absurdity, be said to be true, just as "true
knowledge" is an absurd expression because there could not be false
knowledge. But instead of saying this he [sc. Aristotle] says that truth
in another than the ordinary sense is possible with regard to incomposites.
The fault, however, is only in the expression; the distinction is probably
clear enough in his mind.'

Now I submit that Aristotle's own statements are the only safe
clue to what was in his mind. And what Aristotle says here and
in other passages (notably in *Θ* 10. 1051ᵇ 22–1052ᵃ 4 and in the
De Anima) makes it clear that what to his editor is tautologous
and therefore absurd, is to Aristotle a significant and important
doctrine. The simple or incomposite reals are, on Aristotle's view,
the only absolute and perfect reals. They are facts which are
through and through and perfectly intelligible, either because they

---

[1] Cf. Ross, *Aristotle's Metaphysics*, vol. i, p. 365 (Notes on 1027ᵇ 27 and 28) and
vol. ii, pp. 275–6 (Note on 1051ᵇ 17–1052ᵃ 4).

[2] *Metaph.* 1027ᵇ 25: οὐ γάρ ἐστι τὸ ψεῦδος καὶ τὸ ἀληθὲς ἐν τοῖς πράγμασιν, οἷον τὸ
μὲν ἀγαθὸν ἀληθές, τὸ δὲ κακὸν εὐθὺ ψεῦδος, ἀλλ' ἐν διανοίᾳ · περὶ δὲ τὰ ἁπλᾶ καὶ τὰ τί
ἐστιν οὐδ' ἐν διανοίᾳ.

[3] 1027ᵇ 29–1028ᵃ 4.   [4] Vol. ii, p. 275.

are forms without matter, sheer actualities without any residue of
unrealized potentiality (like, for example, God) ; or because, being
the *essential nature* of the substances that are composite of form
and matter, they constitute in them all that is intelligible or
definable, i.e. all that is genuinely real. The only possible apprehension, Aristotle maintains, of these perfectly intelligible, and
therefore supremely real, simple facts is an intellectual act which,
if it takes place at all, must be true, because, in such an act,
thought is in contact with (i.e. is immediately and undividedly
'one' or continuous with) the indivisible whole which is its object.
To apprehend a simple fact or real at all is to apprehend it whole
and wholly ; no partial apprehension and no misapprehension—no
error and no falsity—are possible. The only alternative is sheer
nescience (ἄγνοια), a blank within the faculty of intellectual apprehension, a gap in τὸ νοητικόν.[1]

The intellection or affirmation of a simple real, therefore (the
νόησις or φάσις τῶν ἁπλῶν or τῶν ἀσυνθέτων), is true in a totally
different sense from that in which a silent or spoken judgement (a
δόξα or act of διάνοιά, or a κατάφασις or ἀπόφασις) is true. A judgement is true, if it connects or separates thoughts in accordance
with the real junctions and severances of the elements of a complex
fact : and its truth is opposed to a possible misconnexion or mis-
separation, i.e. to various degrees of falsity and error. But the
intellectual act (the νόησις or φάσις), which apprehends or affirms a
simple real, is true in the sense of infallible: its occurrence is the
self-manifestation of fact, its very being is truth.[2] When Ross says
that 'true knowledge is an absurd expression'—that it is tautologous and therefore absurd to affirm that knowledge is true, he is
using the term 'true' as the opposite of 'false'. The very meaning of
knowledge is a cognizance or a thought which is true not false.
But it would clearly be no less absurd to deny that knowledge was
true. For, indeed, knowledge is truth: truth is its essence.

In this passage, then, if I understand it rightly, Aristotle
maintains that there are acts of conceptual apprehension, of
intellectual intuition, which must be sharply distinguished from
discursive thought or judgement. An act of intellectual intuition
he calls νόησις: and the discursive activity of thinking he calls
διάνοια. In an act of intellectual intuition, in a νόησις, we have a
single indivisible actuality, the very being of which is truth. What

---

[1] Cf. 1052ᵃ 2–4.
[2] Cf. *Metaph.* Θ 1051ᵇ 22–1052ᵃ 4; *De anima*, e.g. 430ᵇ 27–31.

is true, in this case, is one whole: and the whole is simple, i.e. *incomposite*. If we speak of it as a fact (πρᾶγμα), it is, we must remember, a fact, the very occurrence and being of which is a *being-apprehended*, a *being-thought*, or *being-known*. And if we speak of it as a 'thought' or 'thinking', we must remember that it is not διάνοια but νόησις: i.e. not an activity by which the intellect separates or connects its thoughts so as to *represent* the distinguishable elements, and their relation within a complex real, but an indivisible act by which it 'makes contact', and 'becomes one', with the indivisible real which it 'thinks'—so that the latter is whole, and wholly absorbed, in the 'thinking'.[1]

§ 4. *The method of logic is reflective and critical analysis*

Having described in outline the subject-matter of logic—and having explained the terms employed in the description—I have now to explain and justify what I said of its method: that the method of logic, because of the concreteness of its subject-matter, is the method distinctive of all philosophical explanation: viz. reflective and critical analysis.

A. *In what sense is logic an analysis of knowledge-or-truth?*

1. 'Analysis' is a popular term somewhat indiscriminately applied to various intellectual procedures whereby—in everyday life and in scientific investigations—a subject is elucidated. Is there any single principle underlying these various applications? Is it possible, by examining some examples of its common use, to find and formulate an unambiguous central meaning for the term? And, if so, can it then be shown that Analysis (thus understood, but with the qualification 'reflective and critical') properly applies to the method of logic? It seems worth while to make the attempt. Let us consider therefore the following examples.

In a practical perplexity, enlightenment is sought by an analysis of the situation; and we expect to understand an unusual occurrence by an analysis of the conditions of its happening. The geometer explains a figure by analysing it into its spatial elements and their relations; or by a more ultimate analysis which enables him to view it as the result of a construction in accordance with a constitutive equation. In the 'analytical' or 'co-ordinate'

---

[1] Cf., e.g., *Metaph.* Θ 1051ᵇ 22: ἢ ὥσπερ οὐδὲ τὸ ἀληθὲς ἐπὶ τούτων τὸ αὐτό, οὕτως οὐδὲ τὸ εἶναι, ἀλλ' ἔστι . . . τὸ μὲν θιγεῖν καὶ φάναι ἀληθές . . ., τὸ δ' ἀγνοεῖν μὴ θιγγάνειν. 1052ᵃ 1 τὸ δ' ἀληθὲς τὸ νοεῖν ταῦτα · τὸ δὲ ψεῦδος οὐκ ἔστιν, οὐδὲ ἀπάτη, ἀλλ' ἄγνοια κτλ.

geometry of Descartes, for example, the intuitable spatial form (the curve, say, which we perceive or imagine) is explained by an analysis which substitutes for it an algebraical formula expressing the law of its generation. For, since the position of any point in a plane can be uniquely determined by its distance from two inter-secting axes in that plane (its distance along lines parallel to those axes), it is possible (as Descartes showed) to express in an alge-braical formula (a constitutive equation) a law prescribing the suc-cessive positions through which a given point must flow if it is to generate any required intuitable line. The intuitable line is thus explained by analysis—i.e. by resolution into points (or successive positions of a point) each of which is uniquely determinable by the application of a single principle.

A motion, again, is explained by analysis into simple components —as the composition, for example, of the two (or more) simple motions which would have resulted from the operation of two (or more) precisely definable (calculable) forces. Or the chemist explains water and sulphuric acid by analysing them into such-and-such elements, combined in such-and-such proportionate amounts.

Along with this popular and somewhat indiscriminate use of the term 'analysis' there goes an equally popular and indiscriminate use of the complementary term 'synthesis' or its synonyms. Full enlightenment in our practical perplexity demands a synthesis (or is it a re-synthesis?) as well as an analysis; we have to construct (or is it to re-construct or re-constitute?) the situation out of the elements we have reached by analysing. We have to sum or put together the conditions of the complex occurrence. The geometrical figure must be constructed in imagination by a synthesis (or a re-synthesis) of its spatial elements—so that they are viewed in their relations, and the intuitable individuality of the figure (its uniquely characteristic shape) is restored. The curve must be generated by an imaginative construction—by a re-synthesis of the points (or the positions) which have been severally defined (uniquely determined) in accordance with the constitutive equa-tion—so that the successive and discrete positions become a flow, a continuous path with a uniquely individual intuitable character.

A similar reversal of the analytic procedure—a constructive or re-constructive procedure, a synthesis or re-synthesis—is expressed or implied in the other examples. If, for example, the motion of the earth round the sun is to be explained, we have to regard it as though it were the joint (but single) effect of the two simple forces which our analysis has led us to postulate; we have to re-compose in our thought the simple component motions which would have been produced by the separate actions of the force of gravity and of the force of propulsion *ad infinitum* onwards in a straight line. And the re-composition of these hypothetical components has to re-create a motion imaginably single, imaginably circular throughout.

Lastly, the explanation of a compound by chemical analysis has to be supplemented—to put it at its lowest—by a corresponding synthesis. Water, for example, or sulphuric acid has to be conceived—at the very least—as the elements (or their atoms) re-synthesized (combined) in accordance with a determinate structural plan, a characteristic scheme of arrangement. It is clearly no explanation of water to analyse it into a plurality of hydrogen atoms and half as many oxygen atoms. At the very least the plurality must be synthesized and ordered. The atoms must be conceived, for example, as constituting a mosaic with an individual pattern. And the scheme of their grouping—the plan of their synthesis, the pattern of their mosaic—is vital to the 'explanation'. For apart from it there is nothing (in the chemist's account) which could even pretend to explain the glaring contrast between the actions and reactions of the free gases, and the actions and reactions of water.[1]

2. The examples I have quoted differ greatly *inter se*; and the list could easily be extended so as to include many more, differing at least as much both from one another and from those already considered. Nevertheless, it seems, at first sight, a plausible contention that all these various applications of the term 'analysis' embody a single principle; all execute in variations the same theme. The subject of study is something which is in some sense a whole and therefore complex. Because it is complex, it is relatively obscure and stands in need of explanation; and because it is a whole, it must *in some sense* contain or consist of parts, i.e. relatively simple constituents or factors. In a word, the single principle is simplification; to explain is always to analyse, for to analyse is to simplify. In all these examples, it seems, analysis has a central and unambiguous meaning; it is the reduction of a relatively 'complex' subject of study to terms which, being simpler or simple, are relatively or absolutely *self-evident*.

[1] Cf. below, pp. 43-4.

Thus, for example, an extended whole is dissected into its constituent parts, into its simpler spatial elements (the lines and angles and their quantitative relations); or it is resolved into the simplest spatial elements, from which it can be generated, and the law for its genesis. Or a chemical compound is simplified by reduction to the factors which have combined to constitute it, and the law or formula of their combination. Or a motion, which cannot otherwise be understood (i.e. assigned to any known force as its mathematically calculable effect), is explained as the sum or balance of two simple motions—which are not (and are not supposed to be) actually contained within the motion they explain, but which are mathematically calculable effects of forces, the laws of whose operation are known. Or, lastly, an unusual (and therefore obscure) occurrence is elucidated by being shown to be the concluding phase in a single continuous change which (at an earlier phase of its duration) can be resolved into a plurality of simple (and therefore clearly conceivable) constituent events.[1]

But the plausibility of this contention vanishes on examination. In what follows I will try to show (i) that the supposed single principle is not a principle of explanation at all—i.e. explanation is not analysis in the sense of simplification. Next (ii) I shall point out that the examples which appeared to embody this illusory principle do in fact (though very imperfectly) embody a quite different intellectual procedure—the only procedure which is genuinely explanatory. For so far as, in these examples, anything is indeed elucidated and understood, the explanatory process is not an analysis into simples accompanied or followed by a synthesis; it is an analysis which is of necessity synthetic.

3. (i) *Explanation is not analysis in the sense of simplification.* The single principle, which was supposed to underlie, and to be varied in, all our examples, presupposed that whatever is to be explained is in some sense a whole and therefore complex. The

---

[1] Cause and effect, when adequately conceived, differ from logical antecedent and consequent (condition and conditioned) not in principle but because the logical nexus is displayed in a temporal and perceptible change, from which it has to be disentangled and abstracted. It is the logical nexus (the reciprocal necessary implication of condition and conditioned) which is the *essence* of the conception of cause and effect (cf. also below, Study II, p. 166). But, short of adequate and ultimate analysis, we do commonly apply the term 'cause' to the (temporally) preceding phase or stage of a continuous change, and the term 'effect' to the (temporally) subsequent or remaining phase or stage. Cf. Bosanquet's treatment of cause as 'one of the incomplete forms of ground' (*Logic*[2], vol. i, pp. 250 ff.).

explicandum (it was further assumed) since it is a whole must in some sense consist of parts; and the parts must be (relatively or absolutely) simple and therefore (relatively or absolutely) self-evident. Hence to analyse the *explicandum* is to resolve it into constituents which, being simple, are self-evident, and so to 'explain' it.[1] Now, clearly, it is only under one assumption (and an assumption which does not seem to be warranted by the facts) that analysis so understood (viz.—resolution of a complex into its simpler or simple elements) could ever seem to be an explanation. What that assumption is may best be set out by the help of two well-known pronouncements—viz. Plato's assertion in the *Theaetetus* that 'if anything is a whole, the whole of it must be all the parts',[2] and Leibniz's statement, at the beginning of the *Monadology*, that 'a compound is nothing but a collection or aggregate of simple things—i.e. things without parts'.

If we could assume that everything in the universe is either simple or a mere togetherness of simples, and that the simple, because it is simple, is self-evident: then, under these assumptions, there would be a certain plausibility in the view that a method of analysis in the sense of simplification is the only genuine, and the only possible, method of explanation. But, as I must go on to show, even if we were entitled to make these assumptions (and I shall urge presently that we are not), the supposed analysis would not in fact be an explanation.

Before proceeding, however, I ought to guard against a misunderstanding. Neither Plato nor Leibniz does in fact assume (in the sense I am supposing) that everything in the universe is either simple or a mere togetherness of simples. The statements I quoted from them, interpreted in the bare and unqualified sense I have put upon them, do not adequately express their views.

For Plato certainly did not believe that all wholes are nothing but the sums of their parts; nor could he consistently have regarded any mere sum or aggregate as (in any genuine sense) a whole. And in the philosophy of Leibniz the simple things are the Monads. Now the Monad is without parts in the sense that it is not a quantitative sum or an extended whole; but it 'enfolds within itself' or is potentially an infinite qualitative variety (viz. the infinitely graded detail which is 'the Universe', i.e. the total scale or hierarchy of all the Monads). And though the Monad is

---

[1] Cf. above, pp. 29–30.
[2] *Theaetetus* 204 A . . . οὗ ἂν ᾖ μέρη, τὸ ὅλον ἀνάγκη τὰ πάντα μέρη εἶναι.

simple, its simplicity is that of a principle of change; for its *actual being* is the unrolling of a series of changing states or conditions of itself. Each of these passing states is 'a many expressed in one' (i.e. a 'perception'); and every change—every passing from perception to perception—is due to 'the activity of an internal principle' ('appetition') in the Monad.[1]

Consider the first of the two assumptions (the second will occupy us later) under which alone the supposed principle of explanation might seem to be justified. Every *explicandum*, we are to assume, is a togetherness—assemblage, collection, aggregate, or sum—of simples. Now either (*a*) the *explicandum* is genuinely one and whole in virtue of this 'togetherness' of its constituents. If so, the togetherness is essential to its being, distinguishes it from other assemblages and from simples which are not together. The togetherness, therefore, is precisely that which needs to be explained. Yet since the togetherness is not one of the simple constituents which are together, it necessarily eludes the supposed explanatory procedure. For that is analysis, i.e. resolution into simple constituents; and it cannot explain, but can only disintegrate and explain away, the unity and wholeness of the *explicandum* it resolves. Or (*b*) the *explicandum* is indeed nothing but many simples. Their togetherness is illusory; the *explicandum* is not really (but only appears to be) a whole and one. If so, there is nothing to analyse or explain. There is no whole, nothing complex, not even an aggregate. There is no analysis, for there is nothing to resolve; the supposed explanatory procedure is the reiterated assertion of a many against an unexplained illusion of unity. There is *this* and *this* and *this*: many items, each simple and self-evident *per se*. So much was assumed *ab initio*. And so much, and no more, is reiterated to the end. The assemblage or togetherness of the items —the unity and wholeness of the supposed *explicandum*—are swept aside as illusory appearance; and the fact of the illusion is ignored.

The supposed principle, then, is not established—even on the assumption that every *explicandum* is no more than an aggregate of simples and that the simple as such is self-evident. And the assumptions are unwarranted. For within our experience: (*a*) Nothing is simple, and nothing is, *qua* simple, self-evident, and (*b*) No whole-of-parts or one-of-many is ever a mere aggregate or sum. The whole is always more than all its parts; the one-of-many can never be identified with all its items.

[1] Cf. *Monadology*, § 15.

As to the first of these assertions—viz. that nothing is simple and self-evident—this will, I hope, establish itself in the next ensuing Logical Study. There (unless I am mistaken) a reasoned investigation and discussion will force us to recognize that there are no simple elements of reality—or none at least that can be experienced or known. There is no minimal constituent—no unit or atom—of absolute fact, which evidences itself, which is immediately presented, to sense or thought; there is no primary or ultimate *datum*—nothing given and *eo ipso* guaranteed; there is no intuition (whether sensuous or intellectual) which constitutes a unity at once of absolute awareness and of absolute fact.

The second assertion—viz. that *within our experience no one-of-many, or no whole-of-parts, is ever a mere aggregate or sum*—requires some further explanation and defence; for it seems to be exposed to a very obvious objection.

The ones-of-many, which we experience, may be arranged on a kind of scale. At one extreme of this scale there are genuine wholes or unities—e.g. a living organism, a mind. These only the most thoughtless person would identify with aggregates or sums. And at the other extreme of our imaginary scale there are mere aggregates—a heap of stones, a drawerful of papers, a pound of tobacco—which nobody could mistake for genuine ones or wholes.

Between these two extremes there fall a variety of debatable examples—a suit of clothes, a chemical compound, a crystal—which, it might perhaps be argued, are both wholes or unities and aggregates or sums, according as they are considered from one or the other, *equally defensible* though partial, point of view. But (and this is the objection we are to develop and to meet) if we disregard these debatable examples, there are also, in the middle range of our imaginary scale, some indisputable and undisputed examples which must be regarded as aggregates or sums, and yet also as genuinely one and whole: e.g. the numbers and the figures which are the subjects of the mathematician's study.

The number 7, for example (to take first an example from the domain of arithmetic), is on the one hand a mere sum or aggregate. It is so many smaller numbers, and in the end so many units, added together. That is what is meant when, for example, 7 is equated with 6+1, or 5+2, or 1 added to 1 six times in succession. Unless 7 were a mere aggregate, the operations of the arithmetician could not apply to it.

And yet, on the other hand, it is genuinely one and whole. It is an individual integer, distinct from all others. It has its unique position in the series of integers. It possesses arithmetical properties and functions peculiarly its own. Unless 7 were thus uniquely individual, many arithmetical judgements, in which it is the subject—judgements universally accepted as true—would have no meaning or application. It would no longer be true, for example, that 7 and no other number is the square-root of 49.

Or—to take next examples from the objects of geometry—consider the circle, or again the cube. Each beyond question is genuinely one and whole; a uniquely individual type of figure, having its own special position in that conceivable graded system, which would set out exhaustively, and in order, the possible specifications of extended whole (plane surface or solid). And of each, in virtue of its uniquely individual character, certain geometrical propositions must be affirmed and denied, which can be truly affirmed and denied of nothing else. The circle, for example, alone among plane figures, is such that the line, which delimits it, is at all points equidistant from a single point within the figure. The cube must be—and nothing else can be—contained by six equal squares.

And yet each of these extended wholes is the aggregate and collocation of lesser extended wholes which are its parts. For the circle (or the cube) can be disintegrated in thought at any line (or any plane) into constituent parts—into lesser plane figures (or lesser solids). And the ideal division, from which the parts result, leaves them unaltered—at all events, nothing more than ideal aggregation (collocation or juxtaposition in thought) is required to reintegrate them and thus to restore their respective wholes.

Draw in thought a diameter within the circle. You have *eo ipso* effected an ideal separation between two constituent semicircles of the whole; for the conceived (ideally drawn) diameter is their juncture and their cleavage. It is the base of either and of both, and the boundary excluding each from the other. Start, then, in your thought from the two semicircles thus separated by ideal division. Bring them once more together by ideal collocation. Appose them base to base, or limit to limit. You have restored in thought the whole you had in thought divided. Once more the two bases or limits have become—what they were in the original circle—a single ideal diameter, which is for both semicircles the line of cleavage and of juncture, their common boundary, excluding each from the other and confining each within its proper share of the whole.

In general terms, then, the objection may be stated as follows: Amongst the objects of our experience there are genuine wholes or ones-of-many, which, nevertheless, can be explained by an analysis into simple constituents or parts—e.g. the numbers, solids, and plane figures with which arithmetic and geometry are concerned. For these entities, though genuinely whole or individual, are also undeniably sums or aggregates.

And to this objection the answer that must be made is this. It is true that the whole procedure of the arithmetician or geometer presupposes that the numbers and figures, of which the worlds or domains of their sciences consist, do in fact combine these two characters, presupposes that they are, from one point of view, mere aggregates, and yet, from another point of view, individual types, wholes, unities. This is the fundamental assumption (the ὑπόθεσις), without which these sciences could not come into being or work at all.

But it does not follow that there are in our experience genuine wholes which yet are mere aggregates—which therefore can be adequately explained and understood by an analysis of the kind supposed—i.e. an analysis which resolves them into simple constituents. The two characters—wholeness or unity, and being a mere aggregate of simple constituents—if each is taken as absolute, as rigid and without any qualifying conditions, are incompatible. Their combination—which arithmetic and geometry take for granted, and must take for granted for the limited purposes of their investigation—cannot be conceived, i.e. thought out, without self-contradiction; so long, that is, as each is predicated categorically and unconditionally and, so to say, merely side-by-side with the other, of the 'same' (abstractly the same) subject.

One must agree, in the main, with the view taken by Aristotle[1] in regard to the limitations under which arithmetic and geometry and all the special sciences necessarily work. The arithmetician, for example, is concerned only with a single abstracted character or side of things—that in them, or of them, in virtue of which they can be regarded as one or again as many: their countable or numerable aspect. He isolates by definition this feature of the facts—abstracts and substantiates it. And so he is led to postulate

[1] Cf. Arist. *Metaph.* 1077ᵇ 12–1078ᵃ 31. The doctrine Aristotle maintains in this passage, in regard to the 'assumptions' made by the special sciences, seems to me true in principle and in the main; though his exposition is too closely bound up with his special theory of demonstration, and with some of the more disputable of his 'metaphysical' tenets, to be accepted (without modification) in all its details.

a world of sheerly countable entities, i.e. of entities which are nothing but the proper subjects and results of arithmetical operations, nothing but units and aggregates of units. But the world he thus postulates or assumes—and the bare units and integers of which it consists—are fictions: they are (like legal fictions) known to be unreal and impossible, but supposed (for a limited and definite theoretical purpose) to be (not only possible but) 'fact'. They exist (so to speak) and are conceivable only by agreement or convention;[1] for they have been made by exaggerating a single essential moment in the constitution of fact to the suppression of a contrasted moment which is no less essential. They are conceivable only by agreement, not ἁπλῶς: i.e. they cannot be thought out, for to think them out would mean to reconstitute them *ab initio*—to correct the omission in the original ὑπόθεσις—the assumption by which the domain of the science was constituted. To introduce the eliminated moment *ex post facto*—to admit into the context of the science propositions which imply that the supposed mere sums are somehow and also genuinely individual and whole—softens the appearance of paradox, but only at the cost of self-contradiction. It is not to conceive—to think out—the combination of these characters (which, taken in isolation, are conflicting, and mutually destructive) in a single intelligible subject.

But though, in this sense, the arithmetician's assumption is a 'fiction', there is not necessarily any error or falsity in his making or employment of it. On the contrary: as he makes and uses it, his procedure, normally, at all events, is both legitimate and necessary. For his purpose is to emphasize one abstracted character of fact; to study it in isolation, knowing that, so taken, it is not any longer fact or character of fact; and to work out in this (the only possible) manner the full implications of the numerability of things. In so far, however, as he remains true to his initial assumption, his explanatory procedure is artificially restricted, and his results are fictitious entities of a fictitious world.

This shows itself in many ways,[2] one of which we have already

---

[1] Cf. Plato, *Rep.* 533 c: ᾧ γὰρ ἀρχὴ μὲν ὃ μὴ οἶδε, τελευτὴ δὲ καὶ τὰ μεταξὺ ἐξ οὗ μὴ οἶδεν συμπέπλεκται, τίς μηχανὴ τὴν τοιαύτην ὁμολογίαν ποτὲ ἐπιστήμην γενέσθαι;

[2] There is a clear and forcible exposure of the inherent limitations and defects of 'mathematical reasoning' in Bradley, *Logic*[2], vol. ii, pp. 603–7. I quote (from p. 604) a few sentences which summarize the 'fictitious' character of the numerical world. 'Arithmetic appears to require the following postulates. Every unit can be taken as the integer of an indefinite number of units. Every integer can be taken as one among an indefinite number of units in a larger integer. Hence every integer is actually contained in a larger integer, and actually contains all its own

seen. The explanatory procedure which is employed in arithmetic is often supposed to be the proper movement of the intellect as such, i.e. a movement of analysis and synthesis. Yet (as we have seen) within the area defined by the arithmetician's ὑπόθεσις—within the domain he postulates taken strictly as his postulate defines it—there can be nothing to analyse and no determinate product of synthesis, except by the inconsistent introduction of the notion of genuine wholeness and individuality. And, as we have also seen, the complex entities of that domain, the supposed mere sums, are in fact (even within arithmetic) each the sole owner of special properties—and thus by implication (and inconsistently) conceived as genuine ones and wholes.

4 (ii). Our examples imperfectly embody analysis of a different kind. Let us now go back to the examples in which the relatively complex (and therefore obscure) appeared at first sight to be explained by simplification, i.e. by analysis into simpler or simple (and therefore self-evident) constituents. A closer study of them will show that in so far as we really explain the practical perplexity, the unusual occurrence, the intuitable curve, the earth's revolution, or the chemical compound, the explanation is not merely analysis; and the analysis, which *is* contributory to it, is *not* a resolution into simples.

That the explanatory procedure is not merely analysis was virtually admitted in my former description. For, as we saw, there was needed, to complete the explanation, an accompanying or a subsequent reversal of the analysis—a synthesis, construction, composition, combination, or at any rate a re-synthesis or re-constitution. But there is a *suggestio falsi* in this way of describing the explanatory procedure. For it suggests that first the *explicandum* is pulverized by analysis, reduced to a heap of mutually exclusive elements; and that then the inherently repellent items are reunited by synthesis. But if indeed our analysis were a pulverization of this kind, no synthesis of ours—nothing short of a miracle—could reunite the grains of dust.

If our actual procedure, in the examples I have quoted, is to elucidate anything or to explain at all, it must embody a very

smaller units. And every unit can be taken as a unit, and actually is a unit, in a special integer, and also in every other possible special integer larger than itself. But such a world and its processes cannot possibly, to my mind, have more than a relative truth and reality. They hold good, and can be used, that is, only for certain purposes and under certain conditions; and these conditions, or some of them, we throughout, as suits our purpose, ignore.'

different principle. Instead of being an analysis into simples accompanied, or followed, by a synthesis, it must be (from the start and throughout) a *dual* movement—a movement of analysis and synthesis in one. Our procedure must be two-edged; and if we are to give it its proper title, we must not be afraid of *verbal* contradiction, but must call it a 'synthetic analysis' or an 'analytic synthesis'. It must discriminate in connecting and connect in discriminating; and must render the *explicandum* not more simple but more definite, i.e. more explicitly complex.

What I am suggesting amounts to this: in so far as any intellectual procedure is genuinely explanatory, that which is being explained (the *explicandum*) must be (or be taken as) whole or unitary, and must retain this character throughout the process. At first the *explicandum* is relatively vague—vague both as regards its wholeness or structural unity, and as regards the detail, the diversity, by including and unifying which it is itself unitary or whole. But in, and by, the explanatory process, it is gradually made more definite in both respects: both the nature of the detail which is unified, and the nature of the unification, become, gradually and simultaneously (by one and the same process), more distinct. To explain, therefore, is (I suggested) essentially and in principle to exhibit an *explicandum* (which is single in its complexity; which is unitary and whole in, and throughout, a varied detail) as a structurally definite, or well-ordered, system of intrinsically related terms.

An intellectual procedure, therefore, is genuinely explanatory so far as it achieves such an ideal: that is, so far as it brings out, makes distinct, the items of a detail by bringing out and making distinct the modes of their connexion, the structural unity (plan) of that whole, of which they are the detail; in a word, so far as it is a two-edged *discursus*, *analysing by synthesizing* and *synthesizing by analysing*.

That was the suggestion. Let us see how far, on closer consideration, our former examples confirm it.

(*a*) The first two (the practical perplexity and the unusual occurrence) need to be specified.[1] For hitherto there is no more

---

[1] Specification, it may be said, is not enough: *individualization* is demanded. For it is nonsense to speak of an example, unless you set out, in all its singular detail, an actual case of perplexity and enlightenment, and an actual explanation of a given and singular startling event. But so to *individualize* them is, strictly, impossible; and a description, which might pass muster as an individualization (in a loose and popular sense), is beyond the scope of these studies. In any case,

than a vague and general sketch, in which *explicandum* (what is to be explained) and elucidation (the advance in understanding) are equally uncertain.

In the practical perplexity, then, the agent has to make a decision: to refuse or to accept, or to suggest a compromise in regard to, an offer for the purchase of his house. What here is the *explicandum*—the perplexing situation which is to be elucidated? At first it is a vague and ill-defined totality of considerations and interests; one and whole by reference to his present feelings, if I may use that most slippery term to express the formal immediacy and unity of the agent's total present state or attitude of mind, including the vaguely formed and vaguely articulated idea of the field within which his final decision must fall. And if, by taking thought, the agent can obtain enlightenment, it is only because the thought he takes (his intellectual procedure) organizes this vague totality by discriminating items of its detail—items which it *eo ipso* connects and orders in their relevance to (their bearing upon) the alternative possibilities between which in the end he will have to decide. Within the confused mass of circumstances which were comprised in the initial totality—which were loosely unified by falling all together within his 'outlook' or attitude of mind—there gradually emerges, in and by the two-edged activity which is his thinking, a nuclear system of distinct and definitely related elements. And the distinction of these elements is the ground of their connexion: viz. the idea of the articulated field within which the final decision will have to fall. It is this idea which has been present to his mind vaguely from the start, which guides and controls his deliberations throughout and which grows more definite, more precisely articulated, in the process. It is, therefore, this field of the possible alternatives which is explained and better understood as the result of taking thought in his practical perplexity. It becomes more definite in its detail and in the relations to one another of the alternative possibilities of choice within it: and gradually the confused mass of detail, included in the perplexing situation, becomes arranged and cleaned up by reference to its bearing upon one or the other of the 'articulations' in this field of his choice.

Or, again, I am startled by an unusual occurrence—the sudden angry outburst (say) of a colleague at a meeting. What is here the

however, it is possible to confirm the principle, for which I am contending, in specific or typical examples.

explicandum? What is it that startles me; that sets me casting about for an explanation; that in the sequel receives elucidation? What startles me (to sketch the specific or typical form of the problem) is the apparent irrationality of the outburst—its seeming abruptness and want of motive, which isolate it and make it stand out in glaring contrast to the equable flow of a reasoned discussion. From the first, that is to say, the *explicandum* includes (more or less implicitly) a wider context, both contemporaneous with, and preceding, the outburst. It is by contrast to this wider context that the occurrence is startling and sets me thinking. And *the first stage* of my explanatory procedure renders some section within this context more explicit; or (for this is the inseparable obverse of the same process) expands the apparently isolated event into a continuing change, of which it is the culminating phase or climax. I recall, for example, this and that argument in the preceding debate, or this and that tone of the speakers, which I now recognize (working backwards from the outburst) to have been provocative; I recall this and that premonitory warning in my colleague's bearing and gestures—symptoms (as I now see) of the fury gathering in his soul. And so far, my explanatory procedure brings out, within the whole presented and remembered scene, a sectional change— a variety of events unified by a single significant trend. The features I characterize and accentuate are phases of a continuous development culminating in my colleague's angry intervention; it is by their relevance to his state of mind that they are discriminated and *eo ipso* connected. If, in such an example, there is any further advance in understanding, *the next stage* of my explanatory procedure would determine more precisely the outline and the constituent phases of this sectional change. It would both narrow and generalize the *explicandum*: defining it, for example, as the change from calm interest to fury within a human soul, of such and such a character and education, as it responds to such and such influences (such and such changing phases) in its moral and intellectual environment. And finally, perhaps, by an intellectual process still in principle the same—still in principle a synthetic analysis, or an analytic synthesis—there would emerge within the moral or psychological development, as the intelligible law or principle it embodies, a nexus of terms (condition and conditioned, antecedent and consequent) precisely defined and reciprocally necessitating one another.

(*b*) It is sufficiently clear already that, in the three remaining examples, the explanatory procedure conforms to the same general principle. For though it is common enough to speak of the analysis of a compound into its elementary constituents, of the resolution of a curve, or of the composition of a motion, we have already seen the inaccuracy of such phrases. The *explicanda* (water, for example, the intuitable curve, the earth's revolution) are not mere aggregates—even though it is disputable whether, or how far, they are self-coherent, i.e. genuinely whole or individual.[1] And as to the atoms of hydrogen and oxygen, the successive positions occupied by the point in its flow, or the components of the revolution—these supposed simple constituents are either not contained at all, or not contained in their unmodified simplicity, in the compounds or complexes which are being explained.

Thus, as we saw, the chemist's analysis is in principle synthetic. The *explicandum* (for example, water) emerges, in and through his explanatory procedure, not as a mere heap or plurality of hydrogen and oxygen atoms, but as an ordered grouping and arrangement of them. His explanation of water issues in effect in the conception of a mosaic of a very definite pattern—a mosaic in which each atom of oxygen grips firmly to itself two atoms of hydrogen. The simple constituents, therefore, are not contained in their simplicity or as such in the compound. They are contained, if they can be said to be contained in it at all, only in that radically modified state which they assume when locked together in the mosaic. To the eye of scientific faith, no doubt, the hydrogen and oxygen are present in the water; for, if the mosaic be disintegrated, there will be simple atoms, moving freely in their isolation, and exhibiting (if a sufficient number of them is collected) the characteristic properties of these two gases. But so long as the mosaic exists, the grouped atoms behave as no free atoms of oxygen or hydrogen ever dream of behaving; their properties—their actions and reactions—are those of a liquid and not of a gas; and it is thus and only thus (only thus altered beyond recognition by their grouping) that oxygen and hydrogen 'constitute', that is, are contained in, water.[2]

[1] A chemical compound was quoted before (p. 33) as a complex which (like, for example, a crystal or a suit of clothes) was neither indisputably an aggregate, nor beyond question a genuine whole. The curve and the revolution, though individual and whole for intuition or imagination, must be classed with the fictitious entities of mathematical science (cf. above, pp. 33–7).

[2] It remains true that no atom is 'contained' *as such* and *unaltered* in the compound, whether we conceive the atom in the old-fashioned manner (i.e. as a

The intuitable curve (to pass to our next example) contains no points; nor is the flow which generates it a series of fixed positions. Doubtless, whenever I in thought arrest the flow, I conceive a fixed position, uniquely determinable in accordance with the constitutive equation of the curve; an ideal limit, at which the flow is halted and from which it will be resumed. And doubtless, wherever I divide the intuitable curve, I create in thought a point or a duality of points—the ideal limit, which joins and separates the divided portions of the disintegrated whole. But these fixed positions, and these points of juncture and division, are not constituents of the flow or of the curve it generates. And in this respect our former description did less than justice to the paradoxical nature of the geometer's proceedings. The successively defined discrete positions we admitted[1] have to become a flow; the geometer's analysis has to be supplemented by a re-synthesis, by an imaginative construction which generates the curve in its continuous and uniquely individual character. But the geometer's actual procedure is more parodoxical than that. For the discrete positions, as he conceives them, do not *become*, but *are*, a flow; he posits and, in positing, cancels their discretion. He supposes the flow arrested, so that its arrests are fixed definable positions, discriminated from, and serially connected with, one another; and so far the flow is analysed into fictitious constituents and *eo ipso* synthesized by their fictitious relations. But he also supposes (unless, in my ignorance of mathematics, I misunderstand him) that the flow continues unchecked through its arrests; and this supposition contradicts the first supposal, and cancels the discretion and the serial relatedness of the fictitious constituents. Yet unless his explanatory procedure is thus glaringly self-contradictory, it does not even pretend to elucidate the *explicandum*, viz. the intuitable curve.

Finally, the revolution of the earth round the sun may be resolved mathematically into two component movements—viz. a movement tending to persist *ad infinitum* in a straight line, and a movement at right angles to the first—viz. a movement of gravitation towards the centre of the sun. So far, the explanatory procedure is the same two-sided activity, which we found in the

Democritean 'indivisible solid'), or, in accordance with modern developments of physical theory, after the analogy of an infinitesimal solar system, of which the sun and planets are respectively a positive charge and negative charges of electricity (cf. B. Russell, *The A B C of the Atom*, pp. 29–43).   [1] Cf. above, p. 28.

previous examples. For the supposed simple movements are not first discovered and isolated within the revolution, and then re-composed. They are discriminated only as components—the analysis and the composition being the two inseparable sides of a single intellectual activity. But (like the fixed positions and their serial relatedness in the geometrical analysis of the curve, or of the flow which generates it) the components and their composition are fictitious. Neither of these simple movements is actual in the revolution; nor can they be said to make, in fact, each of them, their distinctive contributions to it. Movements, indeed, conform-ing to the law of gravitation alone, and movements tending *ad infinitum* onwards in a straight line, even if they do not actually occur, are at least capable of being clearly conceived. But nobody supposes that such isolated movements did in fact co-operate to produce, or are in fact now integrants of, the earth's revolution. The mathematical explanation affirms only that the revolution takes place as if it were a compromise of the two components—a compromise in which they and their relatedness, their discrimi-nated and connected contributions, are cancelled and absorbed. Or, at the most, it suggests that, were the force of gravity annulled, the earth would travel *ad infinitum* onwards at a tangent to its present orbit; whilst, were the other component eliminated or neutralized, the earth would pull, with a determinately accelerated velocity, towards the sun.

5. Let us pause at this point and consider where we stand.

It was suggested[1] that the *modus operandi* of the intellect is, in principle, one and one only. The intellect *as such*, the intellect *qua vis cognoscens*, has no other method of explaining than the dual procedure, the two-edged activity or 'discursus', whereby and wherein a complex *explicandum* becomes (gradually and *pari passu*) more definite both in its structural unity and in its varied detail. This suggestion was confirmed in the examples we examined. Can we take it, then, as established, and extend it to the philosophical activities of the intellect? Can we assert—not as a provisional suggestion which we believe, and expect the science itself to confirm, but as an established doctrine—that logic, because (and in so far as) it explains its subject-matter, is the Synthetic-Analysis or Analytic-Synthesis of Knowledge-or-Truth?

To such a question the answer is clearly 'No'. What was originally suggested, neither can nor need be established within,

[1] Above, pp. 37–8.

and for the purposes of, an introductory study like the present.[1] To establish it would mean to verify, throughout the range of our explanatory activity, the specified and graded embodiment of a single principle. Nothing less than the philosophical study of knowledge—i.e. nothing less than logic itself in its actual system or self-fulfilment—would suffice as an adequate test (as a solid proof, or even as a disproof) of the suggestion.

The suggestion, though *pro tanto* confirmed, is not proved. This being admitted—or rather emphasized, since it follows from the very nature of a preliminary sketch of logic—the next step is to dispel two probable misunderstandings. When that has been done it will be possible to take the final step—viz. to distinguish the *modus operandi* of the intellect in its logical activity (in its philosophical explanation of knowledge) by the reflective and critical character which its Synthetic-Analysis (Analytic-Synthesis) assumes in this region.

(*a*) The first misunderstanding may be stated most simply in terms of a well-known Cartesian doctrine. Descartes[2] attributed to the intellect (or *Vis cognoscens*) two irreducible functions, in which its nature is exhaustively expressed. Of these, one (*Intuitus*) is a power of intellectual insight or vision. By it the intellect apprehends immediately—in a single cognizant act, complete at once and at a stroke—a simple self-evident *datum*, or primary element of reality and knowledge. The other fundamental function of the intellect (*Deductio*) is a power of infallible illation—a power of mediate or discursive cognizance. By it the intellect advances from *datum* to *datum*, linking them together by an intelligent *discursus*—i.e. a *discursus* natural and proper to itself; and is thus enabled to construct, out of the simple self-evident truths which it possesses by the exercise of its intuitive function, those long chains of reasons (or implicatory sequences) which form the content of a 'science'.[3]

Now it may be thought that our two-edged discursus is in no sense immediate—is, in effect, the function which Descartes con-

---

[1] Cf. above, p. 1 and p. 16.

[2] Cf. *Regulae*, R. III, vol. x. 368, &c.

[3] Cf., e.g., *Discours* (vi. 19): 'Ces longues chaisnes de raisons, toutes simples et faciles, dont les Geometres ont coustume de se servir, pour parvenir a leurs plus difficiles demonstrations . . .'; and cf. *Regulae* (R. V–VII, vol. x. 379–92), where Descartes tries to work out the conception of his method as a *graduated* analysis followed by a *graduated* re-synthesis—and (in doing so) conceives the domain of a science as a network of implicatory sequences.

trasts with 'Intuition'.[1] And, if so, it will be rightly objected, the intellect by its activities could explain nothing. A *mere* discursive movement (even if it be analytic and synthetic at once) could not constitute an understanding of a complex *explicandum*. For it would be a sheer succession of discrete events, without continuity or wholeness. If a discursive process is to explain, there must be a single consciousness pervading, developing in, and unifying its steps or stages.

But this is to misunderstand what was suggested. The assumption we are to make is that the intellect in all its explanatory activities is discursive, its discursus being in principle two-edged; but not that it is sheerly discursive. The understanding of a complex *explicandum* is essentially discursive; it is a cognizant *activity*, an explanatory *process*. But it is *cognizant*, it is *explanatory*, in virtue of a unitary consciousness which is unfolding and developing itself throughout the activity, which is immanent and growing in all the stages of the process; and therefore from this (no less essential) point of view, the understanding of a complex *explicandum* is, in its entirety, an unbrokenly single comprehension of the explained—a beholding of it, intuitive and immediate. It is only in part, we may agree with Bosanquet,[2] 'that our thought is discursive; it has also an intuitive aspect, in which it remains within itself secure in the great structures of its creation'. It is a caricature of the intellect—the *vis cognoscens*, or whatever we ought to call the power which is at work at all the levels of our cognizant experience, for example, in our perception of fact, in our scientific reasoning and philosophical speculation—to identify it with a faculty which, in exercise, is a *mere* discursive movement. An intellect thus truncated is a fiction. It is the purely formal and subjective faculty, which (as I urged before) has no existence outside the limits of an untenable theory; the fictitious source of mere thinking or of thought sheerly relational and discursive.[3] It is the supposed function of formal analysis and synthesis—a function unable to operate, unless materials are presented to it by

---

[1] This is not true—at least not without considerable qualification—of Descartes. There is a sense in which (as he recognizes) *Deductio* is, or collapses into, an immediate cognizance. And the content of an *Intuitus* is an immediately necessary nexus of *Implicans* and *Implicatio*; e.g. the 'simple proposition' that $2+2=4$, &c., 'that self-consciousness implies existence' (cf. *Regulae*, vol. x. 369, 370, 379, 383, &c.). Cf. also below, Study II, p. 169.

[2] *Principle of Individuality and Value*, p. 55.

[3] Cf. Bradley, *Appearance and Reality*, especially chap. xv.

some other and separate faculty of the mind (by some faculty of immediate intuition whether sensuous or conceptional). And as such it is, in its own right, neither cognizant nor contributory to knowledge. For its formal analysis and synthesis could only *seem* to disjoin and connect its 'data' or 'materials'—since it cannot penetrate them, or make them its own, or understand them.

On the other hand, the assumption we are to make does involve the denial that any intellectual act, any thought or act of cognizance, is *sheerly* immediate. To this denial I have already committed myself[1] in anticipation of a later discussion.[2] The intellect has no separate function of intuition, whereby it immediately apprehends—takes in at a stroke, or sees, without discursus of any sort—certain things or facts or simple self-evident items which are the elements of reality and knowledge. In that sense, at all events, we must hold with Kant[3] that 'it is impossible to form any notion of an understanding' (i.e. intellect) 'which intuits the real things'.

It may be worth while to add that, even if such simple cognizant acts occurred, they could not—whether isolated or summed—constitute understanding; nor could the simple elements be said to be explained or understood merely *qua* self-evidencing in (and as) these intuitive acts. For understanding clearly requires that what is understood should be a many (or at least a duality) in one: two (or more) elements which nevertheless constitute a unity, or two (or more) differences in (or of) an identity.

(*b*) So much by way of guarding against the first misunderstanding. We are to assume that the *modus operandi* of the intellect in explaining is one, and one only, in principle; is, in principle, always the same two-edged discursus—but we are not to interpret this as meaning that it is a merely discursive process which is in no sense 'intuitive', therefore in no sense one, total, comprehensive; in no sense immediate and direct. We are not to identify the whole explanatory procedure of his *vis cognoscens* with the 'deductive' or 'illative' function which Descartes ascribed to it as one of its powers, contrasted with an opposite power of 'Intuition'.

Nor—to come now to the second misunderstanding which is to be forestalled—must 'one, and one only' be interpreted as 'therefore in no sense varied or pluralized', nor must 'the same' be

---

[1] Cf. above, p. 33.   [2] Cf. Study II.
[3] Cf., e.g., *Prolegomena to any Future Metaphysics*, § 34, footnote.

read as 'therefore in no sense different'—differentiated neither in type nor in degree.

Every explanatory process expresses the same theme—but the theme exists, and maintains its sameness, only in its variations. Or, every explanatory process embodies a single principle: but the principle lives in its particular embodiments, and their differences are necessary to its singleness, to the unity of its life.

The point at issue can be stated more simply without these musical and biological metaphors. Unity and identity are by a common tradition conceived abstractly: what is one is taken to exclude plurality, what is the same to exclude difference. In that sense only the creatures of abstraction are one, or are the same: only, for example, the fictitious entities of mathematics (units, points, instants, atoms) and their fictitious relations, or only the so-called abstract universals. Nothing real or actual is in that sense one or the same. The unity of the intellect—for the intellect is emphatically *real*—has nothing to do with, for example, punctual simplicity (the unity of a point); and the sameness of its functioning— a functioning which is emphatically *actual*—is the reverse of tautological monotony.

What we are to assume is that the *modus operandi* of the intellect is one in the plurality, and the same in the variety, of its explanatory activities: that its unity and identity are concrete.

Now that which is concretely one must be distinguished from (at least) three varieties of abstract unity. It must be distinguished (1) from the one-beyond-the-many (τὸ ἓν παρὰ τὰ πολλά) ; (2) from the common predicate (the one predicable without variation) of many (τὸ ἓν ἐπὶ πολλῶν, τὸ κοινῇ κατηγορούμενον) ; and (3) from the atomic element persisting unchanged in many different settings—from the one merely in (surrounded by) many. Thus—to give examples—(1) if a Platonic Form be conceived as absolutely simple, as a transcendent and unique specimen in a super-celestial museum, it is one, but its unity is abstract: the same is true (2) of straightness, that is conceived as a single character predicable in a single unvaried sense of many lines; and (3) of the soul (in some philosophical theories) which is a Monad persisting unchanged throughout the individual's life. It is true, also, of the unity of the atom of oxygen which is to-day associated with two atoms of hydrogen to form a molecule of water, and to-morrow conjoined with an atom of carbon to constitute a molecule of carbon monoxide.

Similarly, that which is concretely identical (concretely the same with itself) must be distinguished from (at least) three varieties of abstract identities (or self-sameness). (1) A common content, which thought may abstract from (or rather, which the imagination may conflate out of) many particulars or singulars by blurring or eliminating their differences, is 'the same with itself'—but its identity is abstract. The same is true (2) of the so-called abstract universal concept which thought may form provisionally to mark, in vague outline, an area for investigation; and (3) of a nucleus which is taken to persist unvaried through changing contexts, or to be the essential nature, the specific nature, repeated without being modified in a multiplicity of different embodiments (or individuals).

Thus (1) the general idea in the sense of the generalized image of man, horse, is 'the same', the same with itself; but its identity is abstract. By the generalized image I mean the result of a process whereby the mind 'conflates' many singular and definite ideas or images, by eliminating or blurring their differences, into (so to speak) a composite photograph—the exact likeness of none, but the vague 'common notion' of all.[1] (2) Abstract, also, is the 'sameness' of a genus or generic character conceived provisionally as the common basis, the as yet undeveloped potentiality of disjunctive specification.[2] So conceived the genus or generic character is 'the same without difference'; and *this* sameness is abstract because it depends upon ignoring what the concept essentially implies. For when, with the advance of knowledge, the concept is rendered distinct, the *genus* (or generic character) will be developed into a closely affiliated group of complementary species (or typical specifications of the generic character). Each member of the group will be a different actualization of the potential (generically common) basis (cf., for example, equilateral, isosceles, scalene—three different actualizations of the possibility of bounding a plane by three straight lines, or forming a plane figure with three angles which are together equal to two right angles). In all of them together—and not otherwise—its sameness will obtain full and distinct expression. But so expressed, its sameness (far from excluding difference) involves differentiation in its very constitution, and is a concretely articulated identity. Lastly (3), abstractly

[1] Cf., e.g., Spinoza's account of the *notiones universales* in *E*. II. 40, S. 1.
[2] Cf., e.g., the 'abstract universal' triangle—triangle *qua* defined at the outset of Euclid's treatment.

the same is the essential nature (or cohering group of essential elements), if (as usually happens in text-books of formal or Aristotelian logic) that is taken to persist as the unchanged and unchangeable form (the εἶδος or τὸ τί ἦν εἶναι) of the singular perceptible substance (the σύνολον, σύνθετος οὐσία, the αἰσθητόν, τόδε, &c.) ; or, again, if it is taken as the specific form (the ἄτομον εἶδος) identically repeated in many different (coexistent and successive) singular embodiments.

In short: what is concretely one is not a simple element or simple content externally related to, or predicable of, a many. Nor is it a simple element or unit in many contexts or in many complexes. It is a one essentially 'pluralized'. And what is concretely identical is not the same without differences—whether this blank sameness is conceived by blurring and conflating differences, or by provisionally disregarding differences and concentrating upon their as yet undeveloped basis. Nor is it the same in (surrounded by) differences. It is a 'same' essentially differentiated.

B. *In what sense is the method of logic reflective and critical?*

6. What, then, are the differences in which the *modus operandi* of the intellect maintains, displays, and fulfils its concrete unity and identity? What are the variations in which, and as which, the intellect plays its single theme—its Synthetic-Analysis or Analytic-Synthesis?

(*a*) There are, *first*, differences of kind or type. These are correlative to the different types of *explicanda*. They condition, and are conditioned by, the different types of complex facts or wholes[1] with which the intellect is concerned in its explanatory (or theoretical) activities.

(*b*) There are, *secondly*, differences of degree or power. Neither of these terms is adequate, but they must serve in default of a better. These different degrees or powers severally characterize the intellect (or *vis cognoscens*) as it works at three broadly distinguishable levels of cognizant experience—viz. the matter-of-fact or common-sense level of ordinary (intelligent) perception (δόξα μετ᾽ αἰσθήσεως), the level of scientific explanation and theory (διάνοια, ἐπιστήμη), and the level of philosophical speculation (φιλοσοφία, διαλεκτική).[2]

---

[1] Cf. above, p. 33.

[2] Cf. the passage quoted from T. H. Green (above, p. 14). Plato's terms are added only as rough indications of what is meant.

At each and all of these levels there is, constituting or contributing to constitute the theoretical experience, a two-edged activity of synthesis-and-analysis-in-one. Without it, except by virtue of it, not one of them would be possible, or could possess the character it actually has. But the intellect—or whatever we call the *vis cognoscens* which is the source of this activity—is functioning, so to speak, at different degrees or powers of itself. Thus, in constituting the cognizant experience we call 'perceptual', the *vis cognoscens* is working blindly or instinctively. If the two-edged activity, which is an indispensable factor in perception—of this blind and instinctive analytic-synthesis or synthetic-analysis—is 'thinking', it is a 'thinking' of which the percipient is unaware; and if the source of the activity is intellect, it is an intellect functioning without consciousness of its own activity. It is only by subsequent reflection upon his perceptual experience, and upon the character of the things and facts perceived, that the percipient may come to recognize that his mind in fact was (or must have been) active —and sometimes, by further reflection, may recognize the nature of this activity.[1]

On the other hand, at the level of scientific explanation and theory, the *vis cognoscens* is aware of its activity. In the demonstrative and experimental sciences alike, the exercise of the intellect is deliberate. The mathematician or the student of nature sets himself to explain and think. He knows that the activities in which he is engaged are—in some degree, at any rate—initiated by his intellect and under its control. Here, therefore, the *vis cognoscens* is working consciously and deliberately. The two-

[1] Cf., e.g., J. Cook Wilson, *Statement and Inference*, vol. i, pp. 45–7. 'The apprehension of the characteristics of what we perceive involves a comparison; and comparison we take to be thinking.' But in perception 'we are really comparing but do not recognize that we are'.—The question of nomenclature is primarily a matter of convenience. Kant, perhaps wisely, restricted the terms 'intellect', 'intellectual', 'thought' (*Verstand, Denken*, &c.) to the *vis cognoscens* operating on the self-conscious level; and called the same *vis cognoscens* 'imagination' (*Einbildungskraft*), when regarded as the source of the blind and unconscious (or instinctive) synthesis which is indispensable to constitute the most rudimentary cognizance of an object —perception. Cf. Kant, *Kritik der reinen Vernunft*[2], pp. 103 and 105, with Caird's commentary and criticism. Thus, e.g., 'There is necessary to the genesis of *perception as such*, as opposed to sensation on the one hand and to the mere forms of sense on the other, an activity which Kant attributes to the understanding: though not to the understanding in that conscious activity which is manifested in the application of the Categories, but in an *unconscious* activity, to which he gives the name of imagination' (*The Critical Philosophy of Kant*[2], vol. i, p. 311); '... the same faculty [viz. the imagination] which, when it ceases to be blind and becomes self-conscious, is called the understanding' (ib. p. 358: and cf. pp. 326–30).

edged operation of analysis and synthesis is the procedure of a mind fully awake, self-directed in the explanation of a complex which it has itself selected as its *explicandum*. But though the mind is fully awake (or self-conscious), it is not yet *reflectively* self-conscious; not turned upon its own activities and the knowledge they help to constitute; not reflecting upon it and them, nor critical in its reflection. It is this final power of the mind's 'awakeness'—its reflective and critical self-consciousness throughout its intellectual activities—which is distinctive of the level of cognizant experience called philosophy. The method of logic—the *modus operandi* of the intellect in its philosophical explanation of knowledge-or-truth—is still 'Synthetic-Analysis' or 'Analytic-Synthesis'. But the method of logic is, nevertheless, essentially different from the method of science. For, in logic, the two-edged activity is raised to the power of the intellect (*vis cognoscens*, mind) which it expresses (which is actual in it); and is therefore reflective and critical in a sense I must endeavour to make clearer.

7. Let us go back and reconsider the general description of explanation which hitherto we have taken for granted. We laid it down[1] that every *explicandum* is in some sense complex, a one-of-many or a whole; and that to explain (or understand) it, is to exhibit it—by a two-edged activity which brings out and defines both its unity and its diversity—as an ordered system of intrinsically related terms.

But this general description does not apply, strictly and commensurately, to philosophical explanation and to the *explicanda* which form its subjects. For the objection to which I referred before—viz. that subject-matter and method in philosophy are too intimately connected to admit of separate treatment[2]—returns now in a final and inescapable form. The spiritual realities which are the subjects of philosophical study do indeed constitute and maintain themselves in the speculative movement itself; and thus are ones-of-many, wholes and systems of a uniquely peculiar kind —if indeed these terms are applicable to them at all. Hence, *explicandum* and explanatory process on the philosophical level of cognizant experience determine, and are determined by, one another in a manner which I have not yet sufficiently recognized: and the general description of explanation with which, hitherto, I have been working does not strictly apply to philosophical explanation.

[1] Cf. above, pp. 37–8.   [2] Cf. above, pp. 15–16.

Perhaps, then, a fuller consideration of this somewhat paradoxical character of the subjects of philosophical study will throw
some light upon the sense in which the method of logic is reflective
and critical; and so at last enable us to bring this preliminary outline to a conclusion.

(i) Let us begin by considering a paragraph in Green's *Principles
of Political Obligation.*[1]

'Rights,' Green says, 'are made by recognition. There is no right
"but thinking makes it so"; none that is not derived from some idea
that men have about each other. Nothing is more real than a right, yet
its existence is purely ideal, if by "ideal" is meant that which is not
dependent upon anything material, but has its being solely in consciousness.'

Some of Green's phrases, in this characterization of the spiritual
fact we call a 'right', are perhaps open to criticism. It seems an
exaggeration to say that a right 'has its being *solely* in consciousness'; that it is 'not dependent' (if that means in no sense dependent) 'on anything material'; and to speak of its being 'made
by recognition' or by 'thinking'. But Green's own treatment in
the context[2] supplies the necessary qualifications of these rather
unguarded statements; and, properly interpreted, his characterization is beyond question sound. A right has force and binding
effect—a right is actual—only at the level, only in the medium or
element, of the mutual recognition of self-conscious beings. And,
strictly speaking, a right which is not actual is not a right at all.
It is only by an acknowledged abstraction that we can speak of
'unrecognized rights'. A right, no doubt, may be unrecognized
by this or that person; but a right which nobody recognizes—
either directly or by implication—is a contradiction in terms. In
that broad sense, at any rate, 'thinking', 'consciousness', 'intelligent will' are essential to the very constitution of a right. They
are the soil in which alone a right can live—the medium or element
in which alone it can have and sustain its actual being.

Now, in a philosophical study of right and rights, the explanatory
procedure and the *explicanda* have a more intimate relation than
my previous description of explanation suggested. No doubt the
thought which goes to make the *explicanda*, the thought which is
their medium and sustaining element, is not the thought which,

---

[1] *Works*, vol. ii, p. 446.
[2] Cf. the whole preceding discussion on the sense in which 'Will, not Force, is
the basis of the State' (l.c., pp. 427 ff.).

in the form of philosophical speculation, explains them. Obviously the rights must exist and be actual, must have their own independent nature, if the philosopher is to study them; and obviously his business is not to make, or remake, but to understand that nature. And yet, by staring hard at this obvious distinction, we may hypnotize ourselves into forgetting another equally obvious and perhaps more important side of the matter.[1]

For clearly the existence and actuality of the rights, which a philosopher is to study, must imply his recognition of them; that is, from the start, as an indispensable condition of his explanatory thought about them, his thought (i.e. a recognition, of which he is conscious, which passes through and invades his mind, which he consciously adopts and makes his own) must go to make them what they are. In that sense, therefore, in explaining them, he is reflecting upon *explicanda* which depend for what they are—for their own nature and actuality—not, indeed, upon the explanatory activity itself, but nevertheless upon intellectual activities of some kind and at some level; upon intellectual activities, moreover, which he, in explaining, must share—in which his intellect must be engaged. And as the philosophical study of these *explicanda* proceeds, the thought which explains re-fashions, in explaining, the spiritual facts (the rights) it is explaining; and thus does, after all, contribute essentially to their being. For certainly the rights which emerge (and as they emerge) in and through a philosophical theory are very different from the original *explicanda*. The rights which come out at the end (so to speak) are very different from the rights which went in at the beginning of the speculative movement.

Yes, it will be objected, but the difference is merely in the philosopher's clearness of apprehension. The rights themselves remain what they always were. But the philosopher sees them now more clearly; not only recognizes them semi-consciously and instinctively, but recognizes also and reflectively the fact (and the principles) of this original and constitutive recognition.[2]

But this objection misses the point. Clearness of apprehension

---

[1] Cf. J. Cook Wilson, *Statement and Inference*, §§ 24–33, 541–4, 547–51. When Cook Wilson says (§ 33, p. 76) that neither the object apprehended nor the apprehension of it 'can be *reduced to*' one another, he is insisting upon the distinction I here call obvious. But when he adds that neither can be 'expressed or explained in terms of the other', his denial is not obvious, or even (I think) true, except on an arbitrarily restricted interpretation of 'expressed or explained'.

[2] Cf. Cook Wilson (l.c., § 16, p. 50): 'Thought can recognize its own laws, by reflecting upon itself.'

or of vision are but metaphors in this connexion. For what the philosopher apprehends is nothing tangible or palpable; and what he sees does not stand finished before him, waiting for increased illumination and more powerful lenses to reveal more and more of its hidden detail. 'Vision' here is intellectual insight; and 'apprehension' is the union in which thought penetrates, and is penetrated by, its object. 'Demonstrations (and these alone) are the eyes with which the mind sees things and observes them', Spinoza says.[1] It is the demonstrating, it is the speculative movement, and nothing else, which is itself the seeing. There is no mental vision, no intellectual insight, except what comes to us in, and as, the inevitable progress of the proof. 'The process of reasoning', as Cook Wilson expresses it, 'is precisely the activity of knowing'; and 'precisely' must be taken with all possible emphasis.[2] Thus, the rights, which in and through a philosophical analysis (like that set forth by Hegel in his *Philosophie des Rechts*) have vindicated themselves as so many essential 'moments' in the practical fulfilment of the human spirit—as so many inevitable phases in the realization of man's intelligent will, or in his self-expression as a moral agent—have been raised to a new and higher level of actuality. In this medium of reflective and critical recognition rights have acquired a new and profounder significance. They have grown, so to speak, to a fuller stature, in virtue of the whole or system which, immanent and articulated in them, they constitute and express. It is thus and only thus—only in this transfiguration, which is due (in part, at least) to the speculative activity of a philosophizing mind—that the rights which were to be explained (the initial *explicanda*) are fully what they really are. For they are fully actual, they are fully themselves, only in constituting and displaying the spiritual reality which is their whole or system—the spiritual reality which is the self-fulfilment of man's 'practical reason' or 'intelligent will'. In this sense, therefore, it is only in, and through, the speculative movement (only in, and through, the philosophical explanation) that the rights which

---

[1] *Ethics*, v. 25: 'Mentis enim oculi, quibus res videt observatque, sunt ipsae demonstrationes.' Cf. Spinoza, *Tr. Th.-P.*, vol. i, p. 533: 'Nam res invisibiles, et quae solius mentis sunt objecta, nullis aliis oculis videri possunt, quam per demonstrationes; qui itaque eas non habent, nihil harum rerum plane vident. . . .' (Spinoza is arguing that it is nonsense to say 'there is no need to understand' (*intelligere*) God's attributes: it is enough 'omnino simpliciter, absque demonstratione, credere'.)

[2] Cf. *Statement and Inference*, p. 35. If A is 'precisely' B, B is 'precisely' A: i.e. to know is to reason, and to reason is to know.

are its *explicanda* gain and possess that definite nature of their own, which the philosophical study of them endeavours to understand.

So far I have been discussing the spiritual facts called rights, and the spiritual reality they constitute—their whole or system which is the commensurate *explicandum* of a philosophical theory of right (using that term to cover the total self-fulfilment of the human spirit as intelligent will). Within such a theory the *explicandum* is intimately bound up with, and determined by, the explanatory procedure. I have now to take the final step—i.e. to show that all this applies, *mutatis mutandis*, to the subject-matter and method of logic.

(ii) What, then, is the commensurate subject-matter of logic—its *explicandum* as a whole or in its entirety, corresponding to what I have just called right (the whole or system of rights) and have identified with the total self-expression, with the self-fulfilment, of intelligent will? Earlier, it will be remembered, it was proposed to call that total *explicandum* 'knowledge-or-truth'—the object being to cover both inseparable sides of the spiritual reality on which the logician reflects. It is truth (it was suggested), in the sense of reality disclosing itself and disclosed to mind—to any and every intelligent mind; and, being truth, it is also and *eo ipso* knowledge—i.e. the whole theoretical movement, the entirety of the cognizant activities, wherein the mind (any and every mind *qua* intelligent) fulfils and expresses itself by co-operating with, and participating in, the disclosure.[1]

There is a grave difficulty here—whether knowledge-or-truth can be regarded as a whole or system or totality at all—or, if at all, in what precise sense. And there is a further difficulty in regard to the spiritual facts (the logical facts, as I proposed to call them),[2] which (corresponding to the several rights in the previous example) articulate and constitute the total *explicandum*, or which, at any rate, can be regarded as the detailed problems of the logician, as *explicanda* of the subordinate phases, sections, and chapters in logic as a whole; in the total speculative movement, which is the philosophical theory of knowledge-or-truth.

We met both these difficulties before.[3] And, as before, we must recognize that within the present preliminary sketch only a vague and tentative answer—an evasion, rather than a solution—is possible. For nothing but logic itself could furnish (or be) an adequate solution, viz. a reasoned account of the spiritual reality

[1] Cf. above, pp. 20–1.   [2] Cf. above, p. 14.   [3] Cf. above, pp. 7–9, 15–16.

as a whole and the spiritual facts which constitute it. Not an introductory study, but nothing less than the entire discursus which is logic itself could show the nature of the wholeness of knowledge-or-truth, the nature of its articulation, and the nature of the logical facts which are its proper parts, its ultimate implicates or constitutive variety.

Yet, as we saw before,[1] there are certain familiar topics which can be taken for the present purpose as logical facts, since beyond question they fall somewhere within the subject-matter of logic. And to the question, 'What are the logical facts which constitute knowledge-or-truth; which, within this sphere, are to be taken as analogous to the several rights in your former example?', a general answer is, for the present, enough. The logical facts, it is enough to say, the *explicanda* of the subordinate phases and sections of the speculative movement, which in its entirety is logic or the philosophical theory of knowledge-or-truth, are the kinds of topic to which reference was made before. Any portion or fragment, for example, of our cognizant experience; anything, for example, which (prima facie, at least) is a perception of fact or a demonstration of truth, and so an experience in which, in some measure, what is real is manifest to mind—disclosing itself in, and through, the activity of mind. Or, again, any form or law of knowledge-or-truth, any of the fundamental implicates or indispensable conditions of its actuality; or, lastly, any of those structural principles of intelligibility and intelligence in one which were referred to before under the name of 'Categories'.[2]

Now Green's characterization of right and rights obviously applies (*mutatis mutandis*) to the subject-matter of logic and to all the logical facts which fall within and constitute it. If knowledge-or-truth is in any sense a whole, it is a whole which clearly is a spiritual or ideal reality: a whole of which the *esse* is to live and be actual in the medium or element of the mutual understanding of self-conscious minds. And the same is obviously true of every logical fact—of every proper part of such a whole. It is true of every implicate, condition, category, or structural principle, whether of knowledge-or-truth in its entirety, or of this or that contributary level or form thereof (e.g. of perception of fact, or of demonstration of truth or truths in science). There is no knowledge or truth—there is no part or fragment, no implicate or principle, of knowledge-or-truth—which is not (in Green's phraseo-

[1] p. 21.   [2] Cf. above, pp. 14–15 and 19–21.

logy) ideal; none (to borrow his quotation from *Hamlet*) 'but thinking makes it so'; none that exists or is actual otherwise than in the cognizant (the thinking or intellectual) activities of the human spirit.

And, strictly speaking, knowledge (or truths) which is not actual is not knowledge (or truths) at all. No doubt there is knowledge and truth in plenty—and there are many implicates and principles of knowledge or truth—which exist and are actual, while yet the intellectual activities, which constitute and sustain them, do not pass through (and are not the functioning of) this or that person's mind: are not, for example, 'mine', activities in which 'I' share or in which 'my' intellect is engaged. But a truth which lives in nobody's thinking; a knowledge which is affirmed and sustained by nobody's intellectual activity; an implicate or condition, or category or structural principle of knowledge or truth which is in no sense actual—these (except by a deliberate and acknowledged abstraction) are so many contradictions in terms.[1]

It follows that, as in the philosophical theory of right, so in the philosophical theory of knowledge-or-truth (i.e. in logic) explanatory procedure and *explicanda* are intimately bound up with one another; and, in particular, to emphasize the point which is directly relevant to the present discussion, it follows that the explanatory procedure essentially contributes to constitute the *explicanda*.

No doubt the thought which goes to make and sustain the *explicanda* is not the thought which, in the form of logical speculation, explains and understands them. There is an obvious distinction (as we saw) between the thinking, the mutual recognition of intelligent wills, which makes a right (which gives it actuality and force), and the thinking which (in the form of philosophical speculation) reflects upon and explains this spiritual fact. And it is equally obvious that the cognizant activities, or the thinking, in

---

[1] Cf. below, Study III. 'How, then', it may be objected, 'can we speak of knowledge or of truths which are forgotten, or as yet "undiscovered"?' The knowledge or truths, which are not yet (or no longer) actual, are entitled to the names (it must be answered) only by implication in, and by reference to, actual knowledge and actual truth. Again it may be objected: 'Are not truths timeless and eternal? And does not this mean that they were before men came into existence, and will be when all conscious beings have ceased?' Truths (it must be answered) are not timeless or eternal in this temporal sense (they are not sempiternal or everlasting). They are so, because, though their actuality is impossible without activities which occur in time, the special date and duration of this occurrence are irrelevant to their character as truths.

which alone there exists and is actual knowledge-or-truth (in all its forms, at all its levels, in all its implicates and principles), must be distinguished from the speculative thinking of the logician, which reflects upon, criticizes, and explains this spiritual reality and these logical facts. The *first* is a thinking—a process at once analytic and synthetic, a discursus—which is instinctive or 'blind', of which the percipient is not aware; a function, in Kant's terminology, of the imagination, not of the intellect proper (of the 'Einbildungskraft', not of the 'Verstand'). The *second* is the thinking of a mind, which is reflectively and critically self-conscious in, and conscious of, its own activity. And it would be an equally serious confusion to identify *simpliciter* the thought, which is embodied, for instance, in mathematical reasoning and which goes to constitute τὰ μαθηματικά (the numbers and figures of the arithmetician's and geometer's worlds), with the thought of the logician in so far as he reflects upon this scientific form or level of knowledge-or-truth—in so far as he makes of mathematical knowledge or mathematical truth his *explicandum*.

Nevertheless, we must not be hypnotized by this obvious distinction. We must not assume that where there is obviously not identity without *difference*, there there must be sheer otherness—i.e. no identity in any sense or at all. For knowledge-or-truth in all its forms is actual only in the medium of consciousness. And if the logician is to reflect upon and study any of these forms—if he is to study, for example, perceptual or scientific cognizant experience—the intellectual activities, in which alone they are actual, must pass through his mind. His own intellect must be functioning in the constitution of his *explicanda*, as well as in the reflection and criticism by which, as a logician, he is trying to explain them.

In other words, the intellect in its logical work (in its philosophical explanation of knowledge-or-truth) is re-thinking and recapitulating the less-developed stages of its self-expression as a *vis cognoscens*. And this re-thinking is inevitably, to some extent, a refashioning and transfiguring. In entering upon the logical study of perception, for example—and in reconstituting for that purpose the perceptual experience it is to study—the logician's intellect inevitably modifies the original unsophisticated nature of its *explicandum*. Its own reflective activity contributes to determine the perceptual experience it is to study—alters it, at least to the extent that its original blind and instinctive character is destroyed. And this refashioning of the *explicandum* by the activity of the intellect, which is reflecting upon it and explaining it, becomes more and more conspicuous as the work of logical speculation proceeds.

Consider, by way of example, what happens in the progress of Kant's critical analysis of knowledge in the *Transcendental Aesthetic* and in the first division of the *Transcendental Logic* (the division to which he gives the title of *Transcendental Analytic*). In the terminology I have been employing, Kant, throughout this early portion of the *Kritik*, is engaged in logical speculation. His aim—and, so far as his reasoning is sound, his achievement—is to set forth the logical explanation of perception (i.e. perceptual experience as a concrete whole, perceiving together with its inseparable correlate and object, viz. perceptible fact), and of the 'scientific level of knowledge-or-truth' (i.e. the reasoning and explanatory theory of the sciences together with the intelligible systems or worlds which are their inseparable correlates and objects).[1]

What, then, is to be regarded as Kant's initial *explicandum*—the spiritual reality or logical facts which he sets out to study and explain? The first rough answer to such a question would be, I suppose: 'Our actual perceptual and scientific experience—any experience in which fact is perceived or truth inferred.' But our actual perceptual experience and our actual scientific knowledge do not enter, as such and unmodified, into the sphere of Kant's investigation. From the outset, by the mere fact that Kant is reflecting upon them, they have been transformed. In order to study them, in order to take them as *explicanda*, Kant of necessity must re-think and recapitulate them; and so to re-think them is to refashion and transfigure them by raising them to the reflective level. The perceptual and scientific experience, which Kant takes as his *explicandum*, is from the first conceived as the union of

---

[1] It is no part of my present purpose to discuss the success or failure of Kant's critical analysis of knowledge in his *Kritik der reinen Vernunft*. My object in referring to it is simply to illustrate the kind of speculative investigation which I take to be (in principle) logical. It should be remembered, however, that in Kant's language knowledge (in the strict and only proper sense) is science, and science is mathematics and mathematical physics. In other words, Kant restricts the scientific level of knowledge-or-truth to the reasoned theory of a world conceived as the correlate and object of mathematical and mathematico-physical demonstration. According to his view, within the compass of these sciences, or systems of explanatory theory, man's intelligent theoretical experience of an intelligible cosmos finds complete and coherent expression; and the 'domains' they demonstrate, and render intelligible, together constitute the whole known and knowable reality—the complete and total truth.

certain opposites, the product of contrasted factors. But these opposites, or contrasted factors, do not express a variety which actually exists within the original perceptual or scientific experience. They express a variety which (if Kant's theory is sound) must be recognized on reflection upon the original experience. In our actual perceptual experience we do not bring together and arrange under the forms of the sensibility and the Categories (or the schematized Categories) a multiplicity of separately received sensations or impressions. But when we re-think a perceptual experience—when, in order to study it, we recapitulate it on the reflective level—we transform, into such sharply contrasted elements or factors, a diversity which, in the original experience as it actually occurred, was a diversity of moments or phases inseparably fused in concrete unity.

Thus, the logical facts which, in the *Transcendental Aesthetic* and *Analytic*, Kant investigates and explains, are not perception and inference as such and unsophisticated as they actually occur in our everyday reading of the world and in the thinking of the men of science. His *explicanda* are perception and inference refashioned and transfigured—conceived and described in terms of the reflective plane on which his own mind is working. From this point of view, the logical facts, that are to be explained in the *Aesthetic* and *Analytic*, are the elementary constituents, implicates, and conditions of perception and inference—the elements of experience which Kant's reflection has, from the first, distinguished and defined. They are, for example, the manifold of sense and the forms of the sensibility; the Categories, the Schemata, the basal principles of a science of nature; and so forth. And these *explicanda*, it is obvious, are being continually modified and developed in, and by, the whole course of Kant's explanatory investigations. What they really are is what they show themselves to be in the reasoning of the *Kritik der reinen Vernunft*. Their real being crystallizes in itself the speculative movement which explains them—or in which alone their full significance emerges and is manifest. Here, too, therefore, as in the example which I first put forward (rights and the system of rights), the *explicandum* constitutes itself in, is in large measure determined by, the intellectual discursus which explains it.

A well-known passage in Kant's *Prolegomena*[1] may serve to confirm and make clearer the view for which I am contending

---

[1] *Werke*, iv, § 39, pp. 322–3, Berlin edition.

(a view which wears a somewhat paradoxical appearance), viz. that the logical facts grow into their full nature only in, and by the help of, the logical study of them; so that the *explicanda* in this region are really what they come to be in the course, and by means, of the logical explanation of them.

Kant, in that passage, is, in effect, insisting that there is all the difference in the world between, on the one hand, the philosopher's first discovery, extraction, and haphazard enumeration of the categories and principles which he has been employing in the concrete (*in concreto*, implicitly and without reflection), for example, in his perceptual experience and scientific theorizing—and, on the other hand, that final treatment of these categories and principles which would satisfy his desire, that is (we must presume), which would exhibit them as they really are. The philosopher's aim is not merely to collect all the categories and principles which cognizant experience (knowledge of an objective world) implies as its *a priori* (intellectual) conditions. At best such a collection would be an aggregate which he believed—but could not know—to be exhaustive. His aim—an aim which Kant claims to have achieved—is 'to deduce them all, by an *a priori* deduction, from a single principle' ('aus einem Prinzip *a priori* ab[zu]leiten'). In other words, his aim is to exhibit them as the necessary articulations of a systematic whole; and thus to know that there can, and must, be precisely this variety—just these, and just so many, *a priori* conceptions and principles constituting the formal and intelligible structure of knowledge.

'It is easy enough,' Kant says, 'to extract and collect . . . those conceptions which, not being based upon any special experience, are nevertheless to be found in all empirical knowledge [*Erfahrungserkenntnis*], constituting (as it were) the mere form of its connectedness. No great reflection, not much insight, is required for such a task. It is as if, by reflecting upon a language, we were to extract general rules for any and every actual use of its words, and thus to collect the elements of a grammar';

but, having gone so far, were incapable of going further. It is as if, having thus collected the elements of a grammar, we were nevertheless

'unable to explain why every language must have precisely this formal constitution, and no other; and still less able to show that, and why, the formal structure of every language must exhibit just this number and just this variety in its articulations'.

II

THE SEARCH FOR A *DATUM*

§ 5

1. The preceding discussions have sketched the subject-matter and method of logic. Logic has been described as the 'philosophical analysis' (the 'reflective and critical synthetic-analysis') of 'knowledge-or-truth'; and some explanation has been given of the meaning of the terms in this 'formula of orientation'.[1]

But this sketch has committed me to a certain position. It is true, no doubt, that nothing in the nature of proof was attempted or possible. To prove a formula of orientation could only mean to try it out in actual logical reasoning. Nothing else, and nothing less, than logic itself—the actual 'science' or 'system' of logical speculation—could prove (or, for that matter, disprove) the correctness or adequacy of a descriptive outline of this kind. Nevertheless, to set up a formula of orientation implies at least a belief that the position it assumes and summarizes is sound in the main—is likely to be confirmed by the actual course of logical investigation.

Now the position, to which my sketch has committed me, is far from commending itself as probable. It has against it a number of generally accepted theories and distinctions, which find expression in ordinary language, and may claim, therefore, to have behind them the weight of common experience.

'The authority of language', Cook Wilson[2] warns us, 'is too often forgotten in philosophy, with serious results. Distinctions made or applied in ordinary language are more likely to be right than wrong. Developed, as they have been, in what may be called the natural course of thinking, under the influence of experience and in the apprehension of particular truths, whether of everyday life or of science, they are not due to any preconceived theory. . . . On the other hand . . . a philosophical distinction is *prima facie* more likely to be wrong than what is called a popular distinction, because it is based on a philosophic theory which may be wrong in its ultimate principles. . . .'[3]

2. To couple knowledge with truth, and to use both terms together to designate in its entirety the subject-matter of logic, is

---

[1] Cf. pp. 1–5.   [2] *Statement and Inference*, pp. 874–5.
[3] But see below, pp. 104–5, for a criticism of excessive faith in ordinary language.

clearly to stretch both terms beyond their common meanings. But is it not worse than this—is it not a plain distortion of language? Both terms are conspicuous examples of what Aristotle calls τὰ πολλαχῶς λεγόμενα. Each of them, in ordinary usage, exhibits a variety of different and, in some respects, conflicting meanings. Yet one thing at least seems clear: neither 'knowledge' nor 'truth' bears, in ordinary usage, the meaning I attributed to it. Neither of them is, in any of its ordinary meanings, commensurate with the spiritual reality which, according to the preceding argument, is the total *explicandum* of logic. Nor are they complementary designations of the same something—designations which emphasize contrasted moments in the constitution of an identical *designatum*.

Thus, for example, (*a*) knowledge, in ordinary usage, is contrasted with error; and truth (the true) with falsity (the false). Yet knowledge and error, the true and the false, both fall within the total *explicandum* of logic, within the spiritual reality, which it was proposed previously to call 'knowledge-or-truth'.

Again, (*b*) in knowledge we should commonly be said to attain and achieve, to apprehend and embody, truth. Truth is not 'knowledge', but that which we know. And knowledge is 'true', but is not truth—though here ordinary usage tends to waver, for knowledge would be said to 'consist of truths'.

Moreover, (*c*) in ordinary usage, knowledge is often taken as roughly equivalent to the whole sphere of conceptional thought, and contrasted with sentient and sensuous or perceptual experience. Knowledge, that is to say, includes every experience—whether intuitive and immediate, or discursive and inferential—in which we are, in any degree, intellectually cognizant of the nature of things. It includes thought in all its forms, so far as it is in any degree true. It includes, therefore, 'conception', 'judgement', 'inference', if these are distinguishable forms or grades of the thinking function; and it includes the judgements and inferences of 'opinion', as well as those of 'demonstration'. In short (to borrow the terminology used by Aristotle in the *Posterior Analytics*), it includes δόξα, διάνοια, νόησις, and ἐπιστήμη. On the other hand, it excludes 'feeling', 'sensation', and 'perception'—it excludes 'knowing' by way of αἴσθησις—whatever the degree of certainty our sentient and sensuous 'knowing' (awareness) may possess.

Lastly, (*d*) by a further refinement and restriction, knowledge is sometimes taken to exclude the whole sphere of opinion and probable argument, as well as sentient and sensuous experience.

In this last sense knowledge is restricted to what Aristotle calls νόησις and ἀποδεικτικὴ ἐπιστήμη; to *intuitus* and *deductio*, as defined in the *Regulae* of Descartes; or to Locke's 'intuitive and demonstrative knowledge'.[1] For, if language is to be used strictly, nothing can deserve the name of knowledge unless it is inevitably, unalterably, and indubitably true.[2] Knowledge, therefore, is either the intellectual intuition of self-evident *data*—of those 'simple propositions' or 'primary truths' (*propositiones simplices*, ἄμεσοι προτάσεις, ἀρχαί) in which two elements cohere by an immediate (yet necessary) nexus; or it is the equally self-evident and infallible inferential movement of the intellect as it follows the logical implications of the self-evident *datum* or *data*, and traces their expansion into a chain of truths—a chain of links and linkages each self-evident and indubitable.[3] Opinion, on the other hand, is the mere thinking, the mere argumentation, which may indeed be true, but also may be false. Being neither infallible nor unalterable, it must be rigorously contrasted with knowledge.

Similarly, in ordinary usage, the term 'truth' is employed now in a wider and now in a narrower sense—corresponding to these wider and narrower senses of knowledge ((c) and (d)).

Thus, for example, (e) what is presented or 'evident' to sentience (feeling) and sense (or perception) is usually called 'fact' rather than 'truth'. It is contrasted with 'truth'—i.e. with what is manifest to thought, is known by intellectual acts and processes. 'Truth' is thus confined to that which discloses itself to intellectual intuition (to that which is 'conceived'), and to that which is brought before the mind and 'known' in judgement and inference.

Or, again, (f) 'truth' is sometimes given a more restricted meaning. For that which is in a broad sense 'intelligible' is

[1] In so far as Locke's 'intuitive knowledge' and Descartes' *intuitus* include the 'infallible' assurance of feeling and sense (cf., e.g., Locke, *Essay*, iv. 9, § 3; iv. 11, § 9), they extend beyond knowledge in this restricted sense.

[2] Cf., e.g., Aristotle, *Post. Anal.* 72ᵇ 3: εἴπερ δεῖ τὸν ἐπιστάμενον ἁπλῶς ἀμετάπειστον εἶναι (the man of science must know his conclusions to be absolutely certain. He must be 'beyond the reach of argument', because he must know that there neither are, nor can be, any rational grounds on which criticism of the truth he has demonstrated could be based). Locke (Letter to the Bishop of Worcester, quoted in footnote to *Essay*, iv, ch. 1): 'For, with me, to know and to be certain, is the same thing; what I know, that I am certain of; and what I am certain of, that I know', &c.

[3] Cf. above, pp. 44–5.

divided into 'truth' proper (the true *sensu eminenti*) and the 'probable'. Truth, in this strict sense, is the commensurate correlative of the 'knowledge' which cannot by any possibility be, include, or become 'error'. For, if language is to be used strictly, nothing can deserve the name of truth, unless it is, absolutely and unalterably, what it is known to be. What shows itself to 'opinion', on the other hand, what is disclosed in most of our judgements and established in most of our arguments, is at best an ambiguous and spurious truth. For it is, at best, truth relative, conditional, partial; a truth balanced against falsity; infected and weakened by the doubts and errors, over which it has won a precarious and temporary victory—a truth for which the proper name is 'probability' or the probable.

3. My formula of orientation, therefore, is exposed to the criticism not that it rests upon a mere assumption and is unproved, but that what it implies or assumes is incredible. The authority of language (the general and ordinary usage of the terms) is against it: for this (it will be said) bears witness to the existence of certain divisions in the very nature of things, divisions which are incompatible with the view that the commensurate subject of logical study is a single spiritual reality, is a genuine whole or system or one-of-many in any sense whatever.

The formula of orientation, it will therefore be said, is worthless. To call the supposed total *explicandum* of logic 'knowledge-or-truth' neither establishes that it is a whole, nor throws any light upon its character or upon the nature of its unity. It is not knowledge; it is not truth: it is not knowledge-or-truth, in any of the ordinary senses of these terms. To describe it, therefore, as knowledge-or-truth is about as helpful as it would be to call it x-y-z.

4. Instead of attempting a direct defence of the description I have given I propose for the present to turn my back upon it and to begin, so to say, at the other end. I propose to examine the chief of those ordinary senses of 'knowledge' and of 'truth', which seem so definite and plain; to test the distinctions and divisions they imply, and the general principles and theories which underlie them. Starting in the present study with the division of cognizant or knowing experience into 'intuitive' or 'immediate', and 'discursive' or 'inferential', I shall examine the attempt to find a *datum* which the various forms of this division seem to entail. Then, in the third and last of these studies, I shall inquire what it is that is true or false, and wherein its truth or falsity consists;

F

and so endeavour to test the value of those ordinary views, according to which there is, on the one hand, a distinction between 'truth' (as that which is known) and 'knowledge' (as the knowing of it) ; and, on the other hand, a sharp cleavage between truth and falsity corresponding to a similar cleavage between 'knowledge' and 'error'.

§ 6

1. The division of cognizant experience (knowing, knowledge, apprehension) into *immediate* and *discursive* is commonly drawn at two different levels, thus taking two main forms. First, there is the antithesis between sense (including sentience, or feeling, in one of the many senses of that ambiguous word) and thought. And secondly (within thought, thus broadly used to cover all intellectual, as opposed to sensuous, apprehension), there is the antithesis between a thinking, which is immediate or intuitive, and one which is discursive, mediate, or relational. The former is, or is supposed to be, a kind of intellectual perceiving, or conceptual apprehension, by which the mind takes in a total object at a glance ; comprehends it, in its unity and its detail, directly and all at once. An intellectual perception of this kind is sometimes called, not only in popular usage but even in philosophical writings, a 'feeling', in another sense of that misleading term.[1] And, on the other hand, there is, or is supposed to be, a discursive or mediate thinking, which presupposes and works upon (or within) *data* immediately conceived—'objects' of which we feel certain though we cannot as yet support this feeling or intuitive assurance by rational grounds. It is this discursive or mediate thinking which (as 'judgement' or 'inference') proceeds, by its characteristic two-edged activity of analysis and synthesis, to convert the *data* we immediately conceive into precisely defined constituents of an articulated whole or system—or again, according to a different theory, to make explicit the detail and the structure within some immediately felt or conceived totality (some total object of intellectual intuition),

---

[1] Cf. (perhaps) *some* passages in Bradley's *Appearance and Reality, Essays*, and *Logic*[2] ; and the frequent appeal in Cook Wilson's *Statement and Inference* to what we 'feel'. Thus, e.g., i. 26: 'We *feel* that we understand better . . .'; i. 338: '. . . a distinction [sc. that between thought and perception] which we *feel* must somehow be maintained', &c. 'Feeling', in such contexts, appears to mean an experience which is intellectual rather than sensuous—an intellectual experience, of which we are sure, though (so long as it remains feeling) we can give no reasons for our assurance.

and so to bring and hold before the mind the distinct and distinctly related elements which the felt totality implies.

2. In both these forms of the division, the immediate member of the antithesis is supposed to constitute (or to provide) the *datum*, material, or foundation, of the discursive member with which it is contrasted.

Thus[1] (a)—on the lower level of the division—all our knowledge by way of judgement or inference (and by way of conception, if any knowledge comes that way—a point to be considered later)[2] rests, in the last resort, upon a *datum* or *data* of sense which it interprets; upon sensible materials which it forms or elaborates; upon what we feel (i.e. are sentiently aware of), sensate, or perceive, that being the solid foundation guaranteeing its validity and truth.

And again (b)—on the higher level of the division, as we find it set forth, for example, in Aristotle's *Posterior Analytics* or in the *Regulae* of Descartes—the judgements and demonstrations, which form the body of a science, logically presuppose certain primary 'intelligibles'. These primary intelligibles are, in their own proper nature, individual facts or reals; i.e. each of them is a unitary total object, self-evident (or immediately manifest) to an undivided intellectual act (an intuitive or conceptual apprehension). In Aristotle's theory, for example (to work with that as an illustration), such primary intelligibles are the Forms, *Infimae Species*, Essential Natures—ἄτομα εἴδη, τὰ τί ἦν εἶναι. In their own proper nature, each of them is an individual fact or reality, to be apprehended all at once, and at a stroke, by an undivided act of intuitive thought: each of them is a νοητόν, immediately manifest in its concrete unity to an act of νόησις. But these individual facts can be 'unfolded' or analysed—can be expressed in the expanded form of definitions (as διανόητα, in λόγοι). And it is thus that they are used by the discursive thought of science. For all the demonstrations of a science (according to Aristotle's theory) are based, in the end, upon certain immediate (indemonstrable) premisses (ἄμεσοι προτάσεις), and are controlled by (must conform to) certain indemonstrable principles or axioms. The former, in ultimate analysis, are definitions in which the man of science expands his immediate knowledge (his intuitive or conceptual thought) of certain forms or essential natures—in

---

[1] I am only concerned at present to characterize the two main levels or forms of the division roughly and in general: a more detailed and accurate account will be attempted later (cf. below, pp. 68-72). [2] Cf. below, § 11.

Euclidean geometry, for example, definitions of plane figure and its specific types or differentiations (triangle, square, circle, &c.). The latter are the principles of reasoning in general (the 'laws of thought'), and the more special principles (if such there be) of reasoning within each sphere or department of being (the laws of geometrical, biological, moral, reasoning) ; and they too depend, in ultimate analysis, upon an immediate knowledge (a conceptual or intuitive apprehension) of the nature of reality as such and in general, or of the nature of the special sphere of reality in question.[1]

Thus, here too (in this, as well as in the preceding, form of the division), the immediately known provides the materials, and is the basis and guarantee, of the rest of our knowledge—of all that we know by discursive or mediate thinking.

3. Now it seems to follow that any logician, who accepts and works with this division (on either of its levels or in either of its forms), is committed to the search for a *datum* or *data*. If, that is to say, the subject of his study (knowledge, cognizant experience, or whatever may be its most appropriate name) is thus divided, his *first task* must be to set out those facts, realities, or truths, which are self-evident and immediately apprehended, and which therefore constitute the materials and foundations of everything else within this domain. He is bound, it would seem, to point them out and enumerate them—and if possible to show that they are self-evident, and wherein their common character, *qua* self-evident, consists. This, at any rate, is the task which I propose to attempt in the present study.

A. THE DIVISION ON ITS LOWER LEVEL

§ 7

Let us begin with the division on its lower level, and let us first describe it more fully and accurately.

(*a*) What we know immediately is what we feel, sensate, sensuously perceive—facts or a fact with which we are directly in

---

[1] Cf. above, pp. 21–2. The laws of thought, i.e. the κοινὰ ἀξιώματα presupposed in any and every demonstration, are definitions of τὸ ὄν ᾗ ὄν. Similarly (though Aristotle does not expressly say so, and perhaps could not have agreed) if there are any special laws to which the reasoning in each department of reality must conform—axioms or principles, for example, of geometrical, or again of biological demonstrations—they would be definitions of that kind of Being (e.g. of Space, or of Life). And, in ultimate analysis, all these definitions are expanded statements or transcriptions of what we know by a direct and undivided intellectual intuition or conception—in which the central character of reality (or of space, of life, &c.) is given at a stroke, and given infallibly as what it is.

contact—fact which is given or presented. Our knowing is the awareness, the apprehension, of *data* of the outer senses (shapes, colours, sounds, tastes, &c.) ; and of the *data* of what may be called the inner sense (sentience or feeling), for example, the thoughts, desires, passions, &c., occurring in ourselves—to which we may attend, or which we may notice by introspection.[1]

If, in this kind of experience, there is activity or act on our side, this is preliminary to the knowing itself, not a part of it. It is a preparatory adjustment—like the opening, moving, focusing of the eyes, the turning of the ear, the bending of the fingers—like 'the turning our attention back' upon our own inner states or processes which we are to observe or notice in introspection.[2] The knowing itself is a being alive or awake to, a taking in of, a fact which confronts us. The fact, whether physical or psychical, whether of 'outer' or of 'inner' sense, is 'given', 'presented', or 'presents itself'. To know it is simply to 'accept' or 'receive' it as it is in its own independent nature.

In this first kind of cognizant experience, then, we are essentially receptive. Our knowing is, in principle, a passive acceptance. We may call it a sensuous or sentient awareness of given or presented facts, including under 'facts' our own inner states and changes. *Essentially* receptive, passive *in principle*—for even if acceptance or reception implies in some sense an act of mind, is the exercising of a mental capacity or power, still this act of mind is not supposed to determine or modify the *datum*. That, i.e. the fact which, in this immediate experience, we apprehend, is what it is ; presents itself as it is ; and remains what it is, and as it is, indifferently before, during, and after our reception or knowledge of it.

(*b*) This first kind of knowledge, this immediate sensuous or sentient awareness of given fact, is contrasted with (and yet is in some sense the material and basis of) a second kind, a discursive or thinking cognizance. There are different and mutually inconsistent theories of the nature of this second kind of knowledge, the knowledge which takes the form of judgement or inference, and of its exact relation to the first. But on the whole it would be agreed that, in judgement or inference, the mind is active, rather than receptive ; and constructive (or co-operating in a growth or

---

[1] I am borrowing certain phrases from Russell, *The Problems of Philosophy*, pp. 80–1 ; but accommodating them to my own purpose. Russell must not be held responsible for what I say.

[2] The act of 'reflecting', as Locke calls it, *Essay*, ii. 1, § 4, &c.

development), not accepting or beholding a present or presented object. If, that is to say, in judgement or inference, we are in contact with fact, the contact is indirect or mediate. The knowledge, which takes the form of judgement or inference, is primarily and essentially a discursive or mediating activity. Our 'knowing' is the thinking, is the discursus itself, not an awareness to which it leads and in which it terminates.[1]

This last point—viz. that in judgement and inference the discursive movement itself *is* the knowing—comes out clearly in two generally recognized characteristics of judgement and inference. Thus (i) it is a commonplace that there is no object of judgement or inference; i.e. no object to be judged or inferred, as there is an object felt, seen, heard, tasted, perceived. I feel anger or desire, I hear sound, see colour, perceive a face or its contour; but there is nothing which, in any analogous sense, I judge or infer. I 'judge' *that S is P*: not S, or P, or SP as a single concrete fact. I judge, for example, that the dog is mad; not the dog, or mad, or the mad-dog. 'To judge the dog' is to pass judgement upon him; i.e. a mere linguistic abbreviation for judging, for instance, that he is a good or bad specimen of his breed. Similarly, I 'infer' *that S, because it is M, is P*—that the dog, because he is mad, is dangerous. I do not infer S or M or P; or even SMP as a total organized or articulated fact—as an individual object confronting me with its elements in their systematic connexion. It is a mere linguistic abbreviation (analogous to 'judging the dog'), if I am said to infer hydrophobia (from the dog's symptoms) or danger (from the mad dog's bite). Nobody supposes that, if I infer hydrophobia or danger, I am cognizant of them as objects: i.e. directly apprehending them.

(ii) It is sometimes said that to judge or infer is to construct a total object (a complex, or rather 'concrete', fact) by a function of analysis and synthesis—to bring it, bit by bit, before the mind. To say this, is to emphasize rightly that the total object is not there except by being 'brought'. It is, in other words, the active process of constructing, the bringing before the mind, which characterizes this kind of knowledge and distinguishes it from feeling, sensation, sense-perception. But there is an obvious one-sidedness in this account of the matter. 'Construction' suggests a spontaneous and arbitrary activity of our thought; as if 'to judge' or 'to infer' were to create the detail which is being brought before the mind—to create, if not its items, at least their connexions. And if so, judge-

[1] Cf. above, p. 54.

ment and inference would be forms, not of knowledge, but of creative imagination. To judge or infer would be to compose—like the poet or musician—not to know like the man of science. Hence there is a tendency to substitute for this one-sided account another. Judgement or inference, it is said, is essentially an activity or a process—but one of discovery, not of construction. But this account also is plainly inadequate. For what is discovered, is there —or is commonly assumed to be there—before and independently of the discovery. America, for example, was there before Columbus discovered it. It was there, with its own independent existence and nature; for otherwise, though he might have invented it, he could not have discovered it. Philosophical reflection, perhaps, may shake this common assumption, or lead to a more guarded state- ment of it; but *prima facie*, at any rate, it is mere common sense that what is discovered must be there to be discovered, and cannot in any way depend upon or be affected by the process of discovery. But now it does most certainly seem nonsense to say that the intelligible domain of a science is there before, and independently of, the judgements or inferences which are the science. It seems nonsense, for example, to attribute to Euclidean space an existence and a nature before and independently of the science of Euclidean geometry. If, that is, by 'Euclidean space' we mean the system of spatial forms, which is known by way of judgement and inference —the total or commensurate 'domain' of the science of Euclidean geometry; then *that* space, *that* object or reality, exists and is actual only in the sustaining medium of the thought—in and by virtue of the reasoning, which is the science. And its nature, what it really is, is what it grows into, or becomes, by help of the intellectual activity which, according to this inadequate account, is a process of discovery.[1] Moreover, apart from this difficulty, to identify judgement and inference with an activity or process of discovery, is in effect to cancel the supposed essential distinction between two kinds of knowledge ('immediate' and 'discursive'). If, in judge- ment and inference, the activity of the mind is discovery, its knowing is not the discursus, but a direct apprehension or aware- ness which supervenes upon, and terminates, the latter. The process (like Columbus's voyage) is a mere preliminary to a know- ledge as immediate as the explorer's vision of the land.

We must try, therefore, to think of judgement and inference in such a way as to combine what there is of truth in these two

[1] Cf. above, pp. 56 ff.

one-sided accounts, while eliminating their obvious defects. In judgement or inference a detail is emerging, is coming bit by bit before the mind. But this emergence, this coming out, must be recognized, on the one hand, as a genuine self-development of a total object; as a growth into its own full being and stature of a 'reality' or 'objective fact'—and, on the other hand, as a process or activity in which our thought co-operates, which our discursive thinking assists. The emergence, in short, demands on our side an eliciting; the coming out, the coming before the mind, is—if we lay due stress upon the part we necessarily play in the matter—a bringing out, a bringing before the mind.[1]

We are to assume then that the total subject-matter of logic is, in principle, sundered into two sets of cognizant experiences. Experiences in the first set are sensuous and immediate. Those in the second set are intellectual and discursive and founded upon the former. Having made this assumption we are to search for a *datum* or *data* amongst the experiences which are 'immediate'. There are experiences 'in which we are sensuously or sentiently aware of given or presented facts'—'sensations', 'sentiences', or 'feelings' of our 'inner' states, and 'sense-perceptions'. Sensation, sentience, feeling, sense-perception, are vague terms; they are not, in normal usage, equivalents; and they cover an enormous variety of our actual experiences. Is it maintained that all our feelings, sensations, and sense-perceptions are alike and equally entitled to rank as self-evident *data*; i.e. that every one of them guarantees itself, with the same absolute and unquestionable right, as a solid foundation for the discursive 'thinking', which (in the form of judgement and inference) is to complete the edifice of knowledge? If this rather improbable doctrine is to be maintained, then what is the common character of these infinitely various experiences, by possessing which they all are self-evident? Or if it is maintained that some only of these actual experiences are 'immediate apprehensions of self-evident fact', then which are we to select and why? And what are the self-evident facts they reveal?

Consider first sense-perceptions.

[1] Cf. R. L. Nettleship, *Philosophical Lectures and Remains*, vol. i, p. 16: 'Growth of experience, its becoming more, may thus be represented as growth of structure, or a process in which we come to be more "constructive", to put more together, to find more in things, to get more out of them. (All these are equivalent expressions, for our experience *is* "we", and it makes no difference whether we represent ourselves as making it or as finding it; sometimes one, and sometimes the other way of speaking comes more naturally.)'

§ 8. (I) *The search for a* datum *in sense-perception*

1. The experiences, which would commonly be called sense-perceptions, are bewildering in their variety and extent. Let me quote a few examples to give some idea of their range. I 'perceive', for example, the whole of what now falls within the range of my vision; the whole, even, of what has been 'brought' within that range by any artificial arrangement or instrument (by mirrors, say, by a telescope or microscope); and any constituent part of these total fields. One may perceive, for example, the weald of Sussex or a blade of grass; the starry heavens or a flash of lightning; one's own back, when reflected in mirrors; the nerve-cell and its nucleus under the microscope. Similarly one may 'perceive' the whole chorus of the birds at day-break, the chord blending in its unity the contributions of all the instruments of the orchestra: and one may 'perceive' (so it would be said with equal right) the single alarm-note of the blackbird, the voice of a friend, the beat of a drum. All these also one would be said to 'perceive' when 'brought' within the range of one's hearing by, for example, the telephone, gramophone, or wireless. Again, I perceive (feel through the sense of touch) the whole contour of the box I grasp within my hand—or any knob or pattern on its surface. Or, lastly, I perceive the full characteristic flavour (a richly variegated unity) of a vintage port; or (equally) I perceive the distinctive quality of its taste, its special sweetness or astringency.

Is there, then, a definite character or characteristics in which all such experiences agree—and in virtue of which they are, one and all, 'immediate'?

One is inclined at first to say, unhesitatingly, 'Yes'. For, within every sense-perception, we can (or must), on reflection, distinguish two opposed and correlated factors—viz. an experiencing and an experienced, a sense-perceiving and a sense-perceived. And, if we make this distinction, it is not difficult to show (*a*) that every sense-perception is a wholly present, processless, and unbroken totality, and in that sense 'immediate'; and further (*b*) that it is a precise and direct correlation of its opposed factors, and so 'immediate' in a second and more relevant sense. 'If we make this distinction'—for perhaps to make it is *eo ipso* to treat sense-perception as not genuinely immediate.[1] But the view before us can hardly be stated without some such distinction; for if there is

---

[1] Cf. below, pp. 172–8.

to be a *datum*, something 'given' or 'presented', there must be, contrasted with it, an 'accepting' or 'receiving'.

Thus (*a*) a sense-perception is essentially and entirely 'present', unbroken and without process, whether we consider severally the character of its factors, or the character of the whole they inseparably constitute. Considered on its 'subjective' side, as a sense-perceiving, it is a single 'present' consciousness, all 'now' and (if we can apply spatial predicates to it at all) all 'here'. It is an undivided awareness—not two or more (simultaneous or successive) awarenesses linked together. Or if we think of perceiving as an 'act,' rather than a 'state' of awareness—as an active acceptance or apprehension,[1] then the 'act' is 'whole', 'complete,' and 'processless'; it is, in Aristotle's terminology,[2] an ἐνέργεια in the strict and proper sense, not a κίνησις. The 'perceiving', no doubt, 'endures'; but its duration is (for the percipient) comprised, as a timeless and unbroken whole, within what some psychologists call 'the specious present'. This perceiving, though it includes within its span a temporal lapse, is, *qua* perceiving, all undividedly 'now'.

Similarly, the sense-perceived (the whole experience considered on its objective side, as 'an experienced') is immediate in this sense —a single present object. It contains distinguishable (perhaps even separable) parts or elements, qualities, and relations, &c.; and it may comprise successive events or phases; yet, *qua* perceived, it is all at once and all together, indivisibly one and whole. It is wholly present—unbroken within a single 'now' and 'here'. It is all and wholly 'now'—though its 'now' embraces a section of a temporal flow, and is (so to speak) a frozen or timeless duration, thus corresponding to the 'now' (the specious present) of the 'perceiving'. And it is all and wholly 'here'—though its 'here' covers an area which may vary almost indefinitely in extent; or passes into unbroken unity many 'heres' and many 'theres'.

And (*b*) every sense-perception is immediate in the second (seemingly more relevant) sense. For it is nothing but the correlation of *this* 'perceiving' and *its* 'perceived'; and the correlation is direct, neither requiring nor admitting a middle or mediating link. It is immediate, i.e. unmediated and incapable of mediation.

Between the percipient's eye or ear and the objects he perceives, physical *media* (and sometimes also physical instruments) intervene. But that is irrelevant to the immediacy of the sense-perception. For between the percipient's conscious state or act (between

[1] Cf. above, p. 69.　　　　　　[2] Cf. *N.E.* x, ch. 4.

his 'perceiving') and its correlative (the 'perceived') nothing is (nothing need or can be) interposed. Within each sense-perception, 'the perceiving' is of 'the perceived'; and 'the perceived' is by 'the perceiving'. Each is the commensurate and direct correlative of the other; and the sense-perception is nothing but the correlation.

2. We seem then to have got our answer—a plain affirmative. Every sense-perception is immediate in the two senses just explained. It is a wholly present, processless, and unbroken totality; and it is a direct correlation of two commensurate opposites. But neither of these characteristics—let us call the first 'presentness', and reserve the term 'immediacy' for the second—is peculiar to sense-perceptions; and neither of them is really relevant to our present search.

The same presentness and the same immediacy characterize not sense-perception only, but memory also, judgement and inference —all forms of 'cognizant experience' or 'knowledge'. They can be shown to characterize even imagination—an experience which nobody would claim to be an 'immediate apprehension of self-evident fact' and many people would hesitate to regard as an apprehension of fact at all.

Consider a few examples. I *remember* an incident of my schooldays; *picture* the execution of Mary Queen of Scots or the murder of Desdemona; *judge* that there will probably be a parliamentary crisis in France next year or that 'it is the nature of a thinking being to form true and adequate thoughts';[1] *infer* that 'given the economic conditions of life in a modern industrial state, inflation of the currency must ruin certain classes of the population'. Within each of these experiences (within the memory, the imagination, the judgements, the inference) there are an 'experiencing' and 'an experienced', (i) each present and processless in the sense explained; and (ii) each the commensurate opposite of the other in a direct correlation.

(i) Presentness: In judgement and inference beyond doubt, and probably also in memory and imagination, the experiencing is discursive—a movement or a development with distinguishable steps or stages. Yet it clearly is also entire and undivided in its form;—a consciousness formally single and present; 'whole' without parts and their relations, 'now' without internal stages or transitions. There is no memory or imagination, no judgement or inference,

---

[1] Spinoza, *Tractatus de Intellectus Emendatione*, ed. Van Vloten and Land, 1. 25.

unless the act of experiencing, however much it is discursive, is
also a single 'present' remembering, imagining, judging, inferring;
—this undivided and processless 'state' or 'act' of consciousness,
embracing the entirety of 'the experienced' within its formal unity.[1]
'The entirety of the experienced'; for 'the experienced' too is
formally 'present'—undividedly 'here' and unbrokenly 'now'—
in a corresponding sense, although it is also (from another point of
view) a whole developing and constructed, emerging bit beside
bit, and bit after bit, by help of the discursive activity of thought.[2]
The imagined execution of the Queen of Scots is the undivided
entirety of what I am now imagining—a total scene fixed, unified,
and circumscribed by my 'present' imaginative act. The remembered incident is what fills my present consciousness; a complex
detail solidified within a single 'here', and frozen within a single
'now', by this my act of remembering.

It will be objected, perhaps, that 'the experienced' within a
judgement or an inference cannot be regarded in this way. 'The
intellect's function of forming true and adequate thoughts', or
'the necessary connexion of inflation and the ruin of the rentier
class'—neither of these is a 'single present scene' or an 'unbroken,
unitary, event', solid within one 'here' and frozen within one
'now'. Each is a content or a nexus, either timeless and universal,
or at any rate commensurate in duration and extent with the
actual existence and duration of 'thinking beings' or civilized
societies. But the objector has forgotten the assumptions to which
the contention he is criticizing is subject. These assumptions may
prove, on further examination, to be untenable. Still, so long as
they are made, the judgement and the inference are to be considered
as 'actual cognizant experiences'; and within each of them 'an
experienced' is to be distinguished from 'an experiencing'. Now,
such 'an experienced' is obviously not the (relatively) everlasting
and indefinitely extending nexus, to which the objector refers. It is
precisely that fragment of the 'total fact'—that limited and partial
appearance of the 'real' or 'objective' nexus—which is gripped
within this single act, within 'my' or 'your' or 'his' judging or
inferring. 'The experienced', in short, is neither more nor less than
the commensurate correlative of 'the experiencing'; a 'content'
made formally one and formally processless by the formal unity
and 'presentness' of the 'containing' (or 'comprehending')
intellectual act.

[1] Cf. above, pp. 44–6.　　　　　　　　[2] Cf. above, pp. 70–2.

(ii) Directness of correlation: every one of these experiences (every memory, judgement, inference, imagination) is, as obviously as every sense-perception, immediate in the further sense that each of them is a direct correlation of its 'experiencing' and its 'experienced'. Each is a correlation that is direct; i.e. unmediated and incapable of mediation. The directness of the correlation is indisputable—if indeed it is a correlation at all. For correlation, it must be admitted, seems an inadequate notion to apply to the very intimate union which fuses together an act of experiencing and its experienced. For the supposed correlatives—and this criticism applies to sense-perceiving and the sense-perceived no less than to the other 'experiencings' and their 'experienceds'—are the complementary sides of a single concrete fact, rather than two factors in reciprocal relation. Is the curve a correlation of concave and convex? or is that which 'embraces', 'grips', 'contains', in any reasonable sense correlative with that which it contains or embraces?

We are thus thrown back upon our original problem, having advanced not one inch towards its solution. We were 'to search for a datum in sense-perception'; to test the claim that sense-perception is an 'immediate apprehension of self-evident fact'; that in all—or at least in some—of those actual experiences, which are commonly reckoned as sense-perceptions, we are directly (and therefore infallibly) aware of a fact presented, or presenting itself, directly and simply as it is. All that we have done is to show that every sense-perception is immediate, because it is a sense-perceiving, undivided and all-now, directly correlated with a sense-perceived which is (correspondingly) all-one without seam, and all-at-once without process. But even if every sense-perception is such a correlation, this immediacy is not the kind of immediacy which we set out to find. For the characters in which this immediacy consists are the 'presentness' of each of the correlates, and the 'directness' of the correlation. But these same characters must also and equally be attributed to every judgement, inference, memory, and even to every imagination. 'Immediacy' in this sense, immediacy consisting in such presentness and such directness, is purely formal, characterizing all these experiences, *qua* 'actual', in respect of the mere form of their actuality.

Let me try to bring out a little more clearly the distinction between the 'formal' immediacy which characterizes every one of these cognizant experiences, and the immediacy which we set out to find—the immediacy which is claimed to be the special character of our sensuous and sentient awareness. Every actual judgement, inference, memory, or imagination is 'immediate' as regards the form of its actuality. Each of them, that is a direct correlation—and each of the correlata is seamlessly whole and present all at once without process.

But it is observed[1] that, here at all events, the 'experiencing' is also discursive—'a movement or development with distinguishable steps or stages'. And it is equally obvious that (in one sense, at any rate) the 'experienced' transcends any single 'here and now'.[2] 'The essential function of the thinking being', for example, or 'the unequal incidence of the hardships of inflation'—what each of these phrases expresses primarily and naturally, is an objective nexus, a total fact or character of fact, which is 'experienced'—i.e. becomes manifest and known—in the judgement or inference. And obviously 'the experienced', so understood, is other, and more, than the direct commensurate correlative of any 'single, present act' of experiencing. The very act of experiencing either of these total facts—the very act of judging the one, or inferring the other—gives to it, or elicits in it, a character essentially transcending any single 'now' and 'here', transcending the maximum field which could be gripped within the span of a single direct awareness. To judge the one, and to infer the other, is to think of something as articulately (not 'seamlessly') whole; and to think of it as 'complete without process', not because it is comprised entire within a 'specious present', but because it conserves and manifests itself timelessly—i.e. without, and untouched by, temporal change—throughout its whole duration.

Similarly, to touch briefly upon the remaining examples,[3] that which I remember or predict in the natural sense and reference of the terms is not present; not here-and-now; not whole without divisions and connexions, nor complete without process; not such as to be 'given' or to 'give itself', to a directly accepting awareness. It is, on the contrary, such as to be recalled and re-constituted, or to be constructed and inferred, by intellectual activities essentially mediating and discursive. What happened to me at school, what will happen in France next month;—these 'facts' or 'events' are anything but 'seamless unities', anything but 'simultaneities without process', anything but solid items of reality to be apprehended at a stroke by a directly confronting

[1] Cf. p. 75.   [2] Cf. p. 76.   [3] Cf. p. 75.

and accepting consciousness. Precisely so far as we remember or predict, our 'experiencing' transcends the 'now-here'; and the 'experienced', in memory or prediction, must fill a time (and may fill a place) excluding and excluded from our 'present'.

So, to imagine the execution of the Queen of Scots is to visualize it as it occurred, i.e. as a past and distant section of the historical flow. From one point of view, no doubt, such an imagination is the gazing upon the successively presented phases of a single scene—a scene which is framed within the specious present of one visualizing state or act. But the formal unity of our 'present' visualizing presupposes, and focuses, in itself, a vast amount of discursive intellectual activity. The scene is 'presented' and 'present' to us, only because we have collaborated (and are still collaborating) to constitute it. It is essentially constructed out of incidents we remember from our historical reading—though while 'visualizing' the constructed whole we are not conscious of the activities involved in its construction and maintenance.

I have dwelt (perhaps too long) upon these obvious considerations because the character which is claimed for sense-perception stands out, and is defined, by contrast with the mediateness of these other experiences. In short, the immediacy, which is in question, is not 'formal' and abstract, but (like their mediateness) '*material*' and *real*.

We perceive[1] such scenes, things, events, *qualia*, &c., as, for example, the weald of Sussex or a blade of grass, the starry heavens or a flash of lightning, an orchestral chord or the voice of a friend, the full-bodied flavour of a vintage port or its peculiar astringency. What we perceive, in other words (like what we remember, predict, defer or imagine), is—in the only natural meaning of the phrase—the fact, scene, event 'itself'. It is *this*, we suppose, of which we are cognizant in perception; something actual and real, and not the mere formal correlate of the act of perceiving.

The immediacy, then, which is claimed for sense-perception amounts to this: that all or some of these actual scenes, things, events, *qualia*, are (severally) solid and complete within one 'here and now', and in that solidity and completeness manifest themselves entire and at a stroke to our perceiving. The immediacy is 'material and real'. The things themselves and their actual qualities (the *Res* and *Realia*) and the awareness we have of them

[1] See above, p. 73.

in perception, are (it is claimed) through and through, utterly and without reserve, immediate—i.e. in no sense bit-beside-bit or bit-after-bit; in no sense affected in their existence or character by what precedes, succeeds, or environs them; in no sense linked to one another by any third or middle, so that 'perceived' and 'perceiving' unite only through an intermediary to constitute the sense-perception.

3. That, and no less, is the claim we have to examine. And it is a claim for which there is no particle of evidence.

But the claim, it will be said, is precisely that sense-perceptions (all or some) are immediate. 'And if they are immediate, their immediacy—both *that* it is and *what* it is—rests *ex hypothesi* upon nothing but itself. No evidence can (or need) be offered for that which evidences itself.'

It is, then, a claim for which (by the admission of those who make it) there is, and can be, no particle of evidence. But, nevertheless, it is a claim which can be adequately refuted. It is impossible to show, in each and every sense-perception, that its apparent immediacy is illusory; since that would involve proving a negative of each and every member of an infinite or inexhaustible plurality. But it is not difficult to show the 'mediateness', of any single sense-perception which may be produced. The refutation, in short, will take the form of a challenge. 'Produce your sense-perception', we shall say in effect to those who make the claim; 'and we will expose its immediacy. And since the exposure will plainly rest upon its character as sense-perception, and not upon its singularity as *this* (and not *that*) example, we shall be entitled to regard the refutation as adequate.'

We are to take an actual sense-perception—say, this sense-perception in which I now perceive a flash of lightning—and try to show that it is not immediate in the sense supposed: viz. that it is not the direct awareness of an independent fact; of a solid constituent of reality, presenting itself, entire and complete, to the passively accepting observer. And, in this examination of the actual sense-perception, we are to forget—so far as we can—the conclusions which have been reached by philosophical reflection upon perception, by philosophical analysis and criticism of perceptual experience. We are to take the sense-perception—so far as we can—as the unsophisticated percipient himself experiences it; to consider it, as it is *for* the percipient while it lasts and fills his conscious being.

In perceiving this flash of lightning, then, I am cognizant—I take myself to be cognizant—of a 'public event'; a single, individual, change open to the perceivings of innumerable observers.

This public event—this 'real' flash—combines in its singleness, in its individual being, a characteristic variety; and is so far describable. I should describe it, for example, as 'a brilliant streak of bluish light sharply defined against the black sky; with a characteristic (and measurable) zigzag outline; with "its own" singular (and assignable) position, date, and duration'.[1]

Now, no doubt these characters of the 'real flash' are 'present' to all the perceivings, and 'appear' within all the 'perceived fields' (the visual fields or perspectives) which the various perceivings comprise and define. But it is clear, when we consider the matter, that they are not exhausted in these their 'presentments' or 'appearances'—not *thus* 'given' either complete or unmodified. They, in their own proper and 'public' nature as characters of the public event, are neither merely, nor precisely identical with, any (or all) of their 'private' appearances. They are more, and other, than each and all of their presentments within the 'visual fields' or 'perspectives'. For (i) the characters as they are 'presented' and 'appear'—as they are comprised within a 'visual field'—are in part determined by the 'perceiving', and vary with its differences. Different observers, for example, bring to bear in their 'perceivings' powers of eyesight, and attention, varying in acuteness, precision, intensity, &c. Thus, the flash, as it 'appears' (as it is snapshotted) in their visual fields, will present different and conflicting colours and outlines. Its 'blue' will differ in intensity, illumination, and perhaps in shade: its 'zigzag' will vary in degree of definition, &c. But, if so, the 'real' colour and outline of the flash 'itself' are different from some, and perhaps from all, of these 'presentments' —though doubtless 'such as to account for' the latter. Again (ii) the location of the percipient's body (say, at Oxford or at Reading) contributes to determine the orientation and range of his visual field. The flash, therefore, *qua* 'presented' or 'appearing' to different percipients, will vary (to some extent) in position and magnitude. Its 'perceived' position and magnitude are proportioned to the total area of the visual field, and adjusted to the

---

[1] In the end, of course, no *description* can 'singularize' (adequately exhibit the singularity of) the flash, or any of its characters; but, subject to this reservation, it is possible, within what is called 'the' spatio-temporal series, to specify uniquely determinate positions and dates by reference to arbitrary, but commonly accepted, standards.

G

positions and magnitudes of the other constituents which form its context in that 'field'. But the real 'where' (or the real magnitude) of 'the flash itself', though doubtless they must be 'such as to account for' the differences in the 'presented wheres' and 'magnitudes' (to account for them, that is, given the variations of range and orientation, in the visual fields in question), plainly cannot be identified with any of them, or with all of them together. Lastly (iii) each 'perceiving' is *now*, but its 'now' is a specious present, i.e. a duration. And the now of one 'perceiving' (its specious present) need not be identical in span with the specious present, which is the now of another. The flash, as it is 'presented' or 'appears', is always now, i.e. has a duration coincident with the 'specious present' of the correlative 'perceiving'. But this, its 'perceived', duration will vary (even if only infinitesimally) for different observers. Hence its 'perceived' duration cannot be identified with the real duration of the 'flash itself', even if in a given case or cases it may happen to coincide with it. For though doubtless the real duration is 'such as to account for' the varying presentments, it cannot itself vary. It is one, and one only: the same identical fraction of the same identical second in the history of the physical world.

The 'real flash', then, with its 'real' colour, shape, place, and time, is not 'presented', completely and as such, in any visual field. It is not an object of perception, if that means the actual (or even the possible) correlate of an actual 'perceiving', of an awareness 'immediate' so as to exclude mediation. Nor is it an object of perception in the sense (if in that sense the phrase could be used) that it consists, and is made up, of all its actual and possible 'presentments'. It is not a stock, a sum, or collection of the correlates of all actual and possible 'perceivings'; and if, in each 'perceiving', the percipient can be said to take or select a view of the 'real flash', the 'taking' or 'selecting' is, at all events, not the extraction of an actual constituent of the flash itself. The 'real flash' cannot be 'given', precisely and adequately as it is. It could only be *so* 'given', if—and in this case the supposition is plainly absurd—its being were both *percipi* and *percipere*; that is, if, instead of being a 'physical event', an 'abstracted object of cognizance', it were neither more nor less than a 'self-awareness', self-given—i.e. given *to* and *by itself*.[1]

If therefore we ask: 'What is meant by the "real flash"—by the

[1] Cf. below, pp. 134–42.

"public event", of which all the observers are (as they suppose) aware in their perceivings—by the "common object" (as it would be called) of their "perceptions"?' the answer is plain, though it may be disconcerting. The 'real flash' is that which all the observers postulate on the ground of the 'appearing flashes' or presentments—postulate inevitably and instinctively so long as they remain on the perceptual level (i.e. *uncritically* perceptive). It is the product of an inexplicit and confused thinking, a thinking immersed in and inseparable from sensation. It is the hybrid offspring of that blend of sense and thought which goes by the name of 'sense-perception'. And its hybrid character stares us in the face. For 'sense-perception' is a form of 'knowledge', a 'cognizant experience', in which the mind thinks sensuously. There is 'thought' in sense-perception, but not thought free and explicit —not 'thought' which the percipient controls, or of which he is even aware *as* 'thought'. And in sense-perception the percipient 'sensates'; but, in sensating, his mind instinctively interprets the *sensa*, 'forms' or 'constructs' them, analyses and (in analysing) synthesizes them. There is, in sense-perception, no *datum*, no sensuous material, which does not involve in its very constitution this interpretative or formative discursus. And there is no 'thought' in sense-perception (no intellectual discursus) which is not immersed in a *datum* it is contributing to constitute; which is not subdued (so to speak) from its proper 'freedom' as thought, to a lower, quasi-instinctive, level—the level of irreflective or perceptual cognizant experience.

Hence, the so-called object of sense-perception—the 'real flash', for example, clothed in its 'real' perceptible characters—is (properly speaking) neither given nor constructed; neither sensible (or sensed) nor conceivable (or conceived). If these terms are to be used to designate it, it can only be called—by what seems a sheer contradiction—a 'constructed *datum*' or a 'sensible *conceptum*'.

In the account I have just given of the mediate character of sense-perception I have employed terms which belong to the 'reflective' level of knowledge—terms which when used to describe perception proper, perception as it is for the unsophisticated percipient, are apt to be misleading.

Some further explanation—sufficient to guard against the grosser kinds of misunderstanding—will be offered later of the 'inexplicit thinking', of the 'instinctive postulating, constructing, interpreting', &c., which I have mentioned. But, in the meantime, there is a definite negative result to be recorded—a definite failure of the 'search for a *datum* in sense-perception'.[1]

(*a*) We are not cognizant in sense-perception (as *perhaps* we are in more developed forms of knowledge) of anything that is, in any strict and proper sense, 'conceivable' or 'intelligible'. The 'object of perception' is a 'scene', 'thing', or 'event', clothed (as the percipient supposes) in sensible qualities. It is not an intelligible unity or whole—not distinctly conceived elements intelligibly related. It is not such an 'object'—such an intelligible fact or reality—as thought, operating freely and in its own proper nature, might perhaps 'construct', and (in constructing) 'discover' and bring before the mind. (*b*) But neither are we, in sense-perception, confined to the mere presentments and appearances—to the 'visual fields' or 'perspectives' which are correlative to the singular 'perceivings'. The 'object of perception'—for example, the 'real flash'—transcends, is more and other than, the flash *qua* perceived, i.e. any and all of its 'presentments'. And this transcendence means that sense-perception is essentially and in principle 'discursive' or 'mediate'. It is not, as was claimed, 'immediate' in the real and material (and only relevant) sense. It is not a direct awareness of a 'given' fact or reality; not a special kind of 'knowledge', whole and complete without inner division or process, excluding (and contrasted with) a second (and inferior) kind—viz. 'knowledge' mediate and discursive, or 'knowledge' in the form of judgement and inference.

This negative result is only what might have been expected. The instability and confusion of perceptual experience have been exphasized throughout the history of philosophy ever since Plato wrote the famous passage in the *Republic*[2] or even from the days of Parmenides and Zeno. Things and facts, as we 'perceive' them (as we 'know' them on the level of unsophisticated perception) are inherently confused, paradoxical, and even self-contradictory. The more intelligent observers have never been content to take their perceptual experience 'as they find it', 'at its face value'. They inevitably reflect, thus bringing to light the confusions that lie beneath the surface of the 'facts' as they perceive them. And as their reflection and criticism develop, the *inexplicit* interpretative assumptions which control their mind in its perceptual experience are formulated as so many *explicit* theories. Since these theories, when thus formulated, are plainly confused, often paradoxical,

---

[1] Cf. above, p. 73.　　　　　　　　　　[2] 523[a] ff.

and sometimes nakedly self-contradictory, the critics have started on the road that leads first to science and then (by fresh reflection of the mind upon its scientific experience) to philosophy.

4. Though the mediate character of sense-perception has been established, the terms in which it has been described require some further explanation.[1] What exactly is the discursive or mediate process involved? I spoke of 'sensuous' or 'inexplicit' thinking; of 'quasi-instinctive' postulating, conceiving, constructing, interpreting. But 'sensuous thinking' is, on the face of it, a self-contradiction as glaring as a 'standing fall' or a 'square circle'. 'Thinking' is a vague term, capable of wide application; but does it retain any meaning at all, when used beyond the range of explicit conception, judgement, or inference? Yet nobody—except by an elementary confusion of perception with the judgement of, i.e. reflecting upon, perception—could maintain that 'to perceive' is (or implies) *explicit* conception, judgement, or inference. Similarly, 'discursive' and 'mediate' are predicates which—in ordinary usage—qualify intellectual operations performed consciously, if not actually controlled, by the mind; and even if a 'quasi-instinctive postulating, constructing or interpreting' suggests some definite and recognizable process, there seems at first no reason to assume that it is *intellectual*—or that, though not intellectual, it is, like intellectual activity, 'discursive' or 'mediate'.

The issue raised by this objection is nothing less than the nature of thought itself in all its forms and at all its levels; and, in particular, the problem of 'the relation of thought to consciousness', to borrow Bosanquet's convenient formulation.[2] And in attempting to discuss so large a problem, we should lose sight of the main object of this study—viz. the examination of the supposed division of knowledge. It seems possible, however, to throw some further light upon the 'discursive' or 'mediate' character of sense-perception—enough at least to prevent the grosser kinds of misunderstanding.

(*a*) Let me begin by correcting an error the whole preceding treatment may be thought to have endorsed by implication. 'To search for a *datum* amongst our sense-perceptions' suggests that there is within us a host of varied experiences—items of a collection, each waiting to be singled out, to be studied bare and in isolation from the rest. It is as though the mind were a theatre in which various experiences appear and play their parts; as though

[1] Cf. above, p. 83.   [2] *The Nature of Mind*, e.g. p. 159.

the knowing subject possessed feelings, sensations, perceptions, memories, imaginations, or acquired them from time to time—and also, on occasion, exercised a function of discursive thought.

All this is a caricature of 'a-mind-and-its-experiences'. For it leaves out of the reckoning the mind itself, and so distorts the 'facts' it professes to be studying. These facts, after all, are a diversity of a special kind—viz. the diversity in which a special kind of unity is constituted, maintained, and displayed. The unity of a mind throughout its experiences is the unity of a 'self-consciousness', what one may call, in order to have a distinctive name, a spiritual unity; and the experiences, being the many of what is thus one, are a spiritual plurality.

The experiences of a mind bear not the remotest analogy to the items of a collection. It may be necessary for certain sciences to assume that every one-of-many within the field of their inquiry is a sum of units, a complex of simple elements, a collection of items. But it is certain that, so long as we think in terms of such mathematical or mechanical categories, our speculations can have little or nothing to do with a mind and its experiences.

There is a fairly close analogy between a mind and a living thing, between the spiritual and organic types of unity. The unity of a mind in its experiences is comparable in some respects to the unity of an organism in its vital functions or in the stages of its vital (physical) development. But though it is almost inevitable to think of the mind in terms drawn from the category of life—to speak of it, for example, as a spiritual life or development—the likeness must not be exaggerated. For, in the world of our experience, there are not any other 'facts'—any other examples of unity-in-plurality, of identity-in-difference, of permanence-in-change—which are strictly analogous to 'a mind', i.e. to a self-conscious subject of experiences. Though helpful up to a certain point the terminology of 'life' does not apply strictly. For in considering a mind and its experiences, we are dealing with a many which contribute to constitute and mould the one to which they belong; and with a one which though it 'owns', and even (in some sense) 'makes', its many, yet itself is 'in the making', is (in some sense) 'made' or 'shaped' by them.

The mind is one throughout its many experiences: but its unitary being—its individual character—depends upon, is made and moulded by, the special variety it experiences. The 'many' in this case contribute to determine the character of their 'one'.

And at the same time, what each experience is depends essentially upon the individual character of the mind which is experiencing. The 'one', in this case, contributes to determine the character of every item of its 'many'—contributes to make and mould each single experience.

In calling attention to this general principle in regard to the unity of a mind, to this reciprocal determination of a mind by its experiences and of experiences by their mind, my object is merely to emphasize certain conditions which must be satisfied by anything that is to be 'an experience' at all; and so to fix the limits within which our thought must move if we are to study an 'experience' as such—in its proper character as an 'experience' and not in caricature.

To be 'a mind' is to be a self-conscious subject of experiences; and the unity of the subject in its many experiences conforms (more or less, at different levels and in different degrees) to a certain type of union-of-a-manifold. Wherever, whenever, in so far as, there actually are 'experiences', or there actually is 'a mind', there, then and so far, the only way to conceive the facts without distortion is to think of them in terms neither of a mathematical sum, nor of a mechanical system, nor of an organic whole, but of a 'spiritual' union of a 'spiritual' variety. If anything is 'one subject acquiring and owning many experiences', it must be (and be conceived as) immanent in them and modified by them—in some sense, therefore, it must make and mould, and be made and moulded by, its many. And if any plurality is (and is to be conceived as) a many, of which the items are experiences, they must 'interpenetrate one another' (in Bergson's picturesque phrase); they must be, and be conceived as, modes and phases of a single immanent subject. In some sense, therefore, they—these modifications of its 'substance', these varied expressions of its unitary being—must go to make it what it is; must go to mould and individualize their 'one', to constitute it '*this* subject of *these* experiences'.

The use I am going to make of this general principle is not affected by certain difficulties as to its range and manner of application in detail. But it may prevent misunderstanding, if I indicate briefly, without attempting to discuss them, the difficulties I have in view. There is (i) the question whether the non-human animals are 'subjects of experiences' or 'souls', even if not 'self-conscious subjects of experiences' or 'minds'; and, if so, whether they exemplify (in any sense, in any degree, at any level) the type of unity which, according to the general principle, is distinctive of a mind-in-its-experiences. Next (ii) there is the question of undeveloped or broken specimens of humanity—the πηρώματα, the φθοραὶ καὶ λῆμαι ἀνθρώπων, as Aristotle calls them. It is usual to think of children, imbeciles, and lunatics as persons of immature, weak, and disordered minds. But are they, or have they, 'minds' at all (in any sense or degree) within the terms demanded by the general principle? These difficulties, perhaps, are of minor importance—could readily be met, or shown to be irrelevant and set aside. But there remains a (real or seeming) difficulty of a more fundamental kind. For (iii) it may be objected that the type of unity demanded by our general principle for a mind-in-its-experiences is a mere ideal, unrealized and unrealizable in fact. No actual person—not even the most perfect and fortunate specimen of humanity—is, or even approximates to being, throughout his life, a 'spiritual union of a spiritual plurality'. The self-consciousness of any actual person is broken and fitful, interspaced by regular and occasional interruptions (by sleep, reverie, and inattention—to say nothing of swoon, delirium, or of the breaches that may be caused by, for example, anaesthetics). If to be a mind is to be a single self-conscious unity, pervading, constituting, and moulding —and yet also constituted, varied, and moulded by—many mutually interpenetrating experiences;—where are we to find examples of mind in the actual world? The utmost that could be said of any actual person, of any actual self-conscious subject, is, not that in some degree, or at some level, he is, or has, a mind, but that he is, or has, a series of imperfect and fragmentary minds —that, from time to time in his historical life, there occur evanescent unions of a manifold which approximate *longo intervallo* to the ideal 'spiritual union of a spiritual plurality' of which we have spoken.

Stated in these terms the difficulty is unanswerable; but what warrant is there for so stating it? What ground is there for thus taking at their face-value the so-called actual persons—the 'historical' or apparent enactors of the temporal show? Once raise this question and press this line of inquiry to its inevitable conclusion, and the difficulty will evaporate. It is not the general principle that will be discredited, but the supposed 'facts'. They cannot exemplify or realize the principle, because they are themselves unreal—because, as taken, they are not 'facts' at all. The actual persons (as they are called) are, in fact, precisely that which they appear themselves to be when measured by the general principle. Each of them is, at most, a series of evanescent and fragmentary 'minds'; modes of a 'mind': imperfect and transitory individuations of the human spirit. If we are to look for actual examples of that 'spiritual union of a spiritual plurality' which is distinctive of a 'mind-in-its-experiences', we must now turn to the 'spiritual realities' to which reference was made in a former context.[1] We must consider the so-called actual persons—the so-called finite intelligences and wills—in respect solely to the 'infinite' self-conscious subject, the 'universal' mind, *potentia infinita cogitandi*, which fulfils itself (in part, at least) in and through them; which, in their fragmentary knowings and willings, creates, develops, and sustains the realm in which it knows itself (the realm of knowledge-or-truth); the realm in which it wills and enacts itself (the realm which is man's ordered life of freedom and right).

(*b*) From the abstract statement of the type of unity-in-plurality which is distinctive of a mind-in-its-experiences, it follows, as a formal corollary, that there can be no such thing as an isolated or isolable sense-perception. A sense-perception is always one of many interpenetrating experiences, an item of a spiritual plurality; and through them all (pervading, making, and moulding them all) there runs the 'spiritual unity' which is 'a mind'—a unity they help to constitute and shape.

But this formal corollary—this denial of the isolation of sense-perception—may be supplemented by a more positive account. For every sense-perception involves, on the percipient's part, the 'consciousness of a world'. He perceives always within a relatively enduring system of fact, within a reality spatially and temporally 'beyond' the particular perception. Of this larger reality he is, in perceiving, in some sense 'conscious' or 'aware'. What he perceives—that on which his attention is focused, to which he is most 'awake'—fits for him, as he perceives it, into a wider frame. It stands out for him against a background, vaguer perhaps but relatively more stable.

This 'consciousness of a world'—supporting and enfolding the particular perceiving with its primary *perceptum*—is a matter of degree, varying enormously in distinctness. Often, no doubt, the background is so indistinct, the percipient's awareness of it so dim, that it is an exaggeration to speak either of 'consciousness'

[1] Cf. Study I, § 5, pp. 51 ff.

or of 'a world'. Still, every percipient, in every perception, is at least in some minimal degree 'awake to' a wider framework, a more persistent background, a reality larger and more lasting, than the particular object he perceives.

It may be objected that sometimes the percipient is 'all in' a single concentrated perception. 'His whole conscious being', it may be said, 'is absorbed in gazing intently on the weald of Sussex, or on a Velasquez; in listening intently to a melody; in tasting the full flavour of the port.' But the objection will not stand against a closer scrutiny of the facts. For (i) every perception, however single and concentrated it may appear, is *internally articulated*. There is, within the whole self-conscious experience, within the whole perception of which the percipient is aware as 'his', a dividing (though not a separating) into two opposed factors, and a correlating of them in their opposition. In spite of his absorption, the percipient is aware (however dimly) of a gazing, listening, tasting—aware of them as 'activities' with which he specially identifies his 'self'. He is aware also of something other than, and opposed to, each of these activities (and so *his* 'object', but not his 'self'); yet correlated with the activity, determining and determined by it, co-operating with it to form the whole self-conscious experience which is 'his' perception.[1]

And (ii), in every perception, the percipient who gazes, listens, or tastes, carries into these activities, and into the whole experience they help to constitute, some traces of his past and (it must even be said) some prefiguration of his future. However great his absorption in the present perception, he is continuous (even, in some degree, 'sensibly' or 'consciously' continuous) with a subject not yet, and no longer, 'in' this experience. In his present perceiving he is a subject 'moulded' and affected by past experiences; and even now, while he perceives, he is 'open' to future experiences and characterized (to some extent) by this susceptibility.[2]

(c) What I have been urging so far is nothing new. It is usual

---

[1] It must not be supposed that a sense-perception—or any other experience in which a self-conscious subject participates—is nothing but two opposed factors (a 'self' and 'not-self') in correlation. A complete analysis must recognize not only the 'internal articulation' of a self-conscious experience, but the concrete unity which is internally articulated. Cf., for explanation and supplementation, Bradley, *Essays on Truth and Reality*, pp. 416 ff.

[2] We are never 'all in' a single perception; but it does not follow that 'states' (other than perceptions), in which the subject is completely absorbed, do not (or may not) occur. For the question of such 'genuine immediates', see below, pp. 171–8.

to recognize, more or less emphatically, in any account of perception, that the percipient is 'conscious of a world'; that, in perceiving, he is also in some wider sense 'aware of' a reality larger and more enduring than the primary *perceptum*. But this consciousness of a world, this wider awareness, is commonly regarded as a fixed attitude of the percipient's mind—as an antecedent upon which the perception merely supervenes, or as a context which surrounds without penetrating it. But in fact this 'wider awareness' is an 'activity' rather than an 'attitude' of mind—an activity which is continued into the perception, contributing essentially to make it what it is. It is not enough to recognize that this 'consciousness of a world' presupposes explicit intellectual activities of the percipient; that it draws its origin from past experiences which consist largely, often predominantly, of explicit judgements and inferences; that it crystallizes them and concentrates them in itself. We must recognize that, as it now 'characterizes' the percipient, as it now forms the wider mental context which enfolds his 'perceiving', it is far more akin to affirming and constructing, to judging (or inferring), than to a quality or a state, a disposition or an attitude.

That this is so, may be most readily seen in those perceptions which are admittedly confined to 'privileged' or 'expert' percipients—perceptions, for example, of the scientific observer (of the specialist in a given field of investigation), of the artist, critic, connoisseur, &c.

Thus, to quote a few examples: Not everybody, but only the trained student of histology, can 'perceive' the characteristic structure and essential details of the preparation under the microscope. It requires his trained and expert 'eye' to 'see' (to detect at once and to discriminate without difficulty), within a section of nervous tissue, the nerve-cells or 'neurones', each with its 'nucleus' and surrounding protoplasm, and the various processes (the 'axons' and 'dendrons') connecting cell with cell.[1] Only a 'musical ear' perceives *this* sequence of chords—this bar or phrase, say, in Bach's *Chaconne*—accurately and completely: 'hears' it, directly and without apparent effort, in its proper rhythmic, melodic, and contrapuntal character.[2] Not you or I,

---

[1] Cf. McDougall, *Physiological Psychology*, pp. 24 ff., with the diagram on p. 26 from Sir M. Foster's *Text-book of Physiology*.

[2] Cf. J. M. W. Turner's retort to the old lady. 'I never saw a sunset like the one in your picture.' 'Don't you wish you had, Madam?'

but only the connoisseur 'perceives' the 1897 flavour of the port. It requires the expert palate of (say) a member of the wine-committee to taste it as it is.

So far I have expressed the exceptional qualifications of the 'privileged' percipients in 'physical' terms—as special training and refinement of the organ of sense. But it is more relevant to my present argument to stress the complementary one-sided description—i.e. to emphasize the 'psychical' side of their pre-eminence.[1] The scientific observer, the artist, the connoisseur, are privileged percipients, and their perceiving is exceptionally precise or delicate, because of their science, their art, and their cultured power of discernment in some special field of values; because they bring to bear, in their perceiving, special endowment and special education; because their vision, hearing or tasting, is unusually intelligent or 'thoughtful'. In short, to be a privileged percipient is to have attained a certain grade of development in body and mind; and to perceive what the expert perceives, and as he perceives it, is to perceive 'at' (and 'from') a determinate level of physical and psychical culture or refinement.

Now it is in its interpretation of a 'grade of development of the embodied mind' that the view of perception, for which I am contending, parts company with the commonly accepted doctrine—the doctrine that perception is through and through immediate, excluding all process or discursive activity. For two assumptions are necessary to that doctrine: viz. (i) that the 'grade' is (relatively) fixed and quiescent, and (ii) that a given 'perceiving' is—so to

---

[1] The subject of cognizant experience—the 'I' which perceives, judges, and infers—is in some sense 'body and mind in one'. The percipient, that is, is certainly not merely a physiological system (a brain and organs of sense, functioning and developing in accordance with physical or physiological laws); and certainly not a discarnate consciousness or unembodied spirit. It is not necessary (for our present purpose) to ask in what sense the subject of cognizant experience is 'body and mind in one'. If (as I believe and have before suggested) the subject of knowledge is a 'spiritual unity', a unity more than 'organic', then even such phrases as 'embodied-mind' or 'self-conscious organism' are misleading: still more such a phrase as 'body-and-mind-in-one'. For all such phrases suggest the erroneous Cartesian doctrine of two *res completae*, mutually exclusive (a corporeal and a thinking substance), miraculously forming a *compositum* which is the subject of all forms of experience (except 'pure intellection'). Though, therefore, I have been working with the distinction between the 'corporeal' (or 'physical') and the 'mental' (or 'psychical'), and so in effect treating the percipient as a *compositum* of mind and body, it must be remembered that the distinction is at most a provisional (or working) hypothesis, and that to describe the percipient's equipment, training, and grade of development as both physical and psychical is at best less inadequate than to describe them as barely physical or barely psychical.

speak—a detachable component of it, or a consequent annexed to it.

Thus (i) the physical and psychical processes (the training and education), through which the privileged percipient has passed in his development, are taken to 'lie behind him' as he now is. They are excluded from the level, at (or from) which he perceives. His present equipment, which enables him to perceive precisely *this* and precisely *thus*, is a 'state', 'disposition', 'habit', 'structure', of body and mind. He is what he is *in esse*, not *in fieri*. The 'grade' of refinement (the 'level' of culture), to which he has attained, crystallizes in itself the results of past judgement and reasoning; but it is itself quiescent, processless, and passive. And (ii) within the embodied mind at any given 'grade' of its development, there are taken to be 'detachable components'—organs-with-their-faculties. These, it is recognized, are related (*externally*) to one another and to the whole; but they are supposed to have each its several character complete within itself. While, therefore, it is admitted that the expert 'vision' or 'eye' of the privileged percipient goes along with, or presupposes, a trained 'intellect' or 'brain', yet the former—the perceptive faculty or organ—is taken to have its 'expertness' located (as it were) and fixed within itself.

According to our view, on the other hand, both these assumptions are erroneous. As rough expository devices, they are often convenient and sometimes necessary. But they do not adequately express the facts. Thus (i), in studying any continuous movement or development, it is convenient (and perhaps necessary) to 'freeze' it into stages—to treat it as a succession of discrete, arrested, grades. But these 'frozen stages', these 'quiescent grades', are no more than convenient fictions. They are not component parts of the movement. Its components are 'stretches', through which it itself persists.[1] And the 'grade', 'stage', or 'level'—at, and from, which (as we loosely say) the histologist, for example, or the musician, perceives—is in reality a 'stretch' of this kind. It is a stretch within the uninterrupted onward-sweeping movement (physical and psychical), which is his 'life', his 'life' as a self-conscious being. Through it, the activities of his past training and education are continued. Through it, his 'consciousness of a world', already definite and highly organized (amounting in the case of the expert percipient to 'a science' or 'an art'), is steadily changing—growing, it may be, still more definite, or on the other

---

[1] Cf. above, Study I, § 4, pp. 42–3.

hand decaying; but never arrested, never a fixed condition or possession of his mind.

It is common to speak of the privileged percipient as a man whose mental faculties[1] have become established in certain perceptive attitudes, and in certain habits or dispositions of thought. His mind, it is said, 'possesses', or is 'informed by', this or that wealth of experience, such and such a 'science' or 'art'. It has acquired a characteristic 'structure'—into which its past perceptual and intellectual activities have become 'set' and 'solidified'. In so speaking, we are working with the antithesis of capacity (δύναμις), disposition (διάθεσις), habit (ἕξις), and act (ἐνέργεια). But it is important not to misinterpret this antithesis while we work with it. Its contrasted members must not be taken for two kinds of things or facts—existing or occurring in the same sense and on the same level, but reciprocally excluding one another. In this region all that actually exists, or occurs, falls on one side of the antithesis only: is a perceiving, thinking, knowing, &c., i.e. an 'ἐνέργεια'. On the other side of the antithesis, there are no 'things' or 'facts'; nothing 'actual', nothing that exists or occurs. Faculties, dispositions, habits, mental structure (and so forth), are 'real' —if, and in so far as, they are 'real'—in a different sense and on a different level. The 'reality' which belongs to, or can be claimed for, them is the 'reality' of the objects of abstract thought. It is a 'reality' like that of a law of nature; or of a form of physical energy (light, for example, magnetism, electricity); or of the 'entities' which form the subjects of mathematical theory (atoms, the numbers, the types of figure &c.).[2]

The mind of the histologist or musician, then, neither *is*, nor *has*, a group of faculties and dispositions, or a structure storing and embedding experience and knowledge. On certain subjects, the histologist (or the musician) perceives, judges, and reasons with unusual precision, relevance, connectedness, &c. It is such characters of the actual functioning of a mind—characters which pervade, and are themselves differentiated and developed in, its activities (in the 'ἐνέργειαι')—which we abstract, for the convenience of summary description, from the movement in which they exist. Thus abstracted and immobilized, they *appear* to reflect—to express and result from—an immobilized and constant

[1] In what follows, the *physical* side of his qualifications can be disregarded, for the sake of brevity.
[2] Cf. Study I, § 4, pp. 32–7.

'structure', or structural parts and constituents (faculties, dispositions, habits) of the mind.

(ii) The second assumption[1] is, on our view, erroneous because it conflicts with a general principle, on which more than enough (perhaps) has been said already.[2] In considering the present mental equipment (the mind, as it would be called)[3] of the histologist (or the musician) as the source of his expert perception, we are dealing—if that principle be sound—not with a sum of constituent elements, nor even with a group of independent (though co-operating) factors or members, but with a 'spiritual plurality'. For certain purposes it is convenient, and under proper reservations it is legitimate, to distinguish perceptive and intellectual 'faculties'—as, for example, vision and hearing, imagination, memory, judgement, &c.; and it is similarly convenient and legitimate to describe the privileged percipient as a man of 'educated vision' or 'cultured hearing'. But the distinction must not be misinterpreted as a separation, nor the description misunderstood as attributing 'education' or 'culture' to a separated and independent perceptive faculty. Many 'interpenetrating experiences', or many mutually pervading spiritual activities, together constitute the histologist's 'mental equipment'; together determine his present 'consciousness of a world' and, through that, his present power of perceiving. What has been 'educated', and thus grown 'expert', is not his vision alone, but each and all of these contributory activities together. The science of histology—or what the given percipient has learnt of histology—permeates, informs, and controls, all his thinking and perceiving. He perceives as only the expert can perceive, because in perceiving he is necessarily also thinking (imagining, remembering, reasoning, &c.); doing so, moreover (he being what he is), predominantly under the guidance and control of his histological studies.

These considerations, it would perhaps be admitted, apply to the special examples I have quoted. But these examples, it will be objected, these so-called 'expert perceptions', are in reality *complex experiences*. In them, a 'halfpennyworth' of sense-perception is diluted with an 'intolerable deal' of intellectual (or, at any rate, non-perceptive) interpretation. The *complex experience as a whole* implies, no doubt, on the part of the experiencing subject,

---

[1] p. 93.   [2] pp. 85 ff.
[3] 'As it would be called'; for, in fact (cf. above, p. 89), it is at most a transient and fragmentary 'mode' or 'individuation' of a mind.

activities essentially constructive or discursive—activities, it may be admitted, which differ from judgement and inference, only because they 'take place *in* him' rather than 'are performed *by* him'. But below the interpretative wrapping, there is a primitive core of sense-perception which it enfolds and, in enfolding, has transformed. Surely that primitive core, it will be said, is, on the part of the percipient, a passive and processless acceptance of a *datum*? Or consider the unsophisticated perceptions of ordinary folk—those of any adult of average intelligence. What is there of constructive or discursive activity—what is there other than mere passive reception—in, for example, the plain man's perception of a flash of lightning?[1]

This objection owes most of its plausibility (i) to an ambiguity in its formulation by which it covertly assumes what was disposed of long ago;[2] and (ii) to a misconception of the difference between 'expert' and 'ordinary' perceptions. Let us first dispel these two sources of confusion, and then (iii) deal shortly with the comparatively simple difficulty that remains.

(i) It is not possible, in any perceptual experience, to 'get below' the interpretative wrapping to a 'primitive core' of sense-perception unadulterated by 'intellectual' activity. In the histologist's and musician's perceptions, as in all perceptual experiences, 'interpretation' and 'what it interprets' are inseparable. There is not a 'perception' *and* a 'judgement about it'; not a *datum* passively accepted *plus* a free, explicit, intellectual activity exercised upon it.[3] If we speak of a *datum* and 'interpretative processes', these complementary features must not be substantiated into mutually independent and separable constituents. There is nothing in a perceptual experience which is not 'interpreted'— which is not saturated with interpretative activity conditioned, by it, through and through. Nor is there, in a perceptual experience, any interpretation which is not fused with that which it interprets —any intellectual activity which is not immersed in, and constitutive of, the 'material' on which it is exercised.

And (ii) there is no such difference, as the objector supposes, between 'expert' and 'ordinary' perceptions. In a broad sense of the terms, every percipient is 'privileged' and every perception 'expert'. For every perception demands a determinate equipment

---

[1] Cf. above, pp. 80 ff.　　　　[2] Cf. above, pp. 83–4.
[3] So much we may claim to have shown in our previous analysis of the perception of a flash of lightning; cf. above, pp. 80–3, and the summary on pp. 84–5.

of the percipient; is possible only 'at a certain grade'—i.e. within a certain 'stretch'—of the development that is an embodied mind.

No doubt, the 'expert perceptions', which were quoted as examples, demand, on the part of their percipients, a development of some special kind, direction and degree; whereas the so-called 'ordinary' perceptions presuppose no more than the 'stereotyped' development (as it might be called) of the sane and healthy adult. Apart from abnormal defects and misfortunes, everybody—in the course of his everyday experience as he grows from infancy to early youth—develops that kind of degree of 'consciousness of a world' which is the *sine qua non* of these 'ordinary perceptions'. Being thus equipped, he 'perceives', for example, the flash of lightning, as you and I and every 'plain man' would perceive it— 'perceives' it, for example, as a brilliant streak of bluish light zigzagging across the sky. In his childhood, perhaps, in the presence of the same 'public event', he would have 'perceived' a dance of fairies in the sky—or (if he had been born in ancient Greece and nurtured in a Pythagorean household) the thunderbolt of Zeus, 'a visible threat to those in hell'.[1]

(iii) Yet, behind and apart from these confusions, there is a real difficulty to which the objection has drawn attention. For *in one respect* there does seem to be a sharp distinction between the 'expert' and the 'ordinary' perceptions. If I am to perceive *what* the histologist (or the musician) perceives, and *as* he perceives it, I must have pursued, consciously and deliberately, a definite course of practice and study. My 'development' must have been (largely, at any rate) a self-education. For to learn a science or an art, is (at bottom and in the main) to teach it to oneself. There must have been, on my part, conscious intellectual effort and activity, thinking in the form of explicit judgement and reasoning; explicit intellectual activities initiated, controlled, and organized by myself, a 'thinking', moreover, methodically pursued and logically connected or systematic. But no such self-education is presupposed in the percipient, who is to perceive the flash of lightning as the 'plain man' perceives it. The 'ordinary perceptions' require, no doubt, a certain normal or 'stereotyped' development in our 'consciousness of a world'. But the development takes place in us without our conscious effort or control. It is a *natural* growth, a *natural* ripening to maturity, of our 'consciousness of a world'— rather than the result of intellectual activities initiated, directed,

---

[1] Cf. *Post. Anal.* 94^b 32–4.

and organized by ourselves. While our 'consciousness of a world' is ripening, no doubt there is (or may be) on our part unsystematic and sporadic 'thinking'—explicit judgement and reasoning on this or that subject. But we do not cause, or control, the ripening by our 'thinking': we are not educating ourselves—not learning to adopt the plain man's outlook on the world, as the privileged percipient learns (i.e. teaches himself) an art or science.

The real difficulty, then, which gives force to the objection[1] is this:

We have been arguing, in effect, that the 'development' continues into, and through, the perception, which presupposes it; and *must* so continue owing to the very nature of a 'mind' or the 'experiences of a mind'. For a mind, or subject of experiences, is not a thing which develops: it is itself development. A mind (we have insisted) is all, and always, developing. It is impossible to conceive it as passing from fixed level to fixed level of attainment; as *now* in process of transition and travelling, and *now* quiescent at a station. Distinctions between structure and function, faculties and their use, habits and their exercise, have a provisional value for expository purposes; but they are not strictly applicable to a mind. A mind is not half in *esse* or *essentia*, and half in *fieri*; its being is all actual and in act, all ἐνέργεια.

Now this line of argument is, in any case and admittedly, of a general and *a priori* kind. But it has, or seems to have, both relevance and force, so long as the 'expert' perceptions are alone in question. We should all agree that the histologist (throughout his apprenticeship) was 'thinking' in the full sense of the term. In his perception, no doubt, he is no longer 'thinking' with the same explicit consciousness and control. Nevertheless, there is, in his perception, a constructive or interpretative process surviving from, and prolonging, his apprenticeship; and it is reasonable to regard this process as a form of 'thinking'—as a semi-conscious, quasi-instinctive, 'thinking'—in virtue of its continuity with, and affinity to, the explicit judgements and reasonings in which it originated. So far, therefore, *and subject always to the soundness of our assumption in regard to the nature of a mind*, the discursive character of these 'expert' perceptions has been established. There must be, and is, in them an 'intellectual' activity—an activity akin to judgement and reasoning.

But what becomes of this general and *a priori* line of argument,

---

[1] Cf. above, pp. 95–6.

if so sharp a distinction must be drawn between the two 'developments'—if one is a self-educative apprenticeship, and the other a natural ripening into maturity? Even if it be granted that the argument itself, together with the assumption which it unfolds, is sound, it seems to have no relevance or force at all in regard to the 'ordinary' perceptions. For no 'thinking' (in the full sense of the term) contributed, or need have contributed, to the 'growth' of the plain man's 'consciousness of a world'—to the preparatory 'development' which fitted him to 'perceive' the flash of lightning. Even if, therefore, this natural 'growth' is continued into, and conditions, his perception, there is no ground whatever for attributing to the latter a 'discursive' character. There is nothing to show that he is thinking in *any* sense—even semi-consciously or quasi-instinctively—when he 'perceives' the flash of lightning; that there is, in his perception, an 'intellectual' activity—an activity derived from, continuous with, and akin to, explicit judgement and reasoning.

The force of this objection must be admitted; but it must not be over-estimated.

And first as to the 'general and *a priori*' character of the argument which was used to establish the presence of 'thinking' in perception. The argument itself is not challenged by the objection—and therefore we are not called upon to defend its *a priori* and general character. But if the argument itself were attacked on the ground of its *a priori* character, the defence—a sufficient defence—would be, in effect, that there is, and can be, no alternative. If an attempt 'to establish the discursive character of perceptual experience' is to be made at all, no line of argument is conceivable which will not be both 'general' and '*a priori*'—couched, that is, in general terms and based upon a general conception of 'a mind and its experiences' that is, a general conception, assumption, or hypothesis—a conception, that is, which may 'prove' and establish itself in experience, but is not 'generalized' from experience, and is, therefore, *a priori*.

Next, in regard to the attack actually pressed by the objection. The difficulty, which gives it force, is real enough but not insuperable. For the distinction between the two 'developments' is not in fact so uncompromising as the objection supposes. The objection has exaggerated a sharp distinction into a complete cleavage.

'Thinking' in its full sense, in its free and proper form, is explicit judgement or inference. And an explicit judgement or inference is a 'discursive process' (a movement of synthesis and analysis in one), which must not only be *one with* the activity of a finite intellect, but must further be, *for* that finite intellect, *its own*. In that sense, 'I' *make* a judgement or an inference; am conscious of the activity as *mine*; of 'myself' as taking an active part in discovering what would not otherwise disclose itself to me. There is thus, in thinking, a certain measure of initiative and control on the part of the finite thinker. But there is another side to the matter.[1] For it is not true that an explicit judgement or inference is nothing but the activity of a finite intellect, 'one with' it in the sense of bare and mere identity; it is not true that 'I' am its 'only begetter', its spontaneous originator and complete controller. The 'discursive process', of which I am conscious as (in one sense) 'my own', is objective and impersonal, working in, and controlling, 'my' mind. In the judgement or inference, which I 'make', I am in the grip, and under the governance, of a power (a *vis cognoscens*) immanent in, but transcending, and more fundamental than, 'my' intellect and 'its' functioning. When I am 'thinking', in the fullest and most pregnant sense of the term, 'the subject'—so it is commonly expressed—'has taken full possession of my mind'; 'reality', or 'the truth', itself is 'shaping itself in my thought'.

This, then, is the side of the matter which the objection has under-estimated or ignored. And if we are to meet the objection, and to show that the difficulty behind it is not insuperable, this is the side from which we must begin, and which we must stress, in our conception of thought. 'Thought'—we must insist—is, primarily and fundamentally, a power inherent in the very nature of things.[2] It is the power which, working in, and through and as, the (so-called) finite minds, fulfils itself in the self-disclosing and self-discovering of reality—in the self-expression of reality in the form of truth. It is this fundamental discursus which, so far as I am 'thinking' in the fullest and most pregnant sense, I recognize and adopt as 'mine'—as *one with* the natural functioning of 'my' intellect. Setting thus the seal of my self-consciousness upon the working of 'thought' in and through 'my' mind, I share in a discovery which is a self-manifestation of fact. I 'make' a judgement or an inference, which are 'making themselves' in me.[3]

[1] Cf. above, pp. 70–2; below, p. 122.

[2] Cf. above, Study I, § 3, p. 13.

[3] Cf. Bradley, *Essays*, e.g. pp. 121, 218, 327, 337; also cf. Bosanquet, *The Nature of Mind*, e.g. p. 59: 'Thought rather governs consciousness than is an act of consciousness'; p. 65, 'For thought, as the development and self-maintenance

Now the self-educative apprenticeship ('learning' an art or science) is sharply distinguished from the ripening to maturity of the plain man's consciousness of a world. But 'thought' pervades and saturates them both. The 'growth' of the plain man's consciousness is also a learning or self-teaching; and the self-educative apprenticeship of the artist, or man of science, is also the ripening of a natural power, its self-fulfilment in (and as) the perfecting of the intellectual activity of a finite subject. In short, the sharp distinction is a contrast between the extreme or limiting varieties, of which a single development—i.e. a development identical and continuous in its essential characters—is capable; it is not a cleavage between a development which is intellectual, and a *merely* 'natural' (i.e. a non-intellectual) growth.

The answer, therefore, which must be made to the objection is simply this. 'Thought' in the sense explained—an 'impersonal', 'objective', or 'infinite', discursive activity, recognized and adopted by the finite subject as his own—plays the main part in both developments. But the explicit judgements or reasonings, which go to form and make the plain man's consciousness of a world, are not (like those which constitute the self-educative apprenticeship of the artist or man of science) centred on a special and limited subject-matter. The 'thinking', therefore, which equips the ordinary percipient to perceive the flash of lightning, is wider, perhaps less systematic and less profound, than the 'thinking' which prepares the histologist and the musician

of the object in ideal form, is, essentially, the judgment. And the judgment is surely the central act by which reality, operating in and through the mind, becomes a constituent of knowledge and of action'; &c. Cf., further, Bosanquet in *British Contemporary Philosophy*, 1st series, e.g. pp. 60–1: 'Thus, it is an incomplete description even to qualify thought as we did just now, by the term "function of mind", without calling attention to its other aspects as the self-revelation of reality. The "I think" . . . is on one side a deceptive phrase. It would avoid misapprehension if we were rather to say (Mr. Russell has suggested it, and I have urged what amounts to the same point) "It thinks in me" or "My world in me takes the shape that —". As Green said long ago, the essence of thought is not in a mental faculty, but in the objective order of things. We bring the two sides together if we say it is the control exercised by reality over mental process.' Also, ibid., p. 68, in criticism of Gentile's 'distinction between thinking thought, or thought in its pure act . . . and so-called thought which has been thought, or the system of the universe as something pre-supposed and falsely conceived as transcending and limiting the activity of thinking thought, which alone is taken as the reality.' Bosanquet summarizes his own view against this distinction (as it is commonly understood) thus: 'The true life is that of the whole, of which thought in the finite mind is a partial and incomplete revelation. The contrast of "pensièro pensante" and "pensièro pensate" precisely inverts the true relation. What really thinks is something more than any thinking act of ours.'

for their 'expert' perceptions. It is 'thinking', nevertheless, in the full and natural sense of the term; and the ripening of the plain man's consciousness, though a 'natural growth', is essentially an intellectual development, to which undoubtedly our main line of argument applies.

§ 9

(II) *The search for a* datum *among our sensations* is impossible or futile; for there are no sensations in the sense supposed.

1. We have seen that every sense-perception is 'immediate', but only in an abstract and formal sense. Its 'immediacy' is no more than the formal unity and presentness, which characterize every experience *qua* 'actual'; no more than the bare form of its actuality. So far from being 'immediate' in the real and material (and only relevant) sense, every sense-perception is, on the contrary, essentially and in principle 'mediate' or 'discursive'.[1] Every sense-perception ('ordinary', as well as 'expert') is conditioned, saturated, and largely constituted, by activities essentially 'intellectual' in character—activities which differ from explicit 'thinking', only because the percipient is not aware of them as his, does not adopt them as his own, is rather controlled by them than in control of them. The thought—the two-edged activity of synthesis and analysis—which is involved in, and goes to constitute, my perception of the flash of lightning, is *in that sense* not 'free'; it is immersed in the sensuous materials it discriminates and, in discriminating, connects—immersed in the *data* it interprets and, by interpreting, constructs and constitutes. And, again, it is thought 'inexplicit' or 'quasi-instinctive'. For it is an activity in which I am engaged without conscious complicity; a discursive movement carrying me with it—a movement, indeed, of which 'I' am a phase and which, in some measure, 'I' contribute to execute, but neither originate nor control.

The negative result, then, already reached and recorded,[2] stands firm. The 'search for a *datum*' in the wide field of perceptual experience has definitely failed. No sense-perception is 'an immediate apprehension of self-evident fact'. Nowhere in this region is there to be found a basic element of fact and truth in one—a self-subsistent constituent of reality which is also a self-evident foundation of knowledge.

But according to the popular division of knowledge into imme-

---

[1] Cf. above, pp. 77, 79, 84. [2] pp. 84–5.

diate and discursive, 'sense' or 'sensuous knowledge' includes
three different groups of actual cognizant experiences. We are
supposed to know immediately all that we *sensate* and all that we
feel, as well as all we *sensuously perceive*. In addition to sense-
perceptions there are assumed to be (*a*) *sensations*—'direct
apprehensions of *data* of the outer senses', immediate awareness of,
for example, shapes, colour, sounds, and other sensible qualities,
and (*b*) *sentiences* or *feelings*—'direct apprehensions of *data* of the
inner sense', immediate awareness of changes and states of our
conscious being.[1]

Now, if this tripartite classification of our sensuous cognizances
is sound, the 'search for a *datum*', which has failed in sense-perception, must be renewed first in the field of sensating, and then in
that of sentience. Are there (we must ask) *sensations*, in which the
sensating subject is immediately and infallibly aware of genuine
qualities of actual fact—in which he directly apprehends *them as
they are*? And are there *sentience* or *feelings* in which the sentient
subject feels—immediately and infallibly apprehends—his own
state, his own sentient being or a modification of it, as it really is
or occurs?

2. But the more one considers the proposed tripartite classification, the more questionable it appears.

(i) Any grouping or classification is open to suspicion, on the
ground that it presupposes a mechanical or atomistic view of the
mind-and-its-experiences—a view such as I have already repudiated as a 'caricature'. 'It is comparatively harmless', it may be
said, 'to think and speak of a mind as though it were a spiritual
energy or force, operating on different levels or at different
"powers" of itself, and so expressing itself in our various experiences with different degrees of intensity and completeness. But
it is an elementary and serious error to speak of a classification
or grouping of cognizant experiences. Experiences are not units
which can be summed, items which can be collected, or members
which can be grouped. Nor does a mind "contain" its experiences,
or enfold them within its unity, as so many collections, groups or
classes.'[2]

(ii) While admitting the general force of this objection, perhaps
it is possible to defend the notion of a classification of experiences.
All our experiences, we may agree, are the expressions of a concretely single spiritual energy: in some genuine and important

sense, the whole mind, and the mind as a whole, is immanent in every one of them. Yet, as the objector himself insists, the single energy is expressed with different degrees of intensity and completeness; or there are different levels and 'powers' of the mind's fulfilment of itself in act. It seems, therefore, that, in the various experiencings of a mind, now one, and now another, of the many sides or 'facets' of its whole nature—of its concrete singleness as a spiritual energy—obtains emphatic and dominant expression; is *par excellence* displayed. It seems mere pedantry to rule out the convenient metaphor of groups or classes. It is surely legitimate to class, as 'sensations' and as 'feelings' respectively, experiences, in which the self-conscious subject is, primarily and predominantly, sensuously apprehending colour, shape, sound, or other sensible qualities, and primarily and predominantly sentient of its own inner states and changes. In doing so, we need not forget that in these, as in all its experiences, the mind is necessarily engaged in some sense 'wholly' and as a 'whole'.

(iii) Apart from this general objection, however, there are special grounds for distrusting the proposed tripartite classification. Leaving the group of so-called feelings or sentiences to be examined later,[1] and remarking only that, even if there are such experiences, it is far from obvious that they are distinctively sensuous (rather than intellectual) in character, i.e. that they have any special claim to count as examples of 'sense-knowledge' in a division contrasting 'sense' with 'thought', let us scrutinize the group of so-called sensations. There is reason to suspect that it owes its supposed distinct and separate existence to a confusion.

(*a*) And first the use of the name (sensation) for experiences distinguished from feelings has been criticized. Such a case, the critic has urged, implies and encourages an obvious confusion of thought. In the language of the 'plain man', every 'sensation' is a 'feeling', though not all 'feelings' are 'sensations'. We speak indifferently of *feeling* hot or cold, pleased or pained, disgusted or sick—and of having *sensations* of heat and cold, pleasure and pain, disgust and nausea. When, on the other hand, we assume (rightly or wrongly, but without hesitation) that we are apprehending a quality in (or of) the thing (in or of 'the external sensible object' in Locke's terminology), we do not call our experience a 'sensation'. We do not speak, for example, of 'sensations of shape or colour or sound'—any more than of *feeling* 'triangular' or ‘C$\sharp$’,

---

[1] Cf. below, § 10.

or 'blue' (except in another sense). If, therefore, due stress is laid on 'the authority of ordinary language'[1] it must be admitted that confused thinking can alone have suggested, and more confused thinking will be engendered by, the proposed title of our group. It is confused and confusing to give the name 'sensations' to experiences which are—or are supposed to be—distinguished from 'feelings' precisely on the ground that what in them we apprehend is other than a state or change of our own 'inner or sentient being'.[2]

Yet these considerations, even if they are sound, are hardly of themselves sufficient to show that the group of 'sensations'—i.e. sensuous cognizances other than feelings and distinct from (and more rudimentary than) sense-perceptions—has no existence except by confusion. For (i) the authority of ordinary language—of the plain man's views and his expression of them—must not be exaggerated. The proposed use of the term 'sensation' is artificial or technical; but it has behind it a long philosophical tradition, and is common enough in philosophical and psychological literature. And, after all, (ii) the question of nomenclature is of no importance. If 'sensation' is an inappropriate term, by all means substitute another. The point at issue—the question we set out to investigate—is whether, or in what sense, certain experiences exist; not how they ought to be named. And even the plain man, it seems, takes their existence for granted; assumes that our sensuous experiences include (besides, and in addition to, sense-perceptions of things and scenes) awareness of sensible qualities—of shapes, for example, and colours and sounds, of tastes and smells and (more doubtfully, perhaps) of varieties of temperature. In refusing to speak of most of these experiences as 'sensations', he is throwing no doubt upon their existence; he is only insisting that most of them, at all events, are other than 'feelings'.

---

[1] Cf. above, p. 62.

[2] I have been drawing upon a passage in J. Cook Wilson, *Statement and Inference*, vol. ii, p. 736: '. . . in the case of heat every one easily recognizes, without philosophy, that he himself has a definite sensation of heat—we know this to be a sensation inasmuch as we say we feel hot. This is not so with colour. People do not easily recognize that colour is a sensation of their own. On the contrary the belief that it is a sensation, is an inference from a theory scientific or philosophic. We all of us, both the plain and the philosophic, think of colour as in the thing and put it there in a way we never put our sensation of heat. Thus, too, ordinary people say they feel hot, but never say they feel coloured, e.g. feel red. Moreover, whereas they speak of a sensation of heat, they *never* speak of a "sensation of yellow".' Yet, do we not (unless corrupted by science or by doubtful philosophic theory) 'think of heat as in the fire and put it there' as unhesitatingly as we 'put' green 'in' the grass?

(*b*) Discarding, then, the question of nomenclature, let us come to the question of fact. 'But surely', it will be said, 'there *is* no question of fact—no question "whether awarenesses of sensible qualities exist"? Are there not, beyond all possible doubt, actual experiences in which—through, or by the help of, a stimulated and reacting special organ of sense—we see, hear, taste, and so forth? And (call these experiences "sensations" or not, as you please) what else are they but "apprehensions of *data* of the outer senses"—direct sensuous awarenesses of shapes and colours, of sounds and flavours, in short of "sensible qualities"?'

So long as the matter is put in such vague and general terms, we may perhaps agree that there is no question 'whether awarenesses of sensible qualities exist'. Nobody doubts that we see colour and shape, hear sound—in short, are actually cognizant of what are called 'sensible qualities'. But when it is asserted that these awarenesses are through and through, and purely, 'sensuous'— that in them by mere sense we apprehend mere *sensa* or *sense-data* —then there is every doubt whether, strictly so interpreted, they are actual experiences at all, whether or in what sense they exist. Let us try to get the issue clearer.

(i) In describing the perception of a flash of lightning I took 'awareness of sensible qualities'—e.g. of colour and shape—for granted. What is apprehended in that perception is 'a zigzag streak of bluish light'. The flash, as it is perceived, is 'clothed in sensible qualities'; the perception 'includes' (in some sense) awareness of a bluish colour and a zigzag shape. But then, in perceiving the flash the percipient is 'thinking sensuously'—not sensating and also thinking. He is not, by sheer vision, apprehending bare *sensa* and also (or, and then) by pure thinking (by a free and explicit intellectual activity) interpreting and combining the material, thus independently given and received. He is aware of bluish and of zigzag. These awarenesses are in a loose sense 'included' in the perception and 'share its actuality'. But they have within it no separate or separable existence. They do not 'inexist' in it as actual cognizant experiences; they are not constituent apprehensions of which it is composed. They belong inseparably to the whole *perception*. That—the whole perception —is actual and occurs. Its two contrasted 'moments' ('sensating' and 'thinking'), as they inseparably constitute its concretely single and indissoluble being, may be said, perhaps, to 'share its actuality'. But if, reflecting upon the perception and subjecting it to philosophical analysis, we concentrate upon either 'moment' and describe it so as to emphasize it *only* in its contrast with the other—then clearly our result (what we are studying) is neither an 'actual' experience, nor even anything which 'shares the actuality' of an actual experience. It is a 'moment' of an actual experience— but a moment extracted and mutilated; and so no longer, strictly speaking, a 'moment', but an abstraction.

From the admission, therefore, that, 'in perceiving the flash of lightning, the percipient is aware of a bluish colour and a zigzag shape' it does not follow that the supposed 'sensations'—the supposed *sheerly sensuous* apprehensions of colour, for example, and shape—are 'actual', or even 'share in the actuality' of any actual experience.

(ii) In another context 'awarenesses of sensible qualities' were taken for granted. They were quoted amongst the examples of experiences 'which would commonly be called sense-perceptions'.[1] I assumed (without hesitation and rightly) that 'sense-perceiving' is articulated into experiences that fall within the ranges of the various special senses—that 'seeing', 'hearing', 'tasting', 'touching', 'smelling' are so many modalities of 'perceiving'. And I quoted, as examples of perceptions, 'hearing the blackbird's alarm-note or the beat of a drum' and 'tasting the sweetness or astringency of the port'.

Here again there is no 'question of fact'—no doubt that such 'awarenesses of sensible qualities' exist and occur amongst our actual cognizant experiences. But then, *ex hypothesi*, such 'seeing', 'hearing', 'tasting', &c., are not the mere exercise of some faculty and organ of sense. *Ex hypothesi*, in these experiences we are 'perceiving'—i.e. (as I have tried to show) not freely thinking, nor barely sensating, nor thinking *and* sensating, but 'thinking sensuously'. And what, in these experiences, we apprehend is not— does not even approximate to being—a bare sensation. It is an 'object of perception'; and, like every such object, through and through 'categorized'. The colour we 'see', for example, is this singular instance of a particular shade of colour; and one amongst several qualities of a (relatively substantial) fact or 'thing'. The sound we 'hear' is this special note characteristic of the blackbird's alarm; and the flavour we 'taste' is that unique astringency of the port. Unity and plurality; singularity, particularity, universality; substantiality and adjectival being—these and other categorical

[1] Above, p. 73.

antitheses or thought-determinations enter beyond question into
the 'colour', 'sound', 'taste', which are 'perceived' in these
experiences, though (it need hardly be said) we neither see nor
hear nor taste them nor, in perceiving, conceive them explicitly
and as such. We may say, perhaps, that they are formal conditions,
which any *sensibile* or *sensatum* must satisfy if it is to be perceivable
or perceived. They are 'implicit' in the object of perception—
revealing themselves only as the 'form', or 'characteristic definite-
ness', in that which we perceive. But if we try to help ourselves
by using language of this kind—language drawn from, or vaguely
reminiscent of, Kant—we must remember that the distinction
between the 'moment of sense' and the 'moment of thought'
within a perception is not without reservation analogous to the
opposition between matter and form.

There is then no doubt (i) that in every perception the percipient
is sensuously aware of (sees or hears or touches, &c.) a sensible
quality or qualities. Sensation—the sensuous awareness of shape,
colour, sound, &c.—is inseparably included as a 'moment' of
every perception. Moreover, (ii) in many of our perceptions,
what we primarily perceive, what we are principally aware of, is,
for example, a sound, a colour, a taste—i.e. a sensible quality.
And, naturally and rightly enough, such experiences would often
be called '*seeing* a colour', '*hearing* a sound', &c., rather than
'perceiving'. They would be designated, that is, in such a manner
as to suggest that they are this or that 'sensating' or *sense*-aware-
ness—instead of being (what in fact they are) this or that modality
of (sense-) *perceiving*.

Now these experiences—these *perceptions* in which the primary
or principal *perception* is a sensible quality—may be arranged on
a graduated scale, according to the relative dominance in each of
them of the 'sensuous' or the 'interpretation' (thinking) moment.
All the examples I quoted and described before, would fall at or
near the upper limit of the scale—i.e. the thinking or interpretation
'moment' in such experiences as perceiving (hearing) the beat of
a drum, the alarm-note of a blackbird, is at a *maximum*. The
percipient is *all but* explicitly and reflectively conscious of the
thought-determinations which his perceptual experience involves.

That is clearly so, unless perhaps in describing these perceptions
we have exaggerated the interpretation or thinking 'moment' in
the actual experience—in the perception as it actually occurs.
For we must not forget that the perception itself as it actually

occurs—that the actual experience of the percipient—is what Bradley calls 'a many felt in one', rather than (what any description of its context must suggest) clean-cut elements in definite relations. It is a non-relational whole with distinguishable features or aspects—not (as any description is bound to suggest) a whole containing, or made up of, several constituents related to one another, for example, as thing and property, cause and effect, &c., &c.

What I *perceive*, and *strictly as I perceive it*, for example, is not exactly 'the alarm-note of the blackbird'. For (i) in this description an infinity of detail is obviously omitted and, on the other hand, (ii) *what I heard* was not, *as I heard it*, thus explicitly broken up and articulated into a sound and its producer, nor into a sound and the emotion which called it forth, or which it expresses.

At its lower limit, our imaginary scale would be terminated by a perception, in which the sensuous 'moment' so predominated, that only careful analysis would be able to detect the presence of any 'thinking' or interpretation at all. It is difficult to give an example; for, obviously, the more the sensuous character of a perception predominates, the less easy it becomes, by help of a description, to recall it to oneself, and to set it unambiguously before others. Two extreme types, however, may be suggested. In both of them, the thinking 'moment' is at a *minimum*—so that the experience is almost, but not quite, one of those 'sensations' which the tripartite classification postulates, but which (as I am maintaining) do not in fact exist or occur. There are, then, at or near the lower end of our imaginary scale, (*a*) perceptions so dim and faint that the percipient is half-inclined to doubt whether he is 'perceiving' or merely 'imagining'—as when he is conscious of a 'barely perceptible' fragrance or sound. And there are (*b*) perceptions so intense and violent, that the experience tends to lose its cognizant character and to be for the percipient an overwhelming 'sensation' (so he would probably call it) of pain or pleasure.[1]

(iv) If these considerations are right, there are no 'sensations' of the kind supposed; no actual cognizant experiences, in which, by the mere exercise of a faculty and organ of sense, we apprehend (i.e. 'sense' or 'sensate', as opposed to 'perceive') shape, colour, sound, and the other so-called 'sensible qualities'. There are no 'sensations'. But in every perception there is an *inseparable*

---

[1] Cf. also below, pp. 174–5.

'*moment*' *of sensation*. There is a sensuous awareness, for example, of shape or colour or sound, which must be distinguished by reflection and may be isolated and then, by confusion, substantiated (so to speak) into an actual cognizant experience, a pure or bare 'sensation'. And in many of our perceptions, the central or primary object we perceive is a colour, or sound, or taste; so that it is natural and sufficient to speak of the experience as, for example, seeing or hearing or tasting a sensible quality. Some of these perceptions—viz. those in which the sensuous 'moment' predominates, and in which the 'thinking moment' is at the *minimum*—may easily, on a first superficial view, be taken by confusion for bare or pure sensations.

3. It would, perhaps, be wiser to leave the matter there, and to proceed at once to explore the third and last of the supposed 'groups' of our immediate cognizant experiences—the group of so-called *sentiences* or *feelings*. For, if there are no 'sensations'—no sheerly sensuous cognizant experiences—it is futile to search amongst them for a *datum*. It would be absurd to ask whether in any of our 'sensations', or in which of them, we are directly and infallibly aware of a genuine quality of absolute 'fact'.[1] For 'sensations' are myths and fictions. The only actual experiences, in which we are aware of the so-called 'sensible qualities', are sense-perceptions; and these have already been examined and have failed to yield a *datum*.

The proposed short-cut is tempting; yet some further consideration seems inevitable. For (*a*) though I have failed to find 'sensations' amongst our actual cognizant experiences, most people (it may be objected) and many philosophers have been more fortunate. Those very 'sensations' which I have just set aside as right and fitting, figure in Locke's philosophy (to say nothing of, for example, Hume or Kant) as the materials of all our thinking about the 'external sensible objects'—as the foundations of our knowledge, slight though it be,[2] of the physical world. And (*b*) in any case every perception—as we have seen—includes 'sensation as an inseparable moment'. We are aware of colour, shape, sound, and the other so-called 'sensible qualities'. Hence, the real issue (it may be said), the only question of substance, remains untouched.

---

[1] Cf. above, p. 102.

[2] For 'as to a perfect *science* of natural bodies (not to mention spiritual beings) we are, I think, so far from being capable of any such thing, that I conclude it lost labour to seek after it' (Locke, *Essay*, iv. 3, § 29).

Are we, or are we not, in our perceptions, precisely in virtue of their 'moment of sensation', directly aware of facts, or characters of fact, presented, or presenting themselves, exactly as they are?

(*a*) No doubt the popular subdivision of our 'immediate' (or sensuous) knowledge into sense-perceptions, sensations, and feelings is derived from and incorporates, or at least roughly resembles, Locke's doctrine of the 'simple ideas of sensation' and of 'reflection' as the two fountains of all our knowledge. But this affiliation or resemblance, I shall try to show, is a source of weakness, not of strength.

First let us recall the broad outlines of Locke's doctrine by a few quotations from *Essay*, ii. c. i:

'Let us suppose,' he says, 'the mind to be (as we say) white paper, void of all characters, without any *ideas*; How comes it to be furnished? ... Whence has it all the materials of reason and knowledge? To this I answer, in one word, from *experience*. ... Our observation employed either about *external sensible objects*, or *about the internal operations of our minds, perceived and reflected on by ourselves, is that which supplies our understandings with all the materials of thinking*. These two are the functions of knowledge, from whence all the *ideas* we have, or can naturally have, do spring.'

About the *first* 'function' (with which we are at present concerned), Locke proceeds as follows:

'... *our senses*, conversant about particular sensible objects, do *convey into the mind* several distinct *perceptions* of things, according to those various ways, wherein those objects do affect them: and thus we come by those *ideas* [="simple ideas of sensation", as we learn presently] we have of *yellow, white, heat, cold, soft, hard, bitter, sweet*, and all those which we call sensible qualities; which when I say the senses convey into the mind, I mean, they from external objects convey into the mind what produces there those *perceptions*. This great source of most of the *ideas* we have, depending wholly upon our senses, and derived by them to the understanding, I call SENSATION.'

Lastly, in the summary at the end of the chapter,[1] Locke says:

'If it shall be demanded ... "*When a man begins to have any ideas?*" I think the true answer is, when he first has any *sensation*. For since there appear not to be any *ideas* in the mind, before the senses have conveyed any in, I conceive, that *ideas* in the understanding are coeval with *sensation*; which is such an impression or motion, made in some part of the body, as produces some perception in the understanding. ... In time, the mind comes to reflect on its own *operations* about the

[1] ii. i, §§ 23–5.

ideas got by *sensation*, and thereby stores itself with a new set of *ideas*, which I call *ideas of reflection*. These *impressions* that are made on our *senses* by outward objects, that are extrinsical to the mind; and *its own operations*, proceeding from powers intrinsical and proper to itself, which, when reflected on by itself, become also objects of its contemplation, are . . . *the original of all knowledge.'*

Even in its most 'sublime thoughts' and 'remote speculations', the mind

'stirs not one jot beyond those *ideas*, which *sense* or *reflection* have offered for its contemplation. In this part, the *understanding* is merely *passive*. . . . For the objects of our senses do, many of them, obtrude their particular *ideas* upon our minds, whether we will or no. . . . These *simple ideas*, when offered to the mind, *the understanding* can no more refuse to have, nor alter when they are imprinted, nor blot them out and make new ones itself, than a mirror can refuse, alter, or obliterate the images or *ideas*, which the objects set before it do therein produce. . . .'

Partly from these passages, and partly from later chapters in the *Essay*, it is clear that Locke is assuming, and expects his readers to accept, a certain situation—a certain philosophical background—which may be roughly sketched as follows:

We are to suppose an individual subject of knowledge to be on the threshold of his studies; to have a mind as yet utterly uninformed and unexercised, and to be just about to enter, for the first time, upon an investigation of the 'sensible objects' (things, for example, animals and human beings) which confront and surround him. Further, we are to suppose ourselves to know many things in regard both to the environment and to the nature of our hypothetical student. His environment, to put it broadly, is a world of 'sensible bodies'—but they are 'sensible' in a special and restricted fashion. They are solid, extended, shaped, at rest or moving, each of them 'one' and composed of 'many' minute 'insensible' parts; but they are not coloured or sounding, and they are without odour, flavour, or temperature.[1] As to the student himself, he is one amongst these 'bodies'; but he is a 'body' specially developed, which is either itself endowed with spiritual powers, or intimately united (in some unknowable way) with a spiritual substance or mind.[2] He is, in short, a 'cogitative being'.[3] His body includes an *apparatus* for receiving and transmitting impressions—motions or some physical effects produced in it by

---

[1] Cf., e.g., *Essay*, ii. 8, §§ 7–26.   [2] Cf., e.g., iv. 3, § 6.
[3] Sensating, perceiving, thinking, willing, &c.: cf. iv. 10, § 9.

the action of external bodies. He has five[1] 'senses', i.e. special
organs of sense; he has nerves and a brain; and the latter either
itself possesses the power of 'thinking', or is in union[2] with a
'thinking substance'.

All this—and more, which need not here be specified—Locke
assumes, and expects his readers to accept, as true. And all this
he supposes, and expects his readers to suppose, is as yet utterly
unknown to the hypothetical student—the student with the blank
and empty mind.

Now these assumptions have been exposed over and over again
by philosophical criticism. The general situation in which Locke
has planted himself is no longer held by any careful thinker. Still,
let us for the sake of argument try to place ourselves with Locke
in this outworn position and inquire what is the value of his account
of the 'first beginnings and materials' of our knowledge.

In view of Locke's loose and ambiguous terminology and the
many confusions in his thought it is difficult to give a short and
confident answer. But one thing seems certain. The 'simple ideas
of sensation' presuppose on the part of the student, who is to begin
his studies by acquiring or having them, the actual possession of
a knowledge which—according to Locke—is obtainable only by
elaboration out of them. Or (to put the same point in a somewhat
different way) the cognizant experiences, in which we are aware of
'yellow, white, heat . . . and all those which we call sensible
qualities', so far from being direct and merely sensuous apprehensions, are—according to Locke's own description of them—
essentially *inferential* in character. They involve an inference from
effect to cause—or, in Locke's terminology, from the 'idea', as it
is 'barely a perception in the mind', to a quality or 'power' in the
external object which has produced the idea. The inference is not
explicit or free; it is inseparable from and immersed in the whole
experience. Still, it is in principle an inference, though it is doubtful how far Locke would have agreed to call it so;[3] and the
experience, which involves it, would be utterly impossible for the
hypothetical beginner with the empty mind.

(i) We may make this clear to ourselves by considering more
closely Locke's account of the 'physical process', which is presupposed by—or, as he tends to say and sometimes seems to
think, which *produces*—our awareness of a 'sensible quality'. An

---

[1] Or perhaps more, ii. 2, § 3.
[2] As we said, cf. *loc. cit.* iv. 3, § 6.   [3] Cf. below, p. 117.

external body acts upon some organ of sense (eye, ear, &c.) of our
hypothetical student. The action is mechanical, or 'by impulse'—
that being 'the only way which we can conceive bodies operate in'.[1]
By the action, the external body communicates *something* of itself
—some 'motion' or some moving (but of course imperceptible)
particles—to the organ of sense. This communicated *something*
is transmitted or 'continued' by other parts of the student's body
(by his 'nerves or animal spirits') until it reaches his 'brain or seat
of sensation'.[2] So far, therefore, the effect of the physical process
is a change in the student's brain; some displacement or new
configuration or fresh movement of its particles.

Now, before I proceed, I will call attention to the fact that the
whole of this physical process falls utterly beyond the student's
ken. He is, *ex hypothesi*, as yet without the least notion of the
nature, and even of the existence, of any external sensible bodies,
or of his own organs of sense, nerves, and brain, or of 'the ways
which bodies operate in'. In whatever sense, therefore, it may be
true that some such 'physical process' is '*presupposed by*' the
student's first awareness of a sensible quality, the 'presupposition'
is Locke's, or ours, and not the student's. The student cannot be
aware of the 'physical process', or of any part of it, as conditioning,
or contributing to, his first acquisition of a 'simple idea of sensation'. Indeed, we must go farther. For it is obvious—so obvious
that one is almost ashamed to state it—that no percipient, while
in the act, for example, of seeing a colour or hearing a sound, is
ever in fact 'aware of' (in Locke's terminology 'perceives' or
'contemplates') any physical changes in his organs of sense or
nerves (to say nothing of his brain) as a part or condition of his
cognizant experience of the 'sensible quality'. And yet Locke's
statements compel us to suppose that every percipient (including
our hypothetical beginner) is primarily or directly aware of a
physical change in his brain, and indirectly through that 'perception' is cognizant of his 'sensible qualities'.

To return to the 'physical process' which, according to Locke's
account, is presupposed in 'having' or 'receiving' a 'simple idea
of sensation'. As we have just seen, an external sensible body acts
upon an organ of sense: communicates to it by impulse a movement or moving particles or some physical change: this in turn is
communicated to, and transmitted by, the nerves or 'animal
spirits', so that it ultimately reaches and affects the brain—

---

[1] Locke, *Essay*, ii. 8, § 11.   [2] ii. 8, § 12.

appearing there in the form of a physical change, a new configuration (perhaps) of the particles of that central organ.

What exactly happens then? Is this physical change of the
brain *itself*, for example, a sensation of colour? Or does it *produce*
a change in consciousness—a 'sensation', i.e. *awareness*, of colour?
Or is it that, which the sentient subject 'perceives' (apprehends)
when he 'has' a simple idea of sensation?

Locke's own attitude to such questions seems at first quite
frankly non-committal or agnostic. He holds it to be 'a point put
out of the reach of our knowledge' whether the Soul is an '*unex-
tended* thinking substance' or a 'thinking *extended* matter'.[1] He
therefore speaks, indifferently, of 'ideas'—or, sometimes, of 'what
produces ideas'—'being conveyed by the senses into *the mind*' or
into *the brain*.[2] On the whole, however, the metaphor he favours
suggest that he was inclined to the view that 'extended matter'
is that which 'thinks'. And he does not seem to realize that, even
on that hypothesis, 'thinking'—i.e. any form of 'being aware of
something', any cognizant experience—would still be a new and
inexplicable function of extended matter in no way analogous to
its other functions or properties. What happens, for example,
when a white paper is stamped or imprinted; or when a mirror
'receives' an 'image'; or when a 'cabinet' is 'furnished' with
contents—is clearly not in the least analogous to what happens
when the 'brain' (the 'thinking extended matter') 'receives an
idea of sensation'—becomes sensuously aware of colour, for
example, or sound.

But further complication is introduced into Locke's already
rather uncertain and confused attitude by a serious ambiguity in
his use of the term 'idea'—a term which plays a large and important part in his exposition.

By the term 'idea' Locke says he means 'whatsoever the mind
perceives in itself, or is the immediate *object* of perception, thought
or understanding',[3] or 'whatsoever is the *object* of the understanding when a man thinks'.[4] But in this last passage he adds 'I have
used it to express whatever is meant by phantasm, notion, species
or whatever it is which the mind can be employed about in thinking'. Now this seems to imply that Locke agreed in the main with
the traditional scholastic view—the kind of view which Descartes
sketches in the *Regulae*,[5] viz. that the 'object of the understand-

[1] ib. iv. 3, § 6.   [2] Cf. ib. ii. 8, § 12.   [3] ii. 8, § 8.
[4] i. 1, § 8.   [5] Cf., e.g., R. XII, *A.T.*, vol. x, pp. 412–16.

ing, when a man thinks' about a perceptible or material thing, is a φάντασμα or εἶδος, an image, shape, or form, impressed by the external thing on a peripheral organ of sense, by that impressed upon the 'common' or 'central' organ of sense—and so ultimately formed in the (corporeal) organ of imagination or memory.[1] One cannot help suspecting, therefore, that it is not by a mere accident of careless writing that Locke describes *ideas* as being 'conveyed into the mind by the senses'; as being '*offered* to the contemplation of the mind'; or as being 'derived from the senses by the understanding as *materials* for its thinking'. Locke himself, if challenged, would probably have replied: 'My language is strictly in accordance with my explanation of what I mean by *idea*. For the motion or configuration in the brain is the kind of thing which is commonly meant by philosophers—which, for example, is meant by Descartes when he speaks of the modifications in the corporeal *Phantasia*; it is "conveyed in" by the senses; and it is—according to the traditional views of philosophy and according to my own theory—the immediate object of which the percipient inevitably and without his act or choice is aware. The only proper name for it, therefore, according to my definition of the term, *is* "Idea".'

And yet, on the other hand, in many passages (and more than once in chapter 1 of Book II of the *Essay*), Locke identifies 'the ideas we have of yellow, white, heat' and so forth—the ideas 'derived from', or 'got by', sensation—with perceptions; a term which, though very general and broad in Locke's usage, implies the exercise of a faculty of mind, even if only the passive faculty, or capacity, of 'receiving'.[2] The 'simple ideas of sensation' are thus not *objects* of perception or thinking, but the *entire perceptions* or *cognizant experiences* themselves, the actual awareness of a colour, sound, taste, or some 'sensible quality'. And this interpretation of 'the simple ideas of sensation' is confirmed, when we find Locke

---

[1] Heaven forbid that I should enter here into the obscure and intricate topic of φαντάσματα, *species intentionales*, &c., and the role assigned to them in the mechanism of knowledge by Aquinas—in elaboration of Aristotle's statements about the νοῦς παθητικός, in *De anima*, iii. The whole subject is admirably treated by Gilson, *Études de philosophie médiévale*, pp. 146 ff. Cf. also Gilson, *Études sur le rôle de la pensée médiévale* (chap. i). But though no doubt Gilson is right in maintaining that Descartes in his mature work attempted to get rid of these obscure entities (which were neither corporeal nor spiritual, or both corporeal and spiritual) and to substitute for them his 'Innate Ideas', they survive, I think, beyond question in the *Regulae* (written when Descartes was still under the influence of the teaching of La Flèche), and traces of them seem to be left even in his later work (cf., e.g., *Medit. VI, A.T.*, vol. vii, p. 75, ll. 5–20).

[2] Cf., e.g., ii. 9, § 1; ii. 21, §§ 72–3.

speaking of 'ideas *or perceptions* in our minds'[1] and of 'a power to
receive ideas *or thoughts* from the 'operation of any external
substance';[2] and when we remember his insistence that 'to be in
the understanding' *is* 'to be understood',[3] and again that our
ideas 'are nothing but actual perceptions in the mind, which
'cease to be anything when there is no perception of them'.[4]

(ii) Amid all the confusion and ambiguity in Locke's statements,
then, so much at least seems clear—to have a simple idea of sensation would be impossible for the imaginary student whose mind
is 'white paper', an as yet 'empty cabinet', or an untroubled
'mirror'. The 'simple idea of sensation' is an experience which
presupposes a percipient already possessed (like Locke himself) of
a developed theory of the bodies of the external world, of the way
in which they operate, and of the nature and capacities of his
own body and mind. 'Simple ideas of sensation'—on Locke's own
showing—are not primitive cognizant experiences, are not the
'beginnings and materials' of all our knowledge. They are, on the
contrary, abstracted results reached by reflection upon (by critical
analysis of) our 'knowledge'—i.e. upon that system or complex of
outworn theory which Locke (as we saw) mistakes for 'knowledge'
of the physical world, and of the perceiving and thinking subjects
who know it.

Next I have to show, briefly, that an experience in which we are
aware of a colour, a sound, or other sensible quality, is in fact,
according to Locke's own description of it, inferential: that it
involves an inference on the percipient's part, though the inference
is not explicit, and would not perhaps be regarded as an inference
by Locke himself.[5]

Since 'to be in the understanding' *is* 'to be understood', there
is never any doubt as to the *occurrence* of any of our ideas. Whether
we dream or remember, whether we imagine or sensate, we know
with absolute certainty—by what Locke calls 'intuitive knowledge'[6]—that the 'ideas' in question are 'actually in our minds'.
But Locke claims that to have, or receive, a simple idea of sensa-

---

[1] ii. 8, § 7.   [2] ii. 21, § 72.
[3] Cf. i. 2, § 5.
[4] ii. 10, § 2; cf. also ii. 32, § 3; iv. 17, § 8, &c.
[5] Yet cf. perhaps iv. 2, § 14: 'But whether there be anything more than barely
that *idea* in our minds, whether we can thence certainly infer the existence of any
thing without us which corresponds to that *idea*, is that whereof some men think
there may be a question made. . . .'
[6] Cf. iv. 2, § 14.

tion is *eo ipso* to be conscious of it (not merely as 'in our mind', but) as '*actually coming into* our minds by our senses'.

'I ask anyone,' he says,[1] 'whether he be not invincibly conscious to himself of a different perception, when he looks on the sun by day, and thinks on it by night; when he actually tastes wormwood, or smells a rose, or only thinks on that savour, or odour? We as plainly find the difference there is between any *idea* revived in our minds by our own memory, and actually coming into our minds by our senses, as we do between any two distinct *ideas*.'

And a little later in the same passage he refers to this distinguishing characteristic of actual seeing, tasting, smelling, &c.—i.e. of receiving or having a simple idea of sensation—as 'that perception and consciousness we have of the actual entrance of ideas from them [i.e. from the external objects]'.

If we take this description of what it is to 'have a simple idea of sensation' at its face value (if we accept it without criticism), it is clear that the experience, which it describes, is inferential. If 'to have a simple idea of sensation' really is to perceive the actual entrance of an idea through one of the senses from an external object, then clearly the percipient has (consciously or unconsciously) contributed a great deal from his general knowledge to the constitution of this experience. Or, to put it otherwise, 'to have a simple idea of sensation' is clearly impossible for Locke's imaginary beginner with the empty mind—since, *ex hypothesi*, he has no inkling of the existence or nature of any external objects or any organs of sense.

The same result—the inferential character of these experiences of the 'sensible qualities'—emerges clearly when we consider Locke's account of what these 'qualities' are. 'To discover the nature of our *ideas* the better . . .', Locke says,[2] 'it will be convenient to distinguish them as they are *ideas* or perceptions in our minds; and as they are modifications of matter in the bodies that cause such perceptions in us. . . . ' He then proceeds:[3] 'Whatsoever the mind perceives in itself . . . that I call *idea*; and the power to produce any *idea* in our mind, I call *quality* of the subject wherein that power is.' From this he goes on to develop the well-known doctrine that, while the real bodies of the external world are actually characterized by the 'primary qualities' (are actually extended, figured, solid, moving, &c.), they are not actually coloured, sounding, flavoured, &c. (i.e. the 'secondary qualities' do not, as such,

[1] iv. 2, § 14.   [2] ii. 8, § 7.   [3] § 8.

characterize them). If we look at a snowball (to borrow an example
from Locke, l.c., §8), the simple ideas of white, cold, and round, are
conveyed into our mind; and we should commonly speak of
'white', 'cold', and 'round' as 'qualities' of the snowball. In
reality, however, as Locke maintains, though the snowball is
actually 'round', it is not actually 'white' or 'cold'. The 'power'
to produce in us the idea of round is an actual shape of the snowball: a pattern, of which our idea is an image or resemblance. But
the 'powers' to produce in us the ideas of white or cold as they
actually exist in the snowball have no resemblance to the ideas
they produce. White, cold, and the rest of the secondary qualities
are in fact not qualities at all. Locke calls them so 'to comply with
the common way of speaking'.[1] 'In truth' they 'are nothing in the
objects themselves, but powers to produce various sensations in
us by their primary qualities, i.e. by the bulk, figure, texture, and
motion of their insensible parts. . . .'

Locke lays great stress on the importance of this distinction
(derived from Descartes) between 'the primary and real qualities
of bodies, which are always in them' and 'those secondary and
imputed qualities.[2] But—whatever its importance[3]—it does not
affect or impair what in a later chapter[4] he calls the 'reality' or
'truth' of the simple ideas of sensation. All the simple ideas of
sensation—our ideas, for example, of white and cold, no less than
our idea of round—are (he there maintains) 'real and true'. In
all of them we are aware of 'real ideas'—i.e. the idea is for us not
merely a 'perception in our mind', but has a reference to a reality

---

[1] ii. 8, § 10.   [2] ii. 8, § 22.

[3] I say 'whatever its importance'—for, so far as possible, I am anxious to avoid
discussion of the details of Locke's philosophy. But, to prevent misunderstanding,
I ought perhaps to say frankly that, in my judgement, nothing but an antiquarian
interest attaches to Locke's distinction between the primary and secondary
qualities of bodies. The doctrine was killed by Berkeley's criticism—and (to
speak *more Hibernico*) killed again, and more completely, by Kant. It is not
possible to state it so that it will retain even an appearance of plausibility for a
modern student of philosophy. 'The snowball', for example, 'is really round—
round, in and for itself, whether anyone perceives it or not.' What does this
unperceived roundness mean? 'It possesses, in and for itself, a shape such that
all the particles on its circumference are equidistant from a single particle or
point—or centre—within it.' But (the modern student will object) this geometrical
character is essentially relative to thought; it cannot belong to the snowball 'in
and for itself', but only to it as an object of conception. And waiving that objection, it is a quantitative character and not a 'sensible quality'. What meaning
is there in calling it a pattern of our idea of 'round'? How can we suppose that
the latter resembles the 'equidistance of particles', &c.—the 'real shape' as it is
in the snowball?   [4] Cf. ii. 30, § 1 and 2.

without, external to, beyond, our mind. All our simple ideas of sensation (and, for that matter, all our simple ideas whatever their source—sensation, reflection, or both sensation and reflection)[1] 'agree to the reality of things', or have 'a steady correspondence with the distinct constitutions of real beings'.

The upshot of the whole matter, then, is this: 'To have a simple idea of sensation' is to be aware of a real power in an external body as the productive cause of a 'perception' (or 'idea' or 'sensation') in the mind. The experience, which is thus described, is largely *mediate* or *inferential*. We are supposed, no doubt, to be immediately conscious of the idea not only as actually present in, but as actually *coming into* or *being produced in*, the mind. But we are also supposed, in the experience, to be aware of a real power in an external thing as the productive cause of the 'idea in our mind'. And this feature of the experience is, beyond question, mediate or inferential. It requires an act of mind which is, in principle, an inference; and the experience, in this respect, transcends the utmost which (on the most liberal interpretation) could be 'passively received' or 'immediately presented'. Nor does it make any difference (as Locke himself rightly points out),[2] whether, in referring the idea in our minds to a power in the external thing, we conceive the latter as a pattern of the former (as a 'sensible quality' exactly like our 'idea') or, less definitely, as some 'distinct constitution'—some *insensible* character— which is its cause. In either case, we are in fact transcending 'the given'—the idea as it is in, or comes into, our mind—and referring it by an inference to a cause not sensated, but conceived.

4. (*b*) We have still to meet one last objection.[3] For, granted that there are no sensations, there is at least sensating—a 'moment of sensation'—in every perception. And the real issue, it may be said, has hitherto been shirked. For between the perception of a corporeal thing, or physical event, and all other modes of experiencing these objects, there is an unmistakable difference—a difference of which, as Locke expresses it,[4] the percipient is 'invincibly conscious to himself'. To *perceive* the sun blazing in the heavens or a flash of lightning zigzagging across the sky; to *perceive* (i.e. to taste) the bitter wormwood, to *perceive* (i.e. to feel) the scorching fire—this is surely a special and unique mode of experience, indisputably distinct from 'thinking on' these objects, from dream-

[1] Cf. ii. 7.
[2] Cf. ii. 30, § 2.
[3] Cf. above, pp. 110–11.
[4] iv. 2, § 14; cf. above, pp. 117–18.

ing of them, imagining or even remembering them. A perception, in short, has (or includes) a characteristic actuality, which marks it off from an imagination, a dream, or even a memory. It brings with it a peculiar sense of contact with fact—what has been called[1] a 'coefficient of reality' or 'a tang'. Now, the real issue, it may be said, lies in this 'actuality', in this unique and special flavour, of perceptual experience. Whence is it derived? Locke attributed it, as we saw, to the percipient's 'consciousness of the actual entrance' of ideas of sensation from external objects—of their 'actually coming into the mind by the senses'. Such an account must clearly be rejected—vitiated, as it is, by the confusion in his notion of *idea* and in the role he assigns to *ideas* in knowledge. Yet, though indefensible in letter, is it so far wrong in spirit? If, in perceiving a flash of lightning, we see a zigzag streak of bluish light,[2] are not these 'visible qualities' (this shape and colour) *real* characters of a *real* thing or event? And are they not directly presented to our vision, forced upon us as immediate objects of our sensating? If so, then Locke's account seems broadly true. For is it not precisely this 'moment of sensation'—this sensuous contact with directly presented characters of fact—which gives to the whole experience its peculiar 'actuality', and makes of it a *perception*, instead of, for example, a memory, imagination, or dream?

The objection is founded on a 'difference' between perception on the one hand, and dream, imagination, and memory on the other. This difference, it asserts, is 'unmistakable'; and if we allow ourselves to be bluffed by the assertion, the rest of the objector's argument may prove difficult to meet. But what are the facts? Suppose that, *in intention*, and *when rightly applied*, these four terms denote four several modes of experience, each uniquely individual in character, each positively itself and sharply distinct from all the rest. But, actually, in our experiences as we live them, mistake, confusion, self-deception are constant and notorious. We are certain, for example, that *now* we are 'perceiving'; that this our actual experience is a 'perception'; we are 'invincibly conscious to ourselves' of its difference from a memory, a mere imagination, or *a fortiori* from a dream. Yet, the next moment, the whole or the major part of this same experience comes home to us as derived from memory, or as embroidered by imagination; and we are convinced that once again, as often

---

[1] Cf. Alexander, *Locke*, p. 48.   [2] Cf. above, pp. 80–81; 102.

before, we have been deceived by a certain vividness and wealth of detail—the hall-mark, as we rashly assumed, of present and presented fact, of fact 'forcing itself' upon our notice. Or presently, perhaps, we wake; and, waking, find ourselves 'invincibly conscious' that the whole experience (together with our former 'invincible consciousness' that we were 'perceiving') was, after all, a dream. The 'invincible consciousness' of the subject of an experience guarantees nothing—except the bare fact that he is experiencing, or rather that there is an experiencing.[1] His conviction (if, or when, he has it) that he is *perceiving* (not, for example, remembering, imagining, or dreaming) is anything but infallible.

There is, then, no 'special flavour', no peculiar 'actuality' or 'tang', in perceptual experience—none that is an infallible index of our 'contact' with elements or characters of reality. In any strict and literal sense, of course, we are never 'in contact with reality'. 'Touching' is not an adequate mode of knowing even the tangible; nor is the real (if, or so far as, anything 'real' is tangible) adequately known, known in its reality, by 'being touched'.[2] 'Contact', however, and its cognates and derivatives, are convenient, if imperfect, metaphors for 'knowledge'. It is both natural and legitimate to speak of 'knowing' and the 'knowable' or 'known' in terms and phrases drawn from the sense of touch, and its field. Thus to know is to grip or grasp, to apprehend or comprehend, the facts, reality or truth; and the facts are hard or solid, stubborn or unyielding; reality or the truth is such that we must 'lay hold upon it', 'grapple with it', or 'grasp it firmly'. But these metaphors, we must remember, apply—in the broad sense, in which alone their employment is legitimate—not solely, nor even prerogatively, to perception, but to all forms of knowledge, or to every mode of experience so far as it is (even remotely) cognizant. In memory, and even in imagination and dream, as well as in perception, the activity of the mind is controlled (to speak broadly) by 'reality' or 'the nature of things'. In all these modes of experience, therefore, not in perception alone, there is a genuine

---

[1] Cf. below, § 10, 3: especially p. 142.

[2] 'Contact' is an affair of surfaces, a superficial union of body with body. If, through the medium of some bodily part, we touch a body, the 'touching' (i.e. the 'sense' or 'feeling' of the contact) is at most an awareness of the surface of the body we touch—not a knowledge of what it (the tangible body) 'really' is, if 'really' it is anything. Conversely, if anything real is, *qua* real, a body and so tangible, its 'reality' (i.e. its corporeal nature) is most inadequately expressed in the contact; i.e. it does not show what it *really* is in 'being touched'.

sense in which we are (if not passive, at least) receptive—a sense
in which what we remember, and even what we imagine or dream,
as well as what we perceive, is 'forced upon' the mind, comes to
us with a certain 'tang' or 'coefficient of reality'.[1]

But still, it will be said, there is a real issue, which must be
faced. Surely, it will be said, there is an objective difference—a
difference in principle—between perception on the one hand, and
memory (say), imagination, and dream, on the other. The subject
of an experience may, and often does, mistake its nature; but if,
or when, he is in fact 'perceiving'—if, or when, his experience is a
genuine 'perception'—there is actually a mode of cognizant experience, a form of 'knowledge', which is characteristically itself and
characteristically distinct from all other modes. What, then, we
shall be asked, is this special and positive character of perception?
Wherein is it distinct from memory, imagination, and dream?

Observe that this issue was wrongly formulated in the original
objection. For there it was assumed that the special character of
a perception was derived from, and could be assigned to, one
'moment' in the experience. The solution, it was taken for
granted, must be sought in the unique character and object of the
'moment of sensation'. In virtue of that 'moment' (it was suggested), or *qua* sensating, the percipient makes contact with 'real
qualities' of fact. But, obviously, a 'moment', *ex vi termini*, has
as such no object and no character—i.e. none that can be assigned
exclusively to it, none that are 'hedged off' within the total
object and character of the whole experience. A 'moment', *ex
vi termini*, is what it is only in, and by virtue of, the whole it goes
to constitute. To seek for some special character and object in the
'moment of sensation' is to confound a whole with a complex and the
'moments' of the former with the isolable constituents of the latter.

But if our former account of perception is sound, the issue is
still not rightly formulated. The perception, as we saw, embodies,
and further defines, a certain total consciousness of a world; and
in the growth and maintenance of that consciousness the whole
structure of the mind (the mind in the established and organized
totality of its activity, not in this or that isolated function) is
implicated and engaged. There is no 'sharp distinction' (as we
supposed,[2] being misled by Locke's contrast between, for example,
'looking on the sun by day' and 'thinking on it') between perception and memory, between either of these and imagination, nor

---

[1] Cf. above, pp. 99–100.　　　　　　　　[2] Above, p. 121.

even between these three and dream. We are not here dealing with four modes of cognizant experience, each complete and independent, and all on the same level. Perception, no doubt, is often, and rightly, used to denominate a 'mode of cognizant experience' —a typical form or level of knowledge—possessing a relative completeness and independence, a character and being of its own. But (disregarding dream for the sake of brevity) it seems neither so usual nor so defensible to use the terms 'memory' and 'imagination' in the same way. At all events, it is clear that they are inseparably entangled with perception. For to perceive is impossible without remembering and imagining; if we are to 'remember' we must have perceived or imagined, or both; and in 'imagining' we draw upon our perceptions and our memories. Not only so. The very act of imagining requires an object made (so to speak) of sensible stuff, and presupposes the 'actual world' of the perceiving and remembering consciousness—if only as a background, by contrast with which it constructs and sustains its own 'imaginary world' The very act of remembering is possible only for a perceiving and imagining consciousness; and what we remember must fit within the framework of our 'real' (i.e. our perceived or perceivable) world. And, lastly, the very act of perceiving embraces a 'then' as well as a 'now', a 'there' beyond the 'here'; transcends any 'punctual' present, whether of time or place; includes, therefore, more than could be assigned to 'perception', if 'perception' is to be 'sharply distinguished' from memory and imagination. If we are to insist upon a 'sharp distinction', do we *perceive* the flash of lightning; or if we are to speak strictly must we on the contrary say that in part we imagine, and in part complete our view of it by memory?

The real issue raised by (or underlying) the objection seems, then, to be no less than this. By perception is meant a level of knowledge at which some finite subject (this or that embodied-mind) apprehends a thing, scene, or event before him—'present' (i.e. here and now) within the frame and context of his 'actual' (and, as he assumes, *the* actual) world. What is this 'presence' in time and place, which differentiates perception (perceiving and the perceived or perceptible) from other levels of knowledge— from, for example, the 'knowledge' attained and embodied in the reasoning of the sciences, or, again, in philosophical speculation? Is this 'presence' or 'actuality' of perception fixed and definable as an objective locality and date within a 'real' (an objective and universal) order of space and time; or is it merely subjective or personal, a reflex of the shifting 'feeling' of this or that embodied-mind? What, in short, is 'my actual world'—the world which includes all that I can be said to 'perceive'; and which, at the level of perception, I take to be '*the* actual world', a world pre-rogatively (if not exclusively) 'real'?[1]

But if this, or anything like this, is the real issue raised by the objection, we may fairly decline to pursue it further. Certainly a complete philosophical theory of knowledge-or-truth—a system of logic—is bound to face these large and fundamental questions, is bound to characterize the three main levels of cognizant experi-ence (perceptual, scientific, philosophical), which we are taking for granted, and to examine their affiliation—their mutual relations and distinctions. The issue underlying the objection is real; but its discussion is not directly relevant to our present restricted problem, nor would its solution shake the negative conclusion to which we have come. At all the levels of 'knowledge', there is intellectual activity of a finite subject—of which a finite subject is the indispensable channel, and which he contributes to sustain; and in all of them the finite subject is 'receptive', or is controlled in 'his' thinking by 'reality or the nature of things'.[2] In *perception*, the intellectual activity is the 'instinctive' or 'sensuous' thinking which is called 'perceiving'; and the controlling reality appears in the form of an 'actual' or 'historical' world, a world of passing events and their enactors. At the '*scientific*' level of 'knowledge', on the other hand, the intellectual activity is explicit (though abstract) reasoning; and what the finite subject knows—the 'reality' which controls the thinking of a man of science, or which is for him 'the real world'—is a system of essential natures and their necessary laws, a 'domain' timeless and unlocalized, or at least unchanging within a *definable* period and region. But how the 'sensuous thinking', which is 'perceiving', is related to, and distinguished from, the 'reasoning' of the sciences; and how both are related to, and distinguished from, 'speculative' or 'philo-sophical' thinking; or again, how the 'actual' world of perception and the 'domains' of the sciences are related to, and distinguished from, one another and from the 'spiritual realities' (the eternal and concrete 'realms') which are known, or know themselves, in philosophy—such large and fundamental questions are surely

---

[1] Cf. Bradley, *Essays*, pp. 460–9, 'On My Real World'.
[2] Cf. above, pp. 99–100, 122.

irrelevant to our present investigation. For whatever their answer, our negative result, in regard to sensation, would still stand firm. Whatever may be the true account of the 'presence' or 'actuality' which characterizes perception, it is clear at least that nothing real—no real element or quality—is directly given or received in a purely sensuous cognizance. We have argued that there are no 'sensations'. We have argued also that, though there is sensating in every perception, it 'is there' and only as a 'moment' of the whole experience, and (being a 'moment', not a 'constituent') has no character or object peculiar to itself or exclusively its own. Provided, therefore, our arguments are sound, it is certain, whatever may be the solution of the 'larger issue', that there is no *datum* to be sought for, or to be found, either amongst our sensations or 'in' (as the 'content' or 'object' of) sensating.

B. The Division on its Higher Level

§ 10. (III) *Sensation or Feeling*

1. We have reached a turning-point in the present investigation, and it will be worth while considering where we stand.

In this and the following Study we were to start from certain commonly accepted theories in regard to knowledge and to truth. These theories—if sound—stand in the way of the conception of logic which was outlined in the introductory Study. We were, then, to accept them provisionally, and to develop them in order to test them.

In the present Study, what we are thus examining is a supposed division of knowledge into immediate and discursive; and this division is popularly drawn at two different levels. At the lower level—with which we have so far been concerned—*knowledge of sense* (sensuous and sentient knowledge) is taken to be immediate: and contrasted with *knowledge by way of thought*, all thought being 'mediate' or discursive. At the higher level there is supposed to be a division within thought itself—to be a *conceptual knowledge which is immediate*, a thought which is intuitive, an intellectual seeing: and, contrasted with it, based upon it and a development of it, a *knowledge by way of judgement and inference*. The latter is essentially a process, movement, development—logical, if not also temporal.

Now this distinction of levels is part and parcel of the popular doctrine of a division in knowledge. It itself, along with the division, is on its trial in the present Study, and we must not be disconcerted if we find it breaking down; and this is in fact what is happening: and this is why we have reached a turning-point. For it is becoming clear that the distinction of levels (with which we have been working) is a mere popular confusion which cannot be defended. It is becoming evident that there is no *knowledge of sense*, no merely sensuous cognizance other than, contrasted with, and divided from all intellectual cognizance, i.e. *knowledge by way of thought*. All cognizant experience, in short, is intellectual—or at least there is no knowledge *without thinking*.[1] Hence what I have hitherto called the *higher level* of the division is in truth the only level at which *knowledge* could be (or rather, seem to be) divided. We have in fact been examining hitherto, and we shall be examining henceforth, a supposed division of *'intellectual cognizance'*. But we must remember that this 'intellectual cognizance' is not set over against a 'knowledge of sense'. It must be interpreted so as to include whatever of knowledge there is—to include, for example, perception (which, in virtue of its 'moment' of sensation, it is natural to call a 'knowledge of sense'), if (or so far as) to perceive is to 'know' and the perceived is 'known'.

Hitherto, however, accepting the popular distinction, we have been concerned with the 'immediacy' which is supposed to characterize all knowledge of sense. Taking knowledge of sense to cover 'all that we feel, sensate, or sensuously perceive', we proceeded (following a commonly accepted classification, derived in the main from Locke) to distinguish three groups of cognizant experiences (sense-perceptions, sensations, and sentiences or feelings) in which it is embodied and actual. And we set out to test its supposed 'immediacy' by searching methodically in each of the three groups thus indicated (sense-perceptions, sensations, feelings) for a *datum*; i.e. for something which presented and guaranteed itself as fact and truth in one.

As a rough delimitation of the range within which, if anywhere, knowledge of sense may reasonably be expected to fall, this tripartite classification is natural enough. For, if ever we know by sense and not by thought, what we thus know (it seems obvious) must either be felt, or sensated, or perceived; and, if anything is ever 'known by sense and not by thought', the knowing it (it seems equally obvious) must be either a feeling, or a sensating, or a perceiving. Yet, as we have seen, neither in perceptions, nor in the

[1] Study I, p. 13.

supposed group of sensations, is there in fact a knowledge of sense
—i.e. a purely sensuous cognizance of a purely sensible object.
Nothing therefore is left except the sentiences or feelings of our
inner processes and states, which form the third and last group of
the tripartite classification. There—or nowhere—we must look
for 'knowledge of sense', for a purely sensuous cognizance of a
purely sensible object.

2. These 'sentiences or feelings', it will be recalled, are supposed to be 'experiences in which a self-conscious subject is
primarily and predominantly aware of his own inner processes or
states'; in which he apprehends, by a kind of 'inner' or 'internal
sense', the actions and affections of his own conscious being; in
which (to borrow Locke's terminology)[1] the mind, 'reflecting on
its own operations within itself', 'perceives', 'observes', 'takes
notice of' its own 'perception', for example, its own 'thinking,
doubting, believing, reasoning, knowing, willing', and so forth.

Are there such experiences in fact? Do they actually occur—or
are they mere products of confusion and misinterpretation, as
mythical as 'sensations'?

One is inclined to say at first that beyond all question such
experiences occur. 'To doubt their actuality is to doubt the
existence of any mind, or self-conscious subject of experiences at
all. For if a subject is self-conscious he clearly is (or may be) aware
that he is experiencing; aware of his experiences as his own; aware
of himself (or, of his "mind") as active—or at all events as implicated—in them. It is in virtue of this actual or possible return
upon itself of his awareness—this inner consciousness, let us call
it, though, as we shall see, the phrase is dangerous—that a subject
of experiences is "self-conscious", or is a "mind".'

But, granted that a mind or a self-conscious subject can neither
be nor be conceived without 'inner consciousness'; and granted
further that the existence of 'minds' or a 'mind' is not to be
doubted—the supposed 'sentiences or feelings' may still be
fictions. (i) It does not follow that the 'inner consciousness'
which, on these premises, is indisputably actual, exists as a group
of special experiences. And (ii) there is nothing to justify its
supposed affinity to sense.

(i) It belongs to the very nature of a mind—of a self-conscious
subject of experiences—that, in experiencing, it should return upon
itself. All my experiences—my pleasures and pains, desires and

[1] Cf. *Essay*, ii. 1, § 4.

volitions, perceptions and thoughts—are, or may be, precisely in so far as I am a 'mind', *mine for me*. In all of them, I—since I am their self-conscious subject—do (or may) 'feel', 'enjoy', myself. They not only *belong* to me; not only, in and by their difference, fulfil and express my unitary being; not only *are* rays diverging from, and converging on, a single form which is myself. As a mind, as self-conscious, I *'feel' myself* one in and through their variety; I *am 'aware of' myself* as the focus, from which they radiate and to which they return.[1] And in some such general sense, there is (or may be) actual, in each and all of my experiences, an 'inner consciousness', a 'feeling or sentience' of myself.

But 'inner consciousness', or a 'sentience or feeling of myself', thus understood, is clearly not itself one of my experiences, nor a group or set of my experiences. It is clearly not the singular of which the supposed 'sentiences or feelings'—the supposed 'experiences in which I am predominantly aware of my inner states and processes' are the plural. And the actual occurrence of the latter is not in the least guaranteed by the 'indisputable actuality' of the former. For it is one thing to insist that, since—or in so far as—I am a 'mind', my conscious being in all its modes, in all its states and changes, is turned back upon itself; that a *'reflected'* or 'inner consciousness' contributes to, and completes, all the experiences in which I know or am affected by or will what is 'other' than myself. This is to insist that 'inner consciousness' is actual as a 'moment' in all my perceiving, thinking, doubting, desiring, willing, &c.; as a 'moment', without which I should not be (as in fact I am) *self-conscious* in all these 'different actings of my mind'. It is a totally different thing to assume that there are *first* states and changes of my conscious being, whereby I know, or will, or am affected by, 'outer objects' or what is other than myself; and that, beside and distinct from these 'primary' experiences, there occur and are actual, *secondly*, awarenesses of them—experiences of a 'secondary' or 'reflective' order, the 'sentiences or feelings' of the popular classification.

So far, therefore, it is an open question whether the supposed 'sentiences or feelings' occur in fact, are actual experiences; or whether they are as mythical as 'sensations'. 'Sensations', it will be remembered, turned out to be *fictions* resulting from popular

---

[1] All this, I am aware, is very inadequately expressed. It is to be understood in connexion with, and subject to qualification by, the account sketched above (pp. 85-9) of the 'spiritual unity' which characterizes a 'mind'.

misinterpretation of an 'indisputable fact'—viz. the sensuous moment, the moment of sensation, in all perceptions. 'Sentiences or feelings' may turn out to be the products of an analogous confusion, a popular misinterpretation of another 'indisputable fact' —viz. the 'sentience or feeling', the 'inner consciousness', which is actual as a 'moment' in all the experiences of a self-conscious subject.

(ii) 'Naturally', it will be objected, 'the question remains open when thus considered. For after all, it is a question of fact. It cannot be decided by abstract speculations on what is involved in the being—in the essence or conception—of a mind. It can only be answered by a review of the facts, by a scrutiny of the experiences which, in this region, occur and are actual beyond dispute.'

The objection is sound; but the difficulty is to determine what exactly are 'the facts'. Still, let us try to set out roughly what, in this region, it seems safe to accept as fact, as actual beyond dispute. 'Seems safe'—for further consideration may force us later[1] to doubt what here we provisionally set down as 'facts'.

In the first place, 'inner consciousness', in the general sense explained before, seems actual beyond dispute. It is, or seems to be, a 'fact' that I am (or may be) 'aware of myself' in, and through, all my experiences of what is other than myself. In them all—in all my passions, desires, volitions, perceptions, thoughts—there is a 'moment of return' which differentiates them from changes merely happening to a 'soul' or 'conscious being', and completes them into experiences of a mind, i.e. changes in which a self-conscious subject achieves, expresses, and maintains its spiritual unity.

And secondly, in this region, it seems possible to venture farther and to accept certain 'reflective' experiences as 'facts', as actual and occurring beyond dispute. For there seem to be occasions when I concentrate my attention upon the 'inner consciousness', upon the 'moment of return', in this or that experience, and make of it the 'object' and the 'filling' of another and independent experience—an experience of a 'secondary' or 'reflective' order. Thus, for example, (a) my perception of the flash of lightning, since (or so far as) I am a mind, involves (and is completed by) an awareness that *I* am perceiving, and that I am *perceiving*; or again, in feeling angry, I (*qua* self-conscious) am aware that *I* am feeling, and that what I feel is *anger*. And, further, (b) it seems impossible

[1] Below, pp. 134 ff.

to deny that sometimes, in certain secondary or reflective experiences, I abstract, and attend to, the 'moment of inner consciousness' in these or similar primary experiences. Thus, it seems
impossible to deny that I may, and often do, 'observe', 'perceive',
or 'take notice of', that 'acting of my own mind' which was its
'primary' perceiving; or that modification of my own self-conscious
being which was my 'primary' experience of anger.

To assert that the occurrence of such 'reflective' experiences
cannot be denied—that such 'reflective experiences' are actual
beyond dispute and must be accepted as 'facts'—is already,
perhaps, to go too far. Such experiences, we shall be reminded,
so far from being 'actual beyond dispute', are the subject of a
notorious controversy—a controversy concerning the manner and
the possibility of what is known as introspection. For, *while* the
self-conscious subject is perceiving the lightning or feeling angry,
he is wholly and undividedly absorbed in these primary experiences.
If *then* he is (in a sense) 'aware' of the 'acting of his own mind',
this awareness, *this* inner consciousness, is submerged in the primary
experience of which it is an integral and inseparable 'moment'.
It seems impossible that then—i.e. while he is perceiving or feeling
angry—he should simultaneously reflect upon this 'moment',
extract it, and make it the object and filling of a distinct and
'secondary' experience; impossible, because, *ex hypothesi*, he is
whole and undivided in his self-conscious being, and only *thus* the
subject of his primary experiences. When, on the other hand, his
perception or emotion is over, the 'inner consciousness', the
'moment of return', the 'acting of his mind', is over too; for,
whichever of these phrases we prefer, what they were intended to
designate was admittedly a complement—an integrating and completing phase or factor—of the primary experience. How then can
he now—in a subsequent reflective experience—'observe' or
'perceive' the past and vanished actings of his mind? How can he
in any sense 'take notice of', or 'study', them? If he is to reflect
upon *them*, they must presumably be, or be brought, before his
mind. But no revival or recall, short of a re-enacting of them,
could reproduce them *as they were* (and as he wishes to study them).
And yet to re-enact them would be to reinstate them as the present
actings of his mind; and so to relive, after a lapse, the primary
experiences in which these 'actings' were 'moments'. He would
be drawn, in short, once more into a perception or an emotion,
instead of 'reflecting upon' and studying the moment of inner

consciousness which such 'primary' self-conscious experiences involve.

Yet at first sight this argument seems to have proved too much. There seems good reason for disregarding these difficulties. There is an air of unreality, of logomachy, about them; and it looks as if they would vanish before a criticism of the rigid and mechanical disjunctions on which they are based. Is it so certain, for example, that the 'primary experiences', when they 'are' at all, completely fill and absorb the mind—so that *either* I 'perceive' without the possibility of 'reflecting', *or* 'reflect' without a trace of 'perceiving'? Or again, is it not monstrous to assume—as the argument does assume—that the experiences of a mind are insusceptible of degree; and that each of them is either 'actual' or 'over'—i.e. utterly vanished, 'actual' in no sense or no degree at all?[1]

We are, then, to assume (provisionally, at least) that there are certain 'secondary' experiences, in which the mind reflects upon its own emotions, desires, volitions, perceptions, thoughts, &c.; reflects upon them, and takes for the object of its study the 'moment of inner consciousness' which these primary experiences involve. The occurrence of such reflective experiences, we are to assume, is undeniable, an indisputable fact—although (as we have just seen) to make this assumption is to set aside a familiar controversy, and to disregard its arguments as unconvincing and unreal.

(iii) But these reflective experiences are not the 'sentiences or feelings' which figure in the popular classification. For the 'sentiences or feelings', it will be remembered, are supposed to form a subdivision of knowledge of sense. They are put forward as a special group of sensuous (as contrasted with intellectual) cognizances. But there is nothing sensuous about the 'reflective experiences' which we have now set down provisionally as facts. There is nothing in my reflective cognizance to suggest any special resemblance, any special analogy or kinship, with sensuous thinking—with sense-perceiving or with the 'sensating' which that involves.

If this is correct, what justification is there for speaking of inner

[1] I have tried to indicate shortly a line of argument which seems at first to offer a successful solution of the well-known difficulty, or apparent paradox, in 'introspection'. Those who are interested may be referred to the brilliant discussion by Bradley (in his *Essays on Truth and Reality*, pp. 166 ff.) of the problem, which he there puts in the form: 'Can I observe my own present state, and, if not that, what in the end can I observe?'

consciousness and introspection? 'Inner consciousness' suggests that the moment of return in our self-conscious experiences is an awareness of facts within (in contrast to facts without) ourselves. And 'introspection' suggests that to reflect is to look at states and processes inside our body, or our mind, or our embodied-mind. And what right have we to call the cognizance in our reflective experiences an 'observing' or 'perceiving'—as though it were indeed analogous to sense-perceiving, involving the stimulation and reaction of an organ and faculty of 'inner sense', as the latter involves the collaboration of the 'outer senses'?[1]

It must be admitted that the terms in question are misleading. The employment of them is not in the end defensible, though it may be excused on the ground of tradition and common usage, and by the plea that they can only be avoided by long and cumbrous periphrasis.

'*Inner* consciousness' and 'introspection'—even when used by writers whose philosophical outlook has nothing in common with that of Locke—tend beyond doubt to suggest to the careless reader (and most readers are careless) the Lockeian antithesis between the 'external sensible objects' and the 'internal operations of our minds'.[2] They tend to suggest the quite indefensible notion of a realm of physical facts 'outside', and confronting, a realm of psychical facts enclosed 'within' the mind—as though the mind were, so to speak, a box containing its experiences, and itself contained in the larger box which is the spatial world.

And undoubtedly we run a risk of suggesting the same absurdities if we use the terms 'observe' or 'perceive' in connexion with our reflective cognizances—however much we may protest that we mean no more by them than 'to attend to', 'to notice' or 'to study', as, for example, one may 'observe' the logical nexus of an argument, or 'perceive' its principle or its truth.[3]

[1] Cf. Locke, *Essay*, ii. 1, § 4: 'This source of *ideas* [*sc.* Reflection] every man has wholly in himself: and though it be not sense, as having nothing to do with external objects; yet it is very like it, and might properly enough be called internal sense.' 'It is very like it', on Locke's theory, apparently because the 'ideas' we have from reflection, like the 'ideas' we have from sensation, are received by us passively; they present themselves to us, and all we have to do, or can do, is to 'observe' or 'perceive' them. At the same time, if we reflect, we cannot avoid observing them; for they impress themselves upon our 'internal sense', much as the qualities of the external bodies impress themselves upon the outer senses and through them upon the brain (or mind).

[2] Ibid. ii. 1; and above, pp. 111 ff.

[3] Prof. N. K. Smith (*A Commentary to Kant's Critique of Pure Reason*[2]) uses 'inner consciousness' without hesitation. Cf., e.g., p. 148: 'No great thinker except,

I shall try to avoid these misleading terms in the rest of my treatment of 'the moment of return in self-conscious experience', and the 'reflective experiences' in which we abstract, and are cognizant of, that moment. Meantime, a few sentences will be enough to summarize the result we have reached so far. The sentiences and feelings of the popular tripartite classification are as mythical, as much the products of confusion and misinterpretation, as sensations. That they should be supposed to occur—to be amongst our actual experiences—is a surprising testimony to the survival in popular opinion of the influence of Locke's speculations. The entire popular distinction between *knowledge of sense* and *knowledge by way of thought* is worthless, and must henceforth be utterly abandoned.

3. We have committed ourselves provisionally to two assertions: viz. (i) that in all self-conscious experience there is 'a moment of return', and (ii) that there are 'secondary' experiences in which, reflecting on this or that self-conscious experience, we are able to make of this integrant phase of its being—this 'moment of return' —a special object of our study.

Further consideration will force me to qualify, if not to withdraw, the second of these assertions. But before reopening the question of these reflective experiences, I want to dwell a little longer on that 'moment of return'. Is not this integrating complement of every self-conscious experience precisely the kind of *datum* of which we are in search? It is, to begin with, fact or at least an inseparable integrant of fact. And, next, this fact or integrant of fact seems to present and guarantee itself—seems, therefore, in being fact, *eo ipso* to be also truth. For must there not, in virtue

---

Locke, has attempted to interpret inner consciousness on the analogy of the senses.' He is quite clear, however, on the failure of this attempt. Cf., e.g., p. 293: 'The doctrine of inner sense, as expounded by Locke, suffers from an ambiguity which seems almost inseparable from it, namely the confusion between inner sense, on the one hand *as a sense* in some degree analogous in nature to what may be called outer sense, and on the other as consisting in self-conscious reflection.' For Bradley's defence of introspection, cf. above, p. 132. There are, however, it must be admitted, unfortunate (and unconscious) survivals of the influence of Locke in Bradley's early work—particularly in his treatment of 'idea' (the 'psychological idea', 'psychical states or events', &c.) in the first edition of his *Principles of Logic*. Still he would have protested vigorously—and in the main, rightly—if anyone had accused him of accepting Locke's general philosophical assumptions. There is a clear statement of the misleading suggestions involved in the term 'introspection' in Reyburn's *Introduction to Psychology* (pp. 51–3). But the author's attempt to explain and justify his own use of the term (to show that, as he uses it, it does not involve similar absurdities) is not altogether convincing.

of this 'moment', be attributed to all the cognizant experience of a self-conscious subject 'a being which is both *percipi* and *percipere*— is not all of it, in this respect at least, a 'self-awareness, self-given and given *to itself*'?[1]

It must, I think, be admitted, that in 'the moment of return' we have found a *datum*—though (as we shall see) not a *datum* precisely of the kind for which we have been looking. We have found *a datum*; for we have stumbled upon that immediate, yet necessary, nexus between self-consciousness and existence, which Descartes discovered, expressed in its simplest and most convincing form, and established once for all as a principle beyond dispute, because to doubt it is *eo ipso* to affirm or reinstate it. That there is 'thought' cannot be doubted or denied: for the doubt or denial is itself a 'thought'. But though, if we are right, all experience, *qua* self-conscious, guarantees its own actuality, and is therefore (in respect at least to a 'moment', an inalienable phase, of itself) *truth positing itself as fact* or *fact self-guaranteed as truth*—the precise value of the 'find', the exact nature of the *datum*, have still to be determined. And for this purpose, we can hardly do better than follow and examine the exposition of Descartes.

It will be remembered that, according to the doctrine set forth by Descartes in his *Regulae*,[2] two functions, both infallible, together express, and exhaust, the intellect or power of knowing—viz. *intuitus* and *deductio*. By the first—by its function of (intellectual) vision or insight—the intellect is by nature such as to apprehend *infallibly* the primary elements of reality, which are (*qua* thus apprehended) self-evident truths, primary *data* or basal premisses of knowledge. And by the second—by its function of logical illation, of rational *discursus*—the intellect is by nature such as to advance *infallibly* from these primary elements, along the line of their logical implications; and so to link together the self-evident truths, which it *infallibly* 'sees', into 'long chains of reasons', and systems of demonstrated truth, which it infallibly 'thinks'—i.e. 'knows' by an equally *infallible* discursive or inferential movement.

But though the intellect is infallible when—or so far as—it exercises its own natural functions, in our actual cognizant experience (for example, in the opinions we commonly hold, in the theories we accept and elaborate into systems of scientific and philosophical knowledge) we are anything but infallible. Actually and in fact our minds are full of errors which prevent, and choked

[1] Cf. above, p. 82.   [2] Above, pp. 44–5.

with prejudices which pervert, the natural functioning of the intellect.

'It is some years', so runs the opening sentence of the first Meditation, 'since I realised that, from my boyhood up, I had accepted as true many false opinions; that consequently all I had subsequently built on such insecure foundations must itself be doubtful; and that therefore I could never hope to establish any solid or permanent results in the sciences, unless I seriously set myself, once at least in my life, to clear away all the errors I had hitherto believed, in order to build up the edifice of knowledge anew from its foundations.'[1]

Accordingly, in the first Meditation, Descartes reviews the whole range of his experience in order to ascertain whether any single one of his beliefs and opinions is *absolutely* free from doubt—*absolutely* certain. And the result of this critical review is summarized, as we all know, in the conclusion:[2] 'I am compelled to admit that everything I have hitherto believed to be true is open to doubt. Nor is the doubt due to any carelessness or want of consideration on my part; but, on the contrary, it is based upon strong and well-weighed reasons.'

Now, it is precisely when Descartes has reached this conclusion (viz. that there is ground for doubting *everything* he has hitherto taken for certain) that he discovers the absolute certainty of one thing. Certainty begins, just when it seems to have been shown that certainty is impossible. For, as Descartes himself expresses it in the synopsis prefixed to the *Meditations*[3]—'the mind is properly entitled to suppose that none of those things exist, about the existence of which there is any—even the least—ground of doubt; but it is shown in the second Meditation that the mind, which makes this supposition, becomes aware that it is absolutely impossible it should not itself exist while making it'.

This is, in fact, the line of Descartes's thought in the second Meditation. He begins[4] by 'supposing' that all his previous opinions and beliefs are false, since they have been shown, on one ground or another, to be open to doubt in some degree. 'I suppose' (i.e. assume) 'that all I see is false: I believe that none of the events, which my lying memory recalls, ever actually occurred: I have no

---

[1] *Medit. I* (*Latin, A.T.* vii. 17; *French*, ix. 13). In the following exposition of the 'Universal or Methodical Doubt' and of the 'Cogito', I have borrowed freely from O. Hamelin (*Le Système de Descartes*, especially Lectures VIII and IX), though I have not altogether accepted his interpretation.

[2] Loc. cit., vii. 21; ix. 17.

[3] Loc. cit., vii. 12; ix. 7.   [4] Loc. cit., vii. 24; ix. 19.

senses at all: body, figure, extension, motion, space are mere chimaeras.' But why should there not be something beyond, and other than, what he has hitherto experienced and believed; something not touched by the sceptical review in the first Meditation; something which gives not the slightest occasion for doubt? May there not be a God, for example, or some power, who (or which) has originated and inspired his doubts? But there is no reason, he at once points out, to postulate a God; 'for it may well be that I myself am able to originate my thoughts and doubts'. Yet, if so, 'then surely at least I myself am something?'[1]

My thoughts and doubts, it has been suggested, beyond doubt imply the existence of a thinker. They imply, therefore, beyond all possibility of doubt, the existence (if not of God, at least) of myself as their author.

But—and the argument now[2] deserves the closest attention, for Descartes is about to define the precise significance of the principle which he holds to be self-guaranteeing—the suggestion that 'I myself am something' seems in flat contradiction with the arguments of the first Meditation, and the 'supposition' Descartes has agreed to make in consequence of them. It may be, perhaps, that, though 'I have neither senses nor a body', I am so bound up with these corporeal nonentities as to have no kind of being whatever apart from them. But Descartes's 'supposition' went farther than that; for

'I have persuaded myself that there is nothing whatever in the world: —no heavens, no earth, no minds, no bodies. Doesn't that mean that I have persuaded myself that *I too* have no existence?

'Far from it. For how could I persuade myself of anything—or even think of anything—unless *I* was?

'But I supposed a supremely-powerful, supremely-cunning, malignant demon—a spirit of irrationality[3]—devoting all his energies at all times to deceiving me.

---

[1] Loc. cit.: 'Nunquid ergo saltem ego aliquid sum?' 'Moi donc à tout le moins ne suis-je pas quelque chose?'   [2] *Medit. II*, vii. 24–9; ix. 19–23.

[3] On the true significance of Descartes's hypothesis of a malignant spirit (cf. *Medit. I*, vii. 22; ix. 17) see Hamelin (loc. cit., pp. 117–19), whose interpretation seems to me right. Suppose—Descartes is arguing in effect—there is no God. In any case, we are contingent and finite beings—dependent upon hazard, or destiny; or at any rate upon something other than, external to, and more powerful than ourselves. Our intelligence is not pure or free, but subject to circumstances beyond our control. For all we know, these alien influences may be hostile to the natural tendency of our thought towards truth. There may be a fundamental irrationality—a spirit of falsity and deception—in the very nature of our environment. It should be added, however, that Gilson rejects Hamelin's interpretation

'Undoubtedly, therefore, if he deceives me, I am there to be deceived. Let him deceive me as much as he can. His utmost efforts will never turn me into nothing, while and so long as I am thinking that I am something.

'Hence, on a full consideration, the conclusion of the whole matter is this:—The judgment "*I am, I exist*" must necessarily be true whenever I assert it or form it in my mind.'[1]

In the immediately following pages Descartes brings out the full force of this qualification (*whenever*, &c.), with the result that his indubitable *datum*—the self-guaranteeing fact which, when formulated as a judgement (silent or spoken), is the absolutely certain principle of all knowledge—emerges incontestable, but disappointingly meagre.[2]

For (*a*) though, beyond possibility of doubt, 'I *exist*', or '*am*' something, my existence or being is self-guaranteed only while I am actually 'thinking'—i.e. 'conscious that I am experiencing'. 'If I were to cease from all "thinking", for all I can tell, I might, therewith and *eo ipso*, cease utterly to be.'[3]

And (*b*) though, beyond possibility of doubt, 'I am *something*', the something that I am—so far as I know or can know what it is with absolute certainty, i.e. within the limits of the necessary truth affirmed in the principle—is *nothing but that which is now* '*thinking*'. What I incontestably am, is no more than the precisely commensurate 'subject' of this present act of 'thought'—of 'consciousness that I am experiencing'. And this subject—this '*X* now thinking'—is, for all I can know, as momentary in its existence as the flash of self-consciousness it originates, and possessed of no further 'character' or 'what' than precisely the power which therein is actualized and exhausted.

It is true that there is a natural temptation to misinterpret the principle as though it affirmed the incontestable existence of a *spiritual substance*—to which Descartes elsewhere succumbs.[4] On

as fanciful. See his *Études sur le rôle de la pensée médiévale dans la formation du système cartésien*, pp. 238–9.

[1] *Medit. II*, vii. 25: 'Adeo ut, omnibus satis superque pensitatis, denique statuendum sit hoc pronuntiatum [= cette proposition, ix. 19], *Ego sum, ego existo*, quoties a me profertur, vel mente concipitur, necessario esse verum.'

[2] Hamelin (loc. cit., p. 128) says: 'Jusqu'ici la logique de Descartes est inattaquable, et il est le fondateur authentique de l'idéalisme moderne.' The first clause seems true without reservation: the second could only be defended by qualifications which would whittle away Hamelin's intended assertion almost to nothing.

[3] *Medit. II*, vii. 27; ix. 21.

[4] Cf. Def. VI appended *to Answers to Second Objections* (vii. 161; ix. 125). Descartes there defines Mind (*mens*) as 'Substantia cui inest immediate cogitatio';

such a misinterpretation, any and every act of self-consciousness is supposed to guarantee—not merely its own existence, or the existence of an X, precisely commensurate with it, as its 'subject', i.e. exhausted in it as the power which it actualizes and expresses, but—the existence of a 'thinking thing' (a self, a mind) which, both in its existence and in its character, extends far beyond any single act of 'thinking' or flash of self-conscious experience. So interpreted, no doubt, the principle would be a most pregnant truth (if it were a truth at all): a germinal fact (if it were a fact) capable of growing into a most fruitful tree of knowledge. But, unfortunately, there is nothing in the fact that I am 'thinking'— nothing in my present 'consciousness that I am experiencing'—to guarantee 'my' existence as a mind, a self, a spiritual substance. And on the whole Descartes's exposition *in the present passage*—as we have now to see—makes this point sufficiently clear.

'What is it', he asks, 'that I *incontestably* am?' And he answers: 'Precisely and only a thinking thing; viz. a mind, intelligence, reason—terms of which hitherto I have failed to appreciate the true meaning. I am moreover a *real* thing, *really* existing: but what kind of thing? The kind I have already stated: —a thinking thing.'[1] At first sight, this is to attribute to my *incontestable being* (i) a duration beyond the single act of thought, and (ii) a variety of attributes or acts. But, whatever he may say elsewhere,[2] Descartes has already, in the present context,[3] insisted that I exist incontestably only while I am actually thinking. And my *incontestable* being is not characterized by a variety of attributes, by the various 'modes of thinking'; but always and only by a single unvarying 'form of thinking' (the 'moment of return', as I called it above), common to all its 'modes' and without which none of them would be a 'mode' of *thinking* at all.[4]

and, according to Burman's report of his conversation with Descartes at Egmond in April 1648 (v. 156), Descartes explained this definition as follows: 'Praeter attributum quod substantiam specificat, debet adhuc concipi ipsa substantia, quae illi attributo substernitur: ut, cum mens sit res cogitans, est praeter cogitationem adhuc substantia quae cogitat, etc.' Cf. also the passages quoted by Hamelin (loc. cit., pp. 128–30) from *Answers to Third Objections* (those made by Hobbes): vii. 174–6 and 178, ix. 135–7 and 138. Descartes throughout conceives the immediate nexus between thought and existence in terms of the implication of a subject (= ὑποκείμενον) by an attribute (a συμβεβηκός or πάθος); and he tends constantly —and almost inevitably—to take for granted the traditional (Aristotelian) view of subject and its accidents or substance and its attributes.

[1] *Medit. II*, vii. 27; ix. 21.　　[2] Cf. above, p. 138.　　[3] Cf. above, p. 137.

[4] For the technical meaning of Mode, cf. *Princ. Phil.* i, § 53. Extension in three dimensions constitutes the nature of the corporeal substance; thought that of

'What is a thinking thing?' Descartes asks; and answers, 'A thing which doubts, conceives, affirms, divines, wills, is unwilling; imagines too, and sensates or feels.'[1] But though he tries[2] to maintain that all these 'modes of thinking' belong to my 'self' (i.e. to the *real* and *really* existing thing I am) and enrich its character with their variety, he is driven to a very different conclusion. For while he *begins* by urging that 'surely it is I myself, a single identical subject, who am now doubting nearly everything, yet conceiving (understanding) some things, affirming that one thing only is true and denying the rest, desiring to know more, anxiously striving not to be deceived, imagining—and sensating many things'—he ends by making an admission, the effect of which is to cancel all the variety in these modes of thinking in so far as they incontestably belong to my single identical self. The admission in question is made explicitly in regard to imagination and sensation only; but it obviously applies equally to all the other 'modes of thinking', and shows that they belong to my incontestable being not in their distinction, as different modes of experiencing, but in their abstract general character, as all (equally and alike) expressions of my 'consciousness that I am experiencing'.

'Again,' he says,[3] 'it is I, the same I, who am *imagining*. For though perhaps—as I have in fact "supposed"—not a single one of my imaginations is true, still *the power of imagining* does itself really exist, and forms part of my self-conscious being (vis tamen ipsa imaginandi revera existit, et cogitationis meae partem facit). Finally, it is I, the same I, who am sensating—i.e. who receive and know bodily things as it were through the organs of sense. Now, for example, I see a light, hear a noise, feel heat. But, I shall be reminded, all these experiences are illusory: I may be dreaming, as I have agreed to "suppose". Even so, at least *I seem* to see, to hear, to feel hot: *this* at all events cannot be false or an illusion. And it is *this*—this *thinking that* I see, that I hear, that I feel, &c.—

---

mind. Everything else which can be properly attributed to body (e.g. figure, motion) *presupposes* extension, and 'is only *modus quidam rei extensae*'; and all that we find in mind *presupposes* thought. Imagination, for example, sense, volition, 'are only *diversi modi cogitandi*'. On the other hand, extension can be conceived [*intelligi*] without figure or motion, and thought without imagination, sense, or volition. Strictly (cf. *Princ. Phil.* i, § 32) all the 'modes of thought' can be reduced to two general modes; viz. perception (or the operation of the intellect) and volition (the operation of the will).

[1] *Medit. II*, vii. 28; ix. 21.

[2] But see Burman's report (v. 151), according to which Descartes, referring to a point in this part of his argument, said: 'Sed haec nondum hic cognovi, et *de iis confuse solum loquor*.'

[3] *Medit. II*, vii. 29; ix. 23.

which is properly designated by the term "sensation" as it is in me: and *this*, understood precisely thus, is nothing but *"thinking"*.[1]

From this consideration of the arguments of Descartes in the second Meditation, it is clear that the first of the two assertions to which I provisionally committed myself[2] can only be defended on a strict and narrow interpretation of its terms. There is, it is true, a 'moment of return' in every flash of self-conscious experience; and, in virtue of that 'moment', each single flash severally posits and guarantees its own 'existence' or actual occurrence. In this sense—but in this sense only—it is 'safe'[3] to accept 'inner consciousness' as fact, as actual beyond dispute. Each single act of self-conscious experience is, in this meagre sense, a *datum*; its being, or rather its occurrence, is both *percipi* and *percipere*; it is a *self*-awareness, *self*-given and given to *itself*.[4]

To say—as Descartes sometimes says—that every act of self-conscious experience posits and guarantees the existence of a 'thinking thing', a self-conscious subject, is to substitute for an incontestable *datum* a most disputable thesis. For however careful one may be to explain—as Descartes explains in the second Meditation, in the passage we already examined—that nothing is guaranteed beyond the existence of an X which 'thinks' and, while it 'thinks', exists; that the 'thinking thing' or 'self-conscious subject' is incontestably no more, and endures incontestably no longer, than the single flash which it originates—it is hardly possible to avoid a very different interpretation. It is almost inevitable to suppose that what is guaranteed is the existence of 'myself' as the identical subject of many different acts and kinds of experience—past, present, and perhaps to come. Now, it may be true that I myself and other selves—that minds, each the self-conscious subject of a plurality of experiences—exist, endure, are actual; it may be true[5] that in all my experiences I am aware of myself (in virtue of the moment of return in each of them) as a mind which achieves and maintains its spiritual unity in and through their variety. But nothing of the kind is guaranteed by our 'incontestable *datum*'. My 'existence', in that concrete and significant sense, if it is a

---

[1] *Medit. II*, loc. cit.: 'At certe videre *videor*, audire, calescere. Hoc falsum esse non potest; hoc est proprie quod in me sentire appellatur; atque hoc praecise sic sumptum nihil aliud est quam cogitare.' Cf. also, in confirmation, *Letter* 113 of March 1638 (ii. 37–8); *Medit. III* (vii. 34–5; ix. 27); *Princ. Phil.* i, § 9 (viii. 7; and see the French version in ix, second half of volume, p. 28).

[2] Above, pp. 130 and 135.   [3] Cf. above, p. 130.

[4] Cf. above, p. 135.   [5] Cf. above, p. 130.

'fact', is certainly not indisputable; nor is it linked by an immediate yet necessary nexus with each, or with any, single flash of self-conscious experience.

The *datum*, then, which we have found is of the most meagre kind. There is a fact which posits itself as truth—truth which cannot be doubted, since to doubt it is to reinstate it; since doubt is itself thought and so the evidence of the very truth which is being doubted. But in itself this *datum* amounts to very little: what is given and guarantees itself as truth is not more than the bare fact that there is a self-conscious experiencing. And in what sense is it given? Have we not 'found' it by an act or movement of discursive thought?

Descartes himself always expresses his incontestable principle in the form of a mediate judgement or inference: 'cogito, dubito, *ergo* sum.' He denies, indeed, that it is an inference in the sense that it rests for us upon prior truths—it is not a conclusion explicitly drawn from explicit premisses.

'When a man says "I think, therefore, I am or exist", he is not deducing existence from thinking by a syllogism. For that would involve previous knowledge of the major premiss "Everything, which thinks, is or exists"; and this is a truth which, on the contrary, he learns later from experiencing in his own case that it is impossible he should be thinking unless he were existing. For it is the nature of our mind to form its general propositions out of its knowledge of the particulars. "I think, therefore I am", is the recognition of something as self-evident by the simple insight of the mind (. . . sed tanquam rem per se notam simplici mentis intuitu agnoscit).'[1]

But the 'self-evident thing' thus recognized is a necessary, though immediate, nexus between two elements—an *implicans* and an *implicatum*. And however much Descartes may stress the intuitive character of the recognition—its formal 'immediacy', its unitary wholeness—there is an act, or *discursus*, of thought involved. The 'content' of this, as of every, *intuitus* is a 'simple proposition'; and the 'simple insight of the mind' is an 'analytic-synthesis' or a 'synthetic-analysis', by which it distinguishes and holds apart, and *eo ipso* unifies and connects by a logical necessity, the two elements (the antecedent and consequent) of the proposition it views as 'one' and 'whole'.[2]

4. The ground has now been cleared for reconsidering the second

---

[1] From *Answers to Second Objections*, vii. 140; ix. 110.
[2] Cf. above, Study I, p. 45, n. 1.

assertion which we ventured provisionally to make—viz. that certain secondary or reflective experiences must be accepted as 'facts', as existing or occurring beyond dispute. It seems impossible to deny—so far, it will be remembered, we ventured to commit ourselves—that a self-conscious subject can (and often does) reflect upon some one of his primary experiences (upon this or that perception, say, or inference or emotion); abstract (i.e. concentrate his attention upon) 'the moment of return' which is (or was) an integrant phase thereof; make of this abstracted 'moment' the object and the filling of a new (a secondary or reflective) experience; and thus observe (in some sense) or study that 'acting of his own mind' which was (say) its primary perceiving or inferring, or that 'modification of his own self-conscious being' which was (say) his primary feeling of anger.[1]

We were to reopen the question of the existence and nature of these reflective experiences, before searching amongst them for a *datum*. And unfortunately it is only too plain that in my previous description of them there was a serious confusion. For 'the moment of return' is but an integrant phase in the primary experiencing—not *of itself* 'the complete acting of the mind', or 'the entire modification of the subject's self-conscious being', with which in that description it was identified. No doubt I can reflect upon 'the moment of return' in self-conscious experience, making it, and its implication of existence, the object and the filling of a secondary experience, of a reflective study. What else, indeed, have I been doing in the whole preceding consideration of the arguments of Descartes; what else, for that matter, was Descartes himself doing in the arguments in question?[2]

---

[1] Cf. above, pp. 130–1, 135.

[2] A passage in *Answers to Seventh Objections* (vii. 559) should be noticed in this connexion. The critic (a Jesuit, Father Bourdin) had urged that more than 'thought' (if I may use that inadequate term, in default of a better, for the untranslatable *cogitatio* of Descartes) is required to raise 'the thinking substance' above the level of the corporeal. If—he had urged—a substance is to be 'a mind' or 'purely spiritual', it must not only 'think', but must in addition, by a reflective act, 'think' that it 'thinks', i.e. have a [reflective] consciousness of its own 'thought' ('sed insuper requiri ut actu reflexo cogitet se cogitare, sive habeat cogitationis suae conscientiam'). This, Descartes rejoins, is a gross mistake—a mere delusion. If the primary 'thought', through which we apprehend an object, can be attributed to a corporeal thing as its originating source, the secondary or reflective 'thought' can equally be attributed thereto. For the difference between the secondary ('reflective') thought and the primary is no greater than the difference between the former and a (possible) tertiary thought—viz. a 'thought' in which we 'think' that we 'thought' that we 'thought' (i.e. apprehended an object).

Descartes, therefore, conceives reflection or the reflective act as in no way

But even though I can reflect upon, and study, the 'moment of return' in my self-conscious experiences (in a perception, say, an inference or emotion), it does not follow that I can reflect upon, and study, the 'acting of my own mind' in its completeness—i.e. as it actually contributed to constitute the primary experience. It does not follow that my power of reflective study extends beyond 'the moment of return' conceived abstractly and in its general character—as a phase generalized and common to all forms and instances of my experiencing. It does not follow that I can hope to know by reflection any specific 'acting of my own mind'—still less, any individual or singular 'experiencing'; that I can make (say) *perceiving* or *judging* (still less *this or that perceiving*, or *this or that judging*) the object of my study in a reflective experience. And though I can reflect upon the self-positing and self-guaranteeing nexus between experiencing and existence, this secondary reflective experience (so far at least as we have seen) merely repeats— repeats, as it were, within a bracket, and to that extent in a remoter and weakened form—the meagre content of my primary experience, of my direct assurance of the incontestable *datum*. There is no reason to suppose that it adds one particle to my knowledge whether of my experiencing self, or of the specific, or individual, nature of my experiencing, or of the character of the nexus or implication of each (or either) in the other.

It was, then, a serious confusion to identify the 'moment of return' in self-conscious experience with the whole experiencing—

modifying or enriching the primary 'thought'. He views it as simply repeating the original experience within, so to speak, an algebraical bracket. And the bracket—the reflective act—is a formal addition, which (*a*) in no way affects the experience it contains, and (*b*) may itself—on the same principle—be enclosed within a second bracket, and so on *in infinitum*. Such a view of reflection, it must be admitted, is profoundly unsatisfactory. If indeed to 'reflect' is no more than that, reflection is a trivial and nugatory act.

Students of Spinoza will remember that he accepted the same view of reflection, adopting it, presumably, from Descartes. *Cognitio reflexiva* is for him the *idea ideae*, and the latter is no more than a thought turned upon itself, and neither altered nor enriched by the process. It is thus that he conceives 'method' as 'knowledge or truth reflected on itself' (cf. *De Int. Emend.*, § 38); it is thus also that he comes to insist that 'there is no difference between human appetite and desire; for 'a man's appetite remains one and the same, whether he is conscious of it or not' (*E*. iii, *Affectuum Generalis Definitio*, Expl.); and it is thus also that he appears (in one passage, at least) to identify self-consciousness with the '*knowing that*' one 'knows', or the '*thinking that*' one 'thinks', in a still more formal and abstract sense than even the Cartesian 'reflective act'. (Cf. *E*. ii. 21 S.: 'Nam revera idea Mentis, hoc est idea ideae, nihil aliud est quam forma ideae, quatenus haec ut modus cogitandi, *absque relatione ad obiectum* consideratur; simulac enim quis aliquid scit, eo ipso scit, se id scire, et simul scit, se scire, quod scit, et sic in infinitum.')

with that 'acting of the mind' which is the 'perceiving' in a perception, or the 'judging' or 'inferring' in a judgement or an inference. 'Still,' it may be said, 'if we can reflect upon the "moment of return", surely we can also reflect upon "the whole experiencing", and make of *that* in its entirety—as it actually contributes or contributed to constitute a primary experience—the object and the filling of a secondary experience. What is the difficulty in amending the faulty description? Why should it be necessary to reopen the question of the possibility of these reflective experiences?'

The trouble, it must be replied, lies far deeper. There is no difficulty in amending the faulty description. But when the correction has been made and the supposed reflective experiences are adequately described, there remain more reasons than one for doubting whether they do, or can, occur. For consider what, in these 'secondary experiences', I am supposed to achieve. Reflecting upon one of my primary experiences (upon this perception, say, or that judgement), I am supposed to extract therefrom 'the acting of my own mind' (my perceiving, for example, or my judging) and make of *it* the object of my study in a secondary experience.

Now there are at least three difficulties to be overcome before such an experience can be accepted as actual or even possible. The first could be met by a further, and more radical, amendment of my former description; the second is due to a misunderstanding which might be avoided; but the third, if I am not mistaken, is insuperable.

(i) The first difficulty is the real or apparent paradox of introspection. As it was then stated,[1] the paradox arose only if it was assumed that a mind must either 'go whole' or 'not at all' into each of its experiences—so that each of my perceptions, for example, or judgements is either 'actual' without qualification (completely filling and absorbing my self-conscious being at a given time) or 'actual' in no sense and not at all. Since these absolute disjunctions, these rigid alternatives, seemed unwarranted, it was easy to dismiss the paradox, so formulated, as logomachy. Yet, before we have a right to assume the possibility of the supposed reflective experiences, we must surely produce a positive and tenable account of the reflective act they imply. It does not seem to be the *Actus Reflexus* recognized by Descartes and Spinoza: the

[1] Cf. above, pp. 131–2.

act which repeats and encloses within a bracket the primary
experience. For it appears to alter the latter—at least so far that
it analyses and dissects it, and extracts one factor in its constitution. And in any case the Cartesian *Actus Reflexus* is—I admitted
—'profoundly unsatisfactory',[1] though so far I have offered no
alternative account of what reflection is. Can the 'reflective act'
in question be conceived as in fact a kind of introspection, i.e. an
act in some way analogous to 'looking'—an act whereby, without
including or affecting the primary experience, I take in some way
'a view' of it and ideally select (not literally extract) this or that
feature of it for further study? But to 'take a view', to 'look',
are metaphors which it would be difficult to justify—*impossible* to
justify, if I was right before in denying to our 'reflective' cognizance any special resemblance, kinship, or analogy with sense.[2]
Moreover, the possibility of introspection—even if we can give to
the term a meaning free from all suggestions of sensuous vision[3]—
has not been vindicated by showing that certain arguments
against it involve untenable assumptions as to the nature of a mind
and its experiences. Correct those assumptions. Admit that my
total self-consciousness may include at a given time a plurality of
experiences, differing in the degree or intensity of their actuality.
It is still a paradox—a paradox prima facie at least requiring to
be discussed and solved—that a primary experience, however
weakened in intensity and however low the degree of its actuality,
should 'coexist' with a secondary. How can I, with one half of my
mind (as it were) be at the level of perception, be thinking sensuously and instinctively; and yet, with the other half, be at the
level of reflective cognizance (be reflectively conscious of my perception) without *eo ipso* destroying the implicit or instinctive
character of the 'sensuous thinking' which is 'perceiving'?

(ii) The second difficulty is in reality a misunderstanding. But
it must be admitted that the misunderstanding is invited by the
terms in which the supposed 'reflective experiences' have hitherto
been described and illustrated.

The primary experience, on which I am to reflect, we may
imagine that a critic would say, is (or was) a *this*; an individual,
uniquely singular, perception (say) or judgement. And the 'acting
of my mind'—the perceiving or judging—which contributed to
constitute it, shares in its unique individuality. It, too, is a *this*—

---

[1] Cf. above, p. 143, n. 2. [2] Cf. above, pp. 132–4.
[3] Cf. above, p. 133.

uniquely singular, like every actual fact or event—occurring once, and once only, in the 'history' in which the universe unrolls and displays itself in time and place. If so, then obviously the 'acting of my mind' in its proper character (i.e. as it actually or really is) can only be 'lived' or 'felt' or 'enjoyed' (not 'contemplated' or 'studied'). The only way to experience (or know) it, is to 'be' it or 'live' it; and that can happen once, and once only, viz. when and as it occurs. To reflect upon it—supposing that to be possible at all—is to tear (more accurately, to have torn) it out of the historical flow to which it belongs, in which alone it is 'actual', i.e. 'real'; to have de-individualized or de-singularized it, and made of it a perceiving or a judging *in general and in the abstract*—an indeterminate acting of an indeterminate mind.

A difficulty of this kind will seem formidable only to those who —like our imaginary critic—allow themselves to be hypnotized by the actuality and uniqueness which attach to everything in so far as it must (or can) be dated and placed, i.e. regarded as a constituent event of the historical process; only to those who, being so hypnotized, confuse *this* 'uniqueness' with genuine individuality, and *this* 'actuality of existence' with 'actuality of essence'.[1] For to be *thus* 'actual' is, so far, to be determined merely in respect to the 'that' or merely *qua* happening. The determination is external —i.e. indifferent to the 'what', or leaving indeterminate the 'nature', of that which happens or exists. And what is *thus* 'uniquely singular' need not therefore be 'individual' in the genuine or pregnant sense in which 'individuality' is the hall-mark of 'reality'. For to be 'individual' *in that sense* is to be—to put the principle roughly and in general—an inevitable, uniquely definable, and indispensable articulation of a whole, differentiation of a universal, or member of a system.[2]

The critic, in fact, is himself entangled—and is trying to entangle us—in an old puzzle. His difficulty—if it held at all—would extend far beyond the 'reflective experiences' against which he proposes to press it. There is nothing—no object of experience or thought—which is not, from one point of view, 'this', 'here',

---

[1] Cf. Spinoza, *E.* v. 29 S.: 'Res duobus modis a nobis ut actuales concipiuntur, vel quatenus easdem cum relatione ad certum tempus et locum existere, vel quatenus ipsas in Deo contineri et ex naturae divinae necessitate consequi concipimus. Quae autem hoc secundo modo ut verae seu reales concipiuntur, eas sub aeternitatis specie concipimus. . . .'

[2] Lectures on *Universal and Individual*, pp. 112–18; pp. 122–65 of the manuscript contain a development of this point [Ed.].

'now', and 'mine' (i.e. *some* finite subjects). Every perception, for example, and every judgement, involves some definite individual's perceiving and judging at some definite date and place; and that which is perceived or judged—the 'object', 'matter of fact', or 'connexion of content'—*can*, no doubt, be 'singularized' by reference to the singular perceiving or judging. In other words, not only is every cognizant experience, from one point of view, 'this uniquely singular experiencing', and so an 'event'—'actual' as a constituent of the historical process and, like every such constituent, tied down to one place and date, and rendered unique and singular by its special position and context. Every cognizant experience, in respect to its 'object' or what in it is 'experienced', is also, if we please so to regard it, 'uniquely singular' in the same comparatively trivial sense—a sense irrelevant to its nature as a 'type' or 'individual' of knowledge. For certainly, from one point of view, what is experienced is the 'object' as it presents itself to, or is affirmed by, 'me'—i.e. that which is confined or comprehended in this 'my' present perceiving or judging. Now the critic assumes that to be 'actual' in this sense is to be 'real', that to be 'real' is to be thus 'actual'; and he identifies the 'individuality' of that which occurs with the 'unique singularity' conferred upon it by the date, place, and context of its occurrence; and if we follow him in this assumption and identification, we shall have to admit more even than he contends. Not only will it be impossible to reflect upon, to study and know, the 'acting of the mind' which constitutes a primary experience. It will be impossible, *by thinking*, to study or to know anything whatever as it 'really' is—i.e. in its actual and individual being. For all thought (whether popular, scientific, or philosophical) is universal and of a 'such'. It is itself καθόλου, and of that which is καθόλου or τοιόνδε. But the *real*, on this assumption, is 'actual' and 'uniquely singular' in the sense explained; and precisely *qua* thus 'actual' and 'unique', precisely therefore *qua* 'real', it is *this* not *such* (τόδε not τοιόνδε); *here-and-now* not *always and everywhere*, not unaffected by date and place (ποῦ καὶ νῦν not ἀεὶ καὶ πανταχον); 'for' the single experiencing of a single subject only, not 'for' any and every experiencing subject. Just in so far therefore, and just because, anything is 'real'—is 'actual and uniquely singular'—it cannot be an object of thought. The more we think, the more hopelessly we part company with the 'real' nature of the facts.[1]

---

[1] Cf., e.g., Arist. *Metaph.* Z. 1036ᵃ 2–8; 1039ᵃ 15–22; 1039ᵇ 27–1040ᵃ 7.

There is no need to dwell upon these elementary confusions in regard to the 'universality' of thought and its object, and again in regard to the 'actuality' and 'individuality' of that which is 'real'. It will be enough for my present purpose to lay down, broadly and dogmatically, a few familiar principles and fundamental distinctions[1] which must be kept in mind—which the critic has ignored or blurred and so created a gratuitous confusion and raised an imaginary 'difficulty'.

What is real is 'actual'; but its 'actuality' is never only, nor even primarily, presence in the historical process, occurrence singularized by reference to *my* (in contrast to, and exclusion of, *your* or *his*) experiencing. The 'actuality' which must be predicated of everything 'real' (and *pari passu* with the degree of its reality) is 'actualization of essence'. The real is 'actual' because *qua* real it is all 'in act' (*actu*, ἐνεργείᾳ). It is fully and explicitly all that it is capable of being: or its essential nature (its conceivable, definable, universal nature) is fully expressed, completely definite, i.e. individuated.

And *what is real is 'unique'*; but it is by thought, and only by thought, that it can be adequately apprehended in its uniqueness. This is true even of the uniqueness, which is no more than 'uniqueness of occurrence'; for the unique singularity of an event is its unequivocal fixation in one spatio-temporal order. And that can be adequately apprehended (if at all) only by thought—only, for example, by giving an account of it in terms of a network of relations, external to the events, and together necessitating the reciprocally excluding positions of them all, and therefore the 'unique' position of each. For 'in principle[2] uniqueness depends on completeness of explicit conditions and not on designation'.

And, finally, *what is real is 'individual'*—the degree (amount, depth, genuineness) of its individuality being the measure of its reality. But individuality must not be confused with the formal unity—the formal concentration—which is only the obverse of the expulsion or exclusion of others. Anything is 'individual'—to state the principle broadly—in proportion to the wealth and variety of universal characters ('natures', *realia*) which it succeeds in holding and harmonizing within its unity. Completely individual—the absolute individual—is that which holds, intelligibly harmonized in intelligible unity, whatever in any sense and degree has 'being'

---

[1] Cf. (in general) above, Study I, pp. 11–12, 46–9, 55–9.
[2] Bosanquet, *Logic*[2], vol. ii, p. 261, Note C.

or 'exists'.[1] 'A true individual cannot be designated, but it and
it alone can be defined.' To 'define' is to trace the articulation of
an individual whole or system.

It would not be easy, but still it would be possible, by radical
alteration of our former description of the supposed reflective experiences, to overcome the first of these difficulties and to avoid suggesting the confusion which generates the second. The new description
would have to satisfy two conditions. *First*, it would have to bring
out, beyond possibility of misunderstanding, that reflection is a
level, a stage of development or 'power', of mind (of the intelligence or *vis cognoscens*) as such and as a whole: not a special
faculty, function, or act. There is a primary (or instinctive), and
there is a secondary (or reflective), level of cognizant experience.
But within a mind, at any given stage of its development, there are
not two sets of experiences—one primary, and the other secondary,
turned upon the first, reflecting upon and studying them. *Secondly*,
in order to be 'fool-proof', the new description would have to
eschew all terms that invite misunderstanding in regard to the
'actuality' and 'individuality' of the 'objects' of reflection. It
would have to emphasize the obvious, but fundamental, consideration that the 'objects' of the supposed reflection, or reflective
study, are experiences *qua* cognizant—i.e. *qua* types and individuals
of 'knowledge-or-truth'. The 'actuality' here in question—whether
of knowledge itself, as an articulate whole or individual system;
or of the articulations of the whole or members of the system (of
perception, for example) or inference or their more determinate,
more fully specified forms is not an affair of date, location, and
setting in the historical process. It is 'actualization of essence'—
fulfilment in 'the medium of mutual understanding of self-conscious minds',[2] or whatever we ought to call that 'element' in
which knowledge lives and moves and has its spiritual being. No
doubt that medium or element depends—at least in part—upon
the activities of the finite cognizant subjects; and these activities
occur in the historical process. But it is not *qua* historical—not
qua occurring at any special time and place, or in any special
physical or psychical setting—that they contribute to create and
sustain the medium in which knowledge is 'actual'. They contribute to constitute the medium in virtue of 'essence'—i.e. in them

---

[1] The Absolute Individual = the Universe as a 'perfect system': cf. Bradley,
Logic[2], vol. ii, p. 656.
[2] Cf. above, Study I, pp. 56–7.

—which is the same whenever and wherever they occur, and whatever the 'historical' setting of their occurrence.[1]

(iii) Let us try, then, to formulate a new description, satisfying both the foregoing conditions. We are to ask whether a mind (any finite mind), being at the reflective level or 'power' of its development, does—or conceivably can—reflect upon knowledge, upon its specific forms and individual types, in such a way as to study and know the activities which it itself contributes to their constitution. Can—or does—the mind reflectively study and know not 'knowledge', but 'knowing'? Not perception, judgement, inference—but the acts or activities of perceiving, judging, inferring?

And here we encounter the third and (as I think) insuperable difficulty.[2] For in effect we are asking whether it is possible to study the abstracted subject of cognizance,[3] the faculty or function of 'knowing', in abstraction from what thereby or therein is 'known', or *qua* subjective: and merely to ask the question is to contradict oneself.

The terms Subject and Object (Subjective and Objective) denote complementary 'moments' of a concrete fact—'moments' which necessarily emerge as correlated opposites within any and every 'actual' cognizant experience when that is raised (or raises itself) to the reflective level; or when (as I expressed it less accurately before) it is subjected to philosophical ('critical') analysis. The terms mean nothing, except when applied to 'moments' within *their* 'concrete fact'—within some specific form or individual type of 'actual' knowledge; and, when thus applied, each means precisely that which, within the *concretum*, is not (is the contrasted correlative of) that which is meant by the other. Nothing, in short, is a subject or subjective, an object or objective, as such and *per se*. There is no activity of knowing—no act or process, for example, of perceiving, judging, or inferring—which when abstracted from the concrete fact of knowledge (from, for example, the perception, judgement, inference) has any character at all. The activity of knowing (perceiving, judging, inferring, &c.) is one of two

---

[1] Judging, for example, is somebody's judging: but it is irrelevant who the somebody is, except in so far as the difference of 'historical' persons is also a difference affecting the essence of the act *qua* cognizant—a difference (say) of intellectual calibre or education. Subject to that proviso, it is indifferent when or where the judging occurs; whether, in judging, the subject is well or suffering from toothache, sorrowful or happy; i.e. it is indifferent what special items form the detail of that historical setting which, taken altogether, singularizes the act of knowledge *qua* 'actual event'.

[2] Cf. above, p. 145.　　　　　　　　　　　　[3] Cf. above, Study I, p. 30.

'moments' inseparable within, and presupposing, a *concretum*; and, within that *concretum*, both 'moments' deserve, and receive, their respective appellations (viz. subjective and objective) precisely because the one is not, and can never be or become, the other.

A judgement, for example—any individual (i.e. completely individuated or definite type of) judgement, say the singular judgement of perception, or the reciprocal hypothetical judgement of science—is *actual* (*actu*, ἐνεργείᾳ) as a *concrete discursus* within the 'spiritual element' to which I referred.[1] This 'element' is generated and sustained by activities which 'pass through' the finite minds; which require the co-operation of, and so in part depend upon, finite 'subjects of experience', i.e. 'enactors' of the historical process. Now, one 'moment'—one contributory phase—of the 'concrete discursus' (which is the *actual* judgement) is a synthetic-analysis (or an analytic-synthesis) wherein there constitutes and affirms itself a 'complex fact'—wherein it emerges and manifests itself in the form of 'a truth'. In respect to this 'moment' of itself, the judgement is an 'objective' discursus—the self-development of an 'object', in which the 'object' becomes known as what it 'really' is, viz. a 'spiritual fact' or 'a truth'. The other 'moment' —the other contributory phase or side—of the 'concrete discursus' (which is the *actual* judgement) is the complement and contrasted correlative of the first. For the judgement, in respect to the first 'moment', is a self-development in which an 'object' constitutes itself and becomes known; in respect to the second it is a discursive activity in which a finite subject co-operates in that self-development—helps to elicit and know the 'object'. And with special reference to (and emphasis upon) this second 'moment' of its full and 'actual' being, the judgement is a finite subject's act—the 'subjective' process or activity of judging.[2]

§ 11. *Intelligible* Data *and Conceptual Intuition: Genuine Immediates*

1. It will be remembered that the object of the present Study is to clear out of the way the popular assumption that knowledge is divided into two contrasted and mutually exclusive kinds: (i) immediate apprehensions, sensuous or intellectual, of *data*, and (ii) mediate or discursive activities (judgements and inferences) by

---

[1] Cf. above, p. 150.
[2] Cf. above, pp. 69–72, 126; Study III, pp. 250–1.

which the mind derives from the data (or elaborates out of them) 'knowledge' other than, and dependent upon, its immediate apprehensions.

It is necessary to clear this assumption out of the way. For, if knowledge is *in principle* thus divided (no matter where precisely the line of cleavage runs), the provisional description of the subject-matter and method of logic, which was put forward in the first of these Logical Studies, must be rejected as indefensible.

The plan or line of argument has been to accept provisionally the supposed division of knowledge: i.e. to start from it, or within it, and to develop it; and to examine it by testing the supposed examples of *data*—the supposed immediate and infallible apprehensions of facts and truths which are offered to us in the chief varieties of logical theory which take this division of knowledge for granted.

Now so far the search for a *datum* has been prosecuted in the two most likely fields: viz. in sense-perception and self-feeling or self-consciousness—i.e. in the 'sensuous knowledge' we seem to have of perceptible things, qualities, and events, and in the 'sentiences' or 'feelings' we seem to have of 'ourselves' or of our own cognizant activities. And so far the search has failed. The supposed *data* have proved to be either not actual cognizant experiences at all or not sheerly and completely immediate: i.e. *either* 'moments' abstracted from the actual cognizant experiences to which they inseparably belong, and distorted into fictions by the abstraction, *or* experiences not sheerly immediate, i.e. not such that in them we 'apprehend' or 'know' without 'thinking', i.e. without an activity essentially discursive or mediate.

But those who assume the supposed division of knowledge may appeal to a different field or kind of cognizant experience. They need not rest their case only, or even mainly, upon the seeming *data* of sense-perception or self-feeling. Even if they are forced to recognize that no immediate infallible apprehension of fact or truth is to be found in either of these fields of cognizant experience, they may still insist that evidence for the supposed division of knowledge can be drawn from another field—a field not yet examined—the field of conceptual or intellectual intuition.

If, they will say, the *division of knowledge* is to be proved to be a mere unfounded and untenable assumption, two things must still be done. It is necessary first to examine the kind of knowledge, which Aristotle, for example, has in mind when he speaks of the 'infallible intellectual intuitions of the simple (incomposite) reals';[1] or again, to which Descartes is referring when he ascribes to the intellect the power of 'seeing' certain self-evident *data*, the primary elements at once of reality and of knowledge.[2] And in the second place (they will add), this examination of intellectual intuition or conceptual vision will suggest that the failure to find a *datum* in sense-perception or in feeling was in fact due to a misconception of what 'immediate knowledge' means and is. It will suggest, in other words, the need of a re-consideration of the analysis of immediate experience into an experiencing and an experienced—an analysis which up to this point has been taken for granted.

2. *Intelligible data and conceptual intuition.* The contention we are to examine is that all our knowledge by way of judgement and inference (all discursive or mediate cognizance) presupposes, and rests upon, a different kind of knowledge—viz. the cognizance, intellectual indeed, but direct or immediate, of certain intelligible *data*. As I hope to show, there is, underlying this contention and wrongly expressed in it, a fundamental and important truth; and I shall endeavour to bring out this kernel of truth, as well as to destroy the husk of error.

In illustration of the view that all our knowledge rests in the end upon self-evident intelligible *data*, objects of conceptual intuition, I referred to Aristotle's analysis of demonstration and the demonstrative syllogism (ἀπόδειξις and the συλλογισμὸς ἀποδεικτικός or ἐπιστημονικός), and to the closely related doctrine of method in the *Regulae* of Descartes, more particularly to his conception of *Intuitus* and *Deductio* as the two primary and native functions of the intellect.[3] For my present purpose, which is not historical, I need not elaborate in detail the sketches I have already given of these well-known theories. But it is worth while to recall the general drift of Aristotle's account of demonstration and to dwell for a little upon one aspect of it, before passing on to a more direct consideration of our subject. For from Aristotle's account one important point emerges—viz. that the supposed *intelligible data* or *objects of conceptual intuition* fall into fundamentally distinct kinds.

According to Aristotle's analysis,[4] then, to know *sensu strictissimo*

---

[1] Cf. above, pp. 25–7.   [2] Cf. above, pp. 44 ff.
[3] Cf., for Aristotle, pp. 108–9 and 43–8; and, for Descartes, pp. 75–6.
[4] For what follows, cf. *Post. Anal.* A, chs. 2–5, 10, 13, 19–22; B, chs. 11 and 19.

(as, for example, the geometer 'knows') is to 'demonstrate'. And to 'demonstrate' is to establish the commensurate ('universal') nexus of a universal substance or subject ('the Circle', 'Man-as-such') with one of its essential attributes (*propria*) as a '*reasoned truth*'—viz. as the conclusion of a demonstrative syllogism. In a 'demonstrative syllogism' all three terms are universal, and the Middle Term expresses the precisely adequate ground ('the proximate cause') of the inherence of the *proprium* (expressed by the Major Term) in its precisely defined and commensurate subject (expressed by the Minor Term). What is *known*, therefore, in any 'science', or body of knowledge, so far as it fulfils its aim, is a system of reasoned truths, of demonstrated conclusions. And every demonstrated conclusion rests, in ultimate analysis, upon undemonstrated and indemonstrable premisses; and must have been drawn in accordance with undemonstrated and indemonstrable principles.

What, then, are these basal premisses and principles? And how, or in what sense, do we know them? For it is clear that, if they are 'known', they must be 'known' without proof or mediation, i.e. immediately; they must be seized and comprehended, whole and all at once, by a single conceptual act or intellectual vision. It is clear, moreover, that unless they are 'known' with absolute certainty (unless they are truths indubitable, though unproved and unprovable) the rest of our 'knowledge' hangs in the air. None of it—not one of the 'demonstrated conclusions' of 'science'—is secure. Its 'truth' is at best conditional and hypothetical; subject to the truth of premisses and principles which, for all we know, are false.

To these questions, Aristotle answers in effect as follows: Within each sphere of Being there are certain primary 'facts' or 'reals', of which it is (so to speak) composed. These primary constituent members of (say) the world of number, of space, of nature, &c., are so many individual types, or specific forms (ἄτομα εἴδη)— the Number 3 or 5 (for example), the square, the brick, the vine, man-as-such.

Now some at least of the indemonstrable premisses in any science —viz. those which form the minor premisses in its fundamental syllogisms—are purely *analytical* judgements. For the individual types or forms can be unfolded or expanded into essential natures —a plurality of distinguishable but inseparable 'moments'; and in these basal minor premisses there are predicated of, for example, man, the vine, the square, &c., one or more of these 'moments' of their respective essential natures.

And these indemonstrable minor premisses are self-evident truths, because they are thus *the mere analysis* of intelligible data —of intelligible reals, each of which the mind (by its special faculty and function of conceptual intuition) has already grasped in its self-manifest individuality, in its concrete (concentrated but incomposite) unity.

Secondly, there are certain fundamental conditions, which must be satisfied, if anything is to be 'real' in any sense and at all, and so to fall within the scope of rational consideration. It is these *conditiones sine quibus non* of 'being' and of reasoning which, when set out and formulated, appear as 'laws of thought', principles controlling (conditioning the validity of) all demonstrative (indeed all 'syllogistic') reasoning.[1] These too—if I rightly understand Aristotle's doctrine—are self-evident and unquestionable truths, because they are simply the unfolding and the analysis of the central and all-pervading character of reality: a character immediately given to the mind; seized, comprehended, and seen infallibly by its function of conceptual intuition.

Lastly—and here there is a wavering and uncertainty in Aristotle's theory—there are certain indemonstrable principles within each subordinate sphere or kind of being. These are, at all events, fundamental and common to the domains of all the mathematical sciences, the so-called quantitative axioms (for example, the whole is greater than its part; if equals be added to equals, the sums are equal); and similarly Aristotle appears to recognize an axiom or axioms of movement and change, fundamental to the whole domain of physics (δευτέρα φιλοσοφία or φυσική).[2] One would expect Aristotle to regard these indemonstrable principles as having the same relation to the several departments of being—to the worlds of number, figure, matter-in-motion—as the laws of thought bear to being-as-such, to being-in-general or as a whole. If so, they would be self-evident truths, because they merely unfold the dominant character of this or that determinate 'kind' or 'sphere' of being—a character immediately given to, and infallibly seized by, the conceptual intuition of the arithmetician, geometer,

---

[1] The so-called κοινὰ ἀξιώματα: ἀποδεικτικαὶ or συλλογιστικαὶ ἀρχαί (cf. above, Study I, p. 21).

[2] The axiom, for example (if it is an axiom), that all change involves a *terminus a quo*, a *terminus ad quem*, and a *substratum*.

physicist. And they would enter into the special science in question, not as basal premisses, but as controlling principles of its
demonstrations.

On the whole, however, Aristotle's treatment of the quantitative
axioms suggests that he took a different, and less defensible, view.
He certainly appears to identify them with the major premisses of
the basal syllogisms in each branch of mathematics. At all events,
he is at pains to point out that the quantitative axioms are true
not in the same, but only in an analogous, sense in the two main
branches of mathematical science—viz. in arithmetic and geometry; but that this does not affect the validity of the reasoning,
since the arithmetician and the geometer respectively 'use' them
as premisses not in their general sense but only with the restricted
or special meaning under which they are true, in the one case, of
all numbers and, in the other, of all figures.[1]

3. Passing on now to a more direct consideration of this subject,
I begin by suggesting that modern logical analysis of any science,
or body of knowledge, seems to distinguish, amongst its structural
elements and its contents, three kinds of *cognita* which have a
prima facie claim to be accepted as intelligible *data*—i.e. as self-
evident 'truths' or 'intelligible facts', each immediately and
infallibly known, seen complete and all at once, or comprehended
without process in a single act of intellectual vision.

(*a*) *Cognita of the first kind*, when made explicit by reflective
analysis and set out in the form of statements, are the fundamental
principles to which the mind must conform in all its 'thinking'.
They control it if it is to 'think' at all, i.e. if its discursive activity
is to have any bearing whatever upon fact or reality. Such
principles formulate the *conditiones sine quibus non* of intelligibility
and intelligence (of 'knowledge'); the basal character of *all* being
and *all* knowing—the mere 'form' of a coherent structure or
system in general. Under this head there fall (to quote the most
obvious and indisputable, if not the only, examples)[2] the principles
of identity, contradiction, and excluded middle (Aristotle's κοινὰ
ἀξιώματα, or ἀρχαὶ συλλογιστικαί), and the formal principle of
deductive illation.[3]

---

[1] Cf. *Post. Anal.* A. 10, 76ᵃ 37–76ᵇ 2.

[2] It is not necessary for my present purpose to discuss whether, for example,
Leibniz's Principles of the Identity of Indiscernibles and of Sufficient Reason, or
again Spinoza's *Negatio est determinatio*, are, or are not, principles in the sense here
defined.

[3] By this I mean the principle (whatever may be its proper formulation) in

(b) *Cognita of the second kind*, when made explicit by reflective analysis and set out in the form of statements, may be called 'axioms', in default of a better name. What I have in mind are statements defining (or contributing elements essentially required to define)[1] the structural character of the 'domain' of the special science or body of knowledge. Thus understood, the term includes, not only, for example, the 'axioms' of Euclidean geometry, but formulations of 'the fundamental concepts' of (say) arithmetic, physics, biology, or economics—of any determinate science or body of knowledge. By 'axioms', then, I mean principles to which the mind must conform, if its 'thinking' is to have point, significance, and validity, within some special world of fact. They formulate the *conditiones sine quibus non*, not indeed of *all* being and knowing, but of determinate kinds or forms of 'being' and the 'knowing' of them.[2]

Now, at first sight, there is an unanswerable case for maintaining that every *cognitum*, which belongs to either of these two kinds,[3] is an 'intelligible *datum*' precisely in the sense of the commonly accepted view we are examining. For (a) clearly no *cognitum* of the first kind, or the principle into which it may be expanded, is a reasoned or demonstrable truth in any sense or at all; and yet, the infallible assurance of their incontestable truth seems to be an indispensable pre-condition of the 'knowing' of anything. What else, then, can this infallible assurance be, but a 'conceptual intuition of intelligible *data*'? What else, but a non-sensuous (i.e. intellectual) seeing of the non-sensible (i.e. conceivable or intelligible) 'form' (or elements constituting the 'form') of 'knowledge' as a system or structure of some kind or in general? And (b) clearly no *cognitum* of the second kind is a reasoned or demonstrable truth within the body of knowledge, of which it is a pre-condition. The physicist, for example, obviously cannot prove—cannot, *qua*

---

conformity with which the mind advances, inevitably and rightly, from the recognition, or the assumption, that 'M is P' and 'S is M' to the conclusion that therefore 'S must be P'.

[1] In Aristotle's terminology, they are definitory statements of τὸ τί ἐστι, or of some amongst τὰ ἐν τῷ τί ἐστι, of the ὑποκείμενον γένος of a science.

[2] The *cognita* (which, when expanded into statements, I have called 'axioms') correspond roughly to the ὑπόθεσις of a science (cf., e.g., *Post. Anal.* 76[b] 3–6). But— if I am right—they enter into science, not as premisses, but as controlling principles of its reasoning. They correspond also, perhaps, to the 'Categories' or 'Denkbestimmungen' in the philosophy of Hegel.

[3] *Cognita*, therefore, which (cf. p. 157) belong to the structural character of a body of knowledge—not amongst its 'contents'.

physicist, establish by any process of reasoning—the 'fundamental concepts' of physics, or the 'axioms' in which these elements of the structural form of his domain (these indispensable conditions of its 'being' and of his 'thinking') are expanded into statements. For what these 'axioms' express are conditions indispensable alike to the 'being' and to the 'knowing' of the 'world' of his science, *and of everything in it*. Hence, so far as he is concerned, there neither is, nor can be, any (physical) fact or any (physical) truth logically prior to (or even in any sense logically independent of) the *cognita* in question. He must 'know' *them*, if he is to 'know' *anything* in the world of his science; unless they are 'true', nothing is true in physics; and unless he is infallibly assured of their truth, he cannot be certain of a single physical demonstration. What else, then, can this 'infallible assurance' be, but a 'conceptual intuition of intelligible *data*'? What else, but an intellectual seeing of an intelligible structure—that structural form, which being required to constitute a 'world of physical facts', must control the mind in its 'thinking' (in its 'discursive activity') if thereby it is to know such a world or anything in it, i.e. if its reasoning is to be 'physical' or such as to constitute 'physical science'?

So far I have distinguished two kinds of *cognita* which seem—on a first view at any rate—to be 'intelligible *data* immediately and infallibly apprehended by conceptual intuition'. I shall return presently to examine whether indeed—or rather, in what precise sense—they are so. But (*c*) a third kind of *cognita*[1] must first be more fully described. For, amongst the contents of any body of knowledge, there are certain *cognita* which tend to be regarded as truths self-evident and self-contained. They presuppose, indeed, a process of reasoning by which we come to know them; but yet, when and as we know them, they are known (it would be said) by an act of intellectual vision, by a single direct inspection of the mind. It is doubtful, I think, whether (according to modern logical analysis of the contents of any body of knowledge) there is anything precisely corresponding to those basal (commensurate and immediate) connexions of fact which, on Aristotle's theory, entered into a 'science' as indemonstrable minor premisses of the fundamental syllogisms, on which the science as a whole depended. But in the context of a science and amongst the reasoned truths of which it consists, there are certain precise (i.e. reciprocal) implications; and these—though no *primary* premisses, and there-

[1] Cf. above, p. 157.

fore not foundations of the rational superstructure as a whole—are yet, it is sometimes contended, *intelligible data* in the sense that, when and as they are known, they are conceived without process, 'seen' or 'perceived' whole and complete by an infallible intellectual intuition. Truths of this kind (I repeat) are not, like Aristotle's ἄμεσοι προτάσεις or στοιχεῖα, indemonstrable foundations of the *whole* inferential edifice, the *whole* system of demonstrations, which is the science in question. They are demonstrable, and perhaps demonstrated; yet clearly they may be used as immediate premisses and foundations of this or that further demonstration within the whole; as fixed starting-points of this or that section or stage in the inferential movement which (as it rounds itself into *relative* completeness and stability) constitutes what is called 'a science'.

When, for example, the student has mastered the multiplication table, the several implications[1] of which it consists will wear to him the appearance of so many 'intelligible *data*'—each a self-evident truth, standing firm and solid in its own right, and a fit foundation on which to base some further step of his arithmetical reasoning. He knows (or seems to himself to know) infallibly and immediately, for example, that twice two must be four and that four demands two twos as its factors—or that five twos make ten and ten requires two fives. Or when (to take a less imperfect example) the student of Euclidean geometry has re-thought and mastered the demonstration that the angles at the base of an isosceles triangle are equal to one another, the implication (precise or reciprocal) of equal subtending sides and equal subtended angles stands out for him henceforth as a self-evident 'fact' or 'nexus-of-fact'[2]—an intelligible *datum*, a truth which he 'conceives' whole and entire by a processless act of intellectual insight.

There are, it seems, and must be recognized, within the contents of every body of knowledge (of every system of scientific reasoning, of every system of reasoned truth which is the intelligible domain of a science), self-evident intelligible *data* of this kind and the 'conceptual intuitions' wherein they are infallibly comprehended or immediately known. It is, for example, a commensurate implication of this kind which the chemist (and the biologist) establishes—

---

[1] Not all the 'implications', of which the multiplication table consists (indeed, if we remember that every product may be regarded as a multiple of unity, not any of them), are 'pure' (i.e. precise, and therefore reciprocal, connexions of *Implicans* and *Implicitum*). So far, therefore, this example is imperfect.

[2] Below, Study III, pp. 231 ff.

or at least endeavours to establish—whenever he formulates (or tries to formulate) a law of chemical combination, or any causal connexion or law of nature. And when once established and precisely formulated, every such implication,—say the formula of combination of water, or the causal connexion between such-and-such a form of poisoning and such-and-such a form of death—wears the appearance of an intelligible *datum*. It is, or seems to be, a nexus of mutually necessitating terms; a truth self-supporting and self-cohering; guaranteeing itself, and capable of being lifted clean (without loss to its self-evident certainty) out of the reasoned context in which it was established.[1]

4. Modern logical analysis of any body of knowledge distinguishes certain characters of its structure, and certain items of its contents, which have a prima facie claim to rank as intelligible *data*—i.e. as truths self-evident, and known in their self-evidence by a non-discursive act of intellect, by conceptual intuition. There are three kinds of these *cognita*. The first two, when made explicit and set out as statements, take the shape (i) of fundamental principles of the form of system—formal principles of any and every system (*qua* system)—of being and knowing, and (ii) of axioms or structural principles of a determinate system of being and of knowing. There seems an unanswerable case, I admitted, for regarding such *cognita* as intelligible *data*, in the very sense in which throughout this Study we have been searching for *data* in vain. They seem, that is, to be 'truths' (intelligible facts) which can be 'known' only by the immediate inspection of the intellect; and which must be so known, and known with absolute assurance, if we are to know, within the body of knowledge in question, anything whatever discursively or mediately—by way of judgement or inference.

As to the third kind of *cognita*—the implications, which are to be found amongst the contents of every body of knowledge—these also (I admitted) seem, when and as they are known, to be intelligible *data*. They seem to be truths self-evident, known without *discursus* (or 'immediately') by conceptual intuition; and thus available for use as foundations, not indeed of the whole inferential fabric of a science, but of this or that particular inference or 'stretch' of reasoning within it.

---

[1] Here, and in what follows, I am making a free use of Bosanquet's admirable analysis of the hypothetical judgement, the idea of ground and of cause, and the conception of a 'pure case', in *Logic*[2], vol. i, pp. 234-63.

Accepting, then, this suggested analysis, I proceed to test the supposed 'intelligible data', selecting for closer consideration one or more examples from each of the three kinds of *cognita*.

Let us begin with *cognita* of the third kind—implications, as I proposed to call them. There is no doubt that, in every scientific investigation, we endeavour to establish precise (and therefore reciprocal) connexions of ground and consequent, of condition and conditioned, of *implicans* and *implicatum*. There are, then, amongst the contents of every body of knowledge, commensurate cohesions of mutually necessitating terms—truths such as would find appropriate formulation in pure reciprocal hypothetical judgements—in short, what I have called implications. It may be said, indeed, that, in ideal, a body of knowledge is nothing but an intelligible whole or tissue of truths, every single one of which is, in this sense, an implication; and that the degree, in which this ideal is realized, measures the exactness of our reasoning, and the extent to which, in and through that reasoning, some region of reality is 'intelligible' to us or 'known'.

Now, what exactly is contended in regard to these implications —these truths which form part (and, in ideal, perhaps, the whole) of the contents of every body of knowledge? It is contended *not* that they are, *ab origine* and *unconditionally*, 'intelligible *data* intellectually intuited'; but that they acquire that character under certain conditions, and stand henceforth possessed of it in certain relations. Even, therefore, if the contention is sound, it does not follow that they are *data* in the sense which alone is relevant, which alone is under discussion, in the present Study. It does not follow (and this after all is the point at issue) that 'implications' constitute a special set of truths, only knowable and only known by a special function of the intellect; and thus marked off from (and yet the indispensable foundations of) the remaining contents (the truths mediated and known discursively) within the body of knowledge in question. We are dealing, in short, at most with *data* not original but acquired, not absolute but relative; with 'conceptual intuitions' or 'intellectual perceptions' presupposing judgement and inference—and, it may well be, including within themselves the surviving throb and tension of the discursive activity they presuppose. For what was urged before[1] in regard to the expert sense-perceptions of 'privileged' percipients applies, *mutatis mutandis*, to the 'intellectual percep-

[1] Study II, § 8, pp. 91–5.

tions' or 'conceptual intuitions' we are now considering. Not any
and every mind, but only the mind which, in its discursive activity,
moves on a certain plane—which possesses (and is possessed by) a
determinate system of demonstrated truth—'perceives' by intellectual insight the 'implications', for example, in arithmetic, in
Euclidean geometry, in physics, in physiology, or in any other
'intelligible world' or 'body of knowledge'. The commensurate
(reciprocally necessary) nexus of the two equal subtending sides of
the isosceles triangle and its two equal subtended angles, or (again)
of the victim's swallowing so much arsenic and suffering such-
and-such a mode of death, *appears* self-evident, stands out with
the acquired *semblance* of an 'intelligible *datum*', only to those who
have mastered the relevant demonstrations; and the 'conceptual
intuition' they thus are privileged to enjoy draws its whole content
from the inferential *discursus*, in which the particular geometrical
or physiological demonstration is (for the time being and relatively)
the last or 'culminating' stage or 'stretch'. For the time being,
perhaps, the reasoning, the discursive activity, has collapsed. At
all events, it has become concentrated into, and is buried under,
an undivided, quiescent, consciousness, in which the expert
geometer or physiologist 'feels' himself immediately certain or
'assured'. But this assurance is derivative and precarious. It is
grounded in, and (so to speak) quick or tense with, the reasoning
from which it was derived, which in it is concentrated or focused.
It loses its vitality, as the memory of the reasoning fades; and if
(or rather, when) it thus grows fainter, it can only be reinforced or
revived by re-thinking the original demonstration.

That, as I believe, is the true answer to the claim that, amongst
the contents of every body of knowledge, there are 'intelligible
data intellectually intuited'. Strictly and properly speaking, the
claim cannot be admitted. Neither *ab origine* and unconditionally,
nor after a process of demonstration and relatively to a certain
level of education of the mind, are there any elements or items of
the contents of a body of knowledge, which are truths strictly
self-evident—immediately known foundations of other truths that
can be known only discursively, only by judgement and inference.
In every body of knowledge, however, there are truths which,
when once established, *appear* self-evident in the sense and with
the qualifications explained; truths which, when and as they
are known, possess for the knower the *semblance* of 'intelligible
data'. And in ideal, it may perhaps be added, this appearance of

self-evidence, this semblance of being given directly to intellectual vision, or to a conceptual act which is a 'seeing', would attach
to all the contents of every body of knowledge, as a 'sign' (a σημεῖον
= a consequent and symptom) of its *relative* completeness and
coherence—of the *relative* self-fulfilment and self-containedness of
the system of demonstrations which it is.

'But surely', it will be said, 'it is not possible to deny the
genuine self-evidence (even though it be derivative and relative)
of some at least of these implications—these demonstrated truths
within each body of knowledge? In the geometrical illustration,
for example, the implication of the two equal subtending sides
and the two equal subtended angles seems to be a truth, which,
when and as it is known, is nothing but "the commensurate nexus
of two precisely defined and mutually necessitating terms". If
so, is it not—when and as it is known—a self-supporting and self-
guaranteeing cohesion of two intelligible elements? It seems,
therefore, to be an "intelligible *datum* intellectually intuited" in
fact and reality, and not merely in appearance—a truth which,
now and henceforth, *imposes itself, whole and all at once*, upon the
geometrically educated mind.'

What is really at issue is the logical character of an implication.
Hitherto I have spoken of an implication as the precise (or pure)
and therefore reciprocal (or commensurate) nexus of ground and
consequent, condition and conditioned, or *implicans* and *implicatum*. The *connexa*, I have insisted, are to be sharply defined;
and it seems clear enough from the examples that they are to be
genuinely distinct from one another. The sides and angles, for
example, the assimilation of arsenic and the mode of dying—
clearly neither term in these two couples *is* the other, nor *contains*
it wholly or even in part. And so far it seems also clear that the
nexus is sheerly synthetic. An implication, if this were the whole
story, would indeed be 'nothing but the commensurate nexus of
two mutually necessitating terms'—the sheer synthesis of two
sheer distincts.

But if this were the whole story—if this were an adequate
account of an implication—no implication could possibly be
'established' or demonstrated. And indeed an implication would
be, strictly speaking, inconceivable—a contradiction in terms.

For the sheer synthesis of two sheer distincts, if we can regard
it as a 'cohesion' of them at all—as a nexus or necessary connexion of them, and not a mere casual togetherness or conjunction

—is clearly unprovable. To establish or demonstrate *such* an implication—even in any sense to explain or understand it— would plainly be impossible. And if we suppose it to be 'given' or to occur in knowledge, in what sense would it be 'conceivable' or 'intelligible'? 'But it *does* occur; for it presents itself to the intellect, and imposes itself "whole and in the lump" upon it—synthesis and distincts falling together within the *ambitus* of a single conceptual vision.' Then it is 'intelligible', it seems, *a non intelligendo*. For that two terms, each precisely and purely itself, and each sheerly distinct from the other, should yet necessitate or determine one another—what else could *such* a 'given' be to the intellect, which seeks to explain and understand, but an impenetrable mystery or miracle? It would be impossible to formulate a more striking example of the kind of situation which, if indeed it were 'given' and imposed itself as 'fact', would baffle all attempts at understanding. The intellect could neither accept nor believe such an implication unless it were guided by the principle '*credo quia impossibile*'.[1]

But of course this is not 'the whole story'; there is a vital omission in the account I have hitherto given of an implication. If the whole story is to be told, something more must be brought out and made explicit.

For certainly the *connexa* are 'genuinely distinct'. But they are so, and can only be so, because they are differences essential to the genuine (or concrete) identity of something other than, and yet embodied in, them both. And certainly the nexus is genuinely synthetic—a connexion of differences neither of which is contained, wholly or in part, within the other. But it is genuinely synthetic, and can only be so, because it is also analytic of that third something, that 'other'. It is analytic of that third something which, disparting itself into the *connexa*, yet maintains its

[1] Cf. Bradley, *Appearance and Reality*[9], 509: 'For, to be satisfied, my intellect must understand, and it cannot understand by taking a congeries, if I may say so, in the lump. My intellect may, for certain purposes, to use an old figure, swallow mysteries unchewed, but unchewed it is unable in the end to stomach and digest them', &c. Cf. also Kant, *Werke*, ii ('Versuch, d. Begriff d. negativen Grössen in die Weltweisheit einzuführen'), p. 202. '. . . wie soll ich es verstehen, dass *weil Etwas ist, etwas anders sei*?' That *etwas anders sei* must be interpreted as though he had written *Etwas Anderes sei*. It is clear from Kant's examples: 'The Divine Will is one thing: the existing world is *something quite different*. Yet God's Will ⟨is supposed to⟩ contain the real ground for the existence of the world. . . . A body (A) is in motion: another body (B), in the straight line of A's movement, is at rest. A's movement is *one thing*: B's movement *another thing*. Yet the second is posited through the first', &c.

concrete unity and identity in (and only by means of) them both, and is thus the real ground of the necessity both of their distinction and of their relation.[1]

What has just been offered as 'the whole story' may seem far-fetched and abstruse. But it is easy enough to see that nothing less is required to do justice to the geometrical and physiological implications that were quoted as examples. The *connexa* in the geometrical example were not '2 equal angles' and '2 equal sides'; the qualifications 'subtended' and 'subtending' were indispensable. And in those qualifications there is assumed, and there is in part expressed, the *third something*—viz. the uniquely characteristic individual which has and maintains its concrete unity and identity precisely and only in these its differences and in this their synthetic relation. It is this—the isosceles triangle—which is the real ground both of the necessity in the distinctness of the *connexa* and of the necessity of their connexion; and, except as differentiating its self-sameness, they are neither *implicans* nor *implicatum*—nor would their connexion be a nexus (i.e. a necessary connexion), but a mere togetherness or conjunction. So, too, in the physiological example. The *connexa* are not 'poisoning' and 'death',[2] nor even 'swallowing so much arsenic' and 'dying in such-and-such a manner'. If the *connexa* are to be *implicans* and *implicatum*, if they in their distinctness and synthetic connexion are to constitute an implication, they must be—to state the principle in the most abstract and general terms—adjectival to a third *something*, two amongst the differences in which it realizes itself. The 'real ground' in this example was vaguely indicated before[3] as 'the victim'—i.e. the living human organism which 'swallows' and 'dies'. And the 'swallowing' and 'dying', which in their precisely defined distinctness reciprocally cohere with one another (so that the first must be terminated by the second, and the second of necessity presupposes the occurrence of the first), are two of the different functions or processes in which and in which alone *this* life (the life of *this* organism) displays and completes its limited and transient 'individuality', or shows the special character and the limits of its 'concrete identity and unity'.[4] The long and the short of it, then, is this. There is no such thing as a logical nexus (a necessary

[1] On genuine (or concrete) identity and unity, cf. Study I, pp. 46–9.

[2] Cf. above, p. 161.   [3] p. 163.

[4] For the assumption that cause and effect, when adequately conceived, are *in principle* identical with logical antecedent and consequent (*implicans* and *implicatum*) see above, Study I, p. 30, n. 1.

connexion) of differences, unless the differences differentiate an identity. Implications 'hold together', and 'hold', only within, and subject to, the (actual or postulated) being of something concretely one and self-same. They depend upon, and are supported by, some (given or postulated) individual whole or system—something that is One in (and by virtue of) its Many, the same with itself in (and because of) a variety of elements or characters essential to its identity, or a plurality of changing states or phases displaying its permanence. For this and that item of the detail of *such* an individual whole or system, this and that difference of its identity or phase of its permanence, may—taken strictly and purely, and thus precisely defined—imply, condition, necessitate, each the other; may constitute an implication. But obviously no implication—none of these commensurate cohesions of items, differences, phases—is self-supporting. It could not be 'lifted clean'[1] 'out of the reasoned context in which it was established'. It holds, and holds together, only within the framework of its special 'ground'—only in one special context, the context in which alone it was, and could have been, demonstrated, viz the reasoned explication (the Synthetic-Analysis or Analytic-Synthesis) of that 'ground'.

I must not delay longer on these 'implications'; for I am anxious to bring this Study to a conclusion, and I have still to examine the contention that 'axioms' and 'principles' are 'intelligible *data* conceptually intuited'. Yet I will permit myself to make one general remark before leaving this subject. If what I have been maintaining is correct, the classical ideal of knowledge—the ideal which dominates the teaching alike, for example, of Aristotle's *Posterior Analytics* and of the *Regulae* of Descartes—must be condemned as illusory. To conceive a body of knowledge in its ideal fulfilment as a system of truths, some indemonstrable and some demonstrated, but all (when the inferential movement has completed itself and 'come full circle') severally absolute, i.e. self-evident and self-supporting—such a conception is no more than an attractive dream, unrealizable because self-contradictory. Truths thus absolute would be so many items of fact and its awareness: units to be summed or aggregated, atoms of information to be conjoined or collocated. They would be intrinsically incapable of constituting a science, a coherent *body* of knowledge —an intelligible *world* intelligently known.

[1] As was suggested, above, p. 160.

Or (to express the same criticism somewhat differently) no movement can be reduced, whether in fact or in ideal, to a succession of discrete unmoving constituents; and the inferential movement, the movement of illation or mediation, is no exception. The inferential movement, that is, cannot be reduced, in fact or in ideal, to a succession of self-evident steps or premises, each seized immediately (or 'intuited') by (or in) an unmoving act of intelligence. Yet in principle this illusory reduction is offered both by Aristotle and by Descartes as the adequate analysis of an ideally perfect demonstration.[1]

Nowhere amongst the contents of a body of knowledge is there an 'intelligible *datum* intellectually intuited'. But what of its 'structural elements'—the *cognita* which (for want of

---

[1] Compare the account given by Aristotle in, for example, *Post. Anal.* 84^b 31–85^a 1 of the demonstrator's aim and procedure with the view explicitly maintained by Descartes in many passages of the *Regulae* in regard to the relation of *deductio* to *intuitus* (e.g. *Reg. III*. Cf. also, above, Study I, p. 44). 'According to Aristotle'—if I may quote my Inaugural Lecture of 1919, *Immediate Experience and Mediation*, pp. 13–17—'the man of science, as the result of certain preliminary investigations . . ., is enabled to formulate various προβλήματα. Each of these προβλήματα is a judgement, true but as yet unproved, asserting the connexion of a property (D) with its appropriate subject (A). The connexion thus provisionally asserted has to be established—the unmediated judgement (A–D) has to be converted into a demonstrated truth of science. When the demonstrator starts, there is an "interval" (διάστημα) whose ends are marked by the two terms (ὅροι) A and D; and this "interval" between the subject and its property is as yet unfilled for his knowledge. His object is to discover the middle term or middle terms which are required to fill this gap—the links connecting A with D—and thus to substitute, for the unfilled interval A–D, a "close-packed" interval, i.e. an unbroken succession of minimal intervals or immediate judgements (ἄμεσα or ἀδιαίρετα διαστήματα, ἄμεσοι προτάσεις, στοιχεῖα). . . . To demonstrate the necessary connexion of D with A is thus to analyse the "stretch" between them into the indivisible, elementary "stretches" of which it is composed. These simple or indivisible intervals (the judgements A–B, B–C, C–D) are the primary, self-evident, and yet necessary, truths, the immediate premises, which the proof that A must be D presupposes as its logical foundations.' And, it must be remembered (cf. above, pp. 154–6), these primary immediate premises are known, and can be known, only by νόησις—by conceptual intuition. 'Such self-evident and yet necessary truths correspond to the "simple propositions" or "simple ideas" which, according to Descartes, are the intuitively apprehended *data* of all our knowledge. The human intellect, he maintains, is . . . infallible in its acts of "intuition", and infallible in its inferential movement' (cf. above, Study I, pp. 44–5). 'Thus, I can . . . "see", e.g., that "$2+2 = 4$", and that "my self-consciousness involves my existence". And, by an unbroken inferential progress from self-evident to self-evident, my intellect can move to the infallible apprehension of a mediate necessary truth. . . . However long and complex the mediation, however many links the chain of proof may contain, the inference is infallible because each of its steps is an infallible intuition.' (Cf. *The Nature of Truth*, 2nd ed., pp. 69–73.)

better names) I called respectively 'fundamental principles' and 'axioms'?[1]

Consider, for example, the principles of contradiction and of deductive illation[2]—or rather the structural characteristics which these principles express, characteristics common to every body of knowledge because inherent in its very form as an intelligible system. Consider also Euclid's 'axioms', for example, that 'the whole is greater than its part' and that 'two straight lines cannot enclose a space'—or rather the special structural characteristics which they express, characteristics inherent in 'homogeneous space', or whatever we ought to call the special intelligible system disclosed in Euclidean Geometry. Are not these and similar structural characteristics so many conditions, to which the intellect is subject in all its reasoning, if that is to have any bearing—to hold good at all—within the world of homogeneous space? Yet how can it be subject to them—how can they inform and control it in its discursive activities—unless they are *in some sense* 'known' to it, 'known' without judgement or inference?

It looks, then, as though we have at last found a *datum* or *data* of the kind for which we have been searching. For there are—it appears—certain structural characters which must be already 'known' to the intellect, if anything whatever *in the world of homogeneous space* is to become known to it by way of judgement and inference; *cognita*, therefore, which are indispensable pre-conditions of all its discursive activities in this sphere. And similarly, in every body of knowledge, there are, or seem to be, intelligible *data* intellectually intuited; viz. certain structural or formal characters, which logical analysis expands into definitory statements, and formulates as fundamental principles of knowledge in general, and as axioms or fundamental concepts of each several body of knowledge in particular.

Yet this apparent success is illusory. For, on further consideration, it is clear that neither the fundamental principles and axioms, nor the structural characters they render explicit and define, are 'intelligible *data* intellectually intuited'—so long at least as the terms of that phrase retain the meaning they have hitherto borne in our inquiry. For the phrase—or, for that matter, even the single term *datum*—commits those who use it[3] to the assumption that,

---

[1] Cf. above, pp. 158-9, 161.   [2] Cf. above, p. 157.
[3] Those at least who use it, as I have done, without special warning and qualification.

within knowledge, *even if it be immediate*, there must of necessity be two terms, opposed to one another and correlated as subject and object; that knowledge must always be analysable into a *cognitum* and a *cognoscens*, into a 'known' and a 'knower' or 'knowing' of it.

Now it was not suggested—and certainly could not be maintained—that (say) the principle of contradiction and the axiom that 'two straight lines cannot enclose a space' are, *themselves* and *as such*, intelligible *data* intellectually intuited by the Euclidean geometer as pre-conditions of his reasoning. They are not, in their proper form as explicit principles, 'known' to him at all—are not *cognita* for him—so long as he is geometrizing; but only, if at all, when he reflects upon his geometrical reasoning. They are, in short, *cognita* for him not *qua* geometer but *qua* logician. And though for the logician (or for the geometer *qua* logician) these principles and axioms are *cognita*, they clearly are not *data*; nor is his 'knowing' them an intellectual vision of them, i.e. a conceptual intuition without, and distinct from, discursive activity. On the contrary: what is prominent and unmistakable in his 'knowing them' is its discursive character. He is judging; and his *cognitum* is a 'truth' which can only be 'known'—and therefore can only be itself, viz. a 'truth'—in the form of a judgement.[1]

On the other hand, the 'structural characters', which these principles and axioms render explicit—how can they, *as such* (i.e. in *their* proper or inexplicit form) be intelligible *data* intellectually intuited? 'They are', it was suggested,[2] 'conditions controlling the intellect in its geometrical reasoning. They must, therefore, be "known" to it *in some sense*—"known" to it apart from and independently of its discursive activities. They are, in short, *cognita* presupposed by, and pre-conditioning, the latter; intelligible facts given directly to, and seen directly by, the intellect.' But everything in this argument turns upon the qualification 'in some sense'. These structural characters plainly are not '*cognita*' or 'known' in the only sense we have hitherto recognized. They are not objects for a knowing subject or act; they do not fall on one side of that correlation, with which hitherto we have tacitly

---

[1] Cf. above, pp. 141–2, on the discursive character of the Cartesian *Intuitus*. I am not denying the formal immediacy—the formal unity, wholeness and continuity, of the consciousness involved in every act of judgement or inference. But I am denying that to 'know by way of judgement or inference' can ever be anything else than *primarily and essentially discursive*, i.e. an activity synthetic and analytic at once.   [2] p. 169.

identified knowledge. The geometer, it is obvious, does not *in that sense* know them—i.e. they are not 'objects' for him—either before, or during, or after, his geometrical reasonings. And what the logician (or the geometer *qua* logician) knows, is (as we have seen) not these structural characters themselves and as such, but certain definitory propositions—or whatever we ought to call those truths in the form of judgements into which these structural characters have been expanded and translated by his reflective analysis.

5. *Genuine Immediates*. Where now do we stand? The 'search for a *datum*', has been prosecuted, if not exhaustively, at least industriously in all the most likely fields. For those who believe in *data*, when their belief is challenged, tend to put forward, as incontestable examples, experiences drawn from one or other of the three fields we have now explored—viz. the fields of self-feeling, sense-perception, and conceptual intuition. Nothing within these fields has proved so far to be a *datum*; i.e. to be a fact, reality, or truth immediately and indubitably known—given, completely and utterly as it is, to some processless and infallible mode of sentience, or of sensuous or intellectual apprehension.

With that negative result, the main object of the present Study[1] has been achieved. For the popular division of knowledge into immediate and discursive has been 'shaken and discredited' at least to this extent—viz. that those who assume it may fairly be challenged to show why their assumption should be treated with respect. It is for them to produce some fresh example of immediate knowledge—an example this time genuinely incontestable; or else to vindicate, and re-establish, the supposed specimens of immediate knowledge, the supposed *data*, that have been examined and found wanting in the preceding investigation.

This brings me to the consideration of a final topic. For knowledge, it may be said, is based upon a *datum* in a different sense from that in which the term has so far been interpreted; or knowledge, though not *divided* into knowledge immediate and knowledge discursive, is nevertheless rooted in, and is the development and consummation of, a genuinely immediate basis.

Throughout these Studies, it will be remembered, it has been assumed that knowledge can always be analysed into a *cognitum* and a *cognoscens*—into two terms opposed and related to one another as object and subject. But such an analysis, it has been

[1] Cf. above, pp. 152–3.

contended, is *always inadequate*, since at best it ignores a fundamental character of knowledge; and often utterly inapplicable,
because there are forms or levels of knowledge—or experiences
continuous with knowledge—which 'fall below' and 'rise above'
all explicit distinctions and relations, even the opposition and
correlation of subject and object.

(i) *Certainly the analysis is inadequate*, and apt to be misleading
by what it omits or fails to emphasize. *In principle*, indeed, I have
already admitted[1] its inadequacy in insisting upon the concrete
unity and identity, within which, and subject to which, alone a
duality of terms can be genuinely distinct and yet genuinely
related. The point is put very clearly and forcibly in Bradley's
Essays on Truth and Reality;[2] and a few quotations will explain
and drive it home sufficiently for my present purpose.

'There is', he writes,[3] 'an immediate feeling, a knowing and being
in one, with which knowledge begins; and, though this is in a manner
transcended, it nevertheless remains throughout as the present foundation of my known world. And if you remove this direct sense of my
momentary contents and being, you bring down the whole of consciousness in one common wreck. For it is in the end ruin to divide experience
into something on one side experienced as an object and on the other
side something not experienced at all.'

Again,[4]

'at no stage of mental development is the mere correlation of subject
and object actually given. Wherever this or any other relation is experienced, what is experienced is more than the mere relation. It
involves a felt totality, and on this inclusive unity the relation depends. The subject, the object, and their relation, are experienced as
elements or aspects in a One which is there from the first.'

Lastly,[5]

'My self is not my finite centre, and my finite centre is but one amongst
many, and it is not the universe. It *is* the whole universe entire and
undivided, but it is that universe only so far as it appears in one with a
single centre. Feeling is the beginning, and it is the source of all material,
and it forms the enfolding element and abiding ground of our world.
But feeling is not that world, and it is not the criterion of Reality', &c.

The analysis of knowledge into a *cognitum* and *cognoscens* is
always 'inadequate' in the sense explained; knowledge is never
'the mere correlation of subject and object'; that correlation

---

[1] Cf. above, pp. 165–7.   [2] Cf. especially ch. vi and ch. xiv.
[3] Loc. cit., p. 159.   [4] Loc. cit., p. 200.   [5] Loc. cit., p. 420.

logically presupposes a more fundamental whole or unity in which
—to speak metaphorically—it is 'rooted', or within (and from)
which it develops; nevertheless this admission, so far as I can
judge, is not relevant to, does not modify or cancel, the negative
result of the preceding search for a *datum*. What has in fact been
admitted is not 'an immediate feeling, a knowing and being in
one', which exists as an *independent* basis, as a separate or separable *datum*, upon which there may be founded, or out of which
there may develop, the mediate or discursive forms of knowledge.
'Basis' is a misnomer for the fundamental unity or immediacy—
the knowing and being in one—which the correlation of subject
and object implies; a misnomer, or at least a metaphor which must
not be pressed. For the 'basis'—if we *will* call it so—is, in this
case, inseparably one with that which is founded upon it, with that
which is rooted in it, and developed out of it. Nor will it do to
press the imagery in the descriptions I quoted from Bradley. The
main point, I take it, which he is anxious to enforce, is that a
certain character of immediacy, a oneness of knowing and being,
is ineliminable from knowledge—not that it comes first in time,
nor that it ever exists as a complete and independent stage, or
form, of knowledge.[1] It is unfortunate, I venture to think, that
he should speak of it as 'an immediate feeling'; for the phrase
undoubtedly suggests a 'substantial' or complete experience, and
not a character ineliminable from—or a 'moment' contributing
to constitute—every form or stage of knowledge. It is unfortunate
also that he should say 'there is an immediate feeling, with which
knowledge *begins*'. But the misleading suggestion of this phrase
is—in part, at least—corrected by the later passage in which he
says of feeling not only that it is 'the beginning', but that 'it
forms the enfolding element and abiding ground of our world'.

(ii) Admitting, then, that (in the sense explained) the analysis
of knowledge into the correlation of subject and object is always
'inadequate', let us pass on to consider the second contention[2]—
viz. that 'there are forms or levels of knowledge (or experiences
continuous with knowledge) to which the analysis is utterly
inapplicable'. On the face of it—on any strict and literal interpretation—the contention is plainly indefensible. How can there

---

[1] Bradley himself, however, though with considerable hesitation, did in fact
maintain also that 'feeling', both in the race and in the individual, is the beginning
(the first stage in time) of knowledge. See particularly his unfinished essay on
'Relations' in *Collected Essays*, vol. ii, pp. 630–76.

[2] Above, p. 172.

be forms of *knowledge* which 'fall below' or 'rise above' the correlation of subject and object? Knowledge without a *cognitum* or a *cognoscens* is a knowledge where nobody knows and nothing is known. Nevertheless behind this contention—misunderstood or misdescribed by those who make it—there are certain experiences which must be briefly noticed.

(*a*) There are, *first*, certain extremes of agony or rapture—immensities of suffering or delight[1]—which 'fall below' all explicit distinctions and relations, even (it may be said) 'below' the opposition and correlation of subject and object. Such states, perhaps, are utterly and genuinely *immediate*. They are, at all events, without distinguishable elements or parts, without terms to relate or mediate. There is a 'feeling', a 'mode of sentience', an 'experience'—if these terms may be used, in default of better, to designate a state or occurrence such that, while it lasts, there is for me nothing beyond, and there are for me no distinctions within, its overwhelming immensity. There is a 'feeling'. But while this 'feeling' is, there is no world beyond it; there is *within it* no self who feels, no pain or pleasure which he feels; nor is there a sentient subject conscious of the feeling as *his* experience or state. There is nothing but one intense and all-absorbing flood of pain or pleasure; too overwhelming, while it lasts, even to be felt (i.e. recognized) *as* pain or pleasure.

In such an experience, however, we plainly are not cognizant of anything, or at all. An experience of that kind—assuming it to occur, and assuming it to be thus utterly and genuinely 'immediate'—is plainly not a form of knowledge. It is not merely, if I may recall a former suggestion,[2] that like an extremely violent and intense perception, the experience 'tends to lose its cognizant character, and to be for the percipient an overwhelming "sensation" of pleasure and pain'. *Ex hypothesi*, and *ab origine*, this experience had no cognizant character to lose—no 'cognizant character' in the only sense the phrase can bear in the context. For, in it, nobody 'experiences' and nothing 'is experienced'. It never was, and never can be, *for* a percipient or a sentient—or *for* a finite subject at all.

(*b*) But, *secondly*, there are experiences which deserve, if I am not mistaken, to rank as (in a certain special sense) immediate,

---

[1] Extremes also, I ought perhaps to add, of fear and panic, of hate and rage, of love, &c.

[2] Cf. pp. 109–10.

and yet as cognizant or continuous with, and consummations of, knowledge.

In such experiences we seem for the time being to have 'risen clear above' all forms of discursive knowledge; to have transcended whatever of division, and of process—perception, for example, and judgement or inference—involves; and to have become (so to speak) the mere channel through which the fact reveals itself, the glass in which it shows and sees itself as truth.

Thus, there are occasions when, for example, the scientific observer, owing to the very intentness of his study, 'loses himself' (becomes buried and absorbed) in the contemplation of the facts. He is no longer aware (on the one hand) of himself and (on the other) of an object opposed to, and correlated with, his subjective faculties or acts. These, and all other explicit distinctions and relations, are submerged in an experience which is indivisibly one and whole. The experience is whole and undivided, and so far, perhaps, 'genuinely immediate'; yet not because (like the flood of agony or rapture) it is too undeveloped and inarticulate to contain any distinctions and relations, but because (on the contrary) it 'overrides' (i.e. includes and, in including, consummates) them. Or, again, there are occasions when, after a thinker has wrestled long with some baffling problem, or has struggled link by link along some difficult chain of reasoning, the completely reasoned solution—the 'whole truth of the matter'—seems suddenly to flood and possess, to irradiate his mind. In such an experience, he is—or seems to himself to be—not judging or reasoning, but yet *knowing* with supreme and absolute certainty. The experience—he would probably say, if asked subsequently to describe it—is not discursive, but intuitive; not thinking but seeing; not a piece-meal discovery or disclosure, but a sudden grasp or vision, a sudden revelation, of the truth. It is a 'grasp'— he might add—such that the mind, which grasps, is and 'feels' itself one with what it grasps; a 'vision' such that nothing, no part of the total experience, remains opaque or unseen. 'Vision', indeed, and 'grasp' are metaphors obviously imperfect. For the experience *as a whole* (including that which grasps or sees) is 'grasped' or 'seen'. It is less misleading, perhaps, to say of it simply that it is the truth become 'self-luminous'—apprehending, and apprehended by, itself.

The experiences I have been attempting to describe occur, I am persuaded, beyond question in human life. The finite knower, at times and for a time, achieves and enjoys (or, rather, is overtaken and absorbed by) states, in which there is for him neither division and relation between the knowing and the known, nor any piece-meal construction of the truth which yet fills and illuminates his mind. In the sphere of knowledge, as well as in that of art and in religion, the finite subject may, at times and for a time, lose and find himself in an experience which we can best describe in Bradley's phrase as 'an immediate unity of one and many at a higher remove'.[1]

It may be that in insisting upon the occurrence of such states—such immediate cognizant experiences richer, and not poorer, than the predominantly discursive or mediate forms of knowledge they override, I am unduly influenced by my philosophical upbringing, by the consensus (as it seems to me) of Plato and Aristotle and Spinoza. For the two last certainly, and perhaps also Plato, find the goal and consummation of knowledge in the kind of state I have in mind—viz. in an intuition or conceptual vision above the opposition of experiencing and experienced (of see-er and seen, of knowing and known), and enriched by the gradual seeking and emergence of the truth (the dialectic process, the discursive move-ment) which yet it overrides.[2]

But assuming, whether rightly or wrongly, that there occur in human life states 'immediate' in the sense described, and cogni-zant or continuous with knowledge, there are four grounds for doubting whether they need be further considered in the present

---

[1] Cf. Bradley, *Essays on Truth and Reality*, p. 231: 'And an immediate unity of one and many' [= 'the immediate unity which comes in feeling', but] 'at a higher remove is the ultimate goal of our knowledge and of every endeavour.'

[2] For Plato, cf., e.g., *Phaedo* 79 d: *Republic* 490 a–b. But, even in these and similar passages, Plato's language, in regard to the supreme grade of knowledge ($\theta\epsilon\omega\rho\ell\alpha$ or $\nu\delta\eta\sigma\iota s$), implies perhaps rather a kinship and a marriage, than a relationless unity, of the Soul (or intelligence) and the forms (or intelligible reality) ; and it is doubtful whether, on his view, the dialectic process (or the movement of reasoning) is ever merged—even in $\theta\epsilon\omega\rho\ell\alpha$—in a total and unbroken vision, or self-manifesta-tion, of truth. As to Aristotle, see above, Study I, pp. 23–7; cf. what he says of the $\nu\delta\eta\sigma\iota s$ (= $\nu o\hat{\upsilon}s$ actual or in act) in which the intelligence 'makes contact with', and so becomes continuous with, and *is*, the intelligible fact it conceives or knows (e.g. *De Anima* Γ. 4 ff. ; *Metaph.* Θ 10, Λ 7 and 9) ; or again his repeated insistence that knowledge living and actual is identical with that which therein is being known (e.g. *De Anima* 430ª 4, $\dot{\eta}$ $\gamma\grave{\alpha}\rho$ $\dot{\epsilon}\pi\iota\sigma\tau\dot{\eta}\mu\eta$ $\dot{\eta}$ $\theta\epsilon\omega\rho\eta\tau\iota\kappa\dot{\eta}$ $\kappa\alpha\grave{\iota}$ $\tau\grave{o}$ $o\ddot{\upsilon}\tau\omega s$ $\dot{\epsilon}\pi\iota\sigma\tau\eta\tau\grave{o}\nu$ $\tau\grave{o}$ $\alpha\dot{\upsilon}\tau\delta$ $\dot{\epsilon}\sigma\tau\iota\nu$. So also 430ª 20: and cf. *Metaph.* 1072ᵇ 20–22, 1075ª 1–5). *Finally*, for Spinoza's conception of *Scientia Intuitiva*—the third or highest kind of knowledge, the *tertium cognitionis genus*, in which our mind is 'an eternal mode of God's thinking', our knowledge 'a part of God's complete knowledge of himself'—cf. *Ethics*, v. 22–40 [and my *Study of Spinoza's Ethics*, pp. 181, and 305–6].

Study. *First*, a state of this kind comes (if it comes at all) *ex hypothesi* as the result and culmination of discursive knowledge. It is, therefore, not a *datum* on which judgement or inference is founded, but on the contrary a complete fulfilment, *of which* discursive thinking is at the least a necessary pre-condition, *in which* perhaps it is a surviving factor or 'within which'—to borrow a suggestive metaphor from Aquinas—it is a 'passage'.[1] *Secondly*, if it is true to say of such a state that, in it, the finite subject is absorbed and lost, it is no less true to say that, in it, the finite subject has, for the first time, fully found and realized itself. For while on the lower (the explicitly discursive) level it was but one partial factor set over against another part within the whole experience, it is in this state one with, and yet also the owner of, the whole. Clearly, then, the state is not *utterly* immediate, not like the extreme of agony or of rapture. *In some sense* it admits and demands the analysis into *cognitum* and *cognoscens*. *Thirdly*, if, in such a state, knowledge is in one sense consummated; if, while it lasts, it is assurance absolute and entire—yet, while it lasts, the absence of doubt is also an absence of reasoning, and this 'consummation of knowledge' is *pro tanto* indistinguishable from the ungrounded feeling of certainty[2] which is faith. And, *finally*, there seems to be no difference in principle between such a state and a kind of experience—viz. the supposed 'intellectual perception of an implication'—which has been considered more than enough already.[3] The only difference, so far as I can see, is a difference of extent or degree. In the supposed 'intellectual perception', a single nexus between *implicans* and *implicatum* has acquired, for a time and under the appropriate conditions, a semblance of self-evidence and self-support; and in the states, of which I have now been speaking, a whole tissue or web of reasoning (or a mass of detail within a field of observation) has, for a time and for the practised thinker (or observer), collapsed—become concentrated, crystallized, focused, in a larger and more glorious 'conceptual intuition' or 'intellectual perception'; in an experience which is (or seems to him, while it lasts, to be) 'the whole truth of the matter' or 'the fact itself' filling and illuminating his mind.

[1] Cf. perhaps Aquinas, *S. Th.*, 2ª, q. 101 (quoted by Laird, *The Idea of the Soul*, pp. 16–17): 'In angelic intellect there is a certain succession of intelligence though not, indeed, a movement, for it is not development from potency to fulfilment, but a *passage within complete fulfilment*.'

[2] Cf. above, p. 66, on 'Feeling' in the sense of an ungrounded intellectual assurance.   [3] Cf. above, pp. 162–8.

There are, then, to summarize the result of this hurried survey, no forms of knowledge, to which the analysis into a *cognitum* and a *cognoscens* is 'utterly inapplicable'.[1] For the immensities of agony and rapture, which might be quoted as experiences devoid of all distinctions and relations, as 'immediate' absolutely and without reserve, are, precisely on that account, devoid also of all trace of cognizance—not states or forms of *knowledge* at all. And if, on the other hand, the seeker after truth finds the consummation of his quest in a state seemingly above the distinctions and relations that characterized all the stages of the search it presupposes and overrides, neither the *immediacy* of such a state, nor its claim to rank as *knowledge*, can be admitted without reserve.

[1] Cf. above, p. 172.

III

WHAT IS IT THAT IS TRUE OR FALSE? WHEREIN DOES ITS TRUTH OR FALSITY CONSIST?

§ 12

1. AT the beginning of these Studies, it will be remembered, a rather clumsy periphrasis was used to designate the subject-matter of logic—its subject-matter in its entirety or as a whole. Logic was described (in a 'formula of orientation') as 'the philosophical analysis of knowledge-or-truth'.[1] Certain obvious objections to this designation were pointed out.[2] To couple knowledge with truth in this manner conflicts with the meanings usually given to the terms in the language of everyday life; conflicts also with the more technical employment of them in most of the current treatises on logic. Knowledge is true; unless it were true, it would not be knowledge.[3] But many people would hesitate to *identify* it with truth.[4] Truth, they would say, is 'the aim and goal' of knowledge; or (perhaps) its 'object'; or truth is reality in so far as it is known, in so far as there is knowledge of it. Again, if there is such a thing as a total subject-matter of logic, neither knowledge, nor truth, nor both taken together, seem wide enough to cover it. For (both in ordinary usage and in the technical language of the logician) Knowledge is contrasted with Error, and Truth (or the True) with Falsity (or the False). Yet, by the general agreement of writers on logic, and by my own admission,[5] Error-or-Falsity falls within its subject-matter.

My object in the present Study is to remove these apparent objections to the acceptance of the position (in regard to knowledge and truth, knowledge and error, and truth and falsity) which my conception of logic implied. By the criticism and rejection of some generally accepted theories, and by the development of a well-known doctrine, I hope to show that the only adequate answers to the questions 'What is true or false' and 'What constitutes its truth or falsity' support—instead of conflicting

---

[1] Cf. Study I, § 1, § 3.   [2] Cf. Study II, § 5.

[3] Cf. Study I, pp. 25–7.

[4] Cf., however, Cook Wilson, *Statement and Inference*, vol. i, p. 314: 'Truth', he says, 'is nothing but the apprehension of reality'; and, if I understand him rightly, precisely the same must be said of knowledge.

[5] Cf. Study I, p. 21, n. 1.

with—the account of logic and its subject-matter which was sketched at the beginning of these Studies.

2. *What is it that is true or false?* To this question there is a verbal answer we have all been taught to give. 'It is always a judgement, or a proposition,[1] that is true or false. Every judgement must be, and only a judgement can be, true or false. The proper subject of these predicates—i.e., on a strict analysis, their only subject—is a judgement.'

Statements to this effect are made by all, or nearly all, philosophers and logicians. I quote a few at random. 'Truth', Locke says,[2] 'properly belongs only to propositions.' 'Falsity', we are told by Descartes,[3] 'in the proper sense—i.e. formal [= actual] falsity —is only to be found in judgements.' Or again, as Kant expresses it[4]: 'The opposite of truth is falsity which, in so far as it is taken for truth, is called "Error". Hence an erroneous judgement—*for error, as well is truth, is only in the judgement*—is one which confuses the illusory appearance [*Schein*] of truth with truth itself.' Or—to quote from two modern works on logic—'Every judgement makes an assertion, which must be either true or false. . . . This capacity of truth or falsehood is the peculiar distinction of judgement . . .';[5] and 'Truth and falsehood are coextensive with judgement.'[6]

The answer is familiar, but tells us nothing. For if, broadly speaking, all philosophers and logicians agree in making it, their agreement is no more than verbal. They agree (broadly speaking) as to the *name*, but (for the most part) differ profoundly as to the *nature*, of that which is true or false. In short, the value of the answer depends entirely upon what those who give it mean by a 'judgement'.

Now it seems possible and sufficient for our present purpose to characterize in outline and to examine three typical positions within one or the other of which the most generally accepted of the current theories may fairly be said to fall—to which they conform in principle, or so far as their general trend alone is emphasized.

According to the first of these general or typical positions,[7]

---

[1] Using the two terms (without prejudice) as synonymous, to cover any affirmation or negation.

[2] *Essay*, iv. 5, § 2.   [3] *Medit. III*, vii, p. 43 and cf. p. 37.

[4] *Logik*, ix. 53.   [5] Joseph, *Introduction to Logic*[2], p. 160.

[6] Bosanquet, *Logic*[2], vol. i, p. 67.

[7] This and the two following descriptions are purely provisional. They will be more fully explained later, and greatly modified by the explanation.

judgement is an activity of synthesis, performed by the finite subject upon his 'ideas' (upon, for example, his sensations and thoughts), and issuing in a complex or compound 'idea'—a combination of thought with thought, or of thought with sensation. This position I shall call (for convenience)[1] *Subjective*; and to it there belongs the view that truth and falsity, knowledge and error, consist respectively in the agreement and disagreement of 'ideas' with 'facts', of 'thought' with 'reality'.

According to the second of these typical positions—which, again for convenience and without further explanation at present, I shall call *Objective*—the judgement proper is independent of any psychical process or activity, any act or attitude of a finite mind. No doubt, in speaking of a judgement, we usually mean by the term an 'item of knowledge' or an 'error'; i.e. a complex content, a connexion of significant elements, which is actually asserted or believed. We use the term loosely to include, besides the proposition (besides the judgement in its proper logical character), a psychical attitude or act—a believing or asserting, of which the proposition happens, for the time, to have become the object. But the judgement considered logically; the judgement on a strict analysis; taken precisely as that which is true or false—in a word, the *proposition*—must be disengaged from, stripped of, everything psychical or psychological. So purified, and taken strictly in its logical character, it is a complex entity—two simple or simpler elements (terms, concepts, qualities, or whatever its constituents should be called) holding together by a relation (positive or negative). No doubt, the complex entity, which is a proposition, is *such as to be asserted or believed*—i.e. such that it may become the object of the believing or asserting of a mind or minds. But this is, so to speak, a capacity extrinsic to its proper nature. Considered strictly, and as such, the proposition is a self-subsistent, and therefore timeless, nexus of elements; and, in this self-subsistence, is *eo ipso* true or false. According to this position, then, propositions are complex entities, independent of the mind; and their being is a timeless subsistence which *is* truth or falsity. Every proposition is, as such, either an eternal truth or an eternal falsity.

According to the third position—which, again for convenience and without at present offering any explanation of the epithet, I shall call *Idealist*—judgement is neither a synthesis of ideas, nor yet a self-subsistent nexus such as may be asserted or believed,

---

[1] The reason of the epithet will become plain later: cf. below, p. 242.

but a synthesis of fact with idea. Or rather, it is the ideal expansion of a fact—i.e. the self-development of a fact in the medium of the *Discursus* (the Synthetic-Analysis) which is thought, and therefore through the co-operative activity of a thinking mind or minds. Every judgement (to express it roughly, and at the risk of being misunderstood) is a phase in the total self-development—in the infinite self-analysis and self-synthesis, in the infinite dialectic—in (and as) which reality takes intelligible shape and manifests itself as knowledge-or-truth.

To this position there belongs the view that 'Truth is the Whole'—the self-fulfilling dialectic which alone deserves the name of 'knowledge'. Because the Whole is immanent in, and requires, each and every one of its constituent phases, every judgement is (in some degree) true—but also, being no more than a phase, in some degree false. Truth is the Whole; and the Whole in its wholeness is absolutely true, i.e. true-not-false. But no judgement is ever true-not-false or false-not-true, i.e. ever absolutely true or absolutely false; every judgement is always true and false at once, i.e. both *relatively*, or in some degree. For the Whole—the self-fulfilling development—is present in each of its constituent phases, i.e. in every judgement; but in each phase it is present (not *in its wholeness and wholly*, but) partially and in a limited (and varying) degree.

§ 13. (*A*) *Subjective Position*

1. Every judgement is true or false. It is a cognizant experience—an experience in which we endeavour (sometimes with success) to know, or to increase our knowledge of, the facts. But, as an experience, a judgement is itself a fact—a psychical fact, or fact of mind. Nobody doubts that *in some sense* a judgement is something the individual thinker 'passes' or 'makes'. And it is characteristic of the first ('subjective') position to seize upon this side of the matter, to subordinate to it all else—and thus to exaggerate and misinterpret the part played in judgement by the finite subject. Any theory of the judgement, which regards it only—or at least fundamentally and in essence—as a complex fact of mind, as a psychical product made out of psychical constituents by the psychical activity of a finite judging subject, conforms in principle to the first (subjective) position.

A judgement, then, is something the individual thinker makes. *The materials*, out of which he makes it—or the constituents he

combines to form it—are psychical (not physical). They are his
'ideas'—sensations, for example, memories, thoughts, he 'has in
mind'; with which (in Locke's metaphor),[1] his mind is 'furnished';
which are 'in', bound up with, his present conscious state. His
making is his activity of thinking—the exercise of a faculty of
thought, a power of synthesis or analysis, inherent in his mind.
It is a combining or a separating *in thought, of thoughts* (or 'ideas'),
by thinking. And the result of his making—i.e. the judgement itself,
that which is true or false—is a psychical (or 'ideal') product.
It is a complex or compound 'idea', composed of simple (or
simpler) 'ideas'.

But the psychical product, which is a judgement, differs (as we
know) from all other facts of mind—from, for example, an emotion
or a volition, from an imagination, a prayer, or an interrogation—
by its distinctive function or property, which is part of its nominal
definition; viz. that it alone can be, and must be, true or false.
To make a judgement is to combine 'ideas'—but to combine them
so, that my judgement is an assertion (in ultimate analysis, an
inner or tacit assertion, i.e. an 'opinion' or 'belief') about the
facts. And this distinctive property of the judgement depends upon
the special nature of its constituents and the special mode in
which they are combined. For (*a*) the 'ideas' which are its constituents—the sensations, memories, thoughts, which I 'put
together' when I judge—*represent* ('are like', for example, or
'signify' or 'symbolize') elements or characters of the real world
(the world 'without', and independent of, my mind—the world
which, by judging, I hope more fully to know).

And (*b*) if I am to make a judgement, I must 'combine' two
ideas by predicating (affirming or denying) one of the other; and
this is only possible if they 'represent' elements capable of constituting a genuine unity in the world of fact. The 'idea', which in
my thought—in the ideal synthesis which constitutes the judgement—is 'subject', must represent—to take the commonest and
simplest example—a substantial element or substance; and the
'idea', which in my thought (in the synthesis which constitutes
my judgement) is 'predicate', must represent an adjectival
element—an action (say) or passion, a quality or modification, of a
substance. Hence, though the process of judging is an activity
in (and of) the mind; though the combining (or separating) is
'ideal' and not 'real', an arranging in thought and of ideas, not a

---

[1] Cf. *Essay*, ii. 1, § 2; above, Study II, pp. 111 ff.

development in reality and of the fact—yet the product, i.e. the complex fact or state of mind which is the judgement, may (and, when it is true, actually does) 'agree with', 'represent', 'correspond', or 'conform' to, a single (but complex) fact or reality 'without' the mind; i.e. other than, and independent of, the judging mind at least, if not also other than, and independent of, each and every mind.

2. 'What theory of the judgement,' I may be asked, '"conforms in principle" to a position so crude and confused? It is often said, no doubt, and supposed, that nothing *in the end* is true or false but a state or attitude of mind, an "opinion" or "belief"—a mental affirmation or negation which, if expressed in words, would be the assertion that S is (or is not) P. And it is often said, no doubt, that its truth or falsity is its agreement or disagreement with a matter of fact—a real something, actually possessing or not-possessing a real property. But all this is no more than the loose language and loose thinking of unreflecting people.'

On the contrary I venture to think that the position I have sketched, in spite of its crudities and confusions, underlies more than one well-known theory of the judgement and of the truth and falsity which belong to it. And I will try to support this assertion by a brief consideration of Aristotle's account of ἀπόφανσις (the λόγος ἀποφαντικός) and Locke's account of the proposition. For both these theories (though neither of them is entirely consistent with itself, and though in many respects they differ greatly from one another) agree that to judge is (fundamentally and in essence) to combine ideally psychical (or ideal) elements; that a judgement is a complex or compound 'fact of mind', which is true or false owing to the representative character of its constituents and the mode of their combination; and that truth or falsity consists therefore in an 'extrinsic relation', in a relation of 'correspondence or 'discordance' between facts in some sense 'within', and facts in some sense 'without', the judging mind.

(i) *Aristotle's account of ἀπόφανσις (De Interpr.* i–vi). In the account Aristotle gives in the *De Interpr.* of the 'assertion' which is true or false, he is elaborating and modifying a doctrine which Plato had suggested in the *Sophist.*[1] And in order to understand Aristotle's theory, it will be best to begin with the simpler form of it which Plato there puts forward. As Plato there explains, speech (λόγος) is simply thought (διάνοια) expressed in language; the only

[1]   259 E ff.

difference is that '*thought* is the conversation of the soul with itself taking place without voice, while *speech* is the vocal stream issuing from the soul through the lips'.[1] The elements of speech, therefore (the words or terms, at any rate the nouns and verbs), are at the same time elements of thought, or units of meaning. Every term therefore shares the general character of thought—a character which Plato takes for granted—in that it 'reveals', 'signifies', 'is a sign of', some real thing or fact. And, as Plato insists,[2] there is a close parallelism between terms (τὰ τῆς φωνῆς σημεῖα) on the one hand and facts (τὰ πράγματα) on the other; for just as some facts combine and fit together to form a single-yet-complex fact (a fact of a higher order) while others refuse, so some terms combine and fit together (while others will not) to form a λόγος—i.e. a single yet complex significant utterance, a unit of speech of a higher order.

For terms—the elements of significant speech—fall into two groups: viz. those which signify (which mean and name) actions or inactivities (*verbs*: e.g. 'runs', 'walks', 'sleeps'), and those which signify (which mean and name) agents or patients (*nouns*: e.g. 'lion', 'stag', 'horse', 'Theaetetus'). Now if the speaker 'mixes' or 'weaves together' a verb and a noun (*not* two nouns or two verbs), the two units of significant utterance 'fit' and constitute the 'first', or smallest and most rudimentary, 'combination' or 'compound':[3] a single-yet-complex significant utterance which is called a λόγος (a 'statement' or 'proposition'). For, in thus weaving together a noun and a verb, the speaker is not merely naming an agent and an action, but 'putting them together'; he is 'completing' something, bringing about some sort of conclusion, saying something which throws light upon the actual (past, present, or future) state of things.[4]

To this account Plato makes what he calls a 'slight' addition—but in reality the new point, to which he calls attention, is of fundamental importance. 'Every λόγος', he says,[5] 'must be something's (or somebody's) λόγος' (λόγον ἀναγκαῖον . . . τινὸς εἶναι λόγον) and its being true or false is directly connected with this character-

---

[1] I quote Burnet's translation of *Soph.* 263 E: cf. also *Theaet.* 189 E ff., 206 D.

[2] 262 D ff.

[3] Cf. 262 C: τότε δ᾽ ἥρμοσέν τε καὶ λόγος ἐγένετο εὐθὺς ἡ πρώτη συμπλοκή, σχεδὸν τῶν λόγων ὁ πρῶτός τε καὶ σμικρότατος. And cf. 262 D: τῷ πλέγματι τούτῳ τὸ ὄνομα ἐφθεγξάμεθα λόγον.

[4] Cf. *Soph.* 262 D: δηλοῖ γὰρ ἤδη πού τότε περὶ τῶν ὄντων ἢ γιγνομένων ἢ γεγονότων ἢ μελλόντων, καὶ οὐκ ὀνομάζει μόνον ἀλλά τι περαίνει, συμπλέκων τὰ ῥήματα τοῖς ὀνόμασι.

[5] 262 E 5.

istic. For, as he goes on to explain, every λόγος is 'of', i.e. 'about', the thing (viz. the agent or patient) which is signified by its noun; and, in being 'about' it, it is descriptive of it—belongs to it, as *its* description. Thus if I say 'Theaetetus is sitting', I am 'putting together a thing' (a patient) 'and an action' (or inactivity) 'by the help of a noun and a verb',[1] and the result is a significant statement about Theaetetus which at the same time is—or is intended to be —a description or definition of his present state. And it is 'true' or 'false' according as it is a correct or incorrect description of a complex fact—viz. of Theaetetus-in-his-actual-state-of-action-or-inactivity.

The 'combination of noun and verb', which is a 'λόγος' in the sense of a 'judgement', is thus connected with the συμπλοκή ὀνομάτων (the weaving-together of *nouns*, each the name of a simple element of reality) which Plato identifies in the *Theaetetus* with a 'λόγος' in the sense of a definition or descriptive formula.[2] The connexion thus indicated between the λόγος which is a 'descriptive judgement' and the λόγος which is a 'descriptive formula' or definition is plain enough. Suppose, for example, a complex thing with many constituent parts—say, a wagon.[3] The λόγος, which 'puts together' the names of its constituents, is a definition (i.e. a descriptive formula) of the whole—an enumeration of its parts. Similarly, every true judgement *about* Theaetetus, which affirms of him one of his 'actions' or 'inactions', is—so far as it goes— descriptive of him. *What Theaetetus is* would be expressed— Theaetetus would be defined—in the totality of true λόγοι, such that in each of them Theaetetus was the logical subject and one of his characteristics the predicate. But in the *Sophist* Plato's primary concern is to bring out the difference—to distinguish the

---

[1] Cf. 262 E 12: . . . συνθεὶς πρᾶγμα πράξει δι' ὀνόματος καὶ ῥήματος.

[2] Cf. *Theaet.* 201 D ff.—a passage, of which no doubt Plato's account in the *Sophist* is intended to remind the reader. According to the theory which is developed in the *Theaetetus*—a theory introduced as one 'of which Socrates has a hazy recollection', which he 'seems to have heard in a dream'—there are certain elements, certain primary unanalysable constituents, of which we ourselves, and everything else in the universe, are compounded. These simple reals, these 'letters of the alphabet of reality' (τὰ πρῶτα οἱονπερεῖ στοιχεῖα), can only be 'perceived', immediately apprehended, known by 'acquaintance' (they are αἰσθητά). Since they are simple (without parts, unanalysable), it is impossible to describe or define them. They can only be 'named', not elucidated by any rational procedure. They are ἄγνωστα, ἄλογα: cannot be stated or set out in a λόγος. For it is the very essence of a λόγος to be a συμπλοκὴ ὀνομάτων—and therefore no *simple* real, but only a complex of two or more reals, can possess a λόγος.

[3] Cf. *Theaet.* 207 A.

συμπλοκή of a noun and verb, which is a judgement, from the
συμπλοκή ὀνομάτων which is a definition. And here, as we have seen,
he tells us only that, if I judge, I am not merely naming, but
'completing' something—'bringing the matter to a conclusion'.
What he means, however, comes out more clearly in a later
passage.[1] In λόγοι (i.e. judgements), he says, there is a familiar
distinction between affirmations and negations. Now—since λόγος
is simply spoken διάνοια—we must recognize an analogous distinction in *thought*, i.e. in the silent conversation which the soul carries
on with itself (in his ψυχῆς διάλογος πρὸς ἑαυτήν). These silent
analogues of the affirmative and negative 'statements' (or λόγοι)
are (Plato says) what are called δόξαι—i.e. opinions, beliefs. And
he identifies δόξαι with conclusions terminating the inner conversation or discussion.[2] Thus the distinctive function, the
differentia, of the λόγος, which is a judgement (and not a mere
description), is—so apparently Plato means—*to terminate a process
of doubt or debate, to bring an argument* (an argument within the
soul) *to a conclusion*.

It is no doubt with this passage of the *Sophist* in his mind that
Aristotle formulates his own account of the λόγος ἀποφαντικός (the
assertion which is true or false, i.e. the proposition or judgement) in
the *De Interpretatione*.[3] In making that account more definite and
systematic, he introduces certain modifications which can hardly
be regarded as improvements. Thus, Plato (as we saw) was content
to say simply that thought, whether it goes on silently in the soul
or is 'imprinted on' (or 'mirrored in') the stream of articulate
sound issuing through the lips,[4] 'reveals', 'means', 'signifies',
elements of the real world, or real complexes which those elements
combine to form. But in Aristotle's more elaborate (and more
questionable) version, speech draws apart from, and is (not one

---

[1] 263 E–264 B.   [2] 264 B I.

[3] In what follows, I shall be summarizing the account of ἀπόφανσις which
Aristotle gives in the *De Interpr.*, assumes in the *Categories*, and never *explicitly*
modifies or withdraws. As a theory of the judgement, the account is obviously in
many respects inadequate; it fails even to recognize (to say nothing of solving)
difficulties connected with the subject which Aristotle himself draws attention to,
and discusses, elsewhere (e.g. in the *De Anima*, *Post. Anal.*, *Metaph.*). But I am
not now concerned with the historical question what Aristotle's mature and
considered theory of the judgement may have been, or how he would have modified
the somewhat crude and primitive doctrine of the *De Interpr.*, if he had returned
to the subject at a later stage of his philosophical development. For my present
purpose, it is enough to show that the doctrine, which Aristotle in fact puts
forward in the *De Interpr.*, exemplifies the 'subjective position' we are to consider.

[4] Cf. *Theaet.* 206 D.

with, but) related to, the thought which it expresses or utters; and thought 'reveals' fact by resembling it. Articulate utterances, Aristotle says,[1] τὰ ἐν τῇ φωνῇ (spoken words, phrases, sentences), are symbols or signs (σύμβολα, σημεῖα) of what goes on in the soul, of psychical states and changes (τὰ ἐν τῇ ψυχῇ παθήματα, παθήματα τῆς ψυχῆς). *What I say*, therefore, symbolizes a happening in, and of, my soul; expresses or 'interprets', for example, my present feeling, emotion, sensation, thought. If you hear me, my utterance will be to you a 'sign', for example, of a sensation (αἴσθημα) or thought (νόημα) which I am now experiencing; and will provoke in your soul a corresponding πάθημα. If, for example, I say 'horse', you will recognize that the thought of a horse is 'in' my mind—and the thought of a horse will 'occur in' your mind. *Only, however, under certain conditions.* A language is a system of symbols or signs; its articulate sounds express and evoke determinate psychical states and changes. But the connexion between these symbols or signs and the symbolized or signified is not 'natural', but artificial or 'conventional';[2] hence it is not 'universal', but holds and is recognized only within a limited time and area. Every articulate utterance, then, is *for those who understand the language to which it belongs* the sign of a determinate psychical state or change.

Now the changes or states which occur in a soul—at any rate those of which Aristotle is here primarily speaking, viz. thoughts, memories, imaginations, sensations, &c.—are (so he asserts) '*likenesses*' (ὁμοιώματα) *of the 'facts'* (τὰ πράγματα). And since there is one, and only one, set of facts—one, and only one, reality—the 'thoughts' or other psychical states, in which they are mirrored or copied (which are 'likenesses' of them), are *identical* in whatever soul they occur.[3] Hence, articulate utterances, no matter to what language they belong, 'symbolize' thoughts (or other psychical states) which are *the same* for all men, in that they are 'likenesses' of *the same* (i.e. the only) facts. We can therefore neglect, or abstract from, the idiosyncrasies of the different languages, and regard the whole sphere of articulate utterance (all that is spoken; τὰ ἐν τῇ φωνῇ = τὰ λεγόμενα, *Categ.* 1ᵃ 16) as a single system of symbols. Each symbol signifies *immediately* a determinate psychical state, the same in all the souls in which it may occur; and signifies

---

[1] *De Interpr.* 16ᵃ 4 ff.

[2] κατὰ συνθήκην: cf. e.g. 16ᵃ 19–27, 17ᵃ 1–2.

[3] So at least Aristotle says, *De Interpr.* 16ᵃ 6–7; though one would suppose that the thoughts in the different souls are *more or less* like their originals—i.e. *have an identical reference* but are not necessarily themselves 'identical'.

mediately (i.e. through the uniquely determinate psychical state) a determinate fact—one of the facts which constitute the Real World.[1]

Still following in the lines of Plato's sketch in the *Sophist*, Aristotle proceeds to distinguish, within the sphere of significant sound or speech, (*a*) unit-utterances (φάσεις), (*b*) complex or compound utterances (λόγοι) and, as one species of the latter, (*c*) assertions that are true or false, propositions or judgements (λόγος ἀποφαντικός, κατάφασις and ἀπόφασις).

(*a*) A φάσις or unit-utterance symbolizes (expresses and evokes) a single (incomposite and indivisible) thought, and through it 'names' (designates) a single (incomposite) fact or element of fact. The unit-utterance is, so to say, an atomic element of speech conveying an atomic element of meaning; it is significant as a whole, but no part of it is significant by itself. If I say, for example, 'Churchill', 'man', 'white', 'to cut', each of these 'expressions' is a φάσις. No doubt 'Churchill' is a composite noun, and each of its component syllables might be uttered separately; so uttered, each would be a unit-utterance conveying its own unit-meaning. But when I say 'Churchill', the meanings, which 'Church' and 'Hill' would have if they were spoken separately, form no part of the meaning of my utterance. No doubt, also, 'Churchill' as he exists *in rerum natura* is not incomposite; he has many parts and attributes, &c. But still, if I say 'Churchill', my utterance,

---

[1] Cf. *De Interpr.* 16ª 3 ff. Ἔστι μὲν οὖν τὰ ἐν τῇ φωνῇ τῶν ἐν τῇ ψυχῇ παθημάτων σύμβολα, καὶ τὰ γραφόμενα τῶν ἐν τῇ φωνῇ. καὶ ὥσπερ οὐδὲ γράμματα πᾶσι τὰ αὐτά, οὐδὲ φωναὶ αἱ αὐταί· ὧν μέντοι ταῦτα σημεῖα πρώτως, ταῦτα πᾶσι παθήματα τῆς ψυχῆς, καὶ ὧν ταῦτα ὁμοιώματα, πράγματα ἢ δὴ ταὐτά. No attempt is made in the *De Interpr.* to explain or defend the assertion that the παθήματα τῆς ψυχῆς are 'likenesses' of the facts. In the next sentence (16ª 8–9) the reader is referred to the *De Anima* for an account of the παθήματα τῆς ψυχῆς. But in the *De Anima* there is no express reference to this assumption—no repetition or discussion of the view that, for example, αἰσθήματα and νοήματα are mental (psychical) 'copies' of originals external to, and independent of, the mind (soul). In his treatment of perception and thought in the *De Anima* (as in the *Metaph.*) Aristotle works with the conception of a form which, *qua* informing a matter, *is* the reality of the thing or fact, and (*qua* present in the soul or mind) *is* the (adequate) perception or (true) thought thereof; cf. above, Study I, pp. 25–7. Yet perhaps Aristotle would have said that an adequate perception or true thought is 'like' the fact, precisely because the same form is embodied in different matters—in psychical changes and in physical stuff? It is almost incredible to me that Aristotle could have written the *De Interpr.* after the *De Anima*. Hence Maier's proposal (cf. Ross, *Aristotle*, p. 10), to transfer the reference from 16ª 8–9 to 16ª 13 and to take it as relating to *De Anima* iii. 6, does not appeal to me as a satisfactory solution. The reference, I should like to maintain, is a note added by a later editor or scribe.

taken strictly and precisely, names a single fact. The thought it symbolizes is the 'thought', of (according to Aristotle, the 'likeness' of) an individual *qua* single and incomposite.[1]

It is clear that the class of unit-utterances includes all utterances, in which (as Plato expresses it)[2] the speaker 'does no more than name something' (ὀνομάζει μόνον). Hence every 'term' thus spoken might be called an ὄνομα or 'name'. Aristotle sometimes uses ὄνομα in this wide sense, applying it not only to a noun, or an adjective,[3] but even to a verb[4] so far as it merely names an 'action' or 'inaction'.[5] But in defining ὄνομα,[6] he restricts it to nouns;[7] and in defining ῥῆμα,[8] he emphasizes a character which the verb possesses not when uttered in isolation, but only in the judgement, or only by suggesting the supplementation it would receive in a judgement—and so sharply distinguishes it from the ὄνομα.[9]

(*b*) A complex or compound utterance (λόγος) unites within its single meaning—as parts contributing to the whole—the atomic meanings of two or more unit-utterances. Hence the 'thought' or 'state of soul' (πάθημα τῆς ψυχῆς), which a complex utterance expresses and evokes, is complex or compound. It is 'one', but its unity is the union of two or more 'thoughts' or psychical states. It is a whole, symbolized by the λόγος as a whole; and it contains, as its parts, the atomic thoughts (the units of meaning) which are severally symbolized by the φάσεις, i.e. the unit-utterances composing the λόγος. And the fact (πρᾶγμα), which a complex utterance reveals (or designates) by means of the complex thought it symbolizes—the real original, of which the complex thought (the union of two or more unit-thoughts) is (or is intended to be) a 'likeness'—is correspondingly complex, a whole of parts or some kind of union of two or more elements.

(*c*) Now there are several varieties of λόγοι or complex utterances, differing from one another in the kind of unity of the meaning

---

[1] Aristotle calls these unit-utterances 'φάσεις' in contrast to 'judgements' (ἀποφάνσεις, i.e. καταφάσεις or ἀποφάσεις: cf. *De Interpr.* 17ᵃ 17), thus modifying Plato's terminology (cf. *Sophist.* 263 E, where φάσις = κατάφασις). But he does not keep consistently to this use of φάσις as opposed to ἀπόφανσις in his other works: cf. Bonitz, *Index*, s.v.

[2] *Sophist.* 262 D.

[3] Cf. *De Interpr.* 16ᵃ 15.   [4] Cf. *De Interpr.* 16ᵇ 19–21.

[5] Cf. Bywater, *Aristotle on the Art of Poetry*, p. 274.

[6] *De Interpr.*, ch. 2.

[7] And even to nouns in the nominative case. But I must not get entangled in the *minutiae* of Aristotle's doctrine. Cf., on the whole subject, Bywater, l.c., pp. 275–6.

[8] Verb: *De Interpr.*, ch. 3.   [9] Cf. below, pp. 193–4.

they respectively convey (in the structure of the psychical state, the complex 'thought', they respectively symbolize), and differing therefore also in the kind of unity of the complex fact (the πρᾶγμα) of which that complex psychical state is a 'likeness'.[1] And Aristotle proceeds to distinguish the special variety of complex utterance, with which he is concerned in the *De Interpretatione*, from all others—to distinguish the proposition or judgement, the λόγος ἀποφαντικός, from, for example, the λόγος which is a prayer[2] and the λόγος which is a definition.[3]

The complex utterance which is a judgement, so Aristotle points out, differs from all other λόγοι (and indeed from all other utterances) because it not only 'means' something or 'is significant' (is σημαντικός, σημαίνει, &c.) but, taken as a whole, 'declares' being or not-being—'declares' that something 'is' or 'is not'—and therefore is (and must be) either true or false. So the 'complex thought', or combination-of-thoughts,[4] which the λόγος ἀποφαντικός symbolizes—the state of mind it expresses and evokes—is distinguished from all other 'thoughts' and psychical states (from all other παθήματα τῆς ψυχῆς), because it not only is 'a likeness of' (and in that sense represents or presents) a fact, but is (or involves) a tacit declaration (an 'ideal assertion') or belief that the original it resembles is or is not fact, exists or does not exist *in rerum natura*. From this point of view, it is the *state of mind*, rather than the utterance (the spoken or written statement) that symbolizes it, which is (and must be) either true or false. What distinguishes the λόγος ἀποφαντικός from all other λόγοι—from, say, a definition or a prayer—is, strictly and in ultimate analysis, a characteristic

---

[1] Cf. Bywater, l.c., pp. 270, 276-7.

[2] εὐχή: cf. *De Interpr.* 17ᵃ 4.

[3] Ib. 17ᵃ 11-15. I do not know of any attempt in Aristotle's works to characterize the unity of the 'thought' conveyed in a prayer, or the unity of the fact it 'copies'—if it *does* copy any fact. But he carefully discusses the mode of unity which characterizes the definition and the *definiendum*. He maintains that the many 'terms' composing the definitory formula (the complex utterance, which is a definition or ὁρισμός) convey a 'single' thought—viz. the thought of a genuinely single thing (substance or attribute). And he tries to show that the thing defined (at least when the thing defined is a substance) is genuinely one, though the definitory formula contains *at least two* terms and seems therefore to designate two (or more) distinct and separable elements. Cf. the elaborate treatment of ὁρισμός (both of substances and of attributes) in *Post. Anal. B* (particularly 93ᵇ 29 ff.); and, for the unity of the *definiendum* which is a substance, cf. *Met. Z* 12 and *H* 6.

[4] Cf. *De Anima* 430ᵃ 26 ff.: ἐν οἷς δὲ καὶ τὸ ψεῦδος καὶ τὸ ἀληθές, σύνθεσίς τις ἤδη νοημάτων ὥσπερ ἓν ὄντων.

constitution and structure in the thought (the διάνοια, the σύνθεσις νοημάτων) expressed and evoked by this form of speech.[1]

Enough has been said already to show that Aristotle's theory of the λόγος ἀποφαντικός 'conforms in principle' to what I called the 'subjective position'. But (with a view to the criticism of the 'subjective position' which I am presently to attempt) it will be as well to enter a little further into the details of Aristotle's account, so as to bring out more definitely *the kind* of being or not-being which (according to him) the judgement 'declares', and *the sense in which* the declaration must be either true or false.[2]

It will be remembered that, in the *Sophist*,[3] Plato identifies the judgement with the 'first' or most rudimentary 'combination of terms' by which the speaker throws light upon the actual (past, present, or future) state of things. This πρώτη συμπλοκή—this first and smallest of all complex unities or compounds in the sphere of significant speech—is a descriptive (narrative, historical) judgement in which an action or inaction is affirmed or denied of some individual agent or patient. Now Aristotle agrees substantially with Plato in treating the singular descriptive judgement as primary and fundamental; and as typical of all judgements. He seems to hold that all judgements—i.e. all complex utterances, which declare being or not-being, and so are either true or false— are derived from, or compounded out of, a combination of two unit-utterances, which he calls 'the simple declaration' (ἁπλῆ ἀπόφανσις), and which, as he describes it, is in effect identical with the πρώτη συμπλοκή of the *Sophist*. And we must, I think, take it to be his view that the analysis he gives of the constituents and structure of this rudimentary ἀπόφανσις exhibits (so to say) the essence of all judgements.

The simple declaration, then, consists of two φάσεις or unit-utterances only; and they are combined in one or the other of two alternative modes. By one φάσις—a spoken noun—the speaker symbolizes the thought 'of' ('resembling') a substance; i.e. 'names' a substance, viz. (in ultimate analysis) an individual (thing, animal, or person) *in rerum natura*.[4] The other φάσις must

---

[1] Cf., for the above, *De Interpr.* 16ᵃ 9–18, 17ᵃ 3–5, 23ᵃ 32 ff.; *De Anima*, 430ᵃ 26 ff. Cf. also *Metaph.* E 4 and Θ 10 on the 'true' which is opposed to the 'false', and which is ἐν διανοίᾳ or διανοίας τι πάθος. Cf. above, Study I, pp. 24–7.

[2] Cf. (for what follows), in addition to *De Interpr.*, chs. i–iv, the opening pages (1ᵃ 16–2ᵇ 6) of the *Categories*.

[3] Above, pp. 185–7.

[4] The noun—φάσις—signifies the 'subject' (τὸ καθ᾽ οὗ κατηγορεῖται, τὸ ὑποκείμενον)

be a spoken verb; and by it the speaker symbolizes the thought 'of' ('resembling') some action or passion or adjectival element of fact; i.e. names or designates something which is such as to 'belong to' or 'inhere in' a substance. But this second φάσις, besides thus naming an adjectival element of fact (besides thus signifying what in the ordinary text-books of logic is called 'the predicate[1]'), has (or acquires), in so far as it is combined with the first to form a single (though complex) utterance, an additional significance. For if I say, for example, 'Kallias is running' (or 'did not run') the (inflected) verb not only names an action but, in addition, signifies its *present attachment* to (or *past severance* from) the substance, Kallias. It is precisely this additional significance of a dated nexus (of a past, present, or future attachment or severance) that characterizes the 'verbal φάσις' and distinguishes it from the unit-utterance which is a spoken noun.[2]

What Aristotle calls the 'simple declaration', therefore, and treats as typical of all judgements, is a noun and a verb so spoken together as to form a complex utterance which, as a whole, affirms or denies that an adjectival element (B) was, is, or will be, united with (or severed from) a self-subsistent element or substance (A). I say 'affirms or denies'. For though Aristotle regards the affirmative judgement (the κατάφασις) as more fundamental than, and prior to, the negative (the ἀπόφασις), the 'simple declaration' may take either form (the form of an affirmative or negative statement) indifferently. I am making 'a simple declaration', in other words, whether I say 'A is B' or 'A is not-B' and so attribute B or not-B to A; or whether I say 'A is-not B' or 'A is-not not-B' and so remove B or not-B from A.[3] And the simple declaration, whether it takes the form of an affirmative or negative statement, is (and must be) *either* true-not-false *or* false-not-true.[4] For the affirmative

---

of the judgement: and this (in ultimate analysis) is—in the language of the categories—a 'πρώτη οὐσία' or—in Aristotle's more usual terminology—a 'τόδε τι' (= a designable substantial, self-subsistent, somewhat: 'a placed and dated specimen of some definable and substantial nature or kind', cf. J. A. Smith in *Classical Review*, vol. xxxv, p. 19).

[1] In Aristotle's terminology, the 'predicate' (τὸ κατηγορούμενον) covers all that is contributed by the second φάσις—i.e. by the inflected verb or by the attribute *plus* copula. In, for example, 'Socrates is pale' or 'Theaetetus ran', 'is-pale' or 'ran' would be the 'predicates'. What is predicated of Socrates is a present-being-pale, and what is predicated of Theaetetus is a past-act-of-running.

[2] Cf. the definition of ῥῆμα in *De Interpr.* 16ᵇ 6–11.

[3] Cf. *De Interpr.* 17ᵃ 8–37; *Post. Anal.* 72ᵃ 11–14.

[4] i.e. true as opposed to a possible error, and false as contrasted with a possible truth: cf. above, Study I, p. 26.

declaration is true-not-false, if there exists, at and during the appropriate time, *in rerum natura* an original of the complex thought it symbolizes—i.e. an actual complex fact or event, a substance A positively characterized by possessing B, or by being such that it excludes B; while if such an original does not exist, or not at the appropriate time, the affirmative declaration is false-not-true. And similarly, the negative declaration is true-not-false if the complex which it denies (viz. A-united-with-B or A-severed-from-B) is really non-existent (at the appropriate time) in the world of actual fact; while otherwise the negative declaration is false-not-true.[1]

(ii) *Locke's theory of the proposition*. Locke's treatment of the proposition, and of truth and falsehood, is entangled with the intricacies of his philosophical system as a whole. His exposition is encumbered by loosely formulated distinctions of doubtful validity—to which, moreover, he does not consistently adhere; and it is obscured by the ambiguity of his use of the term 'idea'— a source of confusion which we encountered before, in examining his view of 'sensation'.[2] It is therefore difficult to show, by a brief consideration of Locke's account of the proposition, that it, too, 'conforms in principle to', falls within the general framework of, the 'subjective position'.[3] A *brief* consideration may do substantial injustice to Locke. What follows, however, is offered as summarizing, to the best of my belief, the gist of the doctrine which Locke endeavours—not very successfully—to expound.

(*a*) 'Truth', Locke says in the chapter headed 'Of the General Nature of Truth',[4]

'seems to me, in the proper import of the word, to signify nothing but *the joining or separating of signs, as the things signified by them do agree or disagree with one another*. The *joining* or *separating* of signs here meant, is what by another name we call propositions. So that truth belongs only to propositions; whereof there are two sorts, viz. mental and verbal; as there are two sorts of signs commonly made use of, viz. *ideas* and words.'

Taken literally and as it stands, this passage sharply distinguishes two sorts of propositions, and two sorts of truth 'in the proper import of the word'. There are, first, *mental propositions*.

---

[1] So I think, in spite of obvious difficulties and apparent absurdities, Aristotle's doctrine must be interpreted.

[2] Cf. Study II, especially pp. 116–18.   [3] Cf. above, p. 184.

[4] *Essay*, iv. 5, § 2; and cf. ii. 32, § 19.

In these, as Locke explains presently,[1] '*The ideas* in our under-standings *are* without the use of words, *put together or separated* by the mind, perceiving or judging of their agreement or disagree-ment'. And they are true or false according as the ideal junction or severance 'agrees or disagrees to' (i.e. corresponds or fails to correspond with) a real junction or severance of the facts, i.e. of the things signified by the ideas. In respect to *such* propositions, then, Locke's account conforms beyond question to the 'subjective position'. To make a 'mental proposition' *is* 'to combine ideally ideal elements'; to form 'a complex or compound fact of mind, which is true or false owing to the representative character of its constituents and the mode of their combination'; and the truth or falsity of a mental proposition—truth or falsehood of *thought*, as Locke calls it[2]—clearly consists 'in an extrinsic relation, in a relation of correspondence or discordance between facts "within", and facts "without", the judging mind'.[3]

But then (if we are to take this passage literally) there is also a second sort of propositions, viz. *verbal propositions*; and it seems impossible to bring Locke's account of them, and of their mode of being true or false, within the outline of the 'subjective position'. For 'verbal propositions', as he explains, '*are words*, the signs of our *ideas, put together or separated in affirmative or negative sentences*'. To make a verbal proposition, then, is to combine words; and words are not ideal or psychical elements, but physical. They are, at all events, as Locke expresses it, 'the signs made by sounds'. And this 'complex', this affirmative or negative sentence, seems to be true (or false) according as it corresponds (or fails to corre-spond) to a 'mental proposition', i.e. to a junction or severance of ideas as it actually exists, or is made, in the speaker's mind. 'Truth', Locke says, speaking of verbal propositions,[4] 'is the marking down in words the agreement or disagreement of *ideas*, as it is. Falsehood is the marking down in words the agreement or disagreement of *ideas* otherwise than it is.'[5] Thus it appears (if we

---

[1] § 5.
[2] Cf., e.g., l.c., § 3.
[3] Cf. above, p. 184.
[4] In iv. 5, § 9.
[5] Locke includes (it will be remembered) *Identity* or *Diversity, Relation, Co-existence* or *Necessary Connexion*, and *Real Existence*, under the vague heading of 'Agreement or Connexion, and Disagreement or Repugnancy' of ideas one with another (cf. iv. 1, §§ 2–3). He 'supposes' that 'all the knowledge we have, or are capable of' is 'contained . . . within these four sorts of agreement or disagree-ment'. For, he says, 'all that we know or can affirm concerning any of "our *ideas*" is, that it is, or is not, the same with some other [e.g. blue is not yellow: is a colour]; that it does, or does not, always coexist with some other *idea* in the same subject

really are to take these and similar statements of Locke literally and at their face value) that the truth or falsity of a verbal proposition (truth or falsehood *of words*) consists in a relation not between thought and things, but between sound and thought—or rather that, if 'truth of words' consists in a relation (or is a 'correspondence') at all analogous to that which constitutes 'truth of thought', the *proposition* (i.e. the affirmative or negative sentence) is, in this case, the fact 'without', which agrees to (or corresponds with), a fact 'within', the judging mind.[1]

Any such literal interpretation of Locke's statements, it is abundantly clear, would force us to attribute to him an utterly incoherent doctrine of the proposition and of truth. He would be maintaining in effect that there are two sundered and heterogeneous sorts of propositions, and two different kinds of truth 'in the proper import of the word'. And, indeed, it is easy to show, by pursuing the same literal insistence on what he says, that the 'truth of thought' and 'truth of words', which *at the beginning of the chapter* are distinguished within truth in its 'proper import' and connected respectively with mental and verbal propositions, are identified *at the end* with 'Metaphysical' and 'Moral' Truth—i.e. two 'other sorts of truth' which Locke dismisses as not being truth 'taken in the strict sense beforementioned'. For a *verbal proposition* is true if it agrees to the junction or severance of ideas as it is in the speaker's mind. And what else is that but 'Moral Truth', which Locke defines[2] as 'speaking of things according to the persuasion of our own minds, though the proposition we speak agree not to the reality of things'? And a *mental proposition* is true if it agrees to a junction or severance of facts 'in real existence'; and that—and nothing else—is what Locke's somewhat confused description of 'Metaphysical Truth' amounts to.[3]

[*Coexistence or Necessary Connexion*: e.g. iron is susceptible of magnetical impressions]; that it has this or that relation to some other *idea* [e.g. two triangles upon equal bases between two parallels are equal]; or that it has a real existence without the mind [e.g. God is]' (iv. 1 § 7).

[1] Or would Locke have said that a verbal proposition is as much 'within' the mind as is the junction or severance of ideas it signifies? *Sound*, we must remember, is one of the so-called 'secondary qualities'—i.e. not *as such* a quality characterizing the external bodies, but an 'idea' produced in the mind by primary qualities of the insensible parts of the 'real' or external body (cf. above, Study II, pp. 118–20). Moreover, *words* (as we saw) are not 'sounds', but the 'signs made by sounds'. Perhaps, therefore, we ought to say that, if 'truth of words' consists in a 'correspondence' at all, *both relata*, both complex structures which 'correspond' with one another, are 'facts within' the judging mind.

[2] Loc. cit., § 11.   [3] Cf. loc. cit., § 11 and ii. 32, § 2.

(*b*) A philosopher, no doubt, must be held to mean what he says; but what he says must be interpreted liberally as well as literally— or rather, the 'literal interpretation', on which alone we have a duty to insist and a right to rely, must take account of *all* his (relevant) sayings and reproduce not their *bare* letter, but the spirit in their letter. Now even in this chapter[1] there are statements[2] which show that the preceding 'literal interpretation' misses the spirit of the doctrine that Locke is trying (however clumsily) to develop; and if the main outlines of his philosophy are borne in mind, something more like a coherent or unitary theory of the proposition and of truth will suggest itself.[3]

The task which Locke sets himself in the *Essay* is to determine the nature, limits, and validity of knowledge. Now, it will be remembered that by 'idea' Locke means 'whatsoever the mind perceives in itself, or is the immediate *object* of perception, thought, or understanding'.[4] 'It is evident', he says,[5] 'that the mind knows not things immediately, but only by the intervention of the *ideas* it has of them.' It is further evident—so Locke assumes and says —that *ideas* are 'all the materials of our reason and knowledge',[6] that 'our knowledge is only conversant about' ideas[7] and that 'we can have knowledge no further than we have *ideas*'.[8] Hence, in order to achieve his main task, he undertakes, as a necessary preliminary, an exhaustive survey of these materials of our knowledge—a complete inventory and classification of our ideas.

There is no need, for my present purpose, to enter into the details of this 'account of the original, sorts and extent of our *ideas*', to which the second book of the *Essay* is devoted.[9] But it is necessary to dwell for a little upon the first broad division on which Locke's classification is based—the division of Ideas into 'simple' and 'complex'.

(i) *Simple ideas* (as we saw) are those of sensation and of

---

[1] iv. 5.

[2] Cf., e.g., § 6, where Locke distinguishes between a 'truth of words' which is 'purely verbal and trifling' and one which is '*real* and instructive . . . the object of that real knowledge, which we have spoken of already'; and the further development of this distinction in § 8.

[3] It would be going too far to say a 'coherent or unitary theory'. The most that can be said is that Locke's conception of the proposition and of truth is not so utterly incoherent as his exposition in iv. 5 makes it appear.

[4] ii. 8, § 8: cf. above, Study II, p. 115. [5] iv. 4, § 3.

[6] ii. 1, § 2: and cf. ii. 33, § 19, where he hesitates whether to speak of these ambiguous entities as 'instruments or materials of our knowledge'.

[7] iv. 1, § 1. [8] iv. 3, § 1.

[9] Cf., e.g., ii. 33, § 19; iii. 9, § 21.

reflection. They are not '*all* the materials of knowledge', but the 'materials of *all* our knowledge'. Ultimately all our knowledge is based upon and derived from them—or so, at least, Locke thinks and tries to maintain, in spite of admissions to which he is driven. In receiving them, we are passive. We cannot refuse to have them; we cannot alter them, when they are 'offered' to us; we cannot 'blot them out', nor 'make new ones' ourselves. Simple ideas of *sensation* are 'conveyed into our mind by the senses', impressed upon them 'by outward objects'. And simple ideas of *reflection* are 'offered' to our observation so that our mind cannot but have them when it 'reflects'—turns back upon, and attends to, 'its own operations about the *ideas* got by sensation'.[1]

Hence, on Locke's theory, *simple ideas* are all of them 'real', 'adequate', and (in a somewhat loose, but fairly intelligible sense) 'true'.[2] It is almost too little to say of them that they are 'signs' of things. The *simple ideas of sensation*, at all events, are impressed upon us by the things; and they either exactly copy the originals they 'signify', or indicate in them certain determinate 'powers' which are such as inevitably to produce these 'signs' in us.

(ii) But *complex ideas* are 'framed' by the mind itself out of its *simple ideas*—by comparison, abstraction, composition; 'intrinsical powers' inherent in the mind, which it exercises instinctively, without conscious effort or control.[3] And under the head of *complex ideas* Locke includes all our general ideas, all ideas of relations, all ideas of substances, and all ideas of modes (whether 'simple modes'—e.g. numbers, figures—or 'mixed modes', e.g. beauty, murder, theft, gratitude, &c.).[4]

Now knowledge in the strictest sense, of the most perfect grade, is demonstrative knowledge—the kind of knowledge that is already in large measure achieved in the mathematical sciences and, as Locke thinks, *in principle* can be attained also in the fields of morality and religion.[5] And 'demonstrative knowledge' has to do, primarily and chiefly (i.e. not exclusively) with complex ideas; viz. General or abstract ideas—in particular, ideas of mixed modes. and their relations. All (or practically all) the propositions of which demonstrative knowledge consists—the affirmations and negations of the man of science, whether tacit ('mental proposi-

---

[1] Cf. the passages quoted from ii, ch. 1; above, Study II, pp. 111–12.

[2] Cf. ii. 30, § 2; 31, §§ 2 and 33, §§ 13–16.   [3] Cf., e.g., ii, ch. 11, ch. 12.

[4] Cf., e.g., ii. 13, 16, 22. On 'modes', see Gibson, *Locke's Theory of Knowledge*, ch. iv.

[5] Cf., e.g., iv. 3, § 18 (and see Gibson, loc. cit., pp. 157–60).

tions') or spoken or written ('verbal propositions')—'join' and 'separate' *complex ideas*, or the words which signify *them*. And however much Locke may insist that these complex ideas are 'framed out of simple ideas', the 'framing' is the mind's own work, and introduces into the 'materials' of knowledge an element neither copied from, nor produced by, the 'external things'. *Complex ideas*, we must agree with Professor Alexander,[1] 'are the voluntary creations of the mind, which manipulates the materials derived from sensation and reflection; or they might be described as resoluble into these elements *together with an active element of construction referable to the mind itself*' (my italics).

The ideas, therefore, which constitute the bulk of the materials of demonstrative knowledge—the ideas of modes and relations— are not *signs of things* at all. Yet Locke—by a magnificent audacity, quite inconsistent (so far as I can judge) with the funda- mental principles of his philosophy[2]—endeavours to vindicate the 'reality' of mathematical and moral knowledge (i.e. to establish that it has a bearing upon the world of fact and actual existence) on the ground that the complex ideas with which it is concerned (the ideas of which, in such demonstrative knowledge, the mind perceives the 'agreements' and 'disagreements' one with another) are '*archetypes*'; i.e. patterns prescribing conditions to which it is possible that things may conform, and so *in a sense* 'signs' of things, if things be regarded under a certain hypothesis. Thus, for example, he says:[3]

'*Mixed Modes and Relations*, having no reality but what they have in the minds of men, there is nothing more required ... to make them *real*, but that they be so framed, that there be a possibility of existing conformable to them. These *ideas*, themselves being archetypes, cannot differ from their archetypes, and so *cannot be chimerical*, unless anyone will jumble together in them inconsistent *ideas*.'

Or again:[4]

'*All our complex ideas, except those of substances*,[5] being *archetypes* of the mind's own making, not intended to be copies of anything, nor referred to the existence of any thing, as to their originals, cannot want any conformity necessary to real knowledge.'

[1] *Locke*, p. 36.   [2] Cf. below, p. 200, n. 2.   [3] ii. 30, § 4.   [4] iv. 4, § 5.
[5] It is fortunately unnecessary for my present purpose to take any account of Locke's view of our ideas of substances, or of his discussion of the question whether (or how far) a science of physical nature is possible (cf., e.g., iv. 3, §§ 26, 29; Gibson, loc. cit., pp. 160–6).

In short, the ideas which constitute the whole, or the bulk, of the materials of knowledge in its strictest sense and most perfect form, are 'their own guarantee of reality'.[1] The geometer and the moral philosopher, provided the ideas they frame, for example, of a triangle and of murder are not self-contradictory, can be certain (Locke holds) that these *ideas* are 'real', i.e. that there is a 'possibility of existing conformable to them'. And they can be assured that their mathematical and moral propositions hold, not only of 'ideas in their own minds', but also of 'real things existing'. For if it is true of a triangle *as the geometer considers it*—i.e. true of the '*idea*' of triangle as he frames it, and as it exists 'in his own mind'—that 'its three angles are equal to two right ones', the same property will belong also to a triangle 'wherever it really exists', when it has a 'real existence in matter'. And if it is true of '*murder*' *as the moral philosopher considers it*—viz. true of it 'in speculation, i.e. in *idea*'—that it 'deserves death', 'it will also be true in reality of any action that exists conformable to that *idea* of murder'; i.e. if, or when, or wherever, a murder is actually perpetrated, the murderer will in fact deserve to die.[2]

(*c*) We were to reconsider Locke's chapter[3] on 'the general nature of Truth' in the light of his conception of 'Demonstrative Knowledge'—of the 'Archetypal Ideas', which are its materials, and of its hypothetical 'reality', i.e. its applicability to *possibly actual* examples of those Ideas.

[1] Alexander, loc. cit., p. 38.

[2] Cf. iv. 4, §§ 6, 8; Gibson, loc. cit., pp. 131–2. I spoke just now (above, p. 199) of the 'magnificent audacity' of Locke's attempt to vindicate the 'reality' of demonstrative knowledge; but the student who recalls the leading principles of Locke's philosophy will be tempted to use a harsher phrase, and to insist rather upon its '*reckless inconsistency*'. For how—on Locke's general theory—*can* anything 'real' or 'existent' conform to an archetypal idea? 'All things that exist', Locke tells us (iii. 3, § 1), are 'particulars'; and 'when . . . we quit particulars, the generals that rest are only creatures of our own making . . .' (ib. § 11). How, then, can anything that *exists* 'conform to', 'agree with', the abstract ideas which the mathematician and moral philosopher consider—of which they perceive and affirm certain universal and necessary relations? If nothing universal or general can be 'real', how can the triangle, which the mathematician considers, *ever* or *anywhere* 'really exist'—*ever* have a 'real existence in matter'? And, again, the 'murder which deserves death', the 'death' it deserves, and the absolute 'ought' (the synthetic necessity which binds each to the other), belong to the realm of abstract general ideas and equally abstract relations—are 'creatures' of the mind's 'own making'. In Locke's 'real' world—the world of particulars which alone exist—no action can be 'conformable' to the archetypal idea of murder. No action *is*, or can even *embody*, murder pure and simple—murder as such and universal—the murder which the moral philosopher considers, and perceives to deserve death.   [3] iv, ch. 5.

It seems possible to read into Locke's statements, or to extract out of them, a *fairly coherent* theory of the proposition and of truth, as follows:

He begins (as we said) by distinguishing *two sorts* of propositions ('mental' and 'verbal'), and seems to ascribe to each a different *kind* of truth—a 'truth of thought', and a 'truth of words'.[1] But the distinction which he is endeavouring to express is not a distinction of 'sorts' or 'kinds', but of 'aspects' or 'moments'.

A proposition in its full and proper form is *both* mental *and* verbal—it is a synthesis of thoughts expressed in words, *or* it is an affirmative or negative sentence 'marking down' a nexus of ideas.

If one asks how Locke came to speak of *the thought expressed* and *the expression of it* as two *sorts* of propositions, if he really meant only to distinguish two aspects of the full proposition, the answer is to be found in his theory of language and its relation to thought. For Locke's theory of language[2] is substantially the same as the theory set out by Aristotle in the *De Interpretatione*. Words, Locke says, are articulate sounds made 'arbitrarily', or 'by a voluntary imposition', to be 'signs of internal conceptions'. *Primarily*, words 'stand for nothing but the ideas in the mind of him that uses them'; and their proper use is (*a*) 'to record our own thoughts for the help of our own memories' and (*b*) to communicate our own thoughts to others.[3] Men, however, do in fact often (*c*) 'suppose their words to be marks of the ideas in the minds also of other men', and (*d*) 'suppose their words to stand also for the reality of things'—and, in doing so, Locke holds, men *misuse* language, and generate error, confusion, and dispute.[4]

Locke thus conceives *language to be related to thought as sign to signified*: i.e. with him, as with Aristotle, language is separated from (related to, not *one with*) the thought it expresses. Hence it is natural and inevitable for him to speak of two sorts of propositions: (*a*) verbal propositions, i.e. junctions or severances of words *standing for* thought, but not themselves alive with thought; and (*b*) 'mental propositions', i.e. junctions and severances of thoughts *bare of expression*—not expressed in words at all; not even in those silently articulated words which, as Locke recognizes, men tend to use 'in their thinkings and reasonings with themselves', for

---

[1] iv. 5, §§ 2, 3.   [2] *Essay*, iii.
[3] Cf. iii. 1, §§ 1 and 2; 2, §§ 1 and 2; 9, §§ 1–3.
[4] Cf. iii. 2, §§ 2–5.

these silent words (he thinks) are employed as *substitutes for* (not as expressions of) 'ideas'.[1]

The most conspicuous examples of propositions in the full and proper sense of the term—i.e. of mental affirmations and negations adequately expressed in spoken or written sentences, and so 'recorded for the help of the thinker's own memory and communicable to others'[2]—are the propositions of demonstrative knowledge, i.e. those in which mathematical science, theology, and moral philosophy are embodied and set forth. Of every such proposition, it must be said *on the one hand* that it is 'verbal', and that its truth is a 'truth of words'. It is a spoken or written affirmation or negation, in which the thinker records ('marks down in language') an agreement or disagreement of his own ideas, as he 'perceives' it and 'as it is'.[3] But, *on the other hand*, it must also be said of it that it is 'mental', and that its truth is a 'truth of thought'. It presupposes, that is, and adequately expresses, a 'mental proposition'—viz. the joining or severance of ideas, which is the mathematician's or the philosopher's 'belief'. And to this mental proposition there belongs a 'truth of thought'; for, in it, archetypal ideas are joined or separated according to their intrinsic agreements or disagreements. The mental proposition, therefore, is true, possesses truth of thought, or is, so to speak, a piece of 'real' knowledge. For the ideas it joins or severs are archetypes; and therefore their intrinsic agreements or disagreements hold good hypothetically or *in posse* of the world of actual fact, the world of particular things or existents. In that world, there *may* occur particulars 'conformable' to the ideas—and if, or when, or so far as, this possibility is realized, an actual junction or severance will correspond to the ideal agreement or disagreement which is the mental proposition; i.e. it will be an actual 'truth of thought', a complex or compound of thoughts corresponding to a complex or compound of facts.

If this interpretation is substantially correct, Locke's view of the 'Proposition' and of 'Truth' (paradoxical and indefensible though it is) may fairly be said to 'conform in principle' to the 'subjective position'. Truth—so Locke seems to mean—consists, primarily and essentially, in a conformity or correspondence between (*a*) an 'ideal complex' (a junction or severance of ideas or thoughts), whether 'silent', or marked down in a spoken or written sentence, and (*b*) a '*real complex*'—i.e. a junction or severance

---

[1] Cf. iv. 5, §§ 3–4.   [2] iii. 9, § 1.   [3] Cf. iv. 5, § 9.

of facts, of elements actually (or possibly) existing and related in the extra-mental world. The junction or severance of ideas, so far as it is the momentary and personal experience of the individual thinker, a 'belief' he silently forms within his soul, is (no more than) a 'mental' proposition, possessing a truth which is *only* a 'truth of thought'. But when the thinker puts his belief into words—into a spoken or written affirmative or negative sentence—he is making a proposition in the fullest and most proper sense: a 'verbal proposition' including, embodying, and adequately expressing the junction or severance of his ideas. And to such a proposition there belongs a 'truth of thought' permanently recorded for the thinker's own memory and made communicable to others. There belongs to it (what Locke calls) a 'truth of words' which is 'something more' than 'mental truth'; a truth of words not 'purely verbal and trifling', but '*real* and instructive'.[1]

3. In trying to show that 'the subjective position underlies more than one well-known theory of the judgement, and of the truth and falsity which belong to it',[2] I have been drawn into a historical digression, from which I must now return to pick up the main thread of my argument. I proposed to characterize and examine three typical positions, one or the other of which (as I thought) is taken for granted in the most commonly accepted theories of truth and falsity—constituting, so to speak, the theme they elaborate and embroider with varying degrees of consistency and success.[3]

According to the first of these typical positions—to restate its essential features—that which alone is true or false is a judgement, and a judgement in strict and ultimate analysis is a 'fact of mind'. It is a 'fact of mind', because it is made by an individual thinker in his thought, and by his thinking and out of his 'ideas' (sensations, for example, memories, conceptions). In short, it is an ideal product, consisting of ideal elements ideally related, i.e. combined by an ideal activity. The ideal elements (though 'ideas of', and 'in', an individual thinker's mind) *represent* ('copy', 'symbolize', 'stand for', 'refer to') elements of fact, real elements—elements 'without', i.e. independent of, mind, or at least independent of *this* individual thinker's mind. And the 'ideal product', though 'made' by the ideal activity of an individual thinker, may—when made, and taken as a whole—'correspond' to a real compound, a complex fact; i.e. one that is 'without' (independent of) *his* mind,

---

[1] Cf. iv. 5, §§ 6 and 8.   [2] Above, p. 184.   [3] Cf. above, p. 180.

at all events, if not 'extra-mental' altogether, i.e. independent of all minds and their ideal activities. If, or when, there is such a 'correspondence', there is truth; i.e. the ideal product (the 'judgement' or 'complex fact of mind') is true. Failing such a 'correspondence', there is falsity; the 'judgement', the ideal product, is false.

Such, then, is the position which has now to be examined, i.e. tested by a closer scrutiny of its essential features. Are they, severally, assumptions which a sane interpretation of our cognizant experience forces us to make—to recognize as formulating indispensable conditions, subject to which alone an intelligent and intelligible account of that experience can be given? Or are they, on the contrary, mere suppositions—assumptions arbitrary, unwarranted, and perhaps long ago discredited by philosophical criticism? And, again, are they consistent one with another, so that the position as a whole forms a coherent hypothesis? Or, on the contrary, do they, when taken strictly and precisely, collide with one another, so that instead of a single position, a single coherent hypothesis, there is but a medley of mutually incompatible suppositions?

(i) *First essential feature of the subjective position*: 'A judgement, in strict and ultimate analysis, is a fact of mind.' At first sight this is a plain statement of something which every treatment of the subject must recognize—a truism. If it is an assumption, it is one that is inevitable and unquestionable. Indeed, it was made, and emphasized, at the beginning of these Studies. For (it was there insisted) a judgement, in its essential nature (i.e. as a phase, or 'proper part', of knowledge-or-truth) is a 'logical fact'; and a 'logical fact', like a 'moral fact' (like, for example, a right or a duty) is, in a very obvious sense, a 'fact of mind'. As a 'logical fact', a judgement[1] 'exists, or has its being and is actual, in the medium or "element" of the mutual understanding of self-conscious minds'. Its reality is 'ideal' or 'spiritual'. It is made and sustained by thinking; by intellectual activities which pass through one or more of the (so-called individual) human minds; activities, in which these individual minds co-operate, and which so (in a sense) they have made their own.

But that is not the sense in which, according to the subjective position, a judgement is a 'fact of mind'. For the further details of the characterization compel us to put a special interpretation

[1] Cf. Study I, pp. 56-7.

upon a 'mind' and 'its facts', and so convert the seeming truism into a most questionable assumption. For the judgement, we are asked to assume, is a *'fact of mind, because . . . made by an individual thinker in his thought, and by his thinking, and out of his ideas'*. The mind, therefore, of which the judgement is a fact, is one of a multitude of self-closed and mutually exclusive thinking beings. It is, for example, my mind or yours; tied down to, located in, enduring with, my organism or yours. And its facts are whatever occurs 'within' the self-closed—the private and exclusive—conscious stream, the psychical flow, which is its being. To be a 'fact of mind', in short, is to be a constituent phase of a psychical flow; to be a 'psychical' (as contrasted with a 'physical') event.

It seems, then, to be characteristic of the subjective position to assume that a judgement in strict and ultimate analysis—a judgement regarded in its proper nature as that which alone is true or false—is a 'psychical fact' in the sense explained; viz. a phase or section of the temporal flow which is the private being, the inner mental history, of a 'self'. And such an assumption, for a modern student of the subject, is plainly untenable and even ridiculous. To make it would be to revive gratuitously a blunder that could have seemed plausible only in the infancy of logical theory—a blunder which (so far as the study of logic in England is concerned) was exposed and 'beaconed' nearly fifty years ago by F. H. Bradley in the first chapter of his *Principles of Logic*. He there sharply distinguishes: (*a*) the particular psychical images, or other states and changes in (and of) the individual thinker's mind, which may (perhaps must) accompany his thinking—modifications of his conscious being, through which he passes in thinking, and (*b*) the (impersonal, objective, universal) meaning which, precisely *qua thinking*, he brings and holds before his mind. The term 'idea', he points out, may be used in either or both of these very different senses—as psychical event or image, and as meaning, i.e. that which is meant. *If used in the first sense*—and that was the prevailing use of the term in England at the time Bradley was writing—then what it denotes is of no direct interest in a logical study of judgement. For 'ideas' in the sense of 'psychical facts'—events of the individual's mental history, phases and changes of his psychical flow—form no part of, in no way enter into or constitute, a judgement, i.e. a significant assertion that is true or false. *It is only if used in the second sense*, that the term 'idea' (= 'ideal content') denotes what is directly and properly relevant in a logical consideration of the judgement.

'We shall always go wrong' (to quote a well-known paragraph)[1] 'unless we remember that the relations within the content of any meaning, however complex, are still not relations between mental existences. There is a wolf and a lamb. Does the wolf eat the lamb? The wolf eats the lamb. We have a relation here suggested or asserted between wolf and lamb, but that relation is (if I may use the word) not a *factual* connection between events in my head. What is meant is no psychical conjunction of images.'

I am not forgetting that the whole treatment of 'ideas' (of the 'ideal' element in judgement and inference) in the first edition of Bradley's *Logic* has been ferociously assailed by Cook Wilson,[2] and is in fact open to serious criticism. In particular, the brilliant first chapter, to which I have been referring, is marred by many obvious faults—both in the matter of its teaching and in the manner of its exposition. Bradley himself drew attention[3] to, and endeavoured to correct, the chief of these faults—viz. the erroneous view of 'idea' (as an independent form or level of cognizance) which the chapter takes for granted, and various misleading and 'more or less objectionable' expressions, which it contains. But, in spite of all its faults, Bradley's treatment of 'ideas' in the *Logic* (and specially in chapter i) has at least this merit—viz. that nobody, who has studied it, is ever likely thereafter to confuse judgements or inferences with 'psychical facts', or to suppose (if I may borrow and adapt a sentence from Bosanquet's *Logic*)[4] that any 'mere mental occurrences as such', any 'series or combination of particular images' could 'by any possibility be a judgement'.[5]

[1] Vol. i, p. 12.
[2] *Statement and Inference*, vol. i, pp. 279–94.
[3] Cf. *Essays*, published in 1914, p. 29; second edition of *Logic*, published in 1922, Additional Notes to ch. 1, pp. 38–40. *Essays*, p. 29, n. 1, is reprinted from a paper first published in *Mind* in Oct. 1906 [not April 1908 as Bradley erroneously states].
[4] Second edition, vol. i, p. 70.
[5] Cook Wilson's criticism was written before the publication of the second edition of the *Principles of Logic*, but after the publication of *Appearance and Reality* and of many of the articles which were reprinted, with modifications, in 1914 under the title of *Essays on Truth and Reality*. In both these works there are passages (cf., to mention only one, the explanation of 'ideal' and 'identity' in *Appearance and Reality*, pp. 146 ff.) which make it abundantly clear that to criticize the first chapter of the *Principles of Logic au pied de la lettre*, and in entire disregard of its author's other works, is to do Bradley profound injustice. Certainly, Cook Wilson's criticism is of value; but in much of it he was forcing an open door, and in some of it he was tilting against windmills. Its value would have been

'But, after all,' it will perhaps be objected, 'the assumption that "every judgement is a psychical fact" is forced upon us the moment we reflect upon our experience. There is nothing impossible or ridiculous about it. On the contrary, it is made by every competent logician and psychologist. And if Bradley is to be quoted as an authority against it, there are other passages, both in his *Logic* and elsewhere in his writings, in which he seems to defend, and even to insist upon it. Thus (to give a few examples): "Ideas and Judgements", he writes,[1] "when I reflect, are known and recognized by me as things which exist in my head. . . . Judgements all exist psychically as events in me." And again,[2] "In order to be, truth itself must happen and occur, and must exist as what we call a mental event"; or[3] "A truth is no truth at all unless it happens in a soul, and is thus an event which appears in time".'

Behind this objection—one is inclined at first to reply—there is nothing but a very simple misunderstanding. It is one thing to assert that every judgement—considered on one side or aspect of itself, regarded from a certain point of view—is a psychical fact; occurs and happens as a mental event; exists 'in somebody's mind' (or, even, 'in somebody's head'). This is the doctrine which Bradley maintains, and on which at times he emphatically insists.[4] It is quite another thing to maintain, with those who adopt the subjective position, that a judgement *qua* true or false—a judgement in its proper nature as a form or phase of knowledge—is a 'psychical fact'. It is this that is a plainly untenable assumption—an elementary, long-discredited blunder.

But this reply is not entirely satisfactory. 'For' (the objector will presumably retort) '*is* there in fact so sharp a line between the assumption that "every judgement, *qua* true or false, is a psychical fact", and the doctrine, to which Bradley is committed by the statements, for example, that "Truth *necessarily* implies an aspect of psychical existence", or that an "aspect of mental event" is

---

greatly enhanced, had he been less eager to show the 'futility' of all 'attempts to explain or define "judgement" in terms of anything but itself' (l.c., p. 279) and to convict Bradley's exposition of verbal confusion, and more anxious to penetrate to the substance of his teaching. As it is, the critic, from want of sufficient sympathy with the writer he is criticizing, *haeret in cortice*: the criticism is effective, is unanswerable, so far as it goes—but it does not go below the surface.

[1] *Logic*[2], p. 631. [2] Ib., p. 612. [3] *Mind*, N.S. no. 33, p. 31.
[4] Cf., e.g., *Logic*[2], p. 612 (immediately before the sentence quoted in the 'Objection'): 'Truth . . . necessarily implies an aspect of psychical existence'; and (ib., p. 617) 'Every logical process . . . is, viewed from the other side, a psychical happening, and this aspect of mental event is throughout involved inseparably'.

"*involved inseparably*" in every logical process? Yet is it really to be supposed that so careful a thinker as Bradley has made a "plainly untenable assumption"—has committed precisely that elementary blunder which he himself elsewhere mercilessly exposes?'

I must not be drawn aside from the examination of the subjective position into another historical digression—into a full exposition and criticism of Bradley's views. But—at the risk of betraying my own misunderstanding—I will try to explain briefly why it seems to me impossible to defend the side of Bradley's teaching which is here in question.

For in what precise sense can it be maintained that 'truth *necessarily* implies an aspect of psychical existence'; that 'a truth is no truth at all unless it happens *in a soul*'; that a judgement, an inference, a logical process, *must* (or even, *can*) be viewed as events that 'exist psychically *in me*'? *Prima facie*, at all events, taken literally and at their face value, such statements treat the conceptions of a 'Soul and its states' and of a 'Finite Self' with far more respect than they deserve—or than is compatible with the estimate Bradley himself forms of them, when speaking as a metaphysician. The Soul and the Self—the supposed individual and exclusive owners of experiences which are their 'states' existing or happening psychically within their several selves—these, according to the metaphysical theory he sets out in *Appearance and Reality*[1] and *Essays*,[2] are fragmentary, mutilated, confused, and inconsistent 'Appearances' of the 'Absolute'. They are not immediately given and immediately apprehended facts—not so many self-presenting and self-guaranteeing elements of the real. They are 'creatures of an intellectual construction',[3] conceptions or theories rather than 'facts'—and, moreover, conceptions that are rough and ready, confused and inconsistent. They are conceptions which for certain purposes it is natural, convenient, even necessary, to form—e.g. for our practical conduct in everyday life, and for the furtherance of the kind of explanation which is aimed at, and achieved, in what are called the 'special sciences'. But they are conceptions which, however legitimate and serviceable for such limited purposes, are compromises, patchworks, makeshifts, which cannot be *thought out*. They are not 'intelligible' without qualification or completely; they could not be defended against philosophical (metaphysical) criticism—i.e. a criticism that is pushed thoroughly, systematically,

---

[1] Cf. pp. 464–6, 468–9.　　　　　　　　　[2] Pp. 409 ff.
[3] Cf. *Appearance and Reality*, pp. 9, 468.

and without concessions, into all 'sides' and 'corners' of that which is being tested.[1] Thus, for example, Bradley says of the 'Soul':[2]

'If you confine your attention to the soul as a soul, then every possible experience is no more than that which happens in and to this soul. You have to do with psychical events which qualify the soul, and in the end these events, so far as you are true to your idea, are merely states of the soul. Such a conception is for certain purposes legitimate and necessary, and to condemn it, while used within proper limits, is to my mind mistaken. But, outside these limits, what we call the soul is, I agree, indefensible. It is vitiated by inconsistencies and by hopeless contradictions. . . .'

The assumption, then, which seems both essential to the subjective position and 'plainly untenable', is utterly alien to Bradley's philosophical theory. The souls and finite selves—the embodied minds, the individual thinkers—which those who adopt the subjective position accept *tels quels* and at their face value; which are for them absolutely (i.e. without qualification and beyond dispute) self-contained and mutually exclusive subjects of knowledge, each the owner of his own ideas and the originator of judgements;— these are, on Bradley's theory, so many imperfect manifestations, so many appearances, of reality. Their 'self-dependence' is relative, a matter of degree; and their mutual exclusiveness is, *in the main*, illusory.[3] Nor is there in his philosophy (in his metaphysical speculations) any support for the assumption that there exist a multitude of mutually exclusive and self-dependent acquisitive powers of thought or intelligence,[4] each implanted and enclosed in an embodied mind—a mind that is mine-not-yours or yours-not-mine. In the leading passages of *Appearance and Reality*, of the *Essays*, and even of the *Principles of Logic* (most

---

[1] Cf. the definition of metaphysics (*Essays*, p. 444): 'By metaphysics I do not mean the doctrine of any one school, but I include under that term all speculation which is at once resolved to keep its hold upon all sides of fact, and upon the other hand to push, so far as it can, every question to the end.'

[2] *Essays*, p. 415.

[3] 'In the main': for 'there really is within the Absolute a diversity of *finite centres*' (*Essays*, p. 412); and so far, presumably, we must not speak of the mutual exclusiveness of souls and selves as *altogether* illusory. But this side of Bradley's teaching is very difficult, and I suspect not entirely consistent.

[4] By 'thought' or 'intelligence' I mean the *vis infinita cogitandi*, or whatever one ought to call the power of Synthetic-Analysis or Analytic-Synthesis (cf. Study I, pp. 37–8) which, rooted in the nature of things, is the real origin and source of what we call 'our' thinking, 'our' intellectual activity, 'our' judgements and inferences (cf. Study I, p. 24 [also pp. 17 ff., 23–4]; and Study II, pp. 89–90, 99–100 [also pp. 70–1, 123]).

clearly and emphatically, perhaps, in the Notes and Terminal Essays which were added in the second edition), the subordinate nature of the part played by the 'finite subject'—by the so-called 'individual' thinker—is amply recognized and enforced. *My* 'making' of a judgement is my co-operation with a discursive movement, with a self-development, that 'makes' and 'fulfils itself' in me and in others. *My* thinking, *my* intellectual activity, is the adoption and the endorsement, partial, limited, and imperfect, of a phase or stretch in that fundamental dialectic, or *discursus*, which is 'Reality' or 'the Absolute' seeking and finding itself in the form of truth—expressing and fulfilling itself 'ideally', in the medium of 'ideas', or through the co-operation of what is called a 'finite mind'.[1]

How, then, is it possible to reconcile with the general trend of Bradley's metaphysical speculations the statements that 'an aspect of mental event' is '*inseparably involved*' in every logical process; that 'judgements all exist psychically as events *in me*'; that 'a truth is no truth at all unless it happens *in a soul*'? Interpret such statements with every conceivable caution; they still leave standing, and presuppose, the popular notions of a 'Soul' and a 'Finite Self'—they still commit anyone who makes and defends them to the assumption that a knower is *in fact and really* a subject of experiences which are 'no more than that which happens in and to' a Soul, is *in fact and really* one out of a plurality of self-closed, mutually excluding, minds. Or plant yourself firmly within the outlines of Bradley's own metaphysical position, and try, on that basis, to find for these statements an intelligible and defensible meaning. If you hold firmly to Bradley's conception

[1] Cf. (to quote a few passages only in support) *Appearance and Reality*[9], p. 523 (Bradley is there insisting that 'my part in the affair' is not irrelevant): 'To be made and to be found is . . . essential to the development and being of the thing, and truth in its processes and results belongs to the essence of reality.' Ib., p. 550: '. . . The process of the Many, and the total being of the Many themselves, are mere aspects of the one Reality which moves and knows itself within them, and apart from which all things and their changes and every knower and every known is absolutely nothing.' *Essays*, p. 121: 'Truth is a mode of the self-realisation of myself and of the Universe in one. . . . The Universe is nowhere apart from the lives of the individuals, and, whether as truth or otherwise, the Universe realises itself not at all except through their differences. On the other side the individuals, if they are to realise themselves personally, must specialise this common life, of which truth is one aspect. . . .' Ib., p. 218: 'My real personal self which orders my world is in truth inseparably one with the Universe. Behind me the absolute reality works through and in unison with myself, and the world which confronts me is at bottom one thing in substance and in power with this reality.'

of metaphysics, and of the standard of reality and truth that metaphysical speculation demands, the Soul with its states, and the Finite Self with its uniquely private experiences, are no more than confused and inconsistent Appearances of Reality: ways in which the Real imperfectly shows itself to us so long as we move, not on the philosophical level of experience, but on the lower or uncritical levels of scientific explanation or popular theory or the loose thinking that is sufficient to serve the practical purposes of life. The Soul, in short, and the Finite Self, have no being, or reality, or truth, except under qualifications which are meaningless in metaphysics: qualifications which must be set aside as irrelevant if we are even to enter upon a metaphysical investigation at all. Yet when Bradley says that 'truth *necessarily* implies an aspect of psychical existence', that 'a truth is no truth at all unless it happens in *a soul*', and that 'judgements all exist psychically as events in *me*', is he not putting before us assertions which—in his opinion—we are forced to make, not only provisionally (not only as psychologists, for example, and not only for this or that limited purpose) but even when, examining the nature of truth and knowledge as philosophers or metaphysicians, we are resolved to push, so far as we can, our speculation to the end and, in doing so, to keep our hold upon all sides of the problem?

To the foregoing criticism, Bradley himself would presumably have replied: 'But, on *my* theory, Judgement and Inference and even Truth (everything, in short, that can fall within the province of Logic) are themselves no more than Appearances. Not only Psychology, but Logic too is, on my view, a "special science". The Logician, as well as the Psychologist, is bound, and is rightly content, to move on a lower level than the Philosopher or Metaphysician. The Logician, like the Psychologist, works with assumptions which are in part fictitious, and has neither the power nor the drive to reach more than provisional results.'

It would take us too far afield from the main line of our investigation to examine Bradley's attempt to delimit psychology from logic, to conceive both of them as 'special sciences', and to mark them off from philosophy or metaphysics. But admitting for the sake of argument[1] that logic is a ' special science', working within

---

[1] 'For the sake of argument' *only*: for Bradley's theory of the relation of psychology to logic, and of both to metaphysics, is the strangest and least defensible part of his teaching. Cf. also Mure, 'The Marriage of Universals' (*Journal of Philosophical Studies*, July and Oct. 1928).

a hypothesis that cannot perhaps be altogether defended, i.e. that is perhaps metaphysically untenable; admitting, for the sake of argument, that the logician is bound, and should be content, to make unjustified and perhaps unjustifiable assumptions, and to derive from them provisional and in part, perhaps, erroneous conclusions—still, on Bradley's own showing, the logician's conception of the judging subject (of the subject of knowledge) is neither that of a Soul, in which experiences occur as 'states', nor that of a Self uniquely private and excluding all other Selves. These popular notions form no part of the logician's hypothesis—or these largely fictitious entities are not amongst the denizens of the domain, to which logic, as a 'special science', is confined. To say, therefore, that a judgement 'exists psychically as an event in me' is false, in any logical context; for within the logician's world—and it is only there, *ex hypothesi*, that there is such a thing as a 'judgement' at all—there are no Selves of this kind; no Self, which is an I-not-you, or which contains cognizant experiences as psychical events within itself. Nor can a truth—even if, when considered as belonging to the 'special domain' of logic, it is no more than an appearance, an imperfect manifestation of the real—'happen in a Soul'. For in logic at all events (whatever may be the case in that other 'special science' which is psychology) the conception of a 'Soul and its states' is useless, and therefore illegitimate.

(ii) My argument so far has been this: it is absurd to assume that 'a judgement, in strict and ultimate analysis, is a fact of mind', if by a 'fact of mind' is meant a 'psychical fact', i.e. a phase in the mental history of this or that temporal (phenomenal) self. Yet precisely this absurd assumption is an essential feature of the 'subjective' position.

But those who are inclined to adopt the subjective position will protest against this argument, and put up a defence along the following lines. Within a philosophical position (they will say), it is possible to distinguish a detail—a plurality of features. But the features thus distinguished, it must be remembered, are 'characteristic', are 'essential', only *as* features inseparable from one another and adjectival to the whole; they must, that is, be steadily viewed in their context, they must be interpreted and understood subject to such qualifications as the total position imposes upon each and all of them. It is easy enough to reduce any philosophical position to a medley of 'plainly untenable' hypotheses, by isolating each of its characteristic features in turn, and examining it apart from the rest. For when that which is isolated is one amongst many features, all inseparable from one another and all adjectival to a whole, to isolate is at the least to over-emphasize, and so to distort. Now this (they will contend) is exactly what has happened in the present instance. For the 'subjective position' as a whole amounts to this. A judgement (i.e. that which alone, in ultimate analysis, is true or false) is an *ideal* product (a complex of ideal elements ideally related), and so an *ideal* fact, or a fact *of mind*. It is other than, and therefore capable of corresponding (or being discordant) with, facts or complexes not thus qualified—for example, facts of nature or physical (not of mind or mental) ; or complexes not *ideal*, but *real*, composed of *real* elements *really* (or 'factually') related. 'It is true', they will perhaps admit, 'that these ideal elements, if the question of their origin is to be pressed, must be regarded (on our view) as *somebody's ideas*—i.e. as sensations, memories, thoughts, which arise, occur, exist, in an individual mind. It is true, further, that, since in the judgement they are *ideally related*, they must have been combined (or so at least it seems to us) by the psychical activity of some individual thinker. It is true, therefore, finally, that, if we are pressed, we do most certainly maintain that the *ideal product*, which is a judgement, has been brought into being by the *psychical* activity of a temporal self—by an activity which he exercises, and can only exercise, upon *psychical* materials, i.e. upon events or phases "within", and constituting, his *psychical flow*. But it is not essential to our position (to our view of truth and falsity, and of that which is true or false) to insist upon any special theory of the genesis and origin of the ideal product which is a judgement. We are prepared, for the sake of argument, to dispense with our assumption of a self-closed mind, possessing a psychical function of analysis and synthesis, and exercising it upon the psychical states and changes of itself. We fail to see what alternative view of the making of a judgement has better warrant in the facts of our cognizant experience ; and, in particular, we do not admit that the hypothesis of a *vis infinita intelligendi* (a power of Synthetic-Analysis) rooted in the nature of things, and operating in and through the finite minds, is more tenable or less absurd. But the assumption, that has been condemned as untenable and absurd, is not essential to our position. Its essential features are three. *First*, the conception of that which is true or false as an Ideal Product, i.e. a complex of ideal elements ideally related; *secondly*, the assumption that these ideal elements are severally representative of real elements or elements of fact—i.e. elements other than, and independent of, themselves; and *thirdly*, the conception of truth and falsity as (respectively) a correspondence and a discordance between the Ideal Product (the complex of ideal elements) and another and independent complex, consisting of the real elements which the ideal elements severally represent.'

Now the weakness of this 'defence' is obvious. For, suppose the assumption we have condemned is not essential to (and that therefore its absurdity must not be pressed against) the subjective position. Eliminate the hypothesis that the elements of a judgement are psychical events, phases of this or that embodied mind or psychical flow; that their relation in the judgement is 'ideal', because brought about by the psychical activity of this or that temporal self; that, in short, the judgement is an 'ideal' product, because you or I have 'made' it by *our* thinking, out of *our* ideas, and in *our* thought. What positive meaning is left to the term *ideal*? The qualification suggests, it seems, no more than that the elements, relations, and products, which it qualifies, are *other than* (and so capable of corresponding, or being discordant, with) elements, relations, and products which are 'real': but 'real' in this connexion means, in its turn, no more than—in some sense— *not ideal*, or *other than* that which is ideal. For it clearly will not do to identify *real* in this context with *physical*, since that would restrict the so-called 'real' complexes—the complexes, correspondence with which is truth, discordance with which is falsity— to *physical* (i.e. corporeal) facts or matter-of-fact. There could, therefore, be no truth or falsity except in regard to bodies, and the attributes, relations, and incidents of bodies. There could, for example, be no truth or falsity, in regard to the judgement, or any form of knowledge, or any theory of truth and falsity themselves. The assertion that 'a judgement is an ideal product' could not itself be, or express, a 'judgement': i.e. could not be either true or false, since no 'real complex' (if *real* means *physical*) is here in question.

Hence, it seems impossible to deny that the assumption we have condemned is essential to, and ineliminable from, the subjective position. Nevertheless, it may not be unprofitable to forget (so far as that is possible) that the position—being based upon a fundamental misconception of a mind and its experiences—has utterly collapsed; and to examine *ex abundantia* its three remaining 'essential features'—viz. the assumptions that a judgement is a product, that its elements are representative, and that its truth or falsity are its correspondence and discordance with a complex other than, and independent of, itself.

(iii) *Second essential feature of the subjective position*: 'The judgement is a product.' For those who hold the subjective position *ideal*—as we have seen—means (if it means anything positive at all) *psychical*, i.e. in, and of, a self-closed and exclusive mind; and in that sense, at all events, as we have also seen, neither a judgement, nor its elements and their relations (if, indeed, within a judgement there are elements and relations) can be *ideal*. For the time being, however, we are to take the qualification 'ideal' on trust—and to consider only whether, or in what sense, a judgement is a product.

The notion of a product carries with it two antitheses. For, *first*, a product is something composite or complex; and, from this point of view, it is contrasted with simple (or relatively simple) elements, out of which it has been produced, of which it consists or is composed. And, *secondly*, a product is something that has been produced; and, from this point of view, it is a result contrasted with a process. It is, that is, something finished, final, complete—by contrast with the 'producing' from which it emerges. It emerges from a process—i.e. it is itself no stage or part thereof. It finishes or completes the 'producing' as a goal that lies beyond it and terminates it *ab extra*.

To assume, then, that a judgement is a *product* is to assume (*a*) that it contains within itself two (or more) constituents or components; and (*b*) that, while it presupposes a process, in which these constituents were being put together, it is itself a processless state (or timeless act) in which they are together.

Now, if this analysis of the notion of a *product* is correct (and those who challenge it may be invited to explain what else they mean by 'product'), it needs no fresh examination to show that the second essential feature of the subjective position is as unwarranted and indefensible as the first. It is idle, at this stage of our investigation, to ask whether a judgement is a result emerging from, and terminating, a process; or a complex contrasted with certain simple (or relatively simple) constituents, which are related and held together within it; or both a result and a complex together. For these questions have already been answered in the negative. Unless the whole trend of the preceding Study ('The Search for a *Datum*') was wrong, there are, *in the first place*, no elements of cognizant experience simpler or more rudimentary than judgement. Judgement cannot contain any constituents other than, and contrasted in character with, itself; it cannot be something composite or complex. For (so we were forced to conclude) within the whole sphere of our cognizant experiences there is nothing, no actual form or piece of knowledge, which is not itself a judgement—or fundamentally and predominantly of the nature of judgement. There are (we were forced to conclude) no perceptions, sensations, feelings, or conceptions, in the sense of items of immediate knowledge—knowledge other than, and contrasted with, the discursive knowledge which is judgement. What such terms denote are *either* 'judgements'—i.e. cognizances through and through, and essentially, inferential, and so of the nature of judgement—*or* 'moments' inseparable from, though distinguishable by reflection upon, some actual form or piece of knowledge; i.e. *'moments' which presuppose* (for their being, and their being distinguished) a judgement, not *items it presupposes*, not elements of which it consists or is composed.

And, *in the second place*, to suggest that a judgement is a result contrasted with a process, and in that sense and so far a product, is to propound a monstrous paradox. For if the antithesis of result and process is to be applied within the region of our cognizant experiences at all, there can be no hesitation on which side of the division judgements would have to fall. The antithesis, as we argued, is not applicable—or not so as to constitute or mark a division. But amongst those who apply it, and who endeavour to maintain the division, nobody would look to *judgement* as exemplifying the kind of knowledge which is a 'timeless state or act'. On the contrary: a judgement, they would all agree, is the typical example of the kind of knowledge which is a process, i.e. which unfolds itself and develops through a period of time.[1]

It is difficult to treat the suggestion that a judgement is a 'product' with any kind of patience or respect. For the antitheses of result and process, and of complex and constituents, are inapplicable not only to a judgement—not only to anything which, like a judgement, is a 'spiritual fact', a reality that is the experience of a mind.[2] They are inapplicable far below that level. It is, for

[1] Cf. above, Study II, pp. 69–72, 127, 151–2. In other words, if it were possible to apply Aristotle's antithesis between κίνησις and ἐνέργεια so as to divide the forms of knowledge into two contrasted groups, *judgements* would obviously have to be reckoned as κινήσεις—not as ἐνέργειαι.

[2] Cf. Study II, pp. 85–7.

example, impossible to characterize, in terms of these antitheses, the phenomena or the facts which belong to the sphere of life. The living thing—the plant, or animal, or man—is (*qua* living, and not more than living, not sentient, for example, or self-conscious) neither *simple* nor *complex*, but *single-in-complexity* or 'concrete'. It is so, through and through, and in all its proper parts and functions, i.e. in all the detail which, belonging to it *qua* living, is itself instinct with life. There is nothing in it, or 'of' it, which is *simple* as contrasted with complex or *complex* as contrasted with simple. And its life is neither 'process' nor 'result', but an actuality which —if we try to speak of it in these terms—we can only characterize as process and result in one. Thus, there are (it would commonly be said) certain 'vital processes'— digestion, for example, assimilation, circulation of the blood, breathing, &c.—*in which* 'the life' of an animal consists. And the statement is true, if properly understood. Its life *is* these processes, and these processes *are* its life; for its life is the whole which differentiates and integrates itself in them, and the result which, throughout their continuance, is producing, developing, and fulfilling itself. But (it is hardly necessary to add) the life of an animal does not *consist of* these processes—i.e. contain them as separate or separable constituents; nor is it a result beyond them—a processless state to which they lead, in which they terminate. The only state 'beyond them'—the only state to which they lead and in which they terminate—is death.

What, then, it may be asked, becomes of the traditional analysis of the judgement into subject, predicate, and copula, or into subject and predicate? Admitting that 'product' is an unsuitable term to use, still—it may be objected—'nobody can reflect upon a judgement without recognizing that it presupposes, has brought together, and holds within its unity, two distinguishable elements or factors—the *logical subject*, or something about which we are thinking, and the *logical predicate* or something fresh which in the judgement we think about it'.

What we have set aside is not the analysis of the judgement into logical subject and predicate, but a particular—and erroneous— interpretation of it. No judgement is a product; it is neither the result of a process, which it presupposes but excludes, nor is it composed of simpler constituents (elements, parts, factors) colligated by a relation. So much has been denied; and the 'traditional analysis' is not touched by the denial, unless it is misinterpreted. For the analysis—as the objector himself admits—is reached by

reflection upon the judgement, by the philosophical reflection of
the logician. It offers us, therefore, distinguishable phases of the
judgement, not stages preliminary to it, nor factors separable
within it. The logical subject and the predicate, in short, which the
analysis distinguishes, are offered to us not as constituents of a
complex, but as moments constituting a self-fulfilling *discursus*—
a whole essentially 'concrete'.

I will try to make this plainer by commenting briefly upon a
passage in H. W. B. Joseph's *Introduction to Logic*.[1]

'We may distinguish', the author there says, 'three subjects, the
logical, the grammatical, and the ultimate or metaphysical. That the
logical subject is not the same as the grammatical subject of the sentence
is readily apprehended. The proposition *Belladonna dilates the pupil*
may be an answer either to the question *What dilates the pupil?*, or *What
do you know of belladonna?* In either case the grammatical subject is
belladonna; but the logical subject is in the former case *dilating the
pupil*; that is what we are thinking about, and about that the judgement informs us that belladonna will effect it; in the latter case, the
logical subject is *belladonna*, and about that the judgement informs us
that it produces this effect. This distinction of logical subject and
predicate is always present in thought when we judge, though sometimes
the logical subject may be very vague, as when we say *it rains* or *it is
hot*. . . .'

Now, as I understand this passage, the distinction of logical
subject and predicate is said to be 'always present in thought
when we judge'.[2] This distinction is what I have called a distinction of moments constituting the thought (*the judgement*) and not
a *distinction of constituents*—for example, not a contrast between
successive stages of the thought, or separable coexistent components of it. That this is so—that this is what the author means
—is clear, I think, if we bear in mind the context in which this
passage occurs; if, in particular, we attach due weight to the
emphatic statements at the beginning of the chapter[3] that 'judgement is the form in which our thought of things is realized', that
'terms come before us only as elements in a judgement', that 'they
live, as it were, in a medium of continuous judging and thinking',

---

[1] Second edition, pp. 166–7.

[2] Not because in judging we are always aware of the distinction explicitly and
as such (for that is clearly not the case), but because the distinction belongs to
the *judgement proper*—i.e. to the *thought* expressed in the proposition, not to the
linguistic form (the form of the sentence) in which it is expressed.

[3] Loc. cit., p. 159.

and that 'their use in question, command, exclamation, or wish
presupposes judgement'. Every judgement, *qua* significant act of
thought, is a determinate advance in knowledge. It is *either* a
significant act of a given individual's thought—a step forward, so
to speak, in his education, a development by which his knowledge
expands or grows towards the level already attained by the expert
or the man of science; *or* it is a significant act of the expert's
thought—a step forward, so to speak, in the progress of a science,
a development by which the best and fullest knowledge available
at the time expands and grows towards a still higher level. *In
either case*, in every judgement, when the logician reflects upon it,
he must clearly distinguish (*a*) a certain extent and level of knowledge which it develops or expands—what Bosanquet somewhere
calls the 'growing-point' of the knowledge, and (*b*) the 'outgrowth'
—i.e. the expansion or development effected in, and by, the judgement in question. We may call the first the 'logical subject'; and
we may say of it, as Joseph does, that it is 'what we are thinking
about' in the judgement—or, as Bosanquet says, that it is the
'growing-point' of the knowledge embodied in the judgement. But
we must not be misled (and I do not suggest that either Joseph or
Bosanquet is misled) by these descriptions. 'What we are thinking about' is not detachable from what in this, and in other,
judgements we think about it. It is, for example (in Joseph's
example), not a *Belladonna* apprehended by a non-discursive or
conceptual knowledge—not a conceptual constituent to which
another conceptual constituent is added by the judgement. The
Belladonna we are 'thinking about' is something which, as we
think about it, shows itself to require the predicate—i.e. we can
only think about *it*, by completing the judgement. And the
'growing-point', similarly, is not, so to speak, a first part or stage
of the judgement, to which there is annexed or succeeds, as a
second stage, the 'outgrowth'. One must think rather of a germ
which is itself developing throughout the judgement—so that the
growing and that which grows are inseparable sides (not parts or
stages) of the total development, the total advance of knowledge,
which is the judgement.

(iv) *Third essential feature of the subjective position*: the supposed 'representative' character of the ideas (or ideal elements)
of the judgement.

A judgement (we have seen) is not ideal in the only sense of that
term which seems available to the advocates of the subjective

position; i.e. it is not a psychical fact—not a fact of the individual mind, made by its 'psychical' activities out of its 'psychical' states or changes. And in any case no judgement is a *product*. It is neither a result contrasted with a process, nor yet a process contrasted with a result. It is a self-development. It is a 'process' (if we *will* use so inapplicable a term) which most paradoxically does not lead to, but *is* its result; or a 'result' which (again, most paradoxically) is throughout *in process*—i.e. producing and fulfilling itself. Nor are there any elements of which a judgement is composed. Its unity is not that of a compound or a complex; and yet it is not *abstractly one*, not 'one' as a unit, atom, instant, or point, are (severally) 'one'. It is *concretely one*, i.e. its unity is that of 'a whole'. It is 'a whole', however, which has no separable parts—i.e. which is *logically prior* to the conception of its parts, and *really prior* (or, at all events, *not posterior*) to their being.

The subjective position, then, since it involves the impossible assumption that a judgement is a 'product', is itself untenable. Yet it will be instructive to examine the two remaining 'essential features' of the 'subjective position'—to examine them independently, and (so to speak) without prejudice, as though it were still an open question whether the judgement is not, after all, in strict and ultimate analysis, an ideal (i.e. a psychical) product.

These two remaining assumptions, it will be remembered,[1] are concerned with the distinctive character or function of the judgement—viz. that it alone is, and must be, either true or false. They are so bound up together that it is impossible to examine either without *eo ipso* (at least by implication) examining also the other. According to the first, the ideas or ideal elements, of which a judgement is composed, differ from all other simple psychical facts, in that each of them 'represents' a determinate element other than, and independent of, itself. To *represent, stand for, refer to*, a determinate Other—*this* is the characteristic property of every idea (of every sensation, imagination, thought), differentiating it from all other incomposite states or events, which coexist and succeed one another as modes of the embodied mind, as phases of the conscious stream which is its actual being. And, according to the second, these representative elements are so related in the complex psychical fact, which is a judgement, that it must be either true or false. For, taken as a whole, it must either correspond, or be discordant with another 'complex fact', another complex of elements-

---

[1] Cf. above, pp. 182–4, 213.

in-relation—viz. one that is composed of the elements *represented* by the ideas; and precisely such a correspondence *is* 'truth', and such a discordance 'falsity'.

Consider, then, briefly the supposed *representative* character of ideas. A may 'represent' or 'stand for' B in a variety of ways; but two only need in this connexion concern us.

(*a*) A copy—for example, a portrait—'represents' or 'stands for' its original. It resembles it; i.e. it is, for all its difference, visibly in certain respects identical with it; it is a (more or less exact) 'likeness' of it.

In *this* sense, it will be remembered, Locke attributed a 'representative character' to some of the Simple Ideas of Sensation. Some of them, he asserted, are 'exact likenesses' of real qualities of the external bodies.[1] If, for example, I look at a snowball,[2] the action of that external body upon my organs of sense (and nervous system) 'conveys' into my brain (or mind) a number of Simple Sensations; and, amongst them, a Sensation, or Idea, of Roundness which 'represents' a primary quality of the snowball (viz. its shape), as a copy 'represents' its original. The idea, as it occurs and exists, is a psychical event in me, a mode or phase of my 'private' conscious being. It is this—viz. a passing state of my own embodied mind—that I *immediately* perceive. But, in perceiving it, I apprehend, *mediately* through it (through it as 'representative'), the original, from which it was derived, and of which it is a copy—viz. the actual shape of a body in the physical ('public') world.

So too, as we saw,[3] 'Ideas'—i.e. those simple (incomposite) occurrences in the soul, those modifications of it, which are sensations, imaginations, conceptions—are assumed by Aristotle in the *De Interpr.* to *resemble* (and therefore to represent or reveal to us) facts. According to the analysis he there gives of the ἁπλῆ ἀπόφανσις —that simple declaration of historical fact which he treats as the basal and typical form of judgement[4]—the two Ideas, of which it is the combination, are 'likenesses' (ὁμοιώματα) respectively of a substance (for example, *Theaetetus*) and of an act or passion of a substance (for example, *running* or *sitting*).[5]

---

[1] Cf. above, Study II, pp. 111–20.
[2] Cf. Locke, *Essay*, ii. 8, §§ 7–8.
[3] Cf. above Study III, pp. 184–94.   [4] Cf. above, pp. 192–4.
[5] To prevent misunderstanding, let me repeat (above, p. 189, note) that, in view of Aristotle's treatment of perception and conception in the *De Anima*, the statement (*De Interpr.* 16ᵃ 7) that the παθήματα τῆς ψυχῆς are ὁμοιώματα of τὰ

It is unnecessary to spend much time in examining the assumption that ideas—i.e. psychical events, phases, and modes of my conscious being—'represent' facts by resembling them, by being 'likenesses' or 'copies' of them. On this point, Berkeley's criticism of Locke seems unanswerable.[1] The gist of that criticism, as it bears upon the supposed resemblance of the idea of roundness to the real shape of an 'external' body, was reproduced before[2] and need not be repeated.

Ideas, which are conceived *ab initio* as phases of a self-closed consciousness, cannot possibly 'resemble' elements, incidents, or characters of a corporeal reality—i.e. of a reality conceived *ab initio* as excluding (as contrasted with, and independent of) all 'minds' and their 'ideas'. 'An idea' (so Berkeley formulates the principle of his criticism) 'can be like nothing but an idea'; and clearly, if by an idea we are to mean a psychical (in contrast to a physical) fact, there is nothing more to be said. What we are asked to assume is that those psychical events which are 'ideas' are in certain respects identical—perceptibly identical—with physical originals; and obviously, under the circumstances, we cannot make such an assumption without naked self-contradiction.[3]

But A may 'represent' or 'stand for' B—at least, may 'suggest' B or 'have a reference' to it—without resembling it, or being a 'likeness' of it. For A may be a sign or signal of B, or a symbol of it. Thus (to quote a few simple examples) a high temperature is a sign of fever (a σημεῖον, σύμπτωμα, i.e. an effect from which we may conjecture fever as its cause); a red flag a sign or signal of danger (i.e. a warning of it in accordance with an accepted code); the fox a symbol of cunning (i.e. a pre-eminent sensible embodiment of the quality). The connexion between the 'representative' element and that which it represents is different in each of these examples, and it admits, no doubt, of still further variation. But in general we

πράγματα cannot safely be taken as adequately expressing his final and considered doctrine. Nor, of course, must it be supposed that Aristotle would have agreed with Locke that each soul with its modifications constitutes a self-closed sphere, or that in perception and judgement I am *primarily and immediately* aware of psychical occurrences in myself.

[1] Cf. *Principles of Human Knowledge*, part i, §§ 8 ff.

[2] Cf. Study II, p. 119, note 3.

[3] Cf. however, above, Study II, pp. 115–17, on the ambiguity of Locke's use of 'idea'. Would Berkeley's criticism be fatal if an 'idea of sensation' = an image or impression stamped on the brain (a phantasma)? Or even if it equals a state of my consciousness in which I am immediately aware of (= 'enjoying') such a corporeal modification? See (in *Mind*, vol. iv, no. 14) Bradley's article, 'In What Sense are Psychical States Extended?'

can say of it *negatively* that it involves no resemblance of the connected elements, i.e. they are not related as copy and original; and *positively* that the sign, signal, or symbol 'suggests', 'refers' or 'points' to, a determinate object other than itself.

Can we then assume—as Locke[1] at times assumes, and as many logicians appear to hold—that ideas are differentiated from all other psychical events because they are 'signs' or 'signals' or 'symbols' of things; because they 'refer' or 'point' the mind—in which they occur, or to which they belong—to facts or characters of fact beyond and other than itself?

Two considerations are fatal to such an assumption—and fatal also to the preceding form of the assumption which has already been disposed of on other, more special, grounds.

For, *first*, it is manifest that[2] a '"sign" or "symbol"' (and, equally, a 'signal' or a 'copy') 'implies the recognition of its individual existence, and this recognition is not implied in an "idea".' And *secondly*, if it is to *represent* or *refer to* B (whether as a sign, signal, or symbol, or as a copy of it), B must be in some sense known or knowable independently of A. Yet, in the case supposed, it is only through A—viz. only through my 'ideas', in virtue of their representative or mediating function—that I am able, for the first time, to know B (viz. to know the facts they represent).

As to the first of these two considerations: If I am to diagnose fever, to be warned of danger, to think of cunning, to be reminded of the original of a portrait—clearly I must apprehend the rise of temperature, the red flag, the fox, the painted canvas. I must apprehend each of them as it occurs or exists—each as a singular event or fact, having its own nature and existence (its own *what* and *that*). And this 'recognition of the individual existence' of the representative is an indispensable condition of its representing, i.e. of its serving to me as a sign (signal, symbol, likeness) of, anything whatever.

But now consider, on the other hand, an actual cognizant experience—my present perception, say, or judgement.[3] In perceiving—for example, in seeing a red flag or in hearing a chord—I do not see or hear or otherwise apprehend the processes of my seeing or hearing, or any constituent events or phases of those processes.

---

[1] Cf. above, Study II, pp. 120–1; Study III, pp. 197–8.
[2] As Bradley (*Logic*[2], p. 38, note 4) expresses it.
[3] Cf. 'Psychical Process' (*Mind*, N.S. no. 69, § 3). I am drawing freely upon this article in what follows.

Whatever those processes or those events may be—whatever may be the physical and psychical mechanism of my perceiving—at least they are not *what* I see or hear or apprehend when I see the red flag or hear the chord. I am not aware of the image on my retina, nor of the rods and cones, nor of my organ of Corti; not aware of them, nor of any change in them. Nor am I aware (for that is *here* the point) of any 'Idea'—any sensation or perception, any 'psychical event', or 'sequence of events' (or 'process'), which accompanies (or which, on reflection, I may suppose to have accompanied) these physical changes. In short, when I perceive *x* —whatever *x* may be—I do not see, or hear, or otherwise apprehend, any process or mechanism, physical or psychical or psychophysical, which is (or may be) involved in my perceiving. I do not, in perceiving, perceive the processes (or any parts or phases of the processes) of my own percipience. Whatever these processes may be, they are not something *through perceiving which* I perceive *x*; nor are they something which (normally, at all events)[1] I perceive *along with x*. For me, *qua perceiving x*, they are nothing at all.

This is so obvious in the case of perception, that I am ashamed to dwell upon it. Between my perceiving and the *x* (the red flag, the chord) which, in perceiving, I apprehend, there intervenes no idea—no psychical event or process—of which I am immediately aware, and *through which* (as through a sign or symbol or copy) my perceiving is mediated with the *x* which is its object. And this is no less obvious in the case of judgement.

For in the judgement, for example, that *Caesar was a great general*, or that *Philosophy is full of intricate problems*, a total concrete fact—a fact single in its complexity—is developing itself and being constructed, is emerging and being brought before my mind. My judging is a *discursus*—a synthetic-analysis—in which this concrete fact (say, *Caesar's greatness as a general*, or *the intricacy of philosophical problems*) both comes-to-be and is constructed (is produced and constitutes itself), both shows itself and is brought out (i.e. is known).[2] But in *thus* (discursively) 'knowing' the total self-developing fact, I do not know (I am not normally aware of)[3] any process of bringing (or of having) it before my mind. If there is

<hr />

[1] I add this reservation, because I do not wish to deny or to affirm, or to re-open the discussion (cf. above, Study II, pp. 128–32) of, 'Introspection'. The whole question is irrelevant to my present point.

[2] Cf. Study II, pp. 70–2; Study III, pp. 215–20.

[3] I add the same reservation as before (*not normally*), and for the same reason (cf. p. 223).

such a process; if there is 'a psychical process' of judging—neither it, nor the successive psychical events (the 'ideas') which are its constituent phases, are anything *for* the judging subject, in so far as, and while, he is judging. Awareness of these psychical events, or of this psychical process, need not (does not normally) accompany, and is never a condition of, the judgement. Between my judging and the concrete fact, which in (and through) my judging I may be said to 'know',[1] there intervenes no *Idea*—i.e. no psychical event, no phase or change of my conscious being, of which I am immediately aware, and *through which* (as through a sign or symbol or copy) my judging is mediated with the concrete fact 'be-judged' and (*in that sense*) 'known'.

The second consideration[2] is as obvious and familiar as the first. If A is to *represent* B to me, or to *refer me* to B, both elements (B as well as A) must be in some sense 'known' to me, and 'known' each independently of the other. Not only so—the relation of A to B (i.e. the connexion, whatever it is, whereby the first of these independently known elements refers me to the second) must in a sense already be 'known' to me. It must force itself upon my recognition as a particular case of, or as a corollary from, some principle of connexion belonging to an established system, which I 'know' at all events in the sense that I have accepted, and am working with, it. If fever, danger, cunning, were utterly unknown to me, how could I be led to think of *them* by my perception of the rise of temperature in the patient, of the red flag, of the fox? And were it not for my acceptance of (say) the orthodox rules of medical diagnosis, a particular code of signals for the regulation of traffic, a given system of principles of symbolism founded upon a determinate artistic or literary convention—the rise of temperature might be to me a symptom of emotion (not of fever), the red flag a signal of safety (not of danger), and the fox a symbol of speed (not cunning).

Now the assumption we set out to examine is that some amongst my psychical events—some of the uniquely singular and 'private' phases of my conscious being—are distinguished by their *representative character*. They possess, that is, the function of 'representing', each of them, a determinate fact or character of fact in

---

[1] Only in the guarded sense already explained. For (cf., e.g., above, Study II, p. 70) it must not be supposed that *in judging* (or, for that matter, even *in perceiving*) we are confronted with, and directly 'apprehend', an object.

[2] Above, p. 223.

Q

the 'public' world; in a world other than, and beyond, the self-closed conscious flow which is my embodied mind. And precisely because these psychical events possess this representative function, they are (so we are invited to assume) 'ideas', i.e. elements capable of being combined into a judgement—into that ideal product which must be true or false, and so is (or may be) a constituent 'piece' of knowledge. But since (as we have just seen) the *scheme* of representative and represented presupposes knowledge—viz. knowledge of both terms independently of one another, and knowledge also of a principle, of which their connexion is an example or a corollary —it is evidently impossible to make the assumption in question. To make it, is to turn round and round in a maze of self-contradiction. Without judgement, *ex hypothesi*, no truth, and so no knowledge of any kind; and without ideas, again *ex hypothesi*, no judgement. Yet unless I already have knowledge of some kind, my psychical events can 'represent' to me nothing; while, *unless* some of my psychical events possess for me a representative function, I have no 'ideas'—and, having no ideas, I am incapable of making a judgement, and so incapable also of knowledge.

(b) The preceding considerations are fatal to the assumption that some of my psychical events can serve to me as 'signs' or 'symbols' or 'copies', through which I become *for the first time* cognizant of facts beyond, and other than, my own embodied mind, my own conscious existence and its phases. But such an assumption, it must be admitted, was hardly worth examining. It might no doubt be imputed to Locke by a rigid and unsympathetic interpretation of some of his statements. But it is not in this sense that any modern logician would dream of attributing a 'representative function' to ideas. When ideas are said to represent facts—to have an objective reference, to be 'signs' or 'symbols' (or even 'copies') of a reality beyond themselves— something very different, and much more plausible, is meant; and this more plausible form of the assumption must be briefly examined.[1]

Ideas, we are to suppose, are psychical events, are phases of some individual's conscious life. But this does not mean that they are nothing but the lapsing of his consciousness, the occurring of

---

[1] The view I am going to state is akin to (perhaps identical with) the view put forward by Bradley in the first edition of his *Logic* (Chapter I: cf. above, pp. 205–12). But I wish to treat it without raising any historical question—without discussing how far Bradley did in fact maintain it, either at the beginning of his philosophical development, or throughout and to the end.

his psychical events. In every phase there is a *content*; in every event (even in a *psychical* event) there is a *somewhat* occurring. And it is the 'representative function' of its *what* or *content* that distinguishes an idea from every other psychical event or phase of a conscious life.

My ideas, then (considered not *qua* 'occurring' to me, or *qua* 'passing through' my mind, but as the *contents* of these occurrences, or as *what* is thus 'passing'), have a 'representative function'. But here again we must be careful, if we are not to caricature the doctrine. For, *in the first place*, it must be remembered that—if we are speaking of the actual judgement as it is made—ideas are nothing apart from their use. It is not (if we are to speak accurately) the ideas which 'have a representative function'. It is rather that I, in judging, am using the contents of my psychical events—am using what happens and passes in my mind—as images or signs of something beyond, and am thus transcending the privacy of my conscious flow and moving in a common or 'public' world. *Next*, it must be remembered that (normally, at all events) I am not conscious, while I am judging, of the psychical events I transcend, nor of the fact or manner of my transcendence. Normally, at all events, this is a hidden mechanism of the judgement—one, of which the judging subject is unaware. In thinking of, in judging about, an absent friend, 'images' of his face and movements 'rise', no doubt, and 'pass before' and 'through' my mind. But—unless, for some special reason, I wish to reflect upon and study the inner mechanism of my judgement—I am not aware of the images apart from the originals they suggest (not aware of them, that is, in their individual occurrence and content), nor of any act or process of transcendence by which I am led on from the former to the latter. And, *lastly*, when my ideas are said to have a representative function, of course it is not meant that they suggest to me objects or facts, of which otherwise I am totally ignorant. That, as we have seen, is impossible and absurd. But my absent friend, for example, was at one time present to me. And, as I now think about him and his doings, the 'images', which pass through my mind, refer me beyond themselves to an original which in part and in a sense I already know, and know independently of them. 'In part' and 'in a sense'; for what I become cognizant of, through the mechanism of my present judgement, is my friend as he now is and acts—not my friend and his movements as I formerly perceived them. And if *this* (viz. my friend as he now is and acts) is the 'original' which my images suggest and 'represent', it is an original which, in the main and in its completeness, must be admitted to emerge, to constitute itself, and to become known, only in and by the help of my present judgement.[1]

What are the grounds for postulating this latent mechanism in the judgement? So far as I can see, the supposed 'mechanism'—of which, admittedly, the judging subject, *qua* judging, knows nothing, knows neither the 'images' or 'signs', nor their representative action, nor the precise and bare elements they represent—is a fiction. 'But', it may be said, 'if it is a fiction, at least it is based upon a genuine characteristic of human thinking. For it seems indisputable that our thinking is immersed in, inseparably one with, sensuous imagery—varying no doubt in kind (visual, auditory, &c.), in vividness and intensity. At all events, though to judge is most certainly not to imagine, yet, *if we reflect upon the movement of our thought which is our judging*, what we find—always, it seems, and only—is a flow of imagery, a succession of "images" or at least of "signs".'

It will be remembered that the whole question whether it is possible to reflect upon and study this or that specific acting of the mind in its cognizant experiences—perceiving (say) or judging—was discussed at length, and eventually answered in the negative, in Study II.[2] Unless and until the arguments in that earlier discussion are refuted, the negative conclusion, to which they forced us, must be pressed against *all* attempts to discover *by reflection*

---

[1] The view, which I have tried to state, has lost (I fear) most of its plausibility in the statement. For it is, in fact, bound up with certain fundamental assumptions, which were examined and rejected in Study II. To make it plausible, it would be necessary to take for granted the immediacy of sensuous knowledge—i.e. to accept and work with the assumption of facts or elements of reality, which are (or may be) directly and infallibly apprehended in sensation, sentience, or sense-perception. It would be necessary also to take for granted a view of judgement which has been repudiated more than once. We should have to accept and work with the (indefensible) assumption that the reality, the total fact, which we know (or try to know) by way of judgement, does not itself enter into the discursive movement. *Qua* discursive, that is, the judgement is subjective; our intellectual arranging and developing, *our* synthesis and analysis of the contents of *our* psychical events. As a form or way of knowledge, on the other hand, the judgement is an 'act of reference'—a direct affirmation (or negation) that the result of this subjective *discursus* is 'real', actually qualifies (or does not qualify) the unmoving and undeveloping 'reality' or fact. In a true affirmative judgement, for example, the ideal content, which has been elaborated in the *discursus*, is referred to, and accepted as its adjective by, a substantial real—a fact *confronting* us while we judge, much as the *data* of sense and the objects of perception are (erroneously) supposed to confront us while we sensate and sensuously perceive.

[2] Cf. above, pp. 144–52.

the 'inner mechanism' of the discursive movement which is our activity of judging. Every such attempt, it must be insisted, is, in the nature of the case, foredoomed to failure; for it is the self-stultifying endeavour to study the abstracted subject—the abstracted subjective moment—of cognizance, i.e. to study that which *ex vi termini* cannot, without ceasing to be itself, be made or become an object. 'If we reflect upon our judging, what we find—always and only—is a succession of images.' We find, therefore, not characteristics of a cognizant activity, not details of the mechanism of our judging—but *objects* of cognizance, *objects* perhaps not of judging at all but of some other cognizant activity.

'But', it may be said, 'is not our thinking in fact immersed in imagery?' 'Immersed in imagery' is a vague phrase. Let us admit —what seems to be meant and to be true—that imagining or imaging (in one form or another) accompanies all (or most) of our thinking. Let us go farther and admit (what is perhaps more doubtful) that no human mind can think which is not also imagining, and even that imagining is in some manner an indispensable condition of our thinking.[1] It still does not follow that thinking (judging) *is* imagining, nor that imagining—and still less that judging—is a procession or a combination of images.

(v) *Fourth essential feature of the subjective position*: The view that truth is the correspondence, and falsity the discordance, of a judgement (a combination of ideal or 'representing' elements) and a matter-of-fact (a 'real' complex, or a nexus of the elements represented by the ideal elements of the judgement in question).

If, as I have tried to show, there are no ideal elements of the judgement; or none at least which, being psychical events or their contents, 'represent' to the judging subject elements beyond, and independent of, the phases of his conscious being—the last of the four assumptions, which seem essential to the subjective position, has been already, by implication, examined and condemned.[2] It is obviously impossible to conceive truth as the correspondence, and falsity as the discordance, between two complexes of elements-in-relation, each taken as a whole—viz. *between a complex of ideal* (or 'representing') *elements* and *a complex of real elements* (or elements which the former 'represent').

The net result of our 'closer scrutiny' of the subjective position is, therefore, this: Far from being a coherent hypothesis, it is a

---

[1] Cf. Arist., *De Anima*, 431ª 16–17: οὐδέποτε νοεῖ ἄνεο φαντάσματος ἡ ψυχή.
[2] Cf. above, p. 219.

medley of assumptions, severally indefensible, if not mutually incompatible. Within its outlines, or upon the basis they enclose, it is impossible to develop an intelligent and intelligible account *either* of the judgement (as that which is true or false) *or* of its truth and falsity.[1] And with this negative conclusion, we should be justified in passing on to the second of the typical positions (the objective position) which were to be considered.[2] Yet the view that truth is a *correspondence* (falsity a *discordance*) of our discursive knowledge (our judgements) with the facts we think about and *thus* (i.e. *discursively*) know (or strive and fail to know) is so common, and seems at first sight so plausible, that I hesitate to dismiss it without *some* direct examination—more especially because an unconscious prejudice in its favour often blocks the way to the adoption of the theory which, later,[3] I must try to defend.

The view of truth as *correspondence* (so to call it, for short) 'properly belongs' to the 'subjective position';[4] i.e. it is the most natural (indeed, seemingly the only possible) answer to the question '*What is Truth?*', if we start by assuming that knowledge in general, and judgement in particular, fall 'within' (or are phases of) the subject's conscious being, and that what he knows or 'thinks about' (the objects of knowledge) are facts 'external' to ('without') his mind. To adopt the subjective position (it seems clear) is to be committed in principle to the view of truth as correspondence in one form or another—and it is at least doubtful[5] whether it is

[1] Cf. above, p. 204.
[2] Cf. above, p. 181.
[3] Below, § 15.
[4] Above, p. 181.
[5] If I understand him rightly, Mr. Bertrand Russell (*Philosophical Essays*, pp. 170–85) attempts to maintain that truth is correspondence, while repudiating altogether the subjective position in regard to judgement. Judgement, he suggests, is a relation of a mind to a complex-of-terms; and truth is the correspondence of this complex-of-terms (this *objective*, in Meinong's terminology; or this *proposition*, in the terminology of G. E. Moore and Russell himself in other works) with a real complex. Some of his statements, however, suggest a different—but equally unconvincing—theory, viz. that truth is the correspondence of a complex-of-terms *qua related to a judging mind* (i.e. *qua* the 'objective' of, or in, a judgement) with *the same* complex *qua existing in fact* (i.e. as an independent entity apart from relation to a mind). See Bosanquet's criticism, *Logic²*, vol. ii, pp. 276–88. As we shall see presently (below, § 14) Russell in other works maintains yet another view: viz. that propositions—timelessly subsisting entities independent of mind and all the acts or attitudes of mind—are true or false, and that is an end of the matter. Truth and falsity, that is, are qualities immediately characterizing certain self-subsistent entities. (Cf. *Mind*, vol. xiii, p. 523.)

possible to conceive truth as correspondence *except within* the outlines of that position.[1]

Correspondence is a correlation; and in the correspondence, which is truth, each party to the correlation 'corresponds', of course, with the other. But the *correlata* are not on the same level. The ideal complex is subordinate to the real complex. The facts (or the 'matter-of-fact') constitute the standard, *by adjustment to which* our judgement is true. The facts, the matter-of-fact, are *there* in their own right (so to speak), fixed and unalterable; while the judgements are being brought into conformity with them, are being made so that they may correspond 'to' them, or 'with' them. The *real complex*, in short (or the matter-of-fact), stands to the *ideal complex* (or the judgement) as an original which the latter is to resemble or copy (which it is to reproduce in a different medium), or to which it is to provide a non-resembling, but analogous, counterpart.[2]

[1] Notice in this connexion (*a*) a passage in Bradley's *Logic*[2] (p. 43): 'We reflect about judgment, and, at first of course, we think we understand it. Our conviction is that it is concerned with fact; but we also see that it is concerned with ideas. And the matter seems at this stage quite simple. We have a junction or synthesis of ideas in the mind, and this junction expresses a similar junction of facts outside. Truth and fact are thus given to us together, the same thing, so to speak, in different hemispheres or diverse elements.' Starting, that is, as most people do, in the subjective position, it seems obvious to us *at first* that truth is correspondence, or (as Bradley expresses it in effect) that truth is our judgement *qua corresponding with the facts*. (He then, of course, proceeds to show how this, seemingly obvious, view breaks down.)

Notice also (*b*) a passage in Kant's *Lectures on Logic* (*Logik, Werke,* ix, p. 50), the substance of which is repeated in *Kritik der reinen Vernunft* (1st ed., pp. 57 ff.; 2nd ed., pp. 82 ff.). 'Truth, it is said, is the agreement of knowledge with the object. Hence, *according to this purely nominal definition' (Dieser bloßen Worterklärung zufolge*—but Kant, even in the *Kritik der reinen Vernunft*, accepts it as a correct account of the meaning of the term) 'my knowledge, if it is to be accepted as true, must agree with the object. But now *it is only by knowing the object* that I can compare it with my knowledge. My knowledge, therefore, is to confirm itself — ⟨a mode of confirmation⟩ far from sufficient to establish its truth. For since the object is *outside* me and the knowledge *inside* me, all that I can decide by the comparison is *whether my knowledge of the object agrees with my knowledge of the object . . . .*'

[2] The notion of 'correspondence' covers other relations than that of likeness to original, or copy to model. A map, for example, 'corresponds' with such-and-such a town or region; or I may use language corresponding to my feelings or 'equal to' the situation; but clearly neither the map nor the blasphemy are 'like' or 'resemble' ('copy') that with which they 'correspond'. I note this because, in a masterly criticism of the 'correspondence' view of truth (on which I shall be drawing freely), Bradley (cf. *Essays,* pp. 107–20) speaks of it as 'the theory that truth consists in mere copying'. His object in doing so, I take it, is to emphasize the main characteristic of the 'correspondence' view of truth—viz. that true judgement, knowledge, truth, &c., are by it regarded as, so to say, *otiose additions* to a reality, a world of

Thus, to take two examples: there actually occurred a certain detail-of-incidents-in-connexion, which we may call the landing of William the Conqueror. If, in thinking about English History, I *so* think that the belief I form (the judgement I make) 'corresponds' to this matter-of-fact (this fixed and unalterable constituent of the world's process), my belief (judgement) is *true*, and its *truth* is precisely the correspondence thus effected. If, on the other hand, my judgements (beliefs) fail to correspond with this matter-of-fact (misrepresenting the items of its detail, or their connexions, wholly or in part), they will be false, their falsity consisting precisely in their discordance. It would be a false belief, for example, that William landed at Hastings (instead of at Pevensey), or in 1065 (instead of in 1066), or that he never landed in England at all. *Again*, there is *in rerum natura*, timelessly actual, real indifferently at any and every time, a cohesion-of-elements, which we may call the internal structure of the triangle. And if, in thinking about plane geometry, I bring my thoughts or my judgements into correspondence with this matter-of-fact (this fixed and unalterable portion of the world's texture), my beliefs (or judgements) will be true, and their truth will be precisely the correspondence thus effected. Any failure in correspondence—i.e. discordance with this original, whole or partial—will be falsity; it would be, for example, a false belief that the internal angles are greater or less than, or not comparable at all in magnitude with, two right angles.

(*b*) Now, it must be remembered that to form a belief, to make a judgement, is to think *in the assurance* (*under the subjective conviction*) *of thinking truly*. The *differentia* of judgement (viewed on the side of the judging subject, viewed as his experience) is that, in it, the subject not only aims at truth and claims its possession, but is certain that his aim is achieved and feels sure that his claim is unchallengeable. This does not mean that 'to judge' necessarily implies the reflective consciousness of an aim and its achievement. It means that 'to judge' (to 'believe') *eo ipso* is to *think true*; to hold unhesitatingly for real, to be assured that what I judge is fact. The assurance, of course, is 'subjective' or 'psychological'; in being sure, I may be mistaken. Nevertheless, it is the *differentia* of judgement—the 'moment' which distinguishes it, as an experience of the subject, from doubt (say), deliberation, or question.

fact, already complete without them—*not* to suggest that advocates of the view are bound to maintain that the truth of a judgement is its *resemblance* or *likeness* to the facts, of which it is true. Cf. Bosanquet, *Logic²*, vol. ii, p. 276; also *The Nature of Truth*, ch. 1, where I have tried to analyse the notion of correspondence.

Without it—without the ineliminable presence of this subjective assurance—'error' (false judgement, in the strict and full sense) would be impossible; for *to be in error* is to make a judgement, true only partially, in the untroubled assurance that it is true wholly and without reserve. 'Error', if I may quote a sentence in which I tried to summarize this seeming paradox some years ago,[1] 'is . . . that form of false thinking which unhesitatingly claims to be true, and *in so claiming* substantiates and completes its falsity.'[2]

To make a judgement, then, is *to be sure* that what I judge is true; i.e. (according to the theory we are to examine), to be sure that my judgement corresponds with its relevant original. It follows, therefore, that if truth is correspondence the judging subject must, in making a judgement, have already before his mind either the matter-of-fact itself, must in some sense *know* it *ab initio* and independently of the judgement he is making; or at least must have before his mind something, some complex object, which he unhesitatingly accepts as the standard and original of his present judgement. If, for example, I am to make a judgement about the landing of William, I must have already before my mind *either* the actual bit of history itself; *or* at all events a complex object (some imaginary connexion of incidents) which I accept unhesitatingly as the authentic event, as William's landing as it in fact occurred. I must have already before my mind something which is to me the original, or the standard, to which I am adjusting my judgement, and with which I am certain, in the act of judging, that my judgement corresponds. Similarly, if I am to make a judgement about the internal structure of the triangle, I must have already before my mind (*ab initio*, i.e. independently of *this* judgement) *either* the relevant piece of the texture of reality; *or* at all events some complex object (some imaginary cohesion of characters) which I unhesi-

---

[1] *The Nature of Truth*, p. 142. Cf. *On Error*, pp. 131–2, 138, 140–2. Cf. also, perhaps, T. H. Green, *Works*, vol. iii, p. 73; and Bosanquet, *Logic*², vol. ii, p. 280.

[2] On the 'subjective assurance' which is distinctive of the judgement, cf. Bradley, *Essays*, pp. 381–2. 'Our last judgement, and that is our present judgement, must be taken or rather must be treated as infallible. This does not mean that a further reflection may not cause us to reject it. It means that, until that reflection comes, *we must hold the judgement as true*, and that *we cannot, while making a judgment, entertain the possibility of its error.*' . . . 'A mere past judgement, when I reflect on it, loses at once by my reflection its own independent value. I am logically beyond it, while I obviously cannot go beyond my present judgement while that remains present. *My present judgement, therefore, while it exists, cannot possibly be doubted*, and, however strange this may sound, *that judgement cannot be allowed or even suspected to be fallible*' (my italics). Cf. also, for further explanation and qualifications, below, pp. 269–72.

tatingly take to be the real structure of the triangle, the authentic standard or original of my judgement.[1]

(c) The view that truth is correspondence, as I have hitherto stated it,[2] takes no account of this *differentia* of the judgement as an experience of the judging subject. It does not consider the judging subject's assurance of truth, nor the paradox, or seeming paradox, which that assurance entails if truth be correspondence. It does not ask, for example, whether that assurance is ever known to be justified or the reverse, nor what is implied in this knowledge if it occurs. In short (to put the same point otherwise and perhaps more simply), the view that truth is correspondence requires more careful statement. We do not yet know precisely what its advocates assert; for we have not yet been told how the authentic standards of our judgements (and how therefore the correspondence or discordance with those standards, which are truth and falsity) are related to our knowledge.

I will try in a moment to restate the view, so as to remedy this deficiency. I will try to ascertain *for whom* the relevant matters-of-fact 'are there'; *by whom*, for example, the authentic landing of William and the real structure of the triangle are known, and by what manner of cognizance. But it is necessary first to dispose of a possible objection.

'For' (it may perhaps be said) 'truth is one thing, and the knowledge or recognition of truth another; and the first alone is now in question. The theory that truth is correspondence has therefore been adequately stated already; and whether, by whom, or how, the correspondence is known, is totally irrelevant. The advocates of the theory do in fact assert precisely this: "the truth or falsity of a judgement is its correspondence or discordance with an original which *is there* in its own right; which is what it is *in rerum natura*, indifferently whether it happens to be known or not, or even whether it is knowable at all or utterly inaccessible to knowledge".'

If this indeed is what the advocates of the theory of correspondence assert, their theory collides with everyday experience, and is based upon a self-contradictory postulate. Their theory, that is, is both paradoxical and impossible.

(i) As to the first point: truth and falsity (on such an interpretation) are the correspondence and discordance of my judgement

---

[1] Cf. the passage quoted from Kant; above, p. 231, n. 1.
[2] Pp. 230–1.

with a standard, which neither I nor anybody can know *for certain* as it really is; since what it really is, it is in itself. *Strictly speaking*, therefore, I do not aim at *truth*; I neither achieve, nor fail to achieve, *truth*; and I am not, in judging, 'subjectively assured' of thinking *truly*. *Truth* and *falsity*, in the strict and proper meaning of those terms (in the meaning given to them on this theory), are mere by-products of our intellectual activities. *Being-true* or *being-false* attaches to, is conjoined with, every judgement. But the attachment is external, the conjunction fortuitous—a mere accident, so far as concerns the judging subject's endeavour and activity; and an accident, which nobody can know for certain to have occurred. The judgement, as I make it, is *in its essence* indifferent to both, and to either, of these supervening and contingent properties; they are added to it *ab extra*, when (so far as my contribution, my thinking, is concerned) it is already, *qua* judgement, complete. If it happens to be true, I deserve no credit; nor any blame, if it happens to be false. And since I must remain for ever uncertain whether my judgement does in fact correspond, or fail to correspond, with the authentic event or cohesion (which is the relevant standard, but unknown and, for all I can tell, unknowable), there is no such thing as the search for truth, as teaching and learning, or as the advance (or failure to advance) in knowledge.

And (ii) as to the second point: on such an interpretation, the theory that truth is correspondence is based upon a self-contradictory postulate. For it requires a *multiplicity* of self-existent standards, each the measure of a special group of judgements in respect to their truth and falsity. William's landing, for example, is one of many individual items or stretches of history; each itself (having and keeping its uniquely determinate character), and in itself in the twofold sense that it is different from, exclusive of, every other, and independent of (and, for all we know, inaccessible to) our knowledge. So, too, the internal structure of the triangle is one of many self-supporting cohesions-of-universals, *this* one and no other; itself, and in itself, both as excluding all the rest and as indifferent (and, for all we know, inaccessible) to our knowledge. Yet plurality and difference imply relatedness in the many and the differents, and are therefore (one would have thought) inconsistent with their self-existence. And since in any case we are to suppose that each of these absolute events and cohesions—each of these authentic bits of history and pieces of reality—is what it is in complete independence of, and indifference to, anybody's knowledge;

since, in short, the *what* of each is (so to speak) 'its own affair'
—for us, at all events, they are indistinguishable, and we have
no right to assume that one differs from another, or that there is
one and another or others (i.e. a plurality) at all.

(*d*) It is clear, then, that the correspondence which is truth, and
the discordance which is falsity, fall in some sense within knowledge; and that the relevant standard—the authentic event or
cohesion, with which my judgement corresponds if true, and is
discordant, if false—is known or knowable by somebody and in
some manner. In what manner? And by whom? Let us consider
briefly the chief alternative answers which seem available to those
who maintain that truth is correspondence.

(i) They may say that truth and falsity fall in some sense within
the judging subject's knowledge. He himself, in making a judgement, has the relevant standard, the authentic original, before his
mind. Truth, they may agree, is not a relation subsisting between
my judgement and an entity, of which I am blankly ignorant; not
a correspondence into which, or out of which, I stumble by accident
when I make a judgement. Truth is an ideal at which I aim, by
which I am inspired, in judging; an ideal which I believe to be
embodied and realized in my judgement—which in some degree,
perhaps, is in fact so realized and embodied in every judgement.[1]

Such an answer, however, is not yet definite enough. For in
what sense is it contended that 'I myself, in making a judgement,
have the authentic original before my mind'?

It is plain that the judging subject does not know the original
precisely and perfectly as it is. If he did, his 'subjective assurance'
of thinking truly would *be* the possession of truth. Every judgement would *eo ipso* be true, and false judgement would be impossible. Why, indeed, under these circumstances, should he
trouble to make a judgement at all? Knowing the matter-of-fact
itself—possessing the original *ab initio*—he has nothing to gain by
judging. For his judgement, even if true (or rather, even though
under this hypothesis inevitably true), will only be an ideal repro-
duction—a copy or analogue in his thought—of an original known
to him already at first hand, without effort, precisely and perfectly
as it is.

---

[1] For the view here implied—viz. that every judgement is of necessity true
in some degree and therefore also *in some degree* false—see below, § 15. Strictly
speaking, it is incompatible (as I think) with the theory that truth is correspondence; but I cannot discuss the matter at this point.

(ii) The advocates of correspondence will no doubt reply that the judging subject has the original before his mind, without knowing it precisely and perfectly as it is. The judging subject, they may say, is neither blankly ignorant, nor precisely cognizant, of the relevant matter-of-fact. Both alternatives are impossible and absurd. But the disjunction—either blank ignorance or complete knowledge—is not exhaustive. There is a third alternative— the doctrine they maintain. The judging subject knows the original *ab initio*, i.e. independently of the judgement he is to make; but he knows it at the beginning more vaguely, and less adequately, than he will know it in the end—than he gets to know it through his judgement. His knowledge of the original, in short, is vague and incomplete by contrast even with the knowledge of it which he will achieve by making his present judgement—*a fortiori*, by contrast with precise and perfect knowledge of it as it is.

A doctrine of this kind is, in substance, sound. But it means the entire abandonment of the view that truth is correspondence. For the original, as known to the judging subject *ab initio*, is (on this view) not the authentic matter-of-fact (not William's landing as it actually occurred) or cohesion-of-universal-characters (not the triangle's structure as it really is). It is, on the contrary, a relatively confused and imperfect version—an appearance—of the real event or nexus. The judging subject's aim in judging is (on this view) not to adjust his thoughts to the original as he has it at first before his mind—not to form a belief, or make a judgement, corresponding thereto. If he did so, his judgement would yield him a knowledge as confused and imperfect as that with which he starts. On the contrary: his aim is to correct and complete (not to copy or reproduce) the *apparent* facts—the 'facts' as they are already before his mind. Lastly, on this view, 'precise and perfect knowledge of the original as it is' can only be conceived (it seems clear) as the ideal fulfilment of the process, which begins with *this* judgement—the judgement in question, which the subject is now about to make. In making *this* judgement, he has *pro tanto* improved—made more precise and adequate—his 'initial knowledge' of the original, i.e. the relatively confused and vague notion of 'the facts' which was at first 'before' (or 'in') his mind. And, in making *this* judgement, he has embarked upon, or has committed himself to, a self-developing process of thought—a self-fulfilling *discursus*—in which (or as which) alone he may be said to achieve and possess 'knowledge of the original as it really is'.

What the doctrine implies, in short, is that truth is a character inherent in the judgement, or in the growing system of judgements which it presupposes and carries farther. Truth, from this point of view, is (to use what has become the generally accepted term) 'coherence'. Knowledge, that is, is true in so far as it is intelligibly connected or 'coherent'; in so far as it is a self-supporting, self-necessitating, whole or system; such that every part stands and falls with every other, or each member demands and is demanded by each and by all. Whether, or rather how far and with what qualifications, such a conception of truth is sound, need not at present be discussed. It is clear, at all events, that it has nothing whatever to do with the view that truth is the correspondence of a judgement with a 'matter-of-fact'—i.e. with a standard external to, and independent of, the judgement itself.

(e) (iii) Let us make one last attempt to restate the view that truth is correspondence, so as to see precisely what is contended, and what, if anything, can be said in its defence.

We have seen that the correspondence which is truth, and the discordance which is falsity, do not fall within knowledge of the judging subject, *as he makes his judgement*. For, as he makes his judgement, the original, with which (if true) it is to correspond, is not as yet in its full and proper character before his mind. He does not know it precisely and perfectly as it is; but makes his judgement with the aim, and in the hope, of knowing *in and by the judgement itself* 'William's landing', for example, or 'the triangle's structure' (if not as they really are, at least) more precisely and more perfectly than he knew them before.

It must, then, be admitted by the advocates of correspondence that, *as I make a judgement*, I cannot know whether it is true or false. My 'subjective assurance of thinking truly' is nothing but the 'aim and hope', without which I could not judge at all. And if my judgement is true, and if its truth is correspondence, to me at all events the original, with which it corresponds, becomes known—if at all—only in, and by help of, the judgement itself. Yet the advocates of correspondence may still attempt to save their theory. For they may say that truth and falsity fall within knowledge, though not within that of the judging subject as he makes his judgement. 'William's landing', they may contend, 'is known to the historian. It is a fixed and established connexion-of-details, an authentic constituent of that ordered past which is the domain, the world, of the science of history. So, too, the internal structure of the triangle is known to the geometer; it is a fixed and unalterable cohesion-of-characters, an authentic piece of the intelligible domain which is the object of the science of geometry. Truth and falsity, then, fall primarily within the knowledge of the expert—the man of science in each department. He is the critic who knows the relevant matter-of-fact for *my* judgement (i.e. for the judgement of the layman). He knows and sets the standard for the correspondence which is its truth, and the discordance which is its falsity. And though, as I make my judgement, I cannot know for certain whether I am approaching, or receding from, the correlation which is truth—yet if, having made my judgement (i.e. having formed my belief), I publish it or impart it to others, its truth or falsity may be known to them and, through their criticism, to myself. For they may share the expert's knowledge, even if they are not experts themselves; and knowing thus the relevant standard, and comparing with it the published content of my judgement, they will know for certain whether there is correspondence or discordance—i.e. they will know, and can inform me, whether my judgement is true or false.'

Such an attempt to restate the theory of correspondence draws attention to what is obvious enough, but irrelevant to the real issue. For (1) nobody doubts that, for example, in the matter of William's landing and the structure of the triangle, the 'true' judgements for you and me—for the ignorant laymen and beginners in the subject—are those of the historian and the geometer. Relatively to our ignorance, the best available knowledge of the time is '*the* truth'—truth absolute, final, and complete. Our aim, as students, may be described roughly as being 'to bring our thought into agreement, or correspondence, with that of the expert'. It is, in fact, to assimilate his thought and make it our own. For you and me, at the outset of our studies, to make 'true judgements' on these subjects *is* to judge 'scientifically'—i.e. to think as the best, and best-informed, minds think; to raise our own thinking to the highest level so far attained in the advance of knowledge; to make judgements the same as (or, at least, not inconsistent with) those of the historian and the geometer. Nor (2) does anybody doubt that, at any given time and in each department of experience, there is a stock of current beliefs, which are commonly supposed to embody results established and authenticated by science. Each of these beliefs passes, for the time being, as a complete and final truth; its content (or what is believed) is taken to be, without qualification, *actual* and *real*—a matter-of-fact, for example, or complex of incidents, which is a constituent of the world's history; or a real cohesion, a complex of characters, which is a component portion of the world's intelligible texture.

But these obvious considerations are irrelevant to the real issue. For (1) admitting that the judgements of the expert (of the historian, for example, or the geometer) are true (if not absolutely, at least for the layman and relatively to his ignorance), is *their* truth 'correspondence'? If so, what are the originals, with which they correspond? And by whom, and in what manner, are these originals known? The expert, it is clear, knows them—if at all—only in and through the judgements he is making. In *this* case, *he* is 'the judging subject'; and if there is an original, correspondence or discordance with which decides the truth or falsity of his judgement, neither the original, nor the correspondence of discordance, can fall within his knowledge. Thus, the old difficulty remains. The correspondence which is truth, and the discordance which is falsity, must fall *in some sense* within knowledge; yet if we ask in what sense, no clear and defensible answer seems possible.[1] And (2) admitting that, by the general agreement of educated men, or as a matter of current belief, such and such a connexion-of-details or cohesion-of-universals *passes for* the authentic 'landing-of-William' or for the real 'structure-of-the-triangle'—the admission may help us to understand why the theory of correspondence is popular and plausible, but contributes nothing on which a defence of the theory could be based. For, if the student of English history or of Euclidean geometry has raised his thought on these subjects to the level of the best contemporary opinion; if he has assimilated, and made his own, the current beliefs which pass for established truths of history and geometry—it is plausible enough to say that he judges 'truly', *because, and in the sense that,* he has formed opinions, acquired beliefs, in conformity to (or in correspondence with) 'the facts'. But this, after all, is only a loose and popular description. For the facts in question are nothing else than what for the time being has become matter of educated belief. They are nothing but stereotyped extracts from a still advancing movement of speculative inquiry; 'implications'[2] loosely formulated, and abstracted from the context in which alone they hold; coarsened summaries of this or that provisional conclusion in the self-fulfilling *discursus*, which is what is called 'a science'—coarsened

---

[1] Cf. above, p. 235.   [2] Cf. above, Study II, pp. 162–8.

summaries of 'the truth', as it lives and grows and develops itself in actual knowledge: in, for example, the systematic (intelligibly connected or coherent) thought of the historian or the geometer.

Thus, for example, the long and patient labour of many investigators—their critical researches; their testing, sifting, adjusting, of innumerable evidences, documentary and other—has developed a more or less coherent, and therefore a more or less stable, theory of the past history of England. Within this constructed order of events, there are a number of *apparently* discrete and self-supporting complexes or connexions-of-details—as, for example, William's landing at Pevensey in 1066, Charles I's execution at Whitehall in 1649, and so forth. However much historical investigation may advance—whatever fresh light may be thrown upon the Norman Conquest or the Conflict of King and Parliament in the seventeenth century—these complexes, it may be admitted, these *bare connexions of terms*, of person and date and place, will remain, in one sense, unshaken and unmodified. They will figure in every text-book, and continue to serve as rough summary indications of the trend of historical investigation. But it would be absurd to view these text-book summaries, or the orthodox and current beliefs they embody, as items of absolute truth (as self-complete unit-knowledges, as it were, of an ideally complete sum of knowledges which is the science of history); and absurd to suppose that they 'correspond to' authentic matters-of-fact, to absolute events, or constituents of the world's actual process. The current belief that (say) William landed at Pevensey in 1066, or that Charles I was beheaded at Whitehall in 1649, is not 'the last word' of historical science, in the sense of a truth final, complete, and absolute; even though, *in another sense*, it may be 'the last word', inasmuch as the advance of knowledge will never, perhaps, reverse, or even modify, so tenuous and abstract a connexion-of-details. Nor is the content of such a belief an authentic matter-of-fact—an actual bit of the world's process, an event which actually happened, and *as* it happened neither more nor less. On the contrary—it is a mere abstraction, an abstract connexion of abstracted elements, which could not by any possibility occur as such, or as such be actual.

§ 14. (B) *Objective Position*

1. At the beginning of this Study, it will be remembered, three typical positions were set out in rough outline. Current theories

R

of the judgement, and of its truth and falsity, fall—it was suggested—within one or the other of these positions; conform to it in principle, or in their general trend. It was proposed, therefore, to examine them successively, in the hope that, from the examination, it would become clear what truth and falsity are, and how they are 'related' to knowledge.[1]

The examination of the first (subjective) position—far the longest, but also the easiest, part of the work before us—has now been finished, and has yielded only negative results. It is clear that, within its outlines, no adequate theory of the judgement of truth and falsity, or of knowledge and error, can possibly be developed. The position has resolved itself, on examination, into 'a mere medley of indefensible assumptions'; and theories which conform to it, or so far as they conform to it, are condemned to futility from the start.

Looking back upon the preceding criticism of the 'four essential features' of the subjective position, one can see that its fatal vice—its fundamental and irremediable blunder—lies in its misconception of the judging subject; or—for this comes to the same thing—in its exaggeration of the part played in judgement by the finite souls or selves or minds, the so-called individual thinkers. To the 'individual thinker' it ascribes the *making* of the judgement. And by the 'individual thinker' it understands one out of many mutually exclusive souls, selves or minds. Each of these minds is confined within its body; tied down to, and restricted by, local and temporal conditions; and so finite, and exclusive of all others. Yet, in spite of the glaring inconsistency, each of these limited and fragmentary minds is taken to be *whole* and *substantial*. For each, within its limits, or in its finitude, is taken to be a genuine individual, self-dependent and self-closed. It has, or produces, within itself a private manifold—experiences, which are its own psychical states, its own ideas (sensations, thoughts, volitions, &c.). It has also, and exercises, its own inherent power of thinking—its private psychical functions, its activities of ideal analysis and synthesis. And by these psychical activities it *makes*, out of its psychical states—out of its simple or simpler ideas—ideal products, or complex psychical facts; and, amongst them, some that are true or false, i.e. 'judgements'.[2]

[1] Cf. above, pp. 180–1, 182, 203.
[2] Cf. above, pp. 182, 203–12. In calling the first position 'subjective', I had this—its exaggeration of the part played by the finite judging subject—in view.

The position we have next to examine—the second or 'objective'[1] position—is, or professes to be,[2] the polar opposite of the first. For it starts by setting aside as irrelevant all consideration of the part which may (or may not) be played in judgement by a mind, by the states or attitudes or activities of a judging subject. Let us see the ground, the nature, and the development of this initial abstraction.

As the term 'judgement' is commonly used—in everyday life and in most logical theories, certainly in all that belong to the subjective position—a judgement is an actual experience, of a temporally existent soul or self or mind. It is something, the being or reality of which (in terms of an antithesis), as I explained before,[3] is *actuality of existence*, not *actuality of essence*. It is inseparably bound up with a mental or psychical flow: it is 'one with'—and to that extent itself *is*—a psychical event, a constituent in the history of an actual mind. In this sense, every judgement is mine or yours or somebody's; is made (believed, asserted) by a finite judging subject.

But those who conform to the objective position—the 'objective logicians', as we may call them for short—propose to use the term 'judgement' so as to cover neither more nor less than the commensurate subject of the predicates 'true' or 'false'. In this sense a *judgement*, they insist, is something impersonal and timeless, independent of the temporally existent minds and their psychical attitudes or acts. It is neither a belief nor a believing; but a complex-of-significant-elements *which is such as to be believed* (or 'asserted'). For whether in fact it was, is, or ever will be, believed, is irrelevant to its intrinsic—its strictly logical—character: irrelevant to its own proper being as that which alone can (and must) be true or false.

Thus (to take a few examples) *that-Charles-I-was-beheaded, that-the-internal-angles-of-a-triangle-are-equal-to-two-right-angles, that-there-is-no-perpetuum-mobile*—these complexes of significant elements are true, whether anybody is believing (asserting) them or not. Taken bare and in their purity, without any dependence upon or connexion with a mind (with its attitudes or acts), these complexes are subjects of the predicate 'true'. It attaches to them,

---

[1] Cf. above, p. 181.

[2] 'Seems to be': for (as we shall see) it shares with the first position the same misconception of the judging subject, and is wrecked thereby, though in a different manner (cf. below, pp. 251–3).

[3] Cf. Study II, pp. 147–50.

to them precisely and as such; they are true impersonally and timelessly. Similarly, *that-Charles-I-died-in-his-bed*, *that-the-diagonal-of-a-square-is-commensurate-with-its-side*, *that-man-is-not-mortal*—these complexes, barely and precisely as such, are subjects of the predicate 'false'. They are false, as the former complexes are true, impersonally and timelessly—i.e. without dependence upon, or reference to, the actual beliefs, the temporal experiences, of *this* or *that* or *any* mind.

According to the objective position, then, 'a judgement' (in the only sense that is relevant in an inquiry into truth and falsity) is a complex of significant elements—a complex such as to be believed or asserted; and must not be confused with what is commonly, but loosely, called 'a judgement'—viz. an actual assertion or belief, in which (besides the complex believed) there is a believing or asserting, i.e. the psychical attitude or act of an 'individual' (of *this* or *that* finite) mind. Such complexes, it is contended, are 'judgements' *sensu strictissimo*—in the only sense, at all events, which is admissible in a genuinely scientific logic, in a logic that is 'pure', i.e. not infected with irrelevant psychological or epistemological matter. In order, however, to avoid all risk of confusion, let us call these complexes not 'judgements', but 'objectives' or 'propositions'—a nomenclature suggested by many of those who adopt the objective position.[1]

The 'objective' logicians thus make a clean cut between psychology and epistemology on the one hand, and logic on the other. The first two sciences are concerned—psychology altogether, and epistemology in part[2]—with what exists or occurs; with facts and

---

[1] Cf. above, Study II, p. 181, Study III, p. 230; and Bertrand Russell, *Principles of Mathematics*[1] (1903), vol. i, p. ix: '. . . Propositions are commonly regarded as (1) true or false, (2) mental. Holding, as I do, that what is true or false is not in general mental, I require a name for the true or false as such, and this name can scarcely be other than proposition.' See, further, the same author's article, 'Meinong's Theory of Complexes and Assumptions', in *Mind*, vol. xiii (1904), pp. 204 ff., 306 ff., 509 ff., in which Meinong's use of the term 'objective' is carefully explained. Russell himself (*Mind*, l.c., p. 206, and note 2) differs from Meinong, and agrees with G. E. Moore, in identifying 'propositions', 'complexes', and 'objectives'—i.e. in using all three terms as equivalents.

[2] Cf., e.g., Russell (*Mind*, l.c., pp. 204–5). 'The theory of knowledge' (l.c., p. 205) 'is in fact distinct from psychology, but is more complex: for it involves not only what psychology has to say about belief, but also the distinction of truth and falsehood, since knowledge is only belief in what is true. Thus the subject may be approached either through psychology or through logic, both of which are simpler than it is.' The theory of knowledge (or epistemology) is thus a complex science—a blend of logic and psychology: and in so far as it contains, or is

events, and the empirical laws of their coexistence and sequence in the phenomenal or actual world. But logic, they maintain, is (or ought to be) a *pure* science—concerned not with what exists or occurs, but with what 'subsists' in the ideal realm of 'meanings' or 'the intelligible'.[1] It is concerned with what may be called 'essences' or 'ideal entities', both simple and complex, which are such as to be conceived or defined or asserted (e.g. with terms, concepts, universals; and with propositions, or any other complex entities in which two or more of these simple entities, these significant elements, are timelessly related). It is concerned also with the necessary implications that are rooted in these ideal entities— these 'essences', these constituents (whether simple or complex) of the 'realm of meanings', these denizens (so to speak) of the 'intelligible world'. But the entities, with which it is concerned, though they are 'intelligible' (though they are such as to be conceived, defined, asserted, &c.), have their own proper being, or 'subsist', in entire independence of any actual intelligence, of any actual mind or mental attitude or act; and it is thus and thus only —i.e. in their 'extra-mental' 'being' or 'subsistence'—that they are, or ought to be, studied by the logician. And the ideal laws or necessary implications, which are (so to speak) the principles of organization of this intelligible world, though they are such as to be discovered by mental processes or acts (by reasoning, for example, or rational intuition), are (or ought to be) studied by the logician in their independent (i.e. 'extra-mental') 'subsistence'— i.e. as so many relations (positive and negative) which 'are valid' or 'hold' timelessly, whether or no they have been, or will be, discovered by any finite mind.[2]

composed of, psychology, it has to do with what exists and occurs, viz. with psychical (or mental) states and events. Cf. *Nature of Truth*, pp. 36–7.

[1] I am fully aware that a 'realm of "meanings" or "the intelligible"' sounds like —and probably is—nonsense, when all relation to an actual mind (to a somebody who means, conceives, or understands) is taken to be excluded *ab initio*. Yet I hardly know how else to describe the domain of pure logic as it appears to be conceived by, for example, Husserl or Russell. Cf., e.g., Russell's attempt to vindicate for certain concepts—certain constituents of this domain—'meaning in a non-psychological sense': *Principles of Mathematics*[1], vol. i, § 51.

[2] Cf., e.g., Bosanquet's summary of Husserl's conception of pure logic in *Implication and Linear Inference*, pp. 141 ff. 'Logic' (l.c., p. 144) 'speaks about concepts, judgements, and inferences, which sound like mental facts; but, in so speaking, it does not really refer to the facts of psychical life, but to the meanings, propositions, and necessary connections which, true independently of mental apprehension, are discovered and apprehended in the mental processes just referred to. "Its laws" [Bosanquet continues, quoting from Husserl, *Logische Untersuchungen*, vol. i, p. 122] "are all the ideal laws which are grounded purely in the meaning (*essence*,

2. According to the plan, on which I have hitherto been working, this sketch of the objective position ought *next* to be filled in and substantiated by an exposition of one or more of the logical systems, which conform to it in principle—by a connected account of the logical doctrines, for example, of Meinong and Husserl, or Moore and Russell.[1] And, *finally*, the position itself ought to be systematically examined. Its component assumptions (its 'essential features') ought to be set out and tested. Are they severally necessary and legitimate—i.e. forced upon us, each of them, and warranted, by the requirements of a philosophical (an intelligible and intelligent) interpretation of our cognizant experience? And are they mutually compatible—i.e. such as to constitute a single coherent hypothesis?[2]

But so much has still to be done to bring the present Study to a satisfactory conclusion, and so little space remains, that I am forced to the utmost possible compression. The 'objective position', therefore, I shall assume, is already sufficiently 'fixed'—clear, without further illustration, in its outlines and essential character. And, without attempting an exhaustive examination of its essential features, I proceed to criticize it where it seems most evidently open to attack—viz. (*a*) in its severance of propositions from the mind, and (*b*) in its postulate of false propositions.

(*a*) *The severance of propositions from the mind.* Let us begin by defining the scope of this first criticism of the objective position. We are concerned in it with the objective logician's assumption that propositions, considered as such and in general (i.e. whether positive or negative, and the true and the false alike), are entities which being severed in their nature from all that exists and occurs in time, are severed also from, are essentially independent of, every mind and every mental attitude or act.[3]

content) of the notions truth, proposition, object, constitution, relation, connection, law, fact, &c."' Cf. also my own exposition and criticism of the same general view of logic as it is applied by Bertrand Russell and G. E. Moore to *the proposition and its truth and falsity*: *The Nature of Truth*, e.g. pp. 36–8, 56–8. In terms of the antithesis, to which I referred before (above, p. 243), propositions (which, according to the objective position, alone can, and must, be either true or false) are complex entities, the being or reality of which is not *actuality of existence*. Their being or reality would be *actuality of essence*—if they possessed any being or reality at all, and were not the products of vicious abstraction (cf. below, pp. 247 ff.).

[1] Such an account, I ought to add, would show, in all these writers, divergences from (as well as conformity to) the 'objective position'. The position is a *type* only—a type to which actual logical systems conform at most 'in principle', or in their general trend.　　　　　[2] Cf. above, pp. 184, 203–4.

[3] Cf., e.g., Husserl's insistence (*Logische Untersuchungen*, vol. i, pp. 127–30) that

We are not to trouble ourselves with any special theory of the constitution of these extra-mental propositions. We are not, for example, to examine Russell's account of them—viz. that they are complex entities, consisting of simple (or simpler) elements in relation—though there are grounds for doubting whether it could be defended. For we have already seen[1] that the antithesis of complex and simple is totally inapplicable in the analysis of a 'judgement'; and there is every reason to suspect it would prove equally inapplicable in the analysis of a 'proposition'—since a 'proposition' may become (and be for a time) the content or 'object' of a 'judgement', i.e. that which a judging subject asserts or believes. Again, that the elements which constitute these complex entities—these propositions, as Russell conceives them—seem to cohere (or to be coupled) alternatively by a *positive*, or by a *negative*, relation;—this, too, we must leave without examination, remarking only that those who adopt the objective position are likely to find themselves embarrassed, even more perhaps than most logicians, by the problems connected with negation.[2]

Nor are we to trouble ourselves at present with the question of falsity and error. We are not to examine a 'feature' which seems essential to the objective position—viz. the division of propositions into two contrasted groups, those that are timelessly true and those that are timelessly false. This, and the difficulties it involves, will occupy us later.

How does the objective logician come by the notion of these propositions which subsist *per se*—these extra-mental or 'independent' propositions? For, on the face of it, a proposition which subsists, and is true or false, *per se*, is a strange and paradoxical 'entity'. It is an 'entity' which the unsophisticated student would find it as difficult to accept or conceive, as (say) an 'independent volition' or 'resolution'—i.e. a volition which subsists,

propositions—or at least true propositions, truths—'neither appear in, nor vanish from, the flow of psychical experiences'; that they have a 'supra-empirical' or 'ideal' being (the being of essences, ideas or ideals); that they are 'units of validity in the timeless realm of ideas', &c.

[1] Above, pp. 215–19.

[2] In referring to 'Russell's account of propositions', I am thinking partly of certain statements in the *Principles of Mathematics*, in the *Problems of Philosophy*, and in the articles on Meinong's theory, &c., in *Mind*, vol. xiii; partly also of his article 'On Propositions: what they are and how they mean' (Aristotelian Society, supplementary volume ii). But (cf. above, p. 230) no single consistent account of propositions can justly be ascribed to Russell. In the works to which I have referred he maintains two or more mutually incompatible views: cheerfully, to all appearance, and without turning a hair.

and is good or bad, *per se*, apart from every existent will and all the temporal acts of willing. We are most of us accustomed, no doubt, when we reflect upon any experienced-truth or true judgement, to distinguish the truth that is experienced and the experiencing of it—or (as it is often expressed) the 'content' of the judgement (its 'burden' or 'object') and the 'act' of judging or of assertion.[1] And all or most of us would readily agree with the objective logician that any judgement—e.g. Euclid's about the triangle, or this or that historian's about Charles I—is true (if it be true) whenever, wherever, and by whomsoever it is asserted. But why should we agree with him that the 'content' (or 'object', in Russell's terminology[2]) of Euclid's (or the historian's) judgement is an 'independent proposition' having its being and its truth timelessly in itself; so that it would *be*, and *be true*, even though nobody asserted it ever or at all?

The 'facts', on which the objective logician is reflecting—the *phenomena* or 'apparent facts', from which (like any other logician) he starts, which (like any other logician) he sets out to explain— are 'items' of 'knowledge' and 'errors', truths and falsities experienced by somebody. *Who* the somebody is, *when* and *where* the somebody experiences—all this, let us admit or rather insist, is (if properly understood) irrelevant. But, in the 'facts' to be explained, there always is *a* 'somebody'; there always is *some* 'when' and 'where'. To eliminate every 'somebody', and all time and place, on the ground that no special somebody, and no special date and position, are indispensable, is to commit an elementary blunder of analysis. One might as well argue that, because (say) a mare proves fertile when mated with any one of a dozen stallions indifferently, it is legitimate to postulate parthenogenesis in respect to mares, or at all events in regard to this individual mare.

The blunder is, indeed, so elementary and palpable, that we may well hesitate to impute it to the objective logician—to the

---

[1] Russell, if I understand him rightly (cf. *Mind*, l.c., p. 510), would call that which is asserted or believed—i.e. the proposition if, or when, it happens to be experienced—always the 'object', never the 'content' (or 'burden'), of the judgement or belief. The 'content', in his usage, is itself mental or psychical— the *what* of the psychical attitude of believing or act of asserting. Husserl employs the terms *Wesen, Inhalt, Gehalt, Bedeutungsgehalt—essence, content, significant content*—freely and indiscriminately to designate the independent propositions, the truths, which are 'units of validity in the timeless realm of ideas'.

[2] Cf. p. 247.

advocate of a 'pure', or rigorously scientific, logic. *Yet how otherwise does he come by the notion of his independent propositions?*

Perhaps the root and origin of these paradoxical entities lie deeper. The objective logician commits no elementary blunder of analysis, for he comes by his notion—or, rather, his notion comes to him—without any explicit analysis at all. He draws a common and loosely worded distinction; and, in doing so, has already inadvertently assumed the mutual independence of the *distincta*. His notion of independent propositions, in short, is the counterpart and complement of his notion of the judging mind; and both are *given* (taken for granted) in his initial distinction between content (or object) and act of judgement.

For this distinction—even if all, or most, writers on logic are accustomed to use it—is ambiguous. What precisely is covered by each of the *distincta*, and how are they related to one another, and to the judgement as a whole? In an experienced-truth (in, for example, Euclid's judgement about the triangle, or in the historian's judgement about Charles I) how much precisely is 'content' (or 'object'), and how much—or how little—is 'act'? Is the 'act' *nothing* but an event of Euclid's or the historian's psychical existence, a change of their consciousness? Or does it penetrate and permeate the 'content' or 'object'—so that the latter, too, as they experience it, is *in process of being brought out?* But if the truth which they assert or judge—the content or object of their judgement—is thus *being brought out* by the 'act' of judgement, must not the 'act' itself be something more than a mere event in their psychical existence? Must not the 'content' or 'object' of the judgement itself be such as to emerge in, and through, an act or activity of thought? And if so, can we really suppose that the activity of thought, in which the internal structure of the triangle or the complex of incidents called 'the execution of Charles I', respectively, constitute themselves as, and take the shape of, 'truths'—can we really suppose that *this* activity of thought is spontaneously originated by Euclid or the historian?

According to the view of judgement, which was set out and defended in the preceding Study,[1] a judgement is through and through a *discursus* or activity of thought—a movement which

---

[1] Cf. above, Study II, pp. 69–72, 127, 152–3. The view belongs in principle to the third ('idealist') position, which will be considered in § 15 below. Cf. Bradley, *Essays*, e.g. pp. 218, 327, 336–7; Bosanquet, *Implication and Linear Inference*, e.g. p. 148.

is analysis and synthesis in one. And this *discursus* is concrete;
i.e. it is 'one' or 'whole', but so that it unites inseparably in itself
two contrasted moments or complements. In respect to one of
these moments of its indissoluble totality, it is 'objective'; i.e.
the self-development of an 'object', a movement in which an
object constitutes itself and becomes known as what it 'really' is,
viz. as a 'spiritual fact' or a 'truth'. And in respect to the other
complement of its total being, it is a 'subjective' *discursus*; an
activity of thought 'passing through' a finite mind, or one in
which an individual thinker co-operates in the self-development
of an object—helps to elicit it, or helps it to emerge, in the form
of a 'truth'. Now with such a view the distinction between content (and object) and act of judgement is incompatible—or can only
be made compatible by careful qualification of its terms. For the
term 'content' (and still more readily, perhaps, the term 'object')
carries with it the suggestion of something finished and quiescent.
But if the judgement is 'through and through a concrete *discursus*',
there can be nothing in it which is therefore *fixed*, which the
judging subject *merely* finds or apprehends. There can be no 'content' or 'object', which is not developing itself and being shaped—
which is not therefore also and essentially the judgement as an act or
activity of thought. And 'act of judgement' (still more obviously,
perhaps, 'act of judging' or 'asserting') tends to suggest that the
activity of thought *originates* within an individual thinker's mind,
and is *no more* than his private psychical process. But if the
judgement is 'through and through a concrete *discursus*', there
can be no 'act of judging' *confined* to this or that particular mind,
and external to the '*object*', which in the judgement is asserted,
or asserts itself. The only *act* is the single and total *discursus*—the
activity of thought, which is the judgement as a whole. And that
activity is *immanent* in the 'object'—the form of its self-development and emergence as a 'truth'; and *immanent also in* one or
more of the so-called 'finite minds'. For what is called, for
example, a 'finite judging subject', an 'individual thinker', or a
'particular mind', is a *mind* (or *thinks*, or *judges*) precisely in so
far as it co-operates in the self-development of a 'content' or
'object'—precisely in so far as an activity of thought, which is
objective and impersonal, is present in, and appears as a phase of,
its special (its subjective and personal) conscious flow. And it is
a 'finite', 'particular', 'fragmentary', mind or judging subject,
because, and in so far as, this 'immanence' is only a passage;

i.e. the activity of thought, which is the judgement, is neither originated by it, nor wholly present within, i.e. confined to, its conscious flow.

But the objective logician agrees with those who conform to the subjective position in viewing the judgement—i.e. any experienced-truth or experienced-falsity—as something composite or complex. For the objective logician, therefore, to distinguish between content (or object) and act is not to emphasize different moments in a 'concrete whole' or a 'spiritual fact'.[1] It is to mark off constituents which, though for a time conjoined, are separable in principle each from one another, and both from the judgement as a whole. 'Euclid's or the historian's judgement', he would probably say, 'is, if you like to call it so, "a whole"'. It is something complex, something capable of being analysed into simpler constituents or parts. But it is not a *concrete whole*—i.e. one in which there are necessarily distinguishable moments, but no parts; differences that must be emphasized, but no constituents—for that is a contradiction in terms. And Euclid's or the historian's judgement is, if you like to speak loosely, a "fact of knowledge". For it is, or rather, it includes, a "fact of knowledge", i.e. a mental act—an act or state of Euclid's or the historian's mind.[2] But the scientific logician knows nothing of *spiritual facts*. Facts are either mental or physical—facts in (and of) a mind or facts of the external (extra-mental or non-mental) world. A "spiritual fact"—i.e. a fact *neither* within *nor* without, or *both* within *and* without, a mind—is as plain a contradiction in terms as is a "concrete whole".'

The objective logician, then, in distinguishing between content (or object) and act, assumes from the start that the 'judgement', within which he is drawing the distinction, is a complex; that the *distincta* are hard and separable constituents, of which it is composed. And, agreeing so far with those who conform to the subjective position, he agrees with them also in his conception of *one* of these constituents. For he assumes from the start that the *act of judgement* is neither more nor less than, for example, Euclid's or the historian's 'act of asserting' or 'attitude of belief'. Hence, though he appears to reject *in toto* the view of the judgement which is maintained by the 'subjective' logicians—for, while *they*

---

[1] Cf. above, Study II, pp. 85–9.

[2] Cf., e.g., Russell, *Mind*, l.c., p. 205: '. . . knowledge cannot be other than psychical . . .', and p. 510: 'But the judgement itself, *in its purity*, as something *wholly psychical* . . . .'

regard it as, in ultimate analysis, an ideal product made by the psychical activity of this or that individual thinker, *he* insists that the individual thinker and his mental attitudes or acts are utterly irrelevant—yet, after all, he shares with his opponents the same fundamental misconception of the judging subject.[1] It has never occurred to him to question their view of the finite minds: the minds which, in their finitude, in their limited duration and their mutual exclusiveness, are supposed, nevertheless, to be genuinely self-dependent and self-contained—to be creators and originators of thought.

The judging mind, then, is to the objective logician precisely what it is erroneously assumed to be by those who adopt the subjective position; but he relegates it, together with all its psychical attitudes and acts, to the domain of psychology. Hence, when he distinguishes within the complex, which is popularly called a 'judgement', the act of assertion and the content (or object) asserted, the act is only mentioned to be cast aside. It is, on his view, in no sense a constituent of, or relevant to, the judgement with which he, as a logician, is concerned—the judgement in its logical character as the true or false. And, conversely, the judgement, as it interests the logician, is *all of it* 'content' or 'object', entirely free and void of 'act'.

An 'independent proposition', then, is a 'content' which no thought 'contains', and which 'contains' no thought. It is an 'object' with no essential relation to a 'subject' or a subject's act. It is a proposition which nobody proposes; a judgement which is not made or asserted; an entity fixed and quiescent, from which all notion of development by (or in) a *discursus* must be rigidly excluded. It is, moreover, suspended midway between the only two realms of fact—the psychical and physical—which the objective logician himself appears to recognize. And the unsophisticated student,[2] it must be said, is right to reject these 'contents' without a continent, these 'objects' abstracted from every 'subject', these fixed and non-discursive judgements. For it is clear that the assumption of these paradoxical entities, these 'independent propositions', is not 'forced upon us' nor in the least 'warranted by the requirements of a philosophical interpretation of our cognizant experience'.[3]

Far from it. The *independent propositions*, which the objective logician would have us postulate as entities subsisting timelessly

<hr>

[1] Cf. above, p. 242.   [2] Cf. above, p. 248.   [3] Cf. above, p. 246.

in a middle region between the knowing minds and the world of facts they strive to know; and *the knowing minds*, of which they are independent; the minds of *his* psychology, which keep, in their psychical attitudes and acts, each within its private self, and all within a world of merely temporal facts and events—are twin fictions generated by the same faulty analysis, or, rather, by the same abuse of a loosely worded distinction.

3. (b) *The postulate of false propositions.* According to the preceding criticism, the general notion of independent propositions is a paradoxical fiction. The objective logician is led to frame it because, although he rightly recognizes that no adequate theory of the judgement *qua* true and false, and of its truth and falsity, can be developed on the basis of the subjective position, he still, without knowing it, has taken and keeps his stand within its outlines. For, in principle and in the main, he shares with the subjective logicians their conception of the judging minds and of the *ultimately* real—the 'facts' they judge 'about' and strive, in the end, to know.

But this criticism, whether sound or not, will not convince the objective logicians. For 'logic', they will say, 'is a science; and, like all sciences, it not only may, but must, make use of working hypotheses. The notion of independent propositions may be a paradox and a fiction. But if it "works" in logic—if the logician finds it convenient in formulating and solving his problems—it needs no further justification. Nor does it matter what view the logician takes of the judging minds and of the *ultimate* reality— the reality to which, *in the end*, their judgements refer. Logic, like every science, has its own delimited domain. The logician, as such, is concerned with the true and the false, neither more, nor less— with propositions, their constituents, and their implications *inter se*. As to the judging minds—whether they *make* by their thinking, and in their thought, the judgements that are true and false, or whether, as he maintains, they do but "assert" or "believe" the propositions, the truths and falsities, that happen for a time to be their "objects"—they fall in any case beyond the domain of logic, and are the concern solely of the psychologist. And as to the ultimately real—the world of facts, or whatever it may be, to which *in the end* these truths and falsities refer, of which indirectly, and in the last resort, they are valid—that is the concern solely of the metaphysician.'

Earlier in this Study,[1] and in connexion with a very different

[1] Above, pp. 211–12.

theory, we came in sight of the view that logic is a *special science*. *There* it was argued that, because logic is a special science, the logician works with provisional, and perhaps fictitious, assumptions, and must be content therefore with provisional results. He considers truth and falsity, and the judgements and inferences which are true and false, only under a deliberate abstraction. For they all inseparably involve 'an aspect of psychical existence'; they all must exist and occur as events in, and of, an individual self or soul—and this whole side of the true and the false, and of truth and falsity, is ruled out *ab initio* from the logician's treatment by the hypothesis which makes and delimits the domain of his science. *Here* the same contention is used as a premiss for a quite different conclusion. Because logic is a science (so the objective logician argues) its domain is *self-sufficient within its rigidly determined limits*. There is no suggestion or admission that the logician must be content with provisional results. On the contrary: it is assumed that the truths and falsities, of which he treats, are, as truths and falsities, complete within his treatment of them. The judging minds on the one hand, and, on the other, the ultimate reality (or world of facts) about which they judge, fall outside his limited domain; and therefore (so it seems to be argued) he is free to take what view he pleases of them. For the ideal realm of meaning, which is his domain, is a middle region between the two real worlds, the worlds of psychical and of physical fact. It is between them—i.e. isolated from them, and self-sufficient in its isolation.

Because of the self-sufficiency of the science of logic and of its ideal realm of meaning, the logician (so it seems to be contended) is in no way responsible for the fact—if it be a fact—that his working hypothesis entails absurdities—if they are absurdities—in the domains of psychology and metaphysics. He is responsible for one thing, and for one thing only: viz. that his hypothesis should be such as to 'work' within the logical domain. If, therefore, the working hypothesis of the objective logician (viz. his postulate of independent propositions) is to be effectively criticized, the critic must show that it fails to 'work'—that, by making and using this postulate, the objective logician does not in fact succeed in developing a coherent account of the items of knowledge and errors, i.e. the 'apparent facts' which (like every logician) he has set out to explain.[1]

---

[1] Cf. above, p. 248.

Now though it seems certain that in this matter the 'ordinary critic' is right—for it is preposterous to sunder the whole of things into two or perhaps three mutually independent realms, and to split up the whole body of knowledge into a plurality of watertight compartments—still, for the sake of argument, let us take up the challenge. Let us meet the objective logician on his own ground so far at least as to ask whether the postulate of false propositions 'works'—whether, or how far, it enables him to elucidate the fact and the nature of error, and its distinction from knowledge. For that, as we shall see,[1] is the problem which the use of this postulate is expected to solve.

There is a preliminary objection which may perhaps be raised. After all, *is* it essential to the objective position to postulate false propositions at all? Can not the objective logician throw the whole burden of falsity and error upon the judging subject— remove both the fact of error, and any problem or problems it may entail, from the domain of logic altogether, and relegate it to psychology?

Russell, for example, inclines at times to this way of thinking even in his article on Meinong,[2] where in the main he advocates the doctrine he had maintained in the *Principles of Mathematics*,[3] viz. that 'true and false propositions alike are in some sense entities, and are in some sense capable of being logical subjects'. He says, for example,[4] that 'knowledge cannot be other than psychical' and that 'the judgement, in its purity', is 'wholly psychical'; and clearly, if these statements are to be pressed, the logician has nothing whatever to do with the experience (or recognition) of truth—nothing to do with knowledge. The theory of knowledge (epistemology) would no longer be a blend of logic and psychology,[5] but a department of psychology pure and simple. Later, in the same article,[6] two alternative views are set out for discussion. '*On one view*, a complex is the same thing as a proposition, and is always either true or false, but has being equally in either case; *on the other view*, the only complexes are true propositions, and falsehood is a property of such judgements as have no objectives.'[7] Between these two views, he says, 'it is

---

[1] Below, p. 257. [2] Above, p. 249. [3] § 52.
[4] *Mind*, l.c., pp. 205, 210: quoted above, p. 251.
[5] Cf. above, p. 244. [6] *Mind*, l.c., p. 512.
[7] Cf. just below, where this view is differently—and, I think, more accurately— stated thus: 'Judgement has no object except when the object is a *true* proposition' [*true* here is tautologous, since on this view *all* propositions are true]; 'an erroneous

not easy to decide'; and though he does eventually decide in favour of the *first*, he does so only with obvious hesitation—and in a later work[1] abandons it, and advocates the second.

'In his latest theory of truth[2] Mr. Russell . . . rejects the realm of the false: he no longer thinks there are false objectives. Nevertheless the doctrine that our statements are about these objectives . . . remains; only, whereas true statements point towards their objectives, the corresponding false statements point from them. This' (Joseph adds, and the criticism is unanswerable) 'is *se payer de mots*; for what is pointing from the objective "that the sun moves" [or, to take an example I gave before,[3] "that Charles I was beheaded"] except pointing falsely towards it?'

But if falsity and error are to be extruded from the domain of logic on the ground that false judgement is nothing but a special psychical attitude or act, true judgement and knowledge must, on the same principle, be eliminated also from logic and relegated to psychology. For they, too, are acts of asserting or attitudes of believing—transient states and events of temporally existent minds. 'But they have propositions—timeless entities—as their objects.' Are we then to suppose that the object—the independent proposition—vitally affects the asserting or believing, with which it is for a time associated; that it converts a purely psychical phenomenon (one that belongs to the domain of psychology, and is of interest only to the psychologist) into a genuine feature of the timeless realm of meaning, a proper subject of the logician's study? Such a supposition is incompatible with the severance of psychology and logic, and the 'self-sufficiency' of their respective domains; and it would wreck the *independence* of the proposition. A proposition, it seems, is such that it enters into, and radically alters the character of, the assertings and believings of the finite minds; the proposition, for example, 'that the angles of a triangle are equal to two right angles' is such that it transforms Euclid's transient psychical attitude or act into a timeless, impersonal, logical assertion. If so, a full account of this or any proposition, of this or any truth, must recognize (it seems) that *what it is*, it is not *sheerly in itself*—that *what it is* consists, in part

judgement is one which, though it seems to have an object, really has none. On this view truth and falsehood apply most fitly to judgement; the object, when there is one, may be called a fact.'

[1] *The Analysis of Mind*, p. 273.
[2] I quote from H. W. B. Joseph's article in *Mind*, vol. xxxvii, p. 22.
[3] p. 243.

at least, in *what it does* in, and to, the finite minds of which it becomes the 'object'.

True judgements, then, as well as false judgements—the believings which, having propositions for their objects, are 'items of knowledge', as well as those other psychical attitudes (whatever they may be) which are errors—must, *on this principle*, be extruded from the domain of logic altogether. But if so—if true judgements and knowledge, false judgements and error are of no concern or interest to the logician, what are the 'apparent facts' he is studying, and what are the problems of his science? The entire objective position, I submit, will have been reduced to futility.

In short, the preliminary objection,[1] if raised, could not be sustained. To adopt the objective position commits the logician to the postulate of false as well as true propositions. And when Russell, or any other 'objective logician', abandons these eternal false entities, he betrays a deplorable weakening of his faith; for he is surrendering in effect the objective position as a whole. The postulate of false propositions—of independent false connexions subsisting timelessly between terms or concepts or elements of meaning (or whatever we are to call the simple constituents of a proposition), and being such as to become from time to time the objects of those psychical attitudes or acts which are commonly called 'false judgements' or 'errors'—seems, no doubt, a strange one. Still, *within logic*, we are assured, it 'works'; and we have agreed, for the sake of argument, to examine it solely from this point of view.[2]

Let us ask, then, (i) precisely what problem or problems the postulate of false propositions enables the objective logician to solve, and (ii) by what manner of using it he achieves the solution. We can hardly do better than turn to Russell's article on 'Meinong'[3] for enlightenment.

(i) According to Russell, the problem—the chief, if not the only problem—which the postulate of false propositions enables the objective logician to solve, may be set out as follows.[4]

Unless we postulate false propositions—i.e. unless we suppose that *what* we believe in our false judgements or errors are entities having 'some kind of extra-mental subsistence'—we shall be driven to the view that a false judgement or error is a *belief in nothing*. For *what* do we believe in the false judgement (say) 'that

---

[1] Above, p. 255.   [2] Cf. above, p. 255.   [3] *Mind*, vol. xiii.
[4] Cf., for what follows, *Mind*, l.c., pp. 218–19.

the diagonal of a square is commensurate with its side' or 'that
Charles I died peacefully in his bed'? We believe—Russell suggests
—'in a relation between two terms which, as a matter of fact, are
not so related'. And 'thus we seem to believe in nothing: for if
there were such a relation as we believe in, the belief would not
be erroneous'.

It seems, then, that we have to choose between two alternatives.
Either we must admit that, in a false judgement or error, 'though
we believe, there is nothing we believe in': *or* we must suppose that
we believe in an entity, which, though it does not 'exist' or is not
an actual event or matter-of-fact, is, nevertheless, *other than* our
believing, has (in Russell's terminology) 'some kind of extra-
mental subsistence'.

Now the first of these alternatives is absurd. Russell deals too
gently with it when he says that 'the idea of a belief, which is a
belief in nothing, *seems at first sight inadmissible*', or when he refers
to it as a 'possibility' which 'seems too paradoxical to be maintained except *in the last resort*'. To believe, and yet to believe in
nothing, is not to believe at all.[1] The idea *is* inadmissible from first
to last and all the time. It is not a 'possibility' in any sense or at all.
It cannot be 'maintained' even 'in the last resort'; for nobody,
however desperate, can 'maintain' a contradiction in terms.

(ii) Hence the objective logician is forced to embrace the second
alternative—the only remaining alternative, as Russell here
assumes.[2] He is forced to postulate false propositions—falsities
subsisting timelessly 'without' the mind—and to use this postulate
in his analysis of false judgements or erroneous beliefs. The use
he makes of it has the merit of simplicity. What it is we have
seen already, but a summary restatement is perhaps advisable.
The 'apparent facts', which the objective logician (like every other
logician) sets out to explain, are true and false judgements, correct
and erroneous beliefs, items of knowledge and errors. According
to him, these 'apparent facts' are *complex*, and the explanation
of them is an analysis into simple or simpler constituents *plus*

---

[1] Cf. Plato, *Theaetetus* 188 D–189 B (189 A 12: 'Ἀλλὰ μὴν ὅ γε μηδὲν δοξάζων τὸ
παράπαν οὐδὲ δοξάζει); *Parmenides* 132 B [*The Nature of Truth*, § 48].

[2] The assumption, though consistent with the objective position, rests upon
an incomplete disjunction. For an erroneous belief, Russell assumes, is *either* a
psychical event with, *or* a psychical event without, an extra-mental object. But
there is a third alternative; for perhaps a belief (whether erroneous or correct) is
not *in this sense* a 'psychical event' at all. The whole opposition, in short, between
what is *within*, and what is *without*, a mind—as the objective logician works with
it—may prove to be meaningless.

a relation. Further, one of these constituents, he takes it for granted, is always a psychical event—a psychical event, moreover, *the same in character* in every one of these 'apparent facts'. In every item of knowledge, and in every error, *one constituent* is that special change of, and within, a singular mind which is a 'believing'.[1] Now, when the 'apparent fact' is an item of knowledge, the completion of its analysis presents no difficulty to the objective logician. In an item of knowledge—say, in Euclid's judgement that the diagonal of a square is incommensurate with the side—the psychical constituent is 'related to' an entity which (though it does not 'exist', is not a 'fact') is yet (as he thinks) undeniably 'something'. For this entity is a true proposition; and if, strictly speaking, it is not 'real'—since to be 'real' is to exist and occur in time, to be a psychical or a physical event—it has a timeless subsistence (an ideal being), which is (so to speak) more and better than temporal reality. The relation of the psychical constituent (say, of Euclid's believing) to the other constituent is, no doubt, 'peculiar'; for[2] 'one term' (viz. the psychical term, the believing) '*is* nothing but an awareness of the other term'. Still the objective logician notes this peculiarity; calls the relation 'the cognitive relation' to mark its special character; and passes on with the comment that the relation is 'more essential, more intimate, than any other'—since 'the relatedness seems to form part of the very nature of one of the related terms'.[3]

When, on the other hand, the 'apparent fact' is an error (the false judgement, say, that the diagonal is commensurate with the side), the completion of its analysis seems at first sight to present certain difficulties. For is there, besides the psychical event, another constituent in this complex at all? And if there is, what is the relation uniting the two constituents—the erroneous believing and the object in which I erroneously believe? *Over the first of these difficulties* the objective logician triumphs by making and using the postulate of false propositions. The false proposition (e.g. that the diagonal is commensurate with the side) is the second constituent of an error, just as the true proposition is the second constituent of one item of knowledge. Certainly the false proposition—the object, in which I erroneously believe—is not 'real'. It is

---

[1] Russell, as we have seen, calls the psychical constituent sometimes an act of assertion, and sometimes an attitude of belief or a believing. But, so far as I can discover, he regards it *as one and the same in character* in spite of the different names he gives to it.

[2] *Mind*, l.c., p. 510.   [3] Ibid.

not a fact; it does not exist and occur in time. But in that sense, as we saw, the true proposition—the object in which Euclid correctly believes—is not 'real' either. But the false proposition is—no less than the true proposition—undeniably 'something'. Both of them are 'entities', which have a timeless subsistence other than, and superior to, the temporal reality of psychical and physical fact.

As to the second difficulty, the objective logician—so far at least as his views are faithfully represented by Russell—skims lightly over it. The relation between the erroneous believing and its object is, it seems clear, the same 'peculiar' relation; i.e. in error, as in knowledge, the believing '*is* nothing but an awareness of the other term'. But—perhaps because there is, to say the least, a startling inappropriateness in speaking of a 'cognitive relation' between the constituents of a complex which is not knowledge but error—Russell tends to avoid using the term 'relation' altogether in his analysis of the erroneous belief. He substitutes for it the phrase 'attitude towards'. The doctrine, which he 'believes to be correct', is summarized towards the end of the article.[1]

Is it necessary to point out that the objective logician (if, as there seems no reason to doubt, Russell's article fairly presents his views) has thrown no light whatever by such an analysis on the nature of error and its distinction from knowledge? The analysis, after all, amounts to no more than this: a correct belief (an item of knowledge) is believing a truth, and an erroneous belief (an error) is believing a falsity. And if we ask, 'What then is a truth, what is a falsity, and how do they differ from one another?', we have to be content with the answer: 'Both are independent propositions—i.e. complex entities, which are not *facts*, which do not *exist* either within or without the mind, but which have a timeless subsistence—and they differ *immediately* from one another.' 'What is truth and what falsehood', Russell says frankly at the end, 'we must merely apprehend, for both seem incapable of analysis.'[2]

[1] *Mind*, l.c., p. 523. 'It may be said—and this is, I believe, the correct view—that there is no problem at all in truth and falsehood; that some propositions are true and some false, just as some roses are red and some white; that belief is a certain attitude towards propositions, which is called knowledge when they are true, error when they are false.' After pointing out what to most of us would seem a fatal objection, and after a short and most unconvincing discussion, the article ends with reiterating the view in question (p. 524).

[2] l.c., p. 524. There is an attempt in the *Principles of Mathematics* (§ 52) to distinguish a true from a false proposition, on the ground that a proposition when it 'happens to be true, . . . has a further quality, over and above that which it shares with false propositions'. 'This further quality', Russell says, 'is what I

§ 15. (C) *Idealist Position*

1. The subjective and objective positions agree fundamentally in two respects. Certainly there are obvious points of contrast between them. *According to the first*, judgement is a synthesis of ideas made by a particular mind; and it is the proper subject of the predicates 'true' or 'false', because it must either correspond, or be discordant, with a real cohesion or a matter-of-fact. *According to the second*, not judgement, but the proposition—a timeless nexus of elements, which subsists *per se* and in no way depends upon a particular mind or minds—is the proper subject of the predicates 'true' and 'false'. The nexus subsists—and as subsisting is either an eternal truth or an eternal falsity.

Yet, that they agree in two respects is no less obvious. For (i) according to both, the *experience* of truth or falsity is the merely private affair of the particular mind. Hence, as we saw, *in theories conforming to the subjective position* truth and falsity themselves (i.e. the judgements which are true or false) tend to become infected with the privacy, particularity, and transience which are supposed to characterize the judging minds and their synthetic activity; while, *in theories conforming to the objective position*, truth and falsity, because in their proper nature impersonal, universal, and eternal, tend to vanish from human experience altogether— to become 'entities', mere 'somethings' we know not what unless we happen, like the objective logicians, to be gifted with a special intuition of things-in-themselves and their immediate differences from one another. And (ii) according to both positions, 'true' and 'false' are mutually incompatible predicates—predicates, therefore, belonging to different subjects. The judgement—or, again, the proposition—must be either true-not-false or false-not-true; i.e. some judgements (or propositions) are true and others false, as some squares on a chess-board are white and others black[1]—or (as Russell expresses it) as 'some roses are red and others white'.

mean by assertion in a logical as opposed to a psychological sense.' But in a previous chapter (§ 38) the same mysterious quality—'a quality which, in a non-psychological sense, may be called being *asserted*'—is invoked to distinguish a proposition proper (e.g. 'A is greater than B') from 'a proposition considered merely as a complex concept' (e.g. 'A's being greater than B'). The attempt therefore must be dismissed as a failure. For one and the same quality—however mysterious—cannot serve *both* to constitute a proposition in distinction from a mere complex concept, and to distinguish, amongst genuine propositions, the true from the false. Cf. *The Nature of Truth*, p. 38.

[1] I borrow the comparison from Bosanquet, *Implication and Linear Inference*, p. 154: 'If it were the case that truth and falsehood were scattered through our

The idealist position rejects *a limine* and *in toto* both these assumptions in which the subjective and objective positions agree. For (i) according to it, the true and the false must be experienced; but the experience is never the merely private affair of a particular mind. No mind is particular in the sense supposed—i.e. such that its experience, or even its experiencing, is merely its private affair. In theories that conform to this position, the proper subject of the predicates 'true' and 'false' is called a 'judgement'; but they mean by the term *neither* a 'psychical product' (something made by this or that mind out of *its* ideas and by *its* spontaneous function of synthesis), *nor* a 'proposition'—i.e. a self-subsistent nexus, which need not be experienced at all, but which, when (or if) it is experienced, becomes the object of a 'believing', of a psychical attitude private and confined to this or that mind. Those who conform to this position mean by 'a judgement' (as we saw before) the ideal expansion of a fact—its self-development in the medium of the *discursus* which is thought, and therefore through the co-operative activity of a judging mind.[1]   And (ii) according to the idealist position, no judgement is true-not-false or false-not-true. Every judgement is true because, and in so far as, it is an indispensable constituent phase of a relatively self-contained (or total), a relatively coherent (and so stable) stage of the infinite advance of knowledge; because, and in so far as, it is an indispensable constituent of the totality of knowledge-or-truth which possesses, and is pursued by, the human spirit as it exists, and is embodied, at a given period of the world's history.[2] But it is a phase which supplements, and is supplemented by, other equally indispensable phases; and what truth it has, it has (or is) only in the cohering totality of this context. It is true because, and in so far as, it stands and falls with a whole system of judgements which stand and fall with it.[3] Taken by itself, as this single judgement,

---

assertions and reasonings like black and white squares on a chess-board, some absolutely one thing and some absolutely the other, and no gradation between the other and the one' [the problem set by error would be insoluble].

[1] Above, p. 182. Cf. again Bosanquet, who (*Science and Philosophy*, p. 107) sums up in a few words the *essential* contrast I wish to emphasize: 'The judgment is not the response of a punctual centre, but the self-shaping of a full world.'

[2] There is, of course, a very serious difficulty here, of which I am fully aware, and to which I shall return: viz. whether, or in what sense, knowledge-or-truth can and must be regarded also as *the complete and infinite whole of all the stages of its own advance*. But this difficulty does not directly affect my present point.

[3] Cf. above, p. 210.

it is not only an incomplete, but a mutilated, fragment of knowledge or of truth. And because of, and to the extent of, that mutilation—because of all the supplementation it requires and implies, but cannot possibly include and express within (so to speak) its own four corners—every judgement is, strictly and by its very nature, false. The judgement, in short, is 'the proper subject of the predicates "true" and "false"' in the sense that every judgement is, and must be, both true and false: i.e. *neither* absolutely, but *each* (and *both*) relatively and in some degree.[1]

2. We have thus come back to the position which was pre-supposed, at the beginning of these Studies, as the background and the basis for a provisional description of the subject-matter and method of logic—for the 'formula of orientation' given in the introductory Study. We have come back to it, as to the only tenable position—the only position within which, notwithstanding certain manifest difficulties, it seems possible to frame adequate answers to the questions: 'What is it that is true or false, and wherein does its truth or falsity consist?'[2] The assertion of this position is now significant, because we have seen the chief mistakes which, in affirming it, we negate. Within its outlines, if anywhere, there is a prospect of forming a clear conception of truth and falsity, and of their 'relation' to knowledge;[3] and so of developing eventually a philosophical interpretation (i.e. an intelligent and intelligible account) of the 'apparent facts' of our cognizant experience.[4]

Let me try, then, in conclusion, (*a*) to recapitulate once more the leading features of this position (the position I have called 'idealist'), (*b*) to draw attention to two very large and manifest difficulties, which are often supposed to be fatal to it; and (*c*) to indicate the lines of solution and defence which seem open to those of us who accept it in principle.

3. (*a*) Logic is philosophy, and its subject-matter, therefore, is concretely real both in its totality and in its detail, is 'real' in the only full and genuine sense of the term, viz. such that its being is 'spiritual'. The realm or world of logic is, in other words, a spiritual reality. It is the self-fulfilment of mind as the '*vis cognoscens*' or theoretical spirit. And the constituents of that

---

[1] Cf. above, p. 182; and for the general view of the judgement, according to the idealist position, see pp. 249–51 and the passages there cited.

[2] Cf. above, p. 181.

[3] Cf. above, p. 242.

[4] Cf. above, pp. 204, 246.

realm, the facts in that world, are phases, stretches, stages of that self-fulfilment.

This spiritual reality—this self-fulfilment of the *theoretical* spirit —is the *total* subject-matter of logic: i.e. the philosopher *qua* logician moves throughout within it; is engaged throughout in the critical or reflective analysis of it; and exhibits it in its fully intelligible structure or coherence in so far as his speculation rounds itself into the 'system' or 'science' of logic. 'Knowledge' —or, to avoid a possible misunderstanding, 'knowledge-or-truth' —was suggested (in the introductory Study) as the most convenient term (or phrase) to designate this *total* subject-matter of logic.[1] But if we so designate it, we must keep firm hold of the sense, in which alone these terms are appropriate. We must not be led astray by this or that interpretation which is put upon 'knowledge' or 'truth' in other logical theories or in popular discussion. (i) The knowledge, for example, or the truth, of which logic is the reflective analysis, is *not 'of' or 'about' reality*. Neither knowledge, nor truth, is a mental process or product, contrasted with a non-mental or extra-mental 'object'; something *within* the mind referring, or related to, or perhaps 'representing', an *external* reality, a fact or world of facts *without* the mind. Or, again, (ii) knowledge (the knowledge, of which logic is the reflective analysis) is not one term in the so-called 'cognitive relation', and 'truth' the other. Knowledge, that is, is not the abstracted subjective act, nor truth the abstracted object, of cognizance; nor is either of them *one* of these abstractions *together with* a relation (or reference) to the other. Knowledge, in other words, is not 'knowing'—even if you add 'a knowing which, though within the mind, refers, or is related, to a fact outside'. Nor is truth a self-subsistent nexus, without and independent of the mind—even if you add 'such that it may be known, i.e. may become one of the two contrasted terms which are held apart and together by a cognitive relation'.

The knowledge, then, or the truth, of which logic is the reflective analysis, is not *about* reality. 'Knowledge', we must insist, 'is reality itself *qua* known; and reality, *in* becoming and being known, is constituting and maintaining itself in the form of truth.'[2]

[1] Cf. above, Study I, e.g. pp. 11–21.
[2] Cf. Bosanquet, *Implication and Linear Inference*, p. 148. He urges that truth 'is reality' and 'is in the form of ideas'; that it is 'the form which reality assumes when expressed through ideas in particular minds'. He then adds, in a footnote: 'The phrase "it is about reality" suggests that its quality depends on representing

(iii) Even this way of putting the matter is not entirely free from ambiguity. It still fails to emphasize sufficiently that the phrase 'knowledge-or-truth' is intended to designate a *self*-fulfilment or *self*-development—a *discursus* or dialectic, which differentiates itself into contrasted moments (e.g. into judging minds and facts ideally expanding, into knowing subjects and objects known), and, in and through this self-differentiation, is continuously integrating itself, thus affirming and keeping its spiritual (i.e. its concrete) unity and self-identity. For a spiritual reality is 'one' and 'the same with itself' by the continuous unifying of a continuously self-generated plurality, by the continuous synthesizing of the differences it continuously creates by self-analysis.[1] Perhaps, then, it is less misleading to speak—in the language I used before[2]—of 'the total self-development—the infinite dialectic, the infinite self-analysis and self-synthesis—in (and as) which reality takes intelligible shape, and manifests itself as knowledge-or-truth'. (iv) Yet even this way of speaking may still be misunderstood. For the 'reality', which 'takes shape' and 'manifests itself', is nothing behind and apart from the *discursus* these metaphors describe. That which 'takes shape' is, here, one with the taking shape and with the shape it takes; 'reality', here, is all of this, and the whole of it, and nothing less than it. And if reality 'manifests *itself* as knowledge-or-truth', *this* reality *itself* clearly is the manifesting and the manifestation. (v) To be real—to be actual as a spiritual reality—is to be more, no doubt, than the self-development which is knowledge-or-truth. For logic is not the whole of philosophy; and the spiritual reality, which is its subject-matter, is the self-fulfilment of spirit considered abstractly —considered in one only of its modalities or forms, and not in all. *Still, this form or modality is indispensable.* To be real is at least to be actual as the self-fulfilment (or as a phase or stage of the self-fulfilment) of the theoretical spirit, of spirit in its theoretical modality; to be actual in the form of knowledge-or-truth, and therefore to be (or to belong to) the subject-matter of logic.[3]

4. (*b*) If we are to maintain a position of this kind, we must be prepared to encounter many difficulties—some really formidable, others formidable only in appearance, but all certain to be urged

---

something outside it. But this is upside down; it is reality which becomes truth when it takes ideal form.'

[1] Cf. above, Study I, pp. 46–9.   [2] Cf. above, Study III, p. 182.
[3] Cf. above, Study I, pp. 9–10, 14–15, 51–9.

by critics of various schools. Two of the most serious criticisms—based upon difficulties which lie at the root of all the rest—may be set out briefly as follows.

(i) *The fact of error*—so the first of these criticisms will insist—*is fatal to the idealist position.* For if one could assume that there is no difference between falsity and partial truth, between error and incomplete knowledge, then doubtless every judgement—and every group and subordinate system of judgements—would be both true and false, part only of knowledge and *eo ipso* an error. On that assumption—but not otherwise—every judgement, or group of judgements, being less than the available totality of knowledge, is knowledge incomplete and therefore erroneous; or must be false, because only a phase or stretch (or, at the most, a stage) in 'the self-development of reality in the form of truth'—or, to use simpler language, because only a step in the advance of knowledge, a grade in the evolution of truth. But such an assumption conflicts with the plainest facts. Incomplete knowledge of geometry, for example, cannot be identified with geometrical error. The knowledge, say, of the beginner, who has mastered no more than the first proposition of Euclid, is totally different in character from, for example, the error that the diagonal of the square is commensurate with its side. There is a radical difference between a partial truth and a falsity—between (say) the true, but vague and indeterminate, judgement that 'Charles I met a violent death', and the false judgement that 'the end came peacefully to him in his bed'.

And with the recognition that falsity and error have, so to speak, a positive character of their own; are radically different from, and irreducible to, partial truth and incomplete knowledge—the idealist position seems utterly to collapse. For that falsities and errors occur, it does not—and indeed could not—dispute. Yet what account could possibly be given of them within its outlines? They stand out, it seems, in irreconcilable hostility to that 'self-fulfilment of the theoretical spirit' which, according to the idealist position, is knowledge-or-truth.[1]

And (ii) this first criticism will be reinforced by a second. For, the critic will say, there is a fundamental inconsistency in the idealist position. Knowledge-or-truth, we are told on the one hand, is a *discursus* or a dialectic; and our single judgements, our groups and subordinate systems of judgements, are respectively

[1] Cf. above, pp. 248, 254.

phases, stretches, stages of its continuous, onward-sweeping flow. To put it broadly, knowledge-or-truth is essentially *in fieri*; a process or growth in time, advancing, evolving, fulfilling, completing itself—but never finished or complete, never finally developed or fulfilled. But, on the other hand, we are also told that knowledge-or-truth is a 'realm' or 'world', a self-fulfilment of spirit in one of its essential modalities; a spiritual reality which affirms and keeps its concrete unity and self-identity; a *total* self-development; a dialectic which is 'infinite'—not because unending, but because all-inclusive, self-supporting, and timelessly complete.

Now, the critic will insist, between these two ways of conceiving knowledge-or-truth the idealist logician must make his choice. He cannot be allowed to shift from one to the other; for most certainly they are mutually incompatible. Is knowledge-or-truth essentially *in fieri*—a never-ending advance, an evolution pointing always to a fuller stage beyond? Then, clearly, knowledge is of necessity always incomplete, truth always partial. For there is no stage in the advance which will not give place to a fuller and more coherent successor—even if every stage is relatively complete and whole, by contrast with the stages it succeeds or with the mere stretches and phases of itself. Knowledge-or-truth, therefore, being by its very nature always incomplete and partial, is—according to the idealist logician's own theory—error as well as knowledge, false in some degree as well as true. The dialectic, in short, the self-fulfilling *discursus*, is nothing but a procession of errors. Viewed as moments in the continuous advance, its successive phases, stretches, and stages may be said, no doubt, to contribute to 'the truth'—i.e. to a knowledge more inclusive and more coherent than themselves. But this 'truth', to which they contribute, is destined to be merged and superseded in the next stage of the advance; it is part only of a fuller truth that is to be. Hence they must equally be said to contribute always to a falsity and an error larger and more misleading than themselves.

Perhaps, then, the idealist logician will choose, and hold fast to, the other alternative. Perhaps he will maintain that the temporal character of knowledge-or-truth is a mere appearance, belying the real nature of that which is here appearing; that, essentially and in reality, knowledge-or-truth is a timeless whole—an infinite dialectic, eternally self-fulfilling and eternally self-fulfilled. Let us assume, the critic will say, that it is possible so to conceive knowledge-or-truth—a very large and generous assumption. The timeless whole, the infinite dialectic, would doubtless, in its absolute completeness, be knowledge in no sense erroneous or error; and, in its absolute self-supporting coherence, be true wholly and utterly—*the* truth without a trace of falsity. But so to conceive knowledge-or-truth will leave the idealist logician powerless to offer any intelligible account of the 'apparent facts'— of the judgements that seem both true and false; of the knowledge (or the error) that appears to be a growth in time; of the *discursus* which seems to pass in part through temporally existent minds; of the self-development and self-manifestation of fact, in which the finite judging subjects seem to co-operate and play their part. For, measured against the eternal and absolute completeness of the whole (the timeless whole which knowledge-or-truth essentially is), every phase and stretch and stage of the so-called advance of knowledge is equally and utterly worthless and condemned. All, measured by such a standard, are sheerly false. They contribute not at all to knowledge or to truth; for knowledge-or-truth, *ex hypothesi*, is timelessly self-supporting and timelessly complete.

5. (*c*) *Lines of defence*. The formidable nature of the difficulties, which lie behind these criticisms, must at once be admitted. A complete solution of them is not to be found in any of the theories which conform to the idealist position. 'Then', the critic will say, 'the common opinion is right. These difficulties *are* fatal to the idealist position. The conclusion of the whole matter is scepticism; and that, in philosophy, is the confession of bankruptcy.' But the difficulties are formidable, not to the idealist logician alone, but to theories conforming to any and every conceivable philosophical position. They are formidable, because they are real—i.e. inherent in the very nature of knowledge-or-truth. And if the idealist logician is no more able than any other philosopher to offer a 'complete solution', he is able at least to show that a 'complete solution' is, in the nature of the case, impossible. For a 'complete solution' would mean the achievement and possession of absolute knowledge-or-truth here and now and by a particular mind. It would mean the compression and concentration of the infinite dialectic, of the *discursus* in its infinitude and wholeness, within an infinitesimal and transient phase of itself.

The idealist logician, then, will be the first to recognize that, behind these criticisms, lie difficulties which are, and must remain, insoluble. Nevertheless, he has open to him certain lines of defence against the criticisms themselves—i.e. against the special formulation given to the difficulties by the supposed critic. Thus, the fact of error constitutes in one sense a difficulty which no theory of knowledge-or-truth—no logic—can solve. In one sense; but not precisely in the sense represented in the preceding criticism. Against that formulation, the idealist logician has every right to protest. And though there is in error a feature which remains to the end insoluble, the idealist logician is not so helpless as the critic supposes. His theory does not 'utterly collapse'. On the contrary: within limits, which he recognizes and rightly recognizes to be inevitable, he does in fact succeed in offering an intelligible account even of error. Similarly, what, borrowing a phrase from Bradley and applying it in our own manner, we may conveniently call the 'twofold nature'[1] of knowledge-or-truth, constitutes in one sense an insoluble difficulty. In one sense; but, once again, not in the sense represented by our imaginary critic. For the real difficulty is not that the idealist logician is bound to choose one or the other of two alternative views of knowledge-or-truth—both of which ignore or deny its twofold nature—and that, whichever he chooses, his failure is inevitable and ludicrous. The real difficulty is, on the contrary, that he is bound to recognize and accept this 'twofold nature'; and, in doing so, to recognize that no intelligible account is possible of its 'how' or 'why'. For knowledge-or-truth—like every form of spiritual reality, like every modality of self-expression or self-fulfilment of spirit—is eternal and yet appears in time, is infinite and yet displayed in and through the self-limitation by spirit of its infinitude. The fact of this union of contrasted and seemingly incompatible characters is forced upon our recognition throughout the whole range, and in every detail, of our experience; but the whole of our philosophical speculation presupposes it, moves within it, and can hardly be said, perhaps, to render it fully intelligible.

(i) *Against the first criticism*, then, the lines of the idealist logician's defence may be traced as follows:

He will refuse to be bluffed into accepting either of the alternatives, which the critic tacitly assumes to be exclusive; or to be deceived by the superficial plausibility of his examples. He is not

---

[1] Cf. *The Nature of Truth*, §§ 7, 58–9; Bradley, e.g., *Essays*, pp. 86–9, 338–41; *Logic*², p. 629 ('This twofold nature of Reality, by which it slides away from itself into our distinction, so as there to become a predicate—while all the time it retains in itself, as an ultimate subject, every quality which we loosen from and relate to it—is, if you please, inexplicable. But none the less . . . it is a fundamental fact'); Bosanquet, e.g., *Implication and Linear Inference*, p. 148, &c.

bound to choose—here, or anywhere—between blank identity and utter difference. A judgement, *qua* false, has a character it does not possess *qua* true; and yet, unless it were true in some degree, unless it were a partial truth, it would not be a judgement at all. Nothing but a partial truth can be a false judgement; though mere deficiency of truth is not of itself enough to constitute its falsity. And knowledge at every stage is incomplete, and nothing but incomplete knowledge can ever be an error; though in the knowledge, which is an error, there is a further feature, there is a positive qualification, besides the mere absence of completeness.

What is this further feature, this positive qualification, which distinguishes the falsity of a judgement from its mere deficiency of truth, the erroneousness of every stage of knowledge from its falling short of being complete? It is bound up with that 'subjective assurance of thinking truly' to which I referred before[1] as the *differentia* of judgement viewed on the side of the judging subject, viewed as his personal experience. If there is to be falsity, in the full and proper sense of the term, there must be a partial truth affirmed (believed) as truth absolute and whole. And if there is to be error, the incomplete knowledge, which now passes through and possesses some particular mind, must be *for* that mind, *as* its experience, complete and final, or absolute.

Now up to a certain point there is nothing in this characterization of error or falsity, which does not harmonize with the idealist logician's general conception of knowledge and of judgement. For, according to the idealist position, it will be remembered, knowledge is a two-sided *discursus*, 'objective' and 'subjective' in one; and every single judgement, as a constituent phase of that *discursus*, shares its two-sided character. Nothing, therefore, is a judgement unless two essential conditions are both fulfilled. If there is to be a judgement, (*a*) there must be a phase of the 'objective *discursus*'. There must be a 'self-development of fact'—a synthetic-analysis in which an 'object' constitutes itself, and makes itself known, as what it really is, i.e. as a 'spiritual fact' or a 'truth'. And (*b*) this phase of the 'objective *discursus*'—this phase of the activity of a power of thought impersonal or rooted in the nature of things— must have a 'personal' or 'subjective' side. It must *pass through* a finite mind, must be present in, and appear as a phase of, its conscious flow. A judgement, that is, is a self-development of fact; yet this self-development requires—somehow, and in some measure—

---

[1] Above, pp. 232–3.

the co-operation of a particular mind. It is the emergence of a truth which is also—somehow and in some measure[1]—being elicited by the contributory act of this or that judging subject, who, in the eliciting, experiences it and is subjectively assured that what he experiences is true.[2]

'But, if so,' the critic will object, 'it follows that, according to the idealist position, every judgement is a falsity, and not true at all; every stage of the *discursus* error, and in no sense knowledge. For, on the one hand, every judgement and every system of judgements (or stage of the *discursus*) must be experienced by a finite knower, by a particular mind—and experienced in the assurance that what is experienced is absolute truth; and yet, on the other hand, no judgement, nor even any system of judgements, can be true except relatively. Its truth is partial and imperfect, subject to conditions it implies but does not include. In order to be true wholly—in order to be and embody absolute truth—every judgement, and every system of judgements—would have to be indefinitely supplemented; to be expanded, to be corrected; to be transformed, perhaps, into we know not what. Hence, according to the idealist position, every judgement, taken as it actually is (taken, that is, in the concrete unity of its twofold character as a spiritual fact), is, it seems, false utterly and without qualification; and, taken similarly in its concreteness, every system of judgements (every so-called "stage in the advance of knowledge") is a mass of errors, error unadulterated.'

This objection betrays a misunderstanding of *the precise scope* of the 'subjective assurance' which, according to the idealist position, is an ineliminable moment in the judgement. My former account,[3] perhaps, was not sufficiently guarded; at all events, what must (as I think) be maintained, is less than the critic supposes. If I am to judge, I must feel absolutely certain that what I judge is true; i.e. that in the given situation, in the actual context which provokes my judgement, any and every judging subject must think *so* and not otherwise. But if I am to judge, I need not feel absolutely certain that what I judge is absolutely true; i.e. true in all situations and contexts, true unconditionally and without respect to any determinate stage of knowledge, an absolute item of absolute truth.

Thus (to take one of the critic's examples)[4] nobody can judge

---

[1] Cf. above, p. 269. [2] Cf. above, pp. 249-51 and 233-4.
[3] Cf. above, pp. 233 ff. [4] Cf. above, p. 266.

that 'Charles I met a violent death', except in the absolute
assurance (the unhesitating feeling of certainty) that, in the given
situation, any and every judging subject must think *so* and not
otherwise. He must feel absolutely certain that what he thus
judges is relatively true; i.e. that it is demanded by, fits in with,
indispensably supplements, 'the whole' (as it would be called) 'of
his present and actual knowledge of English history'. The judgement, as he thus makes it, is a partial truth—a truth provisional
and relative—but not (in the full and positive sense) a falsity or an
error. It would be a falsity or an error only if he affirmed it in the
unhesitating assurance of its absolute truth—affirmed it stub-
bornly as true: wholly, and finally, and without reserve.[1] And
such an assurance of absolute truth is not an essential condition
of our judgements; nor even, fortunately, a very common accom-
paniment of them.

(ii) 'But', the critic will insist, 'what, according to the idealist
position, is this so-called "whole" of the judging subject's present
and actual knowledge of English history? It is a mere stretch or
mutilated stage of the *discursus* as it happens to pervade and
inform a particular mind. It is, therefore, fragmentary and relative,
provisional and shifting—*at most* a whole in the making; a whole,
moreover, such that it can never be finally made. Even as it now
possesses and informs the judging subject's mind, this so-called
"whole of knowledge" is in the very act of expanding and transforming itself into a more inclusive and more coherent system of
more precisely defined constituent judgements—a system, in
which the judgement that "Charles I met a violent death" will
be displaced by the more accurate judgement "was beheaded at
Whitehall in 1649". The given situation, the relevant context, of
the judgement is, in short, a "situation" of error as much as of
knowledge—a "context" conferring upon its constituents (upon
the judgements which imply and supplement it) falsity as well as
truth.'

In trying to meet this objection, we shall at the same time be
tracing our lines of defence against the second of the two criticisms
that were set out just now;[2] for indeed the difficulties, which lie
behind these criticisms, are too closely connected to be kept apart.
What in the end remains insoluble, *in the fact of error*, is precisely
that it involves a stubborn feeling of assurance, on the part of this
or that judging subject, that what he judges is absolute truth.

---

[1] Cf. above, p. 232.   [2] Above, pp. 266–8.

How is it possible or conceivable that this or that finite mind—i.e. this or that transient concentration of the infinite mind, of the *potentia infinita cogitandi*—should ever thus seem to itself to possess, within the compass of its present experiencing, absolute knowledge-or-truth? And what in the end remains insoluble, *in regard to the 'twofold nature' of knowledge-or-truth*, is the same difficulty in a more ultimate and universal form. How is it possible or conceivable that the *potentia infinita cogitandi*, which fulfils itself in knowledge-or-truth, should divide and distribute itself into, and over, a plurality of limited and transient minds—and should eternally have achieved, eternally maintain, the infinite fulfilment of itself *only* by this self-division and self-limitation, *only* through the co-operation of these finite thinkers, and through the temporal (and essentially never complete or final) processes of their thinking?

'My whole present knowledge of English history'—to return to the critic's objection—is, undoubtedly, a mutilated stretch or stage of the *discursus*; not complete, not self-supporting; in short, if the term is to be pressed, not 'a whole' of knowledge-or-truth at all. It is, however, a 'whole', *first*, by contrast with the still more fragmentary phases it includes, and the still more rudimentary and imperfect stretches and stages it has superseded and absorbed; and, *secondly*, in virtue also of its tendency towards wholeness. For—as the critic himself rightly emphasizes—'my present knowledge' (whether of history, or of geometry, or of any subject) is in the very act of expanding and transforming itself; but the trend of this self-development is towards completeness and coherence. The principle, or the mainspring, of the *discursus* is a '*nisus towards totality*'[1] inherent in every phase and stretch and stage of itself.

'My present knowledge as a whole', then, in spite of its manifest imperfection and instability, is the criterion and the measure of the truth of every constituent phase of itself. For me at least, as I make my present judgement, it is the sole and the sufficient criterion. There is nothing '*for*' me—nothing within my actual experience—on which I could base a reasoned doubt or criticism of 'my present knowledge as a whole'—however provisional and incomplete its 'wholeness' must (on the general principles of the 'idealist position') be admitted to be. Every judgement, therefore,

---

[1] The phrase is used, I think, by Bosanquet, though I have been unable to find the passage. But cf. his whole treatment of 'logical stability' and 'truth', both in his *Logic* and in his *Principle of Individuality and Value*.

which contributes essentially to constitute this relatively complete
and relatively coherent system of judgements—to constitute (say)
my present 'total' knowledge of English history, or of plane
geometry—is, *for me as I judge*, true in proportion to the amount,
the value or significance, and the indispensability (the irreplace-
ableness) of its contribution.[1] From this point of view—the point
of view not of practice only, but of theory at all its levels short
of philosophical speculation—every judgement (in the context
in which alone it is, and can be, made) is 'true' *and not false*; and
the whole, to which it contributes (the context which provokes it,
and which it supplements), is 'knowledge' *and not error*. And if
here the critic objects 'But is it, then, *not* false that "the diagonal
is commensurate with the side" or that "Charles I died peacefully
in his bed"? Is it really contended by the idealist logician that
these judgements are true?', the line of defence is plain. *Either*
they are implied by, and contribute essentially to, some present and
actual whole of knowledge—and so contributing, and within that
context, are indeed 'true' and not false. *Or* they are not judgements, not actual beliefs, at all. For as we have already tried to
explain,[2] nothing is a 'judgement', according to the theory of the
idealist logician, unless in it a fact develops itself through the
co-operation of the actual thinking of a particular mind. The mere
grammatical form of the statement does not in the least guarantee
that the thought expressed in it is a judgement—or even that any
thought is expressed in it at all. The plausibility of the critic's
examples, therefore, need not disturb us. For, on a closer scrutiny,
it is plain they are not examples of *judgement* at all. No sane and
intelligent person could *judge*—i.e. could affirm or believe in the
absolute assurance of the relative truth of the 'affirmed' or
'believed'—that 'Charles I died peacefully in his bed' or that 'the
diagonal is commensurate with the side'.

That, then, is the first line of defence for the idealist logician;
but behind it, supporting and supplementing it, he must trace
another. For he has admitted (or rather, insisted) that 'the whole

---

[1] Strictly speaking, the criterion for the judging subject is the organized totality
of his knowledge—the totality of 'his' intelligible world. But it is enough for my
present argument to emphasize the sufficiency of the criterion which is afforded
by the immediately relevant subordinate whole, within which for the time being
the subject's mind is living and moving—this or that sphere or department of his
'total' intelligible world, this or that 'science', i.e. this or that subordinate system
or minor whole within the articulated body of his total knowledge.

[2] Above, p. 270.

of any judging subject's present knowledge' stretched to its utter-most compass—interpreted even, if that be possible, as all the knowledge possessing and possessed by, or available to, the human spirit as it exists and is embodied at a given period of the world's history—remains still a mere section or stage of the *discursus* which is 'knowledge-or-truth'. Indeed, what he has admitted seems even more damaging than that. For the *discursus*, on his view, must be conceived as timelessly whole, as eternally complete. It is the infinite dialectic; it is reality self-shaping and eternally self-shaped, fulfilling itself and eternally self-fulfilled, in the form of absolute knowledge or absolute truth. Now, as we saw before,[1] he cannot be called upon to show *how* the infinite dialectic affirms and maintains its infinite and eternal completeness by appearing as an incompletable advance in time. He cannot be challenged by the critic to explain *how* the *potentia infinita cogitandi*, by the inherent necessity of its own nature, divides and distributes itself into a plurality of finite subjects, affirming and sustaining its timeless actuality only through their co-operation, i.e. only in, and by means of, the temporal processes of their thinking.[2] But he must be prepared to answer one very obvious question: Why must the *discursus* be conceived as timelessly whole, as eternally complete?

The answer he will make to this question is simple and familiar.

We are forced to conceive the *discursus* (of which our actual cognizant experiences are fragmentary phases) as timelessly whole and eternally complete—we are forced, in other words, to identify it with the infinite dialectic, which is reality, half-showing and half-concealing itself in the form of a temporal development—because (1) 'to perceive imperfection is to judge by the perfect';[3] and because (2), when we set out the character of *this* 'perfect', of the ideal implied in our criticism of our cognizant experiences, we shall find it takes no other form than that of a dialectic, which is infinite —which is the eternal synthetic-analysis of spirit in, and by, and for itself.

(1) When we reflect philosophically upon our cognizant experi-ences—upon any of those experiences, no matter what, in which, while we live in them, we feel assured that we are perceiving fact

---

[1] Above, pp. 268–9.

[2] 'Or their willing', I ought perhaps to add. But we are concerned in these Studies *only* with reality in the form of knowledge-or-truth.

[3] I borrow Bradley's formulation of the principle: cf. *Logic*[2], vol. ii, p. 489.

or affirming truth—they show themselves (in various degrees, but one and all) intrinsically 'imperfect'. Intrinsically 'imperfect': i.e. imperfect, because falling short of an ideal, which they themselves suggest. The awareness of fact, i.e. the adequate apprehension of an actual constituent of the 'external' world;—*this* is the perfection, the ideal, which every actual perception 'sets' (so to speak) 'to itself'—and fails to achieve. It is what it 'has in it' to be, what it aims at being and professes to be; and it is also precisely what, in various degrees, it falls short of being. Or again: to affirm and embody truth, the whole truth, neither more nor less, in respect to some matter-of-fact or complex object—*this* is the perfection, the ideal, which every actual judgement 'sets to itself' (so to speak), which it 'has in it' to be, which by its very form it professes to be. And *this* is the ideal, by which it is condemned—the perfection, which (in various degrees, but always and manifestly in *some* degree) it fails to attain.

So far, in the endeavour to simplify the issue, I have been speaking as though each several cognizant experience brought with it its own distinct ideal, its own separate standard of perfection, by which it criticized and condemned itself. But this is to misrepresent the actual situation. For according to the 'idealist' position—the position which is to be defended—there are no *several* cognizant experiences, i.e. none that are isolable, and self-contained or complete in their isolation. There are, always and only, phases, grades, stages of a *single*—infinitely differentiated and endlessly developing—*discursus*. It is this single, continuous and continuing, *discursus*, which philosophical reflection shows to be 'imperfect'—'imperfect' throughout, and in each of the distinguishable phases of its continuous development, because 'coming short' of an ideal which it implies; i.e. which, in that sense, it 'sets to itself' and suggests to the philosopher as the standard of perfection by which he criticizes and condemns it.

(2) What, then, is this ideal? What is this standard of perfection, which the idealist logician, in reflecting upon the *discursus*, recognizes that each and all its phases *imply*, but fail in various degrees to achieve?

'When we set out its character', I asserted,[1] 'we shall find it takes no other form than that of the eternal synthetic-analysis of spirit in, and by, and for itself.' In making this assertion, I was thinking primarily of Hegel's treatment of the matter—for Hegel is the

[1] Above, p. 275.

originator of the 'idealism' I have been trying to maintain. The dialectic, as which (on Hegel's theory) the Absolute displays itself to speculative thought—to thought at its best and cleverest, to the thought which is philosophy—is not a temporal development. It is not a coming-into-being of the Whole, nor its development to a fuller state of itself: it is the timeless self-analysis and self-synthesis, in which the 'being' of the Whole—its spiritual actuality—consists. The Absolute (*die Idee, das Wahre, das Gute*, &c.), Hegel constantly insists, is timelessly perfect, eternally self-fulfilled: the inclusive whole of all the moments and stages of the dialectic 'process', in which it is displayed. No doubt, in calling the dialectic a 'process' or a 'movement', as Hegel constantly does, he exposes himself to misunderstanding, in spite of the care he takes to guard himself against it. But the 'process' in this case (we must remember) *is* the Whole. And the 'movement' is not a passage *towards* perfection, not a movement of transition (a κίνησις); but the living self-expression of the perfect Whole (an ἐνέργεια ἀκινησίας). The order of the terms in this 'process'—in the Hegelian dialectic—is not temporal, but logical; and the logical nexus throughout is determined by the immanence of the Whole in each and all of them, by the immanence of the Absolute in every moment and stage of the dialectic 'movement'.[1]

'But', it will be objected, 'the fact (if it be a fact) that Hegel took this view is not sufficient to justify what was asserted. An appeal to authority is here irrelevant. Granted that Hegel was a great philosopher; granted, further, that Hegel, reflecting upon our actual cognizant experience, conceived it to imply a timeless dialectic as the ideal—as the absolute and perfect reality—of which it is the imperfect temporal appearance. Still, Hegel may have been mistaken. And, apart from that, the point at issue is not how this or that philosopher in fact conceives the ideal, the 'perfect', by which he judges the 'imperfection' of our actual knowledge in all its phases. It was asserted not that the ideal *has been*, but that it *must be*, thus conceived: that it *must*, when set out explicitly, take the form of a dialectic timelessly self-fulfilling and timelessly self-fulfilled.'

Beyond all question this objection would hold against an attempt

[1] Cf., e.g., Hegel, *Encycl.*, vol. i, § 212 and Zusatz; § 213, Zusatz (p. 387); § 214, Zusatz (p. 389); § 237 and Zusatz: also, cf. Hegel's letter on Truth (*die Wahrheit und das Wahre*) to Dubosc (*Briefe von und an Hegel*, 1887 ed., vol. ii, pp. 78–80). And on Hegel's conception of the Absolute as 'the inclusive whole of its stages', see Bosanquet, *Science and Philosophy*, pp. 430–1.

to justify what was asserted by Hegel's, or by anyone's, authority. But the reference to Hegel's treatment of the subject was intended as an appeal not to his 'authority'—which would have been absurd—but to the substance of his doctrine. And the reference was suggested by what seems a not unreasonable reflection. For to maintain that the ideal *must* be conceived in such and such a manner is, in effect, to maintain that such and such is the most adequate conception that can be formed, the truest account that can be given, of it. And it is not unreasonable to presume that this 'truest account' will be found, if anywhere, in the works of those, who have thought most deeply on the subject; it is not unreasonable therefore to turn, in the first instance, for guidance to the account given by Hegel or by some other leading exponent of the 'idealist' view.

But though the objection, as stated, rests upon a misunderstanding, it points to a real omission. For it must be admitted that much more than an appeal to the substance of Hegel's doctrine—much more than a summary characterization of Hegel's conception of the dialectic which is reality—is required to justify what was asserted. The assertion amounted to the challenge: 'Set out the ideal in explicit terms, and you will find it takes no other form than that of an infinite and timeless dialectic.'[1] And the only possible method of justifying this assertion would be to set out the ideal in detail, and to show, in doing so, that it takes—and inevitably takes—this form.

Now in Bradley's *Appearance and Reality* there is an exposition both of the ideal, as (on his view) it must be conceived, and of the line of reasoning, by which (as he thinks) such a conception of the ideal is forced upon us.[2] And in what follows I shall (*a*) reproduce in my own fashion Bradley's account of the ideal; (*b*) draw attention to the one important respect, in which his account of the ideal diverges from that of Hegel, and diverges therefore also (as I think) from the account that must be given—from 'the truest' account or 'most adequate' conception; and, finally (*c*), urge that the reason, which Bradley himself advances for this divergence, is not convincing.

(*a*) Bradley's argument presupposes a very definite and limited conception of 'the intellect' or 'thought'. Thought, as he conceives it, is sharply contrasted with 'Feeling' ('Sentience', 'Im-

---

[1] Cf. above, pp. 275, 276.
[2] Cf. especially *Appearance and Reality*[9], Appendix, Note A, pp. 500–11.

mediate Experience'). It is a *discursus*—i.e. a function of analysis and synthesis in one—but it is a *mere discursus*, a *formal* function. It requires a 'given' on which it operates, or within which it distinguishes and connects. If we are to think, we must have something to think about: something felt or sensed; something of which we are already aware by a form of experience more primitive than (and contrasted with) thought.[1]

This 'given', which thought presupposes, this 'feeling', this felt or presented something (whatever on each occasion it may be), is not 'simple'—i.e. not devoid of inner diversity. It is 'a many felt in one'; an 'immediate union of the one and many'; 'diversity and unity in one whole', but a 'whole' which is 'implicit and not yet broken up into terms and relations.'[2] In short, the more primitive experience which thought presupposes—the 'immediate experience' or 'feeling', from which in thinking we start, and which by thinking we try to render intelligible—contains, fused and confused in its unarticulated unity, many different nuances, aspects, features. It is a *vague* whole, without an explicit structure; and it contains a *vague* diversity—differences implicit, or held in solution, not made explicit and distinct as its constituents or parts.

Our aim and object in thinking, then, is always to understand a 'given'—to render intelligible a felt or presented 'fact' or total situation, a vaguely experienced union of a vaguely experienced plurality. And the intellect (or thought) being what it is—viz. a power (or function) of *formal* analysis and synthesis—its *modus operandi* is, in principle, always the same. Within the confused totality, which is its 'given', it picks out and accentuates differences. As thus selected and emphasized, they have been made, or have become, distinct and definite terms—explicit elements, parts, qualities, constituents. And, so far, the original unity of the 'given' —its vague or implicit wholeness—is broken and destroyed. But the intellect—since it is a power of *analysis and synthesis in one*—in discriminating a plurality of terms within the 'given' is also connecting the many elements or qualities it makes distinct. It sub-

---

[1] Cf., e.g., especially *Appearance and Reality*[9], ch. xv ('Thought and Reality'), pp. 150–2. Substantially and in the main, Bradley insists that the intellect is a formal faculty of synthesis and analysis, depending upon a material or *datum* presented to it by another power of the mind—i.e. upon something which the thinker experiences immediately (by sense or sentience, not by thinking). As we saw before (Study I, pp. 44–6), this is an over-emphasis of one side of the matter —and so a caricature of the intellect or thought. And Bradley himself cannot consistently maintain so impossible a view.

[2] *Appearance and Reality*[9], p. 508.

stitutes—or tries to substitute—a new, and *intelligible*, kind of
unity, for the vague and merely *felt* wholeness, which its analysis
has destroyed. It tries to reunite the many elements or qualities
by precisely conceivable modes of holding a many together, while
yet not blurring their differences, but keeping them emphasized
and well defined.

If this is the aim and object of thinking, it can be expressed, in
a slightly different way, so as to bring out more clearly a fundamental condition, to which its procedure would have to conform in
order to achieve complete success.

We have seen that, by thinking, we try to unify two or more
genuinely different elements or qualities, without cancelling or
blurring their differences. We try, for example, to affirm that the
two elements, A and B, are, each of them, genuinely themselves
and different from one another, and yet constitute a genuinely
individual whole; or that the two qualities, x and y, while emphatically distinct from, and other than, one another, do nevertheless combine to characterize a single identical subject. And our
procedure throughout—on both its sides and as a whole—is to be
'intelligible'. It is to be 'intelligible'—i.e. it is to satisfy the
intellect. And to satisfy the intellect, it must clearly be 'intelligent'
—i.e. express and fulfil the intellect's own nature. Now it cannot
satisfy the intellect, unless it is self-consistent—or if, being self-
contradictory, it violates the very form of intelligence and the
intelligible. Hence the aim and object of thinking, we may say, is
*to unify a many, or to attribute diversity, and in doing so avoid contra-
dicting ourselves.*[1]

In this attempt, Bradley maintains, we always do, and always
in principle must, fail to achieve complete success. For he claims
to have shown that all our thinking—not only the thinking which
guides us in practice and which is embodied in our common-sense
views of the world, but also the thinking which takes the more
elaborate and systematic form of scientific and philosophical
theories—is, in ultimate analysis, 'relational'. Our intellect, that
is, always moves, and can only move, by 'the machinery of Terms
and Relations'.[2] The Schema of *Terms held apart, and held together,
by a Relation* is, he maintains, the one and only device available to,
and employed by, our intellect in its endeavour to affirm the

---

[1] Cf. *Appearance and Reality*[9], p. 506, where the entire work of thought is summarized as 'this attempt to attribute diversity and to avoid contradiction'.

[2] For the phrase, cf. *Appearance and Reality*[9], p. 28.

WHEREIN DOES ITS TRUTH OR FALSITY CONSIST? 281

genuine unity of the genuinely different—and thus to convert the
confused *datum* into an intelligible One of an intelligible Many.
And this device, he claims to have shown, is a mere makeshift.
The Schema of *Terms held apart and together by a Relation* cannot
be defended against metaphysical (philosophical) criticism—i.e.
against criticism which is thorough and comprehensive, resolute or
uncompromising and pushed to the end.[1] It cannot be 'thought
out'. It is impossible to 'think out' the notion of *a Term*, whether
apart from, or together with, its relation to another Term; and the
notion of *a Relation*, whether taken in isolation or taken along
with the Terms it is supposed to connect, is equally devoid of
intelligible meaning. Each of the components of the Schema is
unthinkable by itself, and unthinkable also when taken along with
the other. In employing this Schema, therefore, the intellect, far
from proceeding *intelligently*, is oscillating from one meaningless
abstraction to another, and contradicting itself at every oscilla-
tion.[2]

Our result so far may be summarized thus: The intellect by its
very nature endeavours, and by its very nature fails, to render its
datum intelligible; i.e. to unite explicitly, without contradicting
itself, the differences, implicit in the *datum* which its analysis
makes explicit as many elements or qualities. And by reflecting
upon this result, we can take a further step. For it is clear that we
have reached our result in no other way than by the intellect's own
activity. The intellect itself—i.e. certain processes of thought in
which Bradley's intellect was functioning, and which we have
followed and reproduced and made our own—has informed us
what its own nature is, what its aim and object are, and that, and
why, it fails (and must fail) to achieve complete success. The
intellect itself has doubled the parts of criticized and critic. And
as critic of itself (this is the further step we now can take), the
intellect is using—and therefore must possess—an ideal by which
it criticizes and condemns its own imperfect achievements.

What, then, is this 'ideal'? In its attempt to 'attribute
diversity', or to unify a many, without self-contradiction, 'what
in the end would satisfy the intellect, supposing that it could be
got'?[3] What is the procedure which, being natural to the intellect,

---

[1] Cf. *Essays*, p. 444: 'I include under that term [sc. "Metaphysics"] all speculation which is at once resolved to keep its hold upon all sides of fact, and upon the
other hand to push, so far as it can, every question to the end.'
[2] Cf. *Appearance and Reality*[9], ch. 3 ('Relation and Quality'), pp. 21–9.
[3] Cf. ibid., pp. 567–8.

or perfectly expressing its own nature, would be completely intelligible because completely intelligent?

The actual procedure of the intellect—of the intellect, that is, as *the criticized*, and not *as the critic*—is defective, as we have seen, because it applies an unintelligible schema, and is therefore itself self-contradictory. If we can show in what precisely this self-contradictoriness of the intellect's procedure consists, we shall be able perhaps to suggest the remedy—i.e. to set out in positive terms the ideal procedure, which the intellect *as critic of itself* demands and, in its self-criticism, unconsciously itself employs.

What is the essence of self-contradiction? What is it precisely that the law of contradiction forbids? Bradley discusses these questions,[1] and the doctrine he maintains may be briefly summarized. The law of contradiction forbids the bare identification of the different: 'a thing, for example, cannot *without an internal distraction* be two different things, and differences cannot belong to the same thing in the same point, *unless in that point there is diversity*'.[2] The essence of self-contradiction is 'to unite diversities without any internal distinction'.[3] Or—to put the same doctrine from a slightly different angle—'difference without a reason, i.e. difference in the same relation, *is* a contradiction'.[4]

Now, in the *datum* which thought presupposes, and which it tries to render intelligible, there is (as we saw) diversity freed in unity. But this diversity—before or apart from thought's analysis—is not explicit; and its fusion, its being given or felt or presented together in and as a single experience, is to the experiencing subject so far (i.e. while he is merely accepting what is presented, merely 'feeling') neither perplexing nor self-contradictory. At most, perhaps, there is a *latent* conflict; an as yet undeveloped contradiction between the diversity of aspects and their togetherness in the felt totality; a *potential* conflict or contradiction foreshadowed by a certain tension and instability in the actual 'feeling', the actual immediate experience. But the moment that, by thinking, the philosopher or the logician has accentuated the diversity of aspects into terms—into elements or qualities each distinctly itself and marked off from every other—he has before him a Many which cannot be consistently united, differences which cannot be consistently identified, except on one condition.

---

[1] *Appearance and Reality*[9], pp. 500 ff.
[2] l.c., p. 501: italics mine.   [3] Ibid., p. 504.
[4] Bosanquet, *Logic*[2], vol. ii, p. 130.

This one condition is plain enough. If the intellect is to unify many elements, without self-contradiction, it must recognize in the One which holds the many elements together an internal principle both of their plurality or divergence and of their unification or coalescence; or if the intellect is, without contradicting itself, to attribute different qualities as genuinely belonging to and characterizing a single self-same subject, in the self-sameness of this subject it must recognize an internal principle both of their difference and of their reconciliation. The Many, in short, must be, for the intellect, the *self*-pluralization of a concrete unity; or the differences must be, for it, the *self*-differentiation of a concrete identity. And, conversely, the One must be, for the intellect, an individual unity which eternally makes and maintains itself in and through an eternally self-generated plurality: and *the identity* must be, for the intellect, a subject which eternally makes and maintains its sameness with itself, by eternally reconciling the differences that spring eternally from its own inner being.

The intellect, then, if it is to be satisfied, cannot be content with a procedure which translates the *datum* into terms and relations— i.e. into elements or qualities, which are severally independent, but are held externally together, being conjoined in pairs (or coupled) by bonds that fall between them. It must proceed so as to recognize an internal principle (an inner ground or reason), *both* of the Many and of their union, both of the differences and of their identity. But this means (i) that the intellect, in rendering its *datum* intelligible, must *not* be importing arbitrary distinctions and connexions into it, but (on the contrary) must be tracing and recognizing the self-differentiation and self-integration of the fact, the reality, the object itself; and (ii) that, in thus tracing the self-analysis and self-synthesis of the fact, the intellect must at the same time be following a movement natural and proper to itself. For plainly the intellect could not 'recognize' a principle (a ground, or reason) in the object, which was merely presented to it as a 'given'. To 'recognize', for the intellect, means, and must always mean, to accept and to endorse as *intelligible because intelligent*— i.e. because the expression and fulfilment of the intellect itself.

So far I have been trying to reproduce in my own manner Bradley's conception of the ideal—of that which the intellect demands, and which would completely satisfy it 'supposing that it could be got'—and the line of argument by which he reaches that conception. But there is a short paragraph, in which Bradley himself summarizes the whole matter; and I venture to quote it to confirm, and to throw further light upon, what I have been saying.

'While the diversities[1] are external to each other and to their union' (and Bradley claims to have shown that this must always be the case in the ordinary procedure of the Intellect—the procedure according to the Schema of Terms and Relations), 'ultimate satisfaction is impossible. There must . . . be an identity and in that identity a ground of distinction and connection. But that ground, if external to the elements into which the conjunction must be analysed, becomes for the intellect a fresh element, and it itself calls for synthesis in a fresh point of unity. But hereon, because in the intellect' (i.e. in the *criticized* intellect—the intellect, which Bradley conceives to be a mere function of formal analysis and synthesis, incapable of moving except by the machinery of terms and external relations) 'no intrinsic connections were found, ensues the infinite process. Is there a remedy for this evil?'

'The remedy', Bradley replies, 'might lie here. If the diversities were complementary aspects of a process of connection and distinction, *the process not being external to the elements or again a foreign compulsion of the intellect*, but itself the intellect's own *proprius motus*' (my italics), 'the case would be altered. Each aspect would of itself be a transition to the other aspect, a transition *intrinsic and natural at once to itself and to the intellect*' (my italics). 'And the Whole' (i.e. the universe in its fully intelligible and fully real being, the Absolute) 'would be a self-evident analysis and synthesis of the intellect itself, by itself. Synthesis here . . . has become self-completion, and analysis . . . is self-explication. And the question how or why the many are one and the one is many here loses its meaning. There is no why or how beside the self-evident process, and towards its own differences this whole is at once their how and their why, their being, substance and system, their reason, ground and principle of diversity and unity.'

(*b*) The ideal, which Bradley thus describes, is identical with the dialectic, in which (according to Hegel's philosophy) the 'absolute idea' eternally fulfils itself and is eternally self-fulfilled. That this is so (that Bradley's ideal *is* Hegel's dialectic) is evident from the terms of the description. And, besides, it is expressly stated by Bradley himself in at least one passage of his *Logic*.[2] And yet in

---

[1] *Appearance and Reality*[9], p. 507.

[2] Cf. *Logic*[2]; e.g. 408–10, where the Hegelian dialectic is shown to be a self-development *at once* of the mind and of the reality. In the dialectic process, 'the whole . . . rejects the claim of a one-sided *datum*, and supplements it by that other and opposite side which really is implied—so begetting by negation a balanced unity. This path once entered on, the process starts afresh with the whole just reached. . . . So the process goes on till the mind, therein implicit, finds a product, which answers its unconscious idea; and here, having become in its

one respect Bradley's view of the ideal is fundamentally different from that of Hegel.

For, to Bradley, but not to Hegel, this ideal is a *mere ideal*, an ideal not fully realized in fact. But Bradley's attitude to the ideal is not fairly represented by so crude a statement. If, in one sense, he views it as a *mere* ideal, in another sense he regards it as based upon an absolute standard and criterion of reality and truth—a criterion possessed by our thought; a criterion, by the application of which we achieve absolute knowledge of the *general* nature of the universe. And Bradley's attitude is not only thus complex, subtle, and perhaps inconsistent: it seems to change in his later work, so that in the end it is difficult to see precisely *what failure in actuality* he is imputing to the ideal.

On the one hand—to try to bring out briefly the various sides of Bradley's attitude—the ideal, as we have seen, is a 'way of think-ing' in which the intellect *would* be perfectly satisfied. But the intellect does not, and from its very nature cannot, think in that way. Hence the intellect is not, and never can be, thus fully satisfied in fact. In order to realize its ideal, the intellect would have to possess in itself a principle of self-differentiation and self-integration. It would have to create out of its own concrete unity the differences, which that same unity reconciles, or of which it is the self-maintaining balance and harmony. It would have thus to combine in itself the characteristics, which Bradley attributes to feeling or immediate experience, as well as that function of purely formal analysis and synthesis of a 'given', which (on his view) constitutes the distinctive being, the very essence, of thought.[1] The

own entirety a *datum* to itself, it rests in the activity which is self-conscious in its object.' ('The whole' in the above passage is applied to 'the mind'. But it is clear *from the context* that 'the mind' is conceived concretely—so that, as the development proceeds, the mind, which knows, and that which is known, are together fulfilled as *the whole which is reality manifest to itself in the form of truth*.) Cf. ib. 489–90, where the ideal (the 'perfect', by which we judge the 'imperfection' of the actual procedure of an intellect) is described in substantially the same manner as in *Appearance and Reality*, l.c., and is expressly identified with Hegel's dialectic method in a note added by Bradley in the second edition of his *Logic*. Cf. further, ib. 656–7, where Bradley traces the ideal of 'a perfect system'—i.e. a system absolutely individual and absolutely unique both as a whole and in each of its members. This 'perfect system' is obviously identical with a dialectic eternally self-fulfilling and self-fulfilled—and no less obviously identical with the ideal which Bradley sets out in *Appearance and Reality*, l.c.

[1] Cf. *Appearance and Reality*[9], p. 151. If feeling 'belongs to' perfect thought, 'then thought is different from thought discursive and relational. To make it include immediate experience, its character must be transformed. It must cease to predicate, it must get beyond mere relations, it must reach something other

ideal is thus an 'intellectual ideal'—an ideal, Bradley says,[1] which, 'we know, is not actual fact. It does not exist in our world, and, unless that world were changed radically, its existence is not possible. It would require an alteration of the position in which the intellect stands, and a transformation of its connection with the remaining aspects of existence.'

And yet, *on the other hand*, Bradley strictly maintains that the ideal is not 'a mere delusion. It does not wholly deceive us. It does set before us that which, if it were actual, would satisfy us as thinking beings.'[2] Not only so. The ideal embodies, and makes explicit, certain demands which spring from the very nature of our intellect; demands which, therefore, we, as thinking beings, *rightly* insist must in principle be satisfied if there is to be reality or truth at all. The intellect, no doubt, is only one aspect of the Whole— only a limited and partial appearance of the absolute reality. Still, Bradley insists, it is one 'main aspect' of the Whole—a characteristic and ineliminable side of its total being; and the absolute reality does show itself—does manifest its genuine character—to *some extent* in this, as in every one of its 'appearances'. Hence, Bradley insists, we know, without possibility of doubt or error, that these demands of the intellect are met and satisfied *in principle* and *somehow*—though we cannot know the 'how', or verify the satisfaction in detail. In the absolute experience, we can affirm with certainty, the claims of the intellect are satisfied in full—as are the claims of its other main aspects (of will, for example, and of feeling, if these are the most appropriate names to give them).[3] In this sense, and from this point of view, he goes so far as to say that 'the perfect System'—the whole, which is absolutely unique and absolutely individual, both in its entirety and in each

---

than truth. Thought . . . must have been absorbed into a fuller experience. Now such an experience may be called thought, [if we] choose to use that word. But if any one else prefers another term, such as feeling or will, he would be equally justified.'

[1] *Appearance and Reality*[9], p. 458.

[2] *Logic*[2], p. 490.

[3] Cf., e.g., *Appearance and Reality*[9], pp. 151–2. 'Let us try to realize more distinctly what this supposed consummation would involve. Since both truth and fact are to be there nothing must be lost, and in the Absolute we must keep every item of our experience. We cannot have less, but, on the other hand, we may have much more; and this more may so supplement the elements of our actual experience that in the whole they may become transformed. . . . [Such a whole] would be experience entire, containing all elements in harmony. Thought would be present as a higher intuition; will would be there where the ideal had become reality; and beauty and pleasure and feeling would live on in this total fulfilment', &c.

of its members—'is realized beyond doubt, and therefore realized everywhere in a greater or less degree'.[1] And yet—as he hastens to add—'its full and assured reality lies in a region, in and through which all intelligence lives and to which it all points, but which is, on the other hand, beyond that which can be actually observed or throughout understood'. The ideal of perfect uniqueness and individuality, though 'realized everywhere in a greater or less degree', is *visibly* [my italics] nowhere realized in complete perfection'.

Or, again, in the passage in the Appendix to *Appearance and Reality* in which[2] (as we saw) Bradley shows that the intellect would be 'satisfied', if 'the Whole' were 'a self-evident analysis and synthesis of the intellect itself by itself', he proceeds at once to explain why, on his view, the intellect is not, and cannot be, thus 'satisfied' in fact. 'If all that we find', he says, 'were in the end such a self-evident and self-complete whole, containing in itself as constituent processes the detail of the Universe, . . . the intellect would receive satisfaction in full.' But since, as he adds, he is himself 'unable to verify a solution of this kind', he is 'led to think' that 'the demands' which the intellect makes—the demands which the intellect 'insists . . . must be, and are, met'—are met (not within our actual knowledge or in our intellectual world, but) 'in, and by, a whole beyond the mere intellect'.[3]

(c) The more this attitude of Bradley's to the ideal is considered, the more difficult it is to defend it. If the intellect is a merely discursive and relational faculty—a power of 'mere thinking', of merely formal analysis and synthesis—it is plainly incapable of being or becoming the transparent dialectic in which the Whole eternally analyses and synthesizes itself. The procedure of such an intellect, it is plain, never is, and never can be, the ideal procedure—perfectly intelligible because perfectly intelligent. But such an intellect, it seems equally plain, could never originate—could never, even dimly, conceive—an ideal so radically contrasted with its own character and procedure.

---

[1] *Logic*[2], p. 657.

[2] Pp. 507–8.

[3] Cf. also *Logic*[2], p. 595, note 25, where Bradley summarizes his position as follows: 'Reality is Experience, but thought and truth are merely one aspect of the whole Universe. This one-sided being—like all other partial appearances—is dimly aware of its own one-sidedness, so as not to be content with itself so long as it remains but partial; while, on the other hand, unless partial, this one-sided being must disappear, as itself and as such. But, on the other hand, any "reality" which excludes thought is no less one-sided, and, offered as such, is itself no more than an unreal abstraction.'

Or (to put the same difficulty from the other side) if the ideal is no merely arbitrary fancy; if it embodies the genuine demands of thought—then, the thought which makes these demands, the intellect which originates them and 'insists that they are, and must be, met', is not the 'partial appearance', not the 'one-sided being', not the mere formal function of analysing and synthesizing a 'given', with which Bradley identifies it. It is the intellect *which criticizes* itself—not the intellect *which is criticized*. And, being thus the critic of itself, it includes within its total being, as moments subordinated to its concrete unity, *both* the 'mere thinking', which is criticized, *and* the aspect of immediacy, for lack of which that 'mere thinking' is condemned.

The difficulty which Bradley's attitude involves may be brought out from a different angle, if we ask what precise failure in actuality he is imputing to the ideal.

Thought makes certain demands; and to these *in principle* the universe conforms, i.e. it answers to the ideal, or actualizes it, by its main outline and general character. The absolute is an individual whole or system of experience, uniting consistently all plurality and harmonizing all differences. So much at least (Bradley claims to have shown) we know positively and beyond a doubt. Further, thought insists that, in the absolute, these demands 'must be, and are, met'; i.e. that *somehow* (though we cannot know 'the how' in detail) the demands of thought are satisfied *in full*. The ideal *is* 'realized beyond doubt, and therefore realized everywhere in a greater or less degree'. This, too (Bradley claims to have shown), we know positively and beyond a doubt.

In what respect, then, does the ideal still fail in actuality? What is it that is lacking in our knowledge of reality, so that our ignorance compels us to regard the Hegelian dialectic as a 'mere' ideal—i.e. as an ideal which we do not positively know, and so must not affirm, to be 'actual fact'?

What we do not, and can never, know—so Bradley appears to be insisting—is how in detail the universe satisfies the demands of thought. In the absolute experience, no doubt, thought and feeling and will are all perfected and fulfilled. But, in their perfection and fulfilment, they all have been transformed; they are no longer the thinking, feeling, and willing which we experience in ourselves, which are the 'main aspects' of *our* (finite) experience. The manner of their transformation and its precise results are necessarily beyond our knowledge. Hence, though we can, or rather must, affirm that in the absolute experience *thought is perfected and fulfilled*, i.e. that, in the absolute experience, thought's ideal is actualized in fact—we are still not authorized to affirm that *our* experience, in which thought is still obviously imperfect, actualizes or embodies thought's ideal. Our experience is not through and through intelligent and intelligible. We cannot 'observe' the actualization or the actuality of thought's ideal. We cannot 'verify' throughout the details of the universe, as they fall within our 'knowledge', the eternal self-analysis and self-synthesis, the infinite dialectic, which is reality knowing itself, and known to itself, in the form of truth. We cannot find the perfect system 'realized in complete perfection' anywhere in our world. None of the finite beings (the things or animals or persons) which fall within our view, are 'visibly' absolutely unique and individual members of an absolutely unique and individual system.

Now, while it is obvious that we, in our limited experience, can do none of these things; while it is obvious, in a word, that we are not, and never can become, 'omniscient';[1] is this our limitation in any sense or manner a *want of actuality* in thought's ideal? What thought demands is that, through and through, and in its most genuine and essential being, the universe should be intelligible and intelligent at once—should be, in other words, the timeless dialectic which is both absolute knowledge and absolute truth. It does not demand (so far as I can see) that the dialectic as a whole, or in any of the moments of its infinite process, should be 'visible'; should take the form of something that could be 'found', 'observed', or 'verified', by this or that finite subject of experience within the range of his admittedly imperfect, and partly sensuous, knowledge. Nor does it demand that we, by our limited and imperfect thinking, should be able to explain everything—or, for that matter, should be able *completely* to explain anything at all. The conclusion, then, seems to be that, in saying that 'the ideal is realized beyond doubt and therefore realized everywhere in a greater or less degree', Bradley has attributed to the ideal *the full and only actuality* which is in point. It is in that sense, and in no other, that Hegel, for example, claims that the real is rational and the rational real. And it is on that score, and no other, that—as I have been trying to show—we are forced to conceive our actual knowledge as the imperfect expression (in the form of a temporal development) of a spiritual reality; viz. of that infinite dialectic,

---

[1] Cf. *Appearance and Reality*[9], p. 458; *Logic*[2], p. 683.

in which absolute knowledge or absolute truth timelessly fulfils itself and is eternally self-fulfilled. If then, the philosopher reflects upon the ideal by which his thought has criticized itself; upon the conception of the Perfect by which his intellect has been guided in condemning as 'imperfect', one after the other, all those categories —organizing conceptions, schemata for combining an intelligible (distinctly conceived) Many in an intelligible Unity which it itself employs in trying to understand and know the world; if he reflects upon this ideal and sets it out in explicit terms, *it does* in fact take the form of an infinite and timeless dialectic; a dialectic which is eternally self-fulfilling and self-fulfilled.

And this ideal is in no sense arbitrary—a mere idea or imagination of the finite mind. It is, on the contrary, the way in which reality must be conceived if it is to satisfy the intellect: it is, that is, reality in the form of truth. Reality as it is in truth must be and is such a dialectic, because unless it were so our actual cognizant experience could not have the character it has and, in particular, could not exhibit the imperfections which reflection upon it compels us to recognize.

Bradley himself, in one passage at least,[1] expresses the necessary implication of the actuality of his own Absolute in all human experience very briefly and forcibly.

'From such imperfect experience as I possess,' he says, 'I not only can but I *must* conclude to an Experience perfect and complete, which, though still Experience, includes and is all that is real. And however much—and we are not to forget this—remains inexplicable, there is nothing whatever which, so far as I can see, stands out as impossible.'

But, if I rightly understand his position, he would not agree that 'from such imperfect *knowledge or truth* as we possess, we not only can but *must* conclude to a *knowledge-or-truth which is perfect and complete*—to an Experience which, though still *theoretical*, includes and is all that is real'. The 'Experience which is perfect and complete, which includes and is all that is real', is—so I understand him to insist—*more than* knowledge-or-truth, *more than* 'intelligible' and 'intelligent', *more than* the self-evident dialectic, self-analysis, and self-synthesis, in which thought fulfils and satisfies itself. And the nature of the unity of the all-inclusive experience—its absolute indissolubility or individuality—forbids us to conceive that the aspects it transcends retain their essential

[1] *Logic*[2], p. 683.

character *untransformed* in the consummation, in the complete experience, in which they are transcended. Bradley's Absolute Experience, therefore, while *not less but more than* knowledge or truth, than intelligible and intelligence, than the dialectic in which thought is timelessly self-fulfilled—is nevertheless (I suppose it must be said) not 'intelligible', not 'thought', not knowledge or truth, &c.

And yet unless 'the Experience perfect and complete', to which we are forced to conclude 'from such imperfect experience as we possess', retains *untransformed* (and as the fundamental condition without which it could not be real at all or include anything real whatever) the character of knowledge or truth—how can Bradley assert of it, for example, that it must be self-coexistent or harmonious? How can he insist (as he does, for example, in the passage quoted above) that 'however much remains inexplicable, there is nothing whatever which . . . stands out as *impossible*'? If thought (knowledge, truth, &c.), in being fulfilled in the Absolute Experience, is transmuted or transformed, it is difficult to see how Bradley can be entitled to fix any limits—or what limits—to the transmutation: difficult, therefore, to see what criterion is still available for him by which he is able to decide what is or is not 'impossible'; what does or does not 'stand out', and conflict with, the individuality of his Absolute Experience.

One last criticism or objection must be briefly noticed. It may be said, 'The whole treatment, in the preceding Studies, is incompatible with the view that the ideal, which our imperfect cognizant experiences necessarily imply—the ideal they inherently profess to be their aim and necessarily fail completely to achieve or embody—is a dialectic eternally self-fulfilling and self-fulfilled. Such a dialectic—such a knowledge or truth—would be, at all events, on one side of itself, immediate, self-evident, intuitive, &c.'

It is quite true that, throughout these Studies, I have stressed that side of our knowledge on which it is discursive, mediate, a movement or development or growth; and that I have minimized its other (no less essential), complementary, side—the side on which it is self-manifest rather than self-manifesting, immediate or an unbroken actuality, rather than a piecemeal construction or a development.

This emphasis has been deliberate, and (as I thought and still think) it is legitimate and necessary to counteract what seems to be the prevailing tendency. For the prevailing tendency (so far as I can judge) is to ignore or to deny—in regard to many forms of our cognizant experience—the ineliminable presence and the importance of the side I have been stressing—the 'discursive' side; and so to maintain that this or that phase of our cognizant experience is *sheerly* immediate: that, for example, perception or certain perceptions, or again some special and particular kinds or forms of thought, are (so to speak) isolable or detachable from the discursus, which is our knowledge-or-truth, our cognizant experience as a self-fulfilling development—and are *in that* isolated, self-evident, immediate bits of absolute knowledge and absolute truth.

INDEX

PRINTED IN GREAT BRITAIN AT THE UNIVERSITY PRESS, OXFORD
BY CHARLES BATEY, PRINTER TO THE UNIVERSITY